THE MAGICAL CHORUS

THE MAGICAL CHORUS

A History of Russian Culture
from Tolstoy to Solzhenitsyn

SOLOMON VOLKOV

Translated from the Russian
by Antonina W. Bouis

Alfred A. Knopf ▪ New York ▪ 2008

THIS IS A BORZOI BOOK
PUBLISHED BY ALFRED A. KNOPF

Library of Congress Cataloging-in-Publication Data
Volkov, Solomon.
The magical chorus : a history of Russian culture
from Tolstoy to Solzhenitsyn / by Solomon Volkov ; translated
from the Russian by Antonina W. Bouis.—1st ed.
p. cm.
"This is a Borzoi book."
Includes bibliographical references and index.
ISBN 978-1-4000-4272-2
1. Russian literature—20th century—Political aspects.   2. Politics and
literature—Soviet Union.   3. Arts, Russian—20th century—Political aspects.
4. Russia (Federation)—Civilization—20th century.   5. Soviet
Union—Civilization.   I. Bouis, Antonina W.   II. Title.
PG3026.P64V65 2008
891.709'358—dc22   2007034204

Manufactured in the United States of America
First Edition

CONTENTS

INTRODUCTION

Culture and politics have always been indivisible, and to maintain the contrary is also making a political statement. A stark and tragic example of that connection is Russian culture in the twentieth century: perhaps for the first time in history did such a brutal experiment of politics being forced into the cultural life of such a huge country take place over such a long period, continuing through world wars, convulsive revolutions, and the most ruthless terror.

That is the subject of this book, the first of its kind in any language: while studies in particular areas of cultural-political interrelationships in Russia in the last century are proliferating, there has not been a unified presentation.

The relationship between rulers and culture is a theme that has interested me since my Soviet childhood. My first collection did not consist of the usual toy soldiers or stamps; following Joseph Stalin's death in March 1953, I clipped newspaper photographs of the late dictator with cultural figures like the writer Maxim Gorky or actors from the Moscow Art Theater. This is how far back the psychological roots of this work go. Later, as a journalist, member of the Union of Soviet Composers and senior editor of its *Sovetskaya Muzyka* magazine, and interviewer of many leading cultural figures, I continually had to deal with the political aspects of Soviet culture, which at the time seemed vastly urgent to us all. As a witness, I have tried to convey that sense of urgency here.

By education and personal inclination I have always had an intense interest in music, ballet, theater, and the art market—all integral parts of Russian culture—which sometimes seems to be terra incognita for other historians, who tend to rely on their teams of researchers and so often end up making egregious errors.[1]

As the reader will see, I focus on such masters as Nikolai Rimsky-Korsakov (and his students Igor Stravinsky and Sergei Prokofiev), Mikhail Vrubel, Mikhail Fokine, Fedor Chaliapin, Pavel Filonov, Andrei Tarkovsky, and Alfred Schnittke, and such cultural milestones as the Moscow Art Theater, the liturgical music of the turn of the century, Diaghilev's Russian Seasons, and the "Amazons" of the Russian avant-garde (as well as the "second avant-garde," still not studied thoroughly), placing all these nonliterary institutions and movements in a political and social context. Together, these exceptionally strong and beautiful voices unite in a "Magical Chorus," to use the poet Anna Akhmatova's evocative metaphorical description.

However, there is no denying the fact that Russia—no matter what the Western view may be—has always been a logocentric country, and therefore writers hold center stage in *The Magical Chorus*. Leo Tolstoy, Maxim Gorky, and Aleksandr Solzhenitsyn each tried to realize the idea later crystallized in Solzhenitsyn's maxim that in Russia a great writer is like a second government.[2] They wanted to influence the regime, while the authorities attempted to manipulate them. None of these giants managed to implement his program fully, but in the process, all three created their enormous personal, heavily politicized legends. It is impossible to overestimate the role played by these writers in Russia's public life.

Political turbulence in the twentieth century increased the worldwide resonance of the Russian Magical Chorus, but at too high a cost: death, ruined lives, and creative devastation. For seventy years, the Iron Curtain separated the Russian mainland from the émigré diaspora. They began merging comparatively recently, and that complex and tortuous process is observed in my book. Another painful ideological split in Russian culture—between "urbanites" and "villagers"—cut across the entire century and is still hurting today. It sometimes seems that this conflict is growing more acute in contemporary Russia.

I am fortunate in having good relationships with major figures in both camps. Paradoxically, I would like to think that my move to the United States, where I continue to write and lecture about the old and the new Russian cultures and have been a longtime commentator on the subject, first at the Voice of America and then for Radio Liberty, gives me the opportunity to be more objective. I recall the words of Joseph Brodsky, who once told me he considered his cultural situation in New York as an observer's position high on a hilltop, with a view of both slopes.[3]

A long-distance view is definitely needed as the globalization of culture increases. There are those in Russia who fiercely attack globalization, some who criticize only its excesses, and still others who warily welcome it; but in fact, Russia has been part of this process since the country opened up to Western Europe in the late seventeenth century. It is just that events have accelerated immeasurably.

Lenin and especially Stalin understood the usefulness of culture as a political tool not only inside the country but in the international arena, too, and they wielded the weapon well. The Bolsheviks were innovators in cultural propaganda, making the constant complaints of the Communist leaders about the West's ideological aggression sound disingenuous: they themselves had created this confrontational arena.[4]

The Nobel Prize in Literature became one such highly publicized political event; it was given to five great Russians: Ivan Bunin (1933), Boris Pasternak (1958), Mikhail Sholokhov (1965), Aleksandr Solzhenitsyn (1970), and Joseph Brodsky (1987). Year after year, the Soviet authorities expressed outrage that the Nobel Prize was politicized. Responding to such attacks, Solzhenitsyn noted reasonably, "Even though the Swedish Academy was always being accused of *politics*, it was *our* barking voices that made any other assessment impossible."[5] Thus, each prize came enveloped in a cloud of controversy, and I give special attention to the behind-the-scenes intrigues leading up to the awards.

Nowadays, every significant local cultural gesture sooner or later takes on a global resonance, usually a political one; when it does not, the reason is also political. There is probably no way back to truly autonomous cultural reservations. Russian culture, even domestically, is more and more judged as part of a global marketplace, a situation the Russian intelligentsia finds unusual and painful after seventy years of isolation.

For me, the best Russian examples of sophisticated cultural analysis were always the writings of Alexandre Benois and Prince Dmitri Svyatopolk-Mirsky (D. S. Mirsky) in their émigré period, when their style, authoritative for connoisseurs and accessible for neophytes, was marked by a rare balance of "gentle anger and ironic love."[6] It still resonates today.

Throughout the years I spent working on this book, my guiding star was the memory of my precious conversations with some of its protagonists: Natan Altman, Anna Akhmatova, George Balanchine, Joseph Brodsky, Sergei Dovlatov, Kirill Kondrashin, Yuri Lyubimov, Anatoli Rybakov, Georgi Sviridov, Viktor Shklovsky, Alfred Schnittke, and Dmitri Shostakovich.

I am also deeply grateful to the following, who generously responded to my queries about those dramatic times: Nikolai Akimov, Vassily Aksyonov, Grigori Alexandrov, Vladimir Ashkenazy, Nina Bruni-Balmont, Rudolf Barshai, Tatiana Bek, Isaiah Berlin, Leonard Bernstein, Andrei

Bitov, Dmitri Bobyshev, Valerian Bogdanov-Berezovsky, Nikita Bogo-
slovsky, Elena Bonner, Alexander Borovsky, Lili Brik, Yevgeny Brusilovsky,
Sergei Chigrakov, Marietta Chudakova, Boris Eifman, Alexander Galich,
Leonid Girshovich, Evdokiya Glebov, Alexander Godunov, Yakov Gor-
din, Vladimir Horowitz, Boris Grebenshchikov, Irina Graham, Sofia
Gubaidulina, Lev Gumilev, Alexandra Danilova, Edison Denisov, Oleg
Efremov, Vyacheslav Ivanov, Natalia Ivanova, Roman Jakobson, Mariss
Jansons, Gia Kancheli, Vassily Katanyan, Nikolai Khardzhiev, Aram Kha-
chaturian, Igor Kholin, Andrei Khrzhanovsky, Lincoln Kirstein, Edward
Kline, Elem Klimov, Leonid Kogan, Alexander Kosolapov, Yuri Kochnev,
Gidon Kremer, Natalia Krymova, Savva Kulish, Sergei Kurekhin, Jay
Leyda, Eduard Limonov, Fedor Lopukhov, Lev Losev, Alexei Lyubimov,
Vladimir Maximov, Berthe Malko, Yuri Mamleyev, Sulamif Messerer,
Czeslaw Milosz, Nathan Milstein, Igor Moiseyev, Yevgeny Mravinsky,
Anatoly Nayman, Ernst Neizvestny, Viktor Nekrasov, Natalya Nesterova,
Irina Nijinska, Rudolf Nureyev, Mikhail Odnoralov, David Oistrakh,
Bulat Okudzhava, Alla Osipenko, Nadezhda Pavlovich, Vladimir Paperny,
Sergei Paradjanov, Viktor Pivovarov, Maya Plisetskaya, Boris Pokrovsky,
Lina Prokofiev, Irina Prokhorova, Lev Raaben, Edvard Radzinsky, Rita
Rait-Kovaleva, Yevgeny Rein, Sviatoslav Richter, Gennady Rozhdestven-
sky, Robert Rozhdestvensky, Maria Rozanova, Mstislav Rostropovich,
Harrison Salisbury, Andrei Sedykh, Marietta Shaginyan, Rodion Shche-
drin, Angelina Shchekin-Krotova, Iosif Sher, Yuri Shevchuk, Konstantin
Simonov, Andrei Sinyavsky, Boris Slutsky, Vassily Solovyov-Sedoi, Vlad-
imir Soloukhin, Arnold Sokhor, Vladimir Spivakov, Anna Sten, Isaac
Stern, Vera Stravinsky, Yevgeny Svetlanov, Flora Syrkina, Alexander
Tcherepnin, Yuri Temirkanov, Nikolai Tikhonov, Alexander Tyshler, Vlad-
imir Ussachevsky, Vladimir Vasiliev, Oleg Vassiliev, Georgy Vladimov,
Andrei Voznesensky, Pavel Vulfius, Vladimir Vysotsky, Maria Yudina,
Leonid Yakobson, Vladimir Yankilevsky, Yevgeny Yevtushenko, Sergei Yut-
kevich, Vyacheslav Zavalishin, and Alexander Zinoviev.

Conversations with Vagrich Bakhchanyan, Alexander Genis, Yuri
Handler, Boris Paramonov, Yevgenia Petrova, Alexander Rabinovich-
Burakovsky, Alla Rosenfeld, Ivan Tolstoy, and Peter Vail were very helpful.
Some ideas in this book were first discussed in the friendly homes of
Grisha and Alexandra Bruskin and Tatiana Rybakov and Elena Kolat.
Naturally, none of them is responsible for my conclusions and opinions.

Thanks to my wife, Marianna, for transcribing the interviews cited here and for her gallery of photographic portraits, which contains some of the most vivid personalities of twentieth-century Russian culture. Some photos were graciously supplied by Natalia and Ignat Solzhenitsyn and by Gennady Krochik. The present book is once again the result of deeply satisfying collaboration with my translator, Antonina W. Bouis, and my editor at Knopf, Ashbel Green.

Part One

THE GATHERING STORM

Chapter One

On November 8, 1910, people all over Russia snatched up the latest editions of newspapers reporting the death of Count Leo Tolstoy on the previous day, at 6:05 a.m. at Astapovo Station. The photographs showed perhaps the most famous writer in the world at that time: an austere, gray-bearded man of eighty-two, with high-set, very large ears and shaggy brows drawn over his piercing (some said "vulpine") eyes.

Another world-celebrated writer, though a lesser light, Maxim Gorky, was living in exile on the Italian island of Capri and wrote when he learned of Tolstoy's death: "This struck the heart, and I howled with hurt and longing."[1] In a letter to a friend, Gorky exclaimed in a typically fanciful manner, "A great soul has departed, a soul that had embraced all of Russia, everything that was Russian—about whom save Tolstoy can that be said?"[2] The cosmopolitan modernist poet Valery Briusov stressed the writer's universality in his memorial essay: "Tolstoy was for the entire world. His words went to Englishmen, and Frenchmen, and the Japanese, and the Buryats."[3] From Paris, the political émigré Bolshevik Vladimir Ulyanov (Lenin), doggedly—as only he could—insisted that Tolstoy's "global significance as an artist and his worldwide fame as a thinker and preacher, both reflect in their own way the widespread significance of the Russian revolution."[4]

As it happens, all three were probably right. We tend to think of Tolstoy as a cultural phenomenon of the nineteenth century, the author of *War and Peace* (1863–77, perhaps the greatest novel in the history of the genre) and such masterpieces as *Anna Karenina* (1873–77) and "The Death of Ivan Ilyich" (1886). Yet this giant dominated both the cultural and the political life of the early twentieth century also. Briusov wasn't exaggerating: Tolstoy combined the fame of Voltaire, the popularity of Rousseau, and the authority of Goethe; he was compared routinely to biblical prophets. In his estate at Yasnaya Polyana, two hundred kilometers south of Moscow, Tolstoy received devotees from all over the world, who flocked to hear his antigovernment and antibourgeois sermons.

Gorky, in his memoirs of Tolstoy (a tour de force of twentieth-century Russian nonfiction), confessed that when he looked at him, he thought, not without envy: "That man is godlike!"

However, Tolstoy was made up of contradictions, containing "multitudes," to use Walt Whitman's phrase. He was simultaneously a born archaist and a natural innovator—in his life, in his writing, and in his passionate religious and political beliefs, which sometimes verged on total anarchism. Gorky noted, somewhat caustically (and in seeming contradiction to his worship of Tolstoy): "Psychologically it would be quite natural for great artists to be larger than life in their sins, as well."[5]

Tolstoy's works, while belonging to the apex of nineteenth-century realism, boldly went beyond its framework: another contradiction. Tolstoy rejected and mocked the modernists, but they made good use of his artistic breakthroughs. It's a surprisingly short distance from Tolstoy's "interior monologue" to James Joyce's stream of consciousness. Viktor Shklovsky, the bad boy of Russian formalism, early on placed Leo Tolstoy among the avant-garde: "Tolstoy in his works, which were constructed as formally as music, used such devices as defamiliarization (calling a thing not by its usual name)" and cited his description of the institution of property through the perceptions of a horse.[6] This "alienation technique" (*Verfremdungseffekt*) was later used and abused by Bertolt Brecht and other European avant-garde writers.

The publication in 1911–1912 of three shabby gray volumes came as a revelation for the Russian public: *The Posthumous Fiction of L. N. Tolstoy* included the short story "Father Sergius"; the play *The Living Corpse,* in which, according to Shklovsky, Tolstoy "captured the living speech of trailing sentences"; and the prophetic novella about the endless Russo-Chechen war, *Khadji Murat,* on which he had worked until 1906. A half century later, Shklovsky, no longer holding the radical views of his youth but still habitually spouting paradoxes, maintained that in *Khadji Murat* Tolstoy had been a forerunner of socialist realism ("documentary subject seen through a romantic prism"). "It is Tolstoy who is the father of socialist realism, not Gorky, as they teach you," Shklovsky told me, still cocky at eighty-two.[7]

Since Tolstoy the writer was cast by critics as the patron saint of everything from realism to socialist realism, it comes as no surprise that politically he was variously labeled as well. Contemporaries tried to pin him down as a repentant aristocrat, or the voice of the patriarchal Russian peasantry, or a Christian anarchist, and even as a diehard revolutionary. It was all true to a point: Tolstoy preached an extreme simplicity of life and took a hard libertarian stance toward government, which he considered immoral and illegal, yet he also rejected all forms of violence. In his famous 1909 article "I Cannot Be Silent," he protested capital punishment in Russia and did not recognize the authority of organized religion. This inevitably led the rebel count into conflict with the autocracy and the Russian Orthodox Church. Many believed that a confrontation with Tolstoy gravely weakened both institutions.

Even in April 1896, just before the coronation of Tsar Nicholas II, Konstantin Pobedonostsev, the all-powerful High Procurator of the Holy Synod, in charge of the affairs of the Russian Orthodox Church, denounced Tolstoy (in approximately the same indignant language that three-quarters of a century later was heaped on Aleksandr Solzhenitsyn by the Soviet Politburo): "He spreads the terrible contagion of anarchy and disbelief throughout Russia. . . . It is obvious that he is the enemy of the Church, the enemy of all government and of all civil order. There is a proposal at the Synod to excommunicate him from the Church, in order to avoid any doubts and misunderstanding in the people, who see and hear that the intelligentsia admires Tolstoy."[8]

So, the Holy Synod excommunicated Tolstoy in 1901; a year later he wrote to Nicholas II (calling the tsar "beloved brother"), putting forth his provocative views on the regime and the church: "Autocracy is an obsolete form of rule. . . . And therefore this form of rule and the Orthodoxy connected to it can be supported, as it is today, only through violence: excessive security measures, administrative exiles, executions, religious persecutions, the banning of books and newspapers, warped education, and all sorts of evil and cruel acts."[9]

Did Tolstoy actually expect his bold address to so influence the tsar that he would "understand the evil he does"? Nicholas II simply ignored him, and the writer decided the tsar was "a pathetic, weak, and stupid" ruler. Tolstoy wanted to teach, not to advise modestly and respectfully, as ritual demanded. Nicholas II (whose advisor then was Pobedonostsev and after 1907, Grigory Rasputin) had no intention of playing pupil. Thus a dialogue did not ensue. Accordingly, Tolstoy's model for the twentieth-century discourse between monarch and great writer, between regime and cultural hero, never took hold. It was this model that later Gorky and Solzhenitsyn—each in his own way—also tried to establish. Solzhenitsyn would depict Nicholas II with sympathy and understanding in his novel *August 1914:* did he perhaps imagine himself as the last tsar's ideal interlocutor and advisor?

The shrewd Alexei Suvorin, the influential publisher of the promonarchist newspaper *Novoye Vremya* [New Times], wrote in his diary on May 29, 1901: "We have two tsars: Nicholas II and Leo Tolstoy. Which is stronger? Nicholas II can't do anything with Tolstoy, he can't shake his throne, while Tolstoy is undoubtedly shaking the throne of Nicholas and his dynasty. Tolstoy is excommunicated by the Synod's decision. Tolstoy replies, the reply is disseminated widely in manuscript form and in the foreign press. Just let anyone try to hurt Tolstoy. The whole world will raise a hue and cry, and our administration will turn tail and run."[10]

Suvorin accurately described the situation, which was unprecedented for Russian society. In Tolstoy, Russia's educated classes had a leader who wanted to dictate his solutions to the tsarist government on key social and political issues: war and peace (literally), the distribution of land, and also administrative and judicial reform. "The strength of his position," wrote Boris Eikhenbaum, the leading Tolstoy scholar, "was that even though he opposed his era, he was still a part of it."[11]

It was that tremendous strength that led Lenin to his famous description of Tolstoy in 1908 as "the mirror of the Russian revolution." For Lenin, Tolstoy was revolutionary because of his "ruthless criticism of capitalist exploitation, his exposé of government coercion and the comedy of the courts and government administration, his baring of the yawning contradictions between the growth of wealth and the growth of poverty."[12]

Yet for Tolstoy, earthly power and influence were not enough. Even as a twenty-seven-year-old, Tolstoy came up with a new religion (he noted it in his diary), and he spent his life shaping it, step by step building his image of demigod. In his scheme of things, Christ and Buddha were mere teachers of human wisdom, alongside whom the writer's "godlike" (in Gorky's phrase) figure could naturally take its place.

Gorky also made the caustic observation that Tolstoy "considered Christ naïve and worthy of pity." True, Tolstoy felt that he was actually in a better position to interpret the teachings of Christ than Christ himself. Surprisingly, this rather immodest assumption was eagerly shared in the early twentieth century by many enlightened people all over the world—from France, where Romain Rolland became an enthusiastic standard-bearer of Tolstoy's Christian socialism, to India, where Mahatma Gandhi successfully took up Tolstoy's concept of nonviolent resistance. In the United States, both William Jennings Bryan and Clarence Darrow, one the prosecutor and the other the defense attorney in the notorious Scopes trial in 1925, were fervent adherents of Tolstoy's moral teachings.

Tolstoy's fame was spread and fanned by the world media, hungry for sensation. Tolstoy, who only pretended to be a hermit in his Yasnaya Polyana and in fact liked giving interviews, manipulated the press masterfully. Consequently, never had a Russian writer enjoyed such fame abroad in his lifetime (the celebrity of Alexander Herzen and Ivan Turgenev, who had actually lived in Western Europe, was much more modest). It is telling that Herzen printed his antigovernment booklets in Europe at his own expense, while Tolstoy was endlessly reprinted throughout the world primarily because his books were international best sellers, particularly his new works on religious themes.

Even though Herzen was among the first to produce "tamizdat" (works addressed to Russian readers published first in the West) and "samizdat" (the same works distributed inside Russia illegally, in manuscript copies), Tolstoy undoubtedly took this phenomenon to a new level. His articles, appeals, and open letters, banned by the Russian censors but printed in the West, circulated everywhere almost simultaneously, and the Western attention greatly helped his reputation at home. (Solzhenitsyn's later situation was similar.) Thus Tolstoy in effect escaped official control.

Unable to subdue him during his lifetime, the Russian government and the Orthodox hierarchy tried to hijack the writer after his death, which became a sorry spectacle when Tolstoy ran away. He had long proclaimed his desire to live according to his teaching, not as a count but as a simple peasant, and abruptly escaped from his estate and his family.

But pneumonia kept him at the small railroad station of Astapovo, which was instantly besieged by journalists and film crews, attending family and close friends (with bitter strife within this group), representatives of the tsar and church, and observers of different political leanings. The family tried to maintain the remnants of decorum in a clearly scan-

dalous situation. The press tried to get as much out of the colossal sensation as they could get away with. And the government tried to prevent
any disorder, which it feared greatly, and which the liberals would have
loved to exploit.

The media naturally won out: this was one of the first examples of
their newfound power in Russia. The world saw the documentary
footage showing how Tolstoy's wife was not permitted to see the dying
count. Endless newspaper reports with photographs from Astapovo not
only made the private death of a genius uncomfortably public but also
revealed the embarrassingly ugly squabble over his will and testament.

Unused to dealing with modern media, the government and the Holy
Synod made one clumsy mistake after another. A monk was sent to Tolstoy to persuade him to reconcile himself with the official church. Tolstoy
had only to say two words: "I repent." The attempt failed. Astapovo was
filled with police agents who sent long coded telegrams to their higher-
ups about the latest contretemps and the comings and goings of the
journalists and other suspicious characters.

The police tried to contain Tolstoy's funeral in Yasnaya Polyana by
sharply limiting access to the public from St. Petersburg and Moscow
and to control the memorial gatherings all over the country, which in
many cases took on markedly oppositionist political overtones. Demonstrators on Nevsky Prospect in St. Petersburg carried posters demanding,
in the spirit of Tolstoy's teaching, the repeal of the death penalty.
Suvorin's *Novoye Vremya* reported that these "disorders" were provoked
by people from the Caucasus and by the Jewish press: "Up to their eyes
in dirty politicking, which Tolstoy had abhorred, they turned the memory
of the wise man into an excuse for banal banner waving."[13] Thus in 1910
the idea of the undue influence of the Jewish media on Russia's domestic policies was already promoted, to be resurrected in the late twentieth
century. Typically, the alarm was voiced by the camp of the conservative
press, which was trying to hang on to its overwhelming political and
economic influence.

Mikhail Menshikov, an influential columnist of *Novoye Vremya*,
claimed that the death penalty was one of the foundations of true Christian civilization, and the Jews were merely using Tolstoy's protests
against it in order "to disarm the government." In turn, the liberal journalists (many of whom were Jewish) pointed at the government and the
church as the real conspirators in this story. The noisy polemics turned

Tolstoy's funeral into one of the biggest media circuses of the first decade of the twentieth century.

Was this what the ironic Anton Chekhov had in mind long before Tolstoy's death in a conversation with Ivan Bunin (who was to be the first Russian to receive the Nobel Prize in Literature)? "Once Tolstoy dies, everything will go to hell!"[14] Tolstoy, however, outlived the reclusive Chekhov by over six years, and Chekhov's death and funeral in June 1904 were a vivid contrast to the spectacle of Tolstoy's farewell. In Bunin's opinion, Tolstoy's grave drew "people alien to him, admiring only his criticism of the church and government and who experienced even happiness at his funeral: that showy ecstasy that always overwhelms the 'progressive' crowd at all the 'civic' funerals."[15]

Chekhov's funeral couldn't have been more different. The only great Russian writer who arguably made no effort to inflate his own image, he died in Badenweiler, a small German resort, at forty four, of tuberculosis that had been eating away at him for fifteen years. His face, as Bunin sadly noted, had turned yellow and wrinkled like that of a very old Mongol. The coffin was brought from Germany to St. Petersburg in a railroad car labeled in big letters, to the horror of those meeting the body, "For Oysters." The writer's widow, Olga Knipper, the famous actress of the Moscow Art Theater, was dismayed that only fifteen or so people had come to the train station. The absurdity of it all belonged in a Chekhov short story.

While Chekhov's funeral at the Novodevichy Cemetery in Moscow was well attended, it nonetheless depressed Gorky, who lamented to another writer friend, Leonid Andreyev: "I am all splattered by the gray mud of speeches, inscriptions on wreaths, newspaper articles, and various conversations. Involuntarily thinking of my own death, I imagine the ideal funeral in this way: a dray cart carries my coffin and it is followed by one indifferent patrolman. A writer in Russia cannot be buried in a better, more noble, more decent way."[16]

If only Gorky could have known how "indecent" his own funeral in 1936 would be by the standards he had defined in 1904: a crowd of one hundred thousand people on Red Square, pompous speeches by Soviet leaders, with police and army on guard. By the end of his life Gorky had been proclaimed by Joseph Stalin to be "the great humanist" and fighter for "all progressive humanity." Chekhov had been more concerned with the happiness of the individual; in the opinion of many people, he did not fight for anything. He simply sang the mundane—that was how he was perceived by critics and readers. They did not like the fact that Chekhov, unlike Tolstoy (and later Gorky and Solzhenitsyn), did not aspire to be a leader or teacher of life. Contrary to the Russian cultural tradition, he was not a prophet, or a *yurodivy* (holy fool), or dissident. That is why Chekhov became so popular on the stages of Europe and the United States. The West is mistaken when it takes Chekhov for a typical Russian writer.

Although he admired Tolstoy greatly, Chekhov nevertheless felt strongly that prophecy was not the writer's job. His alienation reflected the realities of the new Russia, moving from the peasant commune to a developed capitalist society. The "peasant" anarchist Tolstoy wrathfully denounced that path. His ideas, populist and quasi-Christian (with strong Buddhist overtones), had not only formed the consciousness of the modern Russian intelligentsia but had also created an influential paradigm for the behavior of the politically astute writer in general. When Russia's movement toward a Westernized market-based society was interrupted by the revolution of 1917, the Tolstoy model reigned supreme for a long time: in the Soviet era art was seen as a direct tool for improving human nature, and the didactic element in culture came to the forefront. (See Shklovsky's paradoxical idea of Tolstoy as precursor of socialist realism.) In that sense, Chekhov was an opponent of Tolstoy and his followers in life and art. Chekhov's ideology was diffused in the artistic fabric of his work and it is very difficult to separate it out.

This does not mean that Chekhov had no ideals at all, as both liberal and conservative commentators of the day had charged. But those ideals were secular, sober, and incomparably more pragmatic than the views of Tolstoy. Tolstoy was rightly compared to a prophet: his moral sermon was passionate and unambivalent. "Do not kill," "Do not eat meat," "Abstain from sex," "Live according to the Bible," Tolstoy admonished. Many people obeyed, hoping to make their lives better. But Chekhov back in 1894 wrote to Suvorin: "Tolstoy's philosophy affected me strongly and influenced me for six or seven years. . . . Now something within me protests; thrift and fairness tell me that there is more love of mankind in electricity and steam than in chastity and vegetarianism."[17]

After Chekhov's death, Tolstoy compared Chekhov's style to the

Impressionists: "You watch a man seemingly smear whatever paints come to hand without any selection and the strokes seem to have no relationship to each other. But you step back a bit and look, and the whole forms a complete impression."[18] This admiration for Chekhov's innovation extended only to his prose; as Tolstoy himself told Chekhov: "I can't stand your plays. Shakespeare wrote badly, and you're even worse!"[19]

This may appear bizarre now, but Tolstoy was not alone in his dislike of Chekhov the playwright; Gorky, Bunin, and many critics at the beginning of the century had serious reservations about his work. The premiere in 1896 at the Imperial Alexandrinsky Theater in St. Petersburg of Chekhov's first mature play, *The Seagull*, was a disaster with a squall of hostile reviews, like the one in *Peterburgskii Listok*: "This is a very badly conceived and clumsily crafted play, with an extremely strange content, or rather, with no content at all. This is a muddle in poor dramatic form."[20]

It is not clear what would have happened to Chekhov the playwright if a boldly innovative theatrical organization had not sprung up in Russia. It revolutionized the art of the stage not only in Russia but throughout the world. *The Seagull* was produced again in 1898 by the recently formed Moscow Art Theater (MAT). Surprisingly, this enterprise was launched by a mediocre playwright, Vladimir Nemirovich-Danchenko, and an amateur actor, Konstantin Alekseyev-Stanislavsky. These unlikely candidates intended to reform the Russian theater radically; they believed it (correctly) to be in shambles. Routine reigned on the stage then—in direction, which was rudimentary, in wooden acting, and in incongruous scenery.

For these Russian theatrical revolutionaries (Nemirovich-Danchenko was an aristocrat, Stanislavsky from a wealthy merchant family) the guiding star was Chekhov's modern sensibility, which the traditional stage could neither understand nor accept. It is not surprising that the old guard saw it all as a muddle: after all, Chekhov had totally rejected the concept of the "well-made play," with its intricate plot twists, overlong monologues and artificial dialogues resembling opera duets. A Chekhov play is usually put together from bits of detached phrases and the action has been moved to the subtext. In the finale of *The Seagull*, the suicide of one of the characters is introduced this way: "A vial of ether has exploded." In *Uncle Vanya* the line "Ah, it must be very hot in that

Africa—a terrible thing" summarizes the tragic ending of an entire life. People on the stage collide and go their separate ways like microbes under the microscope of a doctor, which Chekhov was by training.

Chekhov's modern ideology was inculcated into the social discourse primarily from the stage of the MAT. This is how the Symbolist poet Alexander Blok described a MAT production of a Chekhov play in a letter to his mother: "It is a corner of the great Russian art, one of the accidentally preserved, miraculously unsullied corners of my vile, filthy, stupid, and bloody motherland."[21] Another poet, Osip Mandelstam, would write later, somewhat ironically: "The Art Theater is the child of the Russian intelligentsia, flesh of her flesh, bone of her bone. . . . From childhood I recall the reverent atmosphere that surrounded the theater. Going to the Art Theater for a member of the intelligentsia meant practically taking communion, going to church."[22]

It is possible that Anna Akhmatova's ironic attitude toward both MAT and Chekhov, which so shocked me when we met in 1965, came from Mandelstam. "Chekhov is not compatible with poetry," said Akhmatova. Her anti-Chekhov stance seemed paradoxical, but it reflected Akhmatova's aversion to the cultural intelligentsia mainstream of her youth, which she felt was strongly influenced by MAT and Chekhov.

The very concept of intelligentsia is specifically Russian. It implies not only an educated person—scientists, scholars, writers, journalists, lawyers, doctors, engineers, teachers, and college students—but a certain liberal outlook. Psychologically, the *intelligent* (with a hard G), unlike the white-collar worker, had a civic conscience, valued freedom, and sought to liberate the lower classes.

The traditional Russian perception is that the *intelligent* was first and foremost an altruist serving the ideals of good and justice. This matched MAT's program, which brought together aesthetics and ethics for the first time in Russia on such a high artistic level on the stage. MAT became a kind of club for the intelligentsia.

Ironically, Stanislavsky and Nemirovich-Danchenko, like Chekhov, abhorred politics. But politics caught up with them, forcing its way into their hothouse of high art. The audiences stayed on after premieres for a lecture by a critic on the play. After the lecture, lively topical discussions continued outside the theater. Young people debated with particular passion.

"People with a deep spiritual wound go to the theater," wrote a reviewer in 1905, speaking primarily of MAT. "The theater is the only place where a Russian citizen feels like a citizen, where he meets with others like himself and involves himself in the formation of public opinion."[23] Andreyev described people leaving MAT after a performance of Chekhov's *The Three Sisters* with the sense that they had to seek a way out of the "black mist" of life that surrounded them. They perceived the play that seemed to have no point or idea as an epitaph for an era.

Chekhov literally created a new audience. After *The Seagull,* all the premieres of his new plays at MAT—*Uncle Vanya* (1899), *The Three Sisters* (1901), and *The Cherry Orchard* (1904)—became milestones not only in the country's public life but in the personal lives of many viewers as well. It was reflected in the enormous number of letters written to MAT, containing gratitude, personal confessions, and requests for advice. Replying to one of these sincere epistles, Stanislavsky sermonized in 1901, "Do you know why I abandoned all my personal affairs and took up the theater? Because the theater is the most powerful pulpit, more powerful in its influence than books or the press. This pulpit fell into the hands of the rabble of humanity, and they turned it into a place of depravity. . . . My task is to explain to the modern generation, to the best of my ability, that the actor is a prophet of beauty and truth."[24]

Chekhov didn't take these self-aggrandizing declarations of Stanislavsky's too seriously. Although many people (including Bunin, who admired and envied him) believed that he owed his fame to MAT, Chekhov actually despised actors, calling them vainglorious and seventy-five years behind the rest of Russian society. He feared lofty sentiments, and sarcastically told Bunin, who had compared his work to poetry, that poets were those who mindlessly use words like "silvery vista" and "chord" and slogans like "forward, ye people, to battle darkness!" One should sit down to write, Chekhov said, only when one felt as cold as ice.

This outward coldness, unusual for Russian literature, unnerved all the political camps. The influential liberal guru Nikolai Mikhailovsky handed down his infamous verdict this way: "Mister Chekhov writes away in cold blood and the reader reads along in cold blood," adding that for Chekhov "it's all the same—be it a man or his shadow, a bell or a suicide." Chekhov responded irritably, comparing critics to the gadflies that keep horses from plowing: "I've been reading criticism of my stories for twenty-five years, and I can't recall a single valuable suggestion, I never heard any good advice. However, once the critic Skabichevsky made an impression on me, predicting that I would die in a drunken stupor under a fence."[25]

The Russian Marxists, flexing their muscles at that time, had the most bones to pick with Chekhov. It must be noted that their leader, Lenin, who was no aficionado of contemporary literature, made an exception for Chekhov and Tolstoy. (Chekhov was also a favorite of the young Stalin.) But Lenin's friend, Vaslav Vorovsky, a leading Marxist critic, described the world of Chekhov's plays as "a Philistine swamp, where frogs croak smugly and fat ducks swim officiously," a world of "star-crossed 'sisters,' miserable 'seagulls,' wretched owners of 'cherry orchards,' and there are so many of them, and they are all oh so gloomy, exhausted by petty suffering."[26]

For the Marxist Vorovsky, Chekhov was a "pessimist and objectivist." He championed another writer—the young Alexei Peshkov, who burst onto the Russian literary scene in 1892 under the pseudonym Maxim Gorky. According to Vorovsky, "while the wan, faded Chekhovian types were limping along on the surface of life . . . in those sad days, Gorky spoke out as the daring herald of the brave."[27]

By the age of twenty-five, Gorky had led a turbulent life. If his own account is to be believed, he had worked many odd jobs, as a laborer, stevedore, and baker, and had traveled around Russia by foot. He was the first to present a new hero in Russian literature—the vividly depicted tramp, the "déclassé element"—and this brought him enormous fame. His first book became a best seller, his name was on everyone's lips, his photographs in all the newspapers, and he could not walk down the street unaccosted by fans. Highbrow commentators were flabbergasted: "Neither Turgenev, nor Count Tolstoy at the time of *War and Peace*, nor Dostoevsky ever had such popularity."

Gorky's impact was similar in Europe and America; Stefan Zweig confirmed that Gorky's works literally stunned Western readers at the start of the century. The shock was political, of course. While Dostoevsky and Tolstoy spoke of the coming violent Russian Revolution as a dangerous disease, Gorky's was the first Russian voice to welcome it unconditionally with no sense of "mystical horror before the future," as Zweig put it.

The relationship between Gorky and Chekhov, eight years his senior, developed in a rather curious way. They first met in March 1899, both tall and with deep voices, but otherwise quite different: Chekhov slender, with a neat beard, easy movements, always tastefully dressed, an ironic gaze above his pince-nez; Gorky stooped, red-haired with a yellow mustache, a duckbill nose (Tolstoy told Chekhov that "only the miserable and the angry have noses like that"), always deliberately clothed in a "simple fellow" manner, waving his arms about like a windmill.

At first Gorky was unreservedly ecstatic about Chekhov, who responded sympathetically; in a letter to a woman friend he wrote, "Gorky, I believe, is a real talent, his brushes and paints are real, but it's untrammeled, swashbuckling talent." He also wrote to her, "In appearance, he's a tramp, but inside he's a rather elegant man."[28] Chekhov defended Gorky publicly in a cause célèbre now known as the Academy Incident.

It happened in 1902, when Gorky at the age of thirty-four was elected honorary academician in the category of belles lettres of the Imperial Academy of Sciences (the president was Grand Duke Konstantin Romanov, an accomplished poet). When Nicholas II learned of the selection, he was infuriated. Even sympathetic historians point out the fateful combustion of lack of will and stubbornness in the tsar's character. His cultural tastes were as unassuming and eclectic as that of a provincial high school teacher: he was simultaneously an admirer of Chekhov, the tabloid *Novoye Vremya,* the popular humor magazine *Satirikon,* and the quasi-folkloric art of the famous singer Nadezhda Plevitskaya, who would die in 1940 in a French prison, arrested as a Bolshevik spy. Regarding Gorky, Nicholas informed the minister of public education: "Neither Gorky's age nor his slim works present sufficient cause for his election to such an esteemed title. . . . I am deeply incensed by all this and order you to announce that on my command Gorky's election is annuled."[29]

The Academy obeyed slavishly, outraging the press. Chekhov, who had been made an honorary academician two years earlier, resigned in protest, thereby fanning the scandal. But in the meantime, offstage, relations between Chekhov and Gorky were deteriorating. A confrontation was brewing, and it was eventually played out by proxy, through their wives.

The French suggest *cherchez la femme* as the source of any conflict.

Look for the politics, as well. Political, artistic, and personal relations often intertwine so that it is impossible to find where one ends and another begins. In 1900, MAT brought its production of *Uncle Vanya* to Yalta, the Black Sea resort where Chekhov was recuperating. Gorky was there, too, having fled from his wife. Chekhov kept teaching Gorky how to pick up women, considering himself, not without reason, to be an expert. Perhaps in order to goad Gorky, who was hesitating, Chekhov began courting two leading actresses of MAT at once—Maria Andreyeva and Olga Knipper. Both were striking, larger-than-life beauties and intellectuals, although Andreyeva was married with two children and Knipper was free. Perhaps this mattered most for Chekhov: he married Knipper the following year. Gorky took Andreyeva, and she became his common-law wife in 1903.

Gorky had become a famous playwright by then. He began writing plays in 1901, urged on by Stanislavsky, as well as by Chekhov, who, however, was underwhelmed by Gorky's first attempt, *The Smug Citizens*, reproaching the author for aesthetic archaism—"an irreparable flaw, like red hair in a redhead." Gorky, in a letter to a friend, had a rather different view of his debut: "I, your Alyoshka, scored honorably on my preliminary test for title of playwright. (Watch out, William Shakespeare!)"[30]

The Smug Citizens, shown by the Moscow Art Theater in 1902, was not a success, even though publicity from the Academy Incident helped. (The play became popular much later, when the Soviet director Georgy Tovstonogov presented it in his Leningrad theater in 1966 with the incomparable Yevgeny Lebedev as the lead; I was lucky to see this legendary production.)

Undeterred, Gorky gave his second play to MAT as well, and this time he hit the jackpot. Originally titled *At the Bottom of Life* in Russian and shortened at Nemirovich-Danchenko's suggestion to *At the Bottom* (known in English as *The Lower Depths*), the play first brought to the Russian stage the castoffs of society—thieves, prostitutes, and tramps. Now it is clear that it is Gorky's best play (perhaps his best work) and a masterpiece of world twentieth-century drama. But critics were outraged after the premiere: "You feel as if you have been dunked forcibly in a cesspit! . . . Gorky plucks on the lowest and vilest strings of the human heart";[31] "Too much cruelty, inhumanity, groaning, and curses. . . . Does life ever look like this?"[32]

The public, however, loved *The Lower Depths*, applauding such catch-phrases as "Lies are the religion of slaves and masters!" and "The truth is the God of a free man!" The character played by the great Ivan Moskvin, the sly wanderer Luka, was deemed controversial: a philosopher who explains and accepts everything. (The poet Vladislav Khodasevich, who knew Gorky well, later suggested that Luka's philosophy in many ways reflected Gorky's personal convictions.) The play was performed fifty times to standing-room-only audiences in just a few months (December 1902–April 1903).

Chekhov, who had considered himself the leading contemporary author of the Art Theater and who had frankly not expected such adroitness from Gorky, grew worried and wrote to Knipper: "I was so pessimistic about *Lower Depths* this summer, and look what success!" She consoled her husband by telling him that Stanislavsky was "dreaming of *Cherry Orchard* and said just yesterday that even though *Depths* was a success, his heart was not in it. It's lies, he says."[33] Stanislavsky, who always felt that political engagement and art "were incompatible, one excludes the other," was probably bothered by the openly political tone of Gorky's triumph. A theater revolutionary, in life Stanislavsky was extremely conservative and cautious, which came in good stead in future complications, particularly in his dealings with Stalin in the Soviet era.

A rift—political, cultural, and personal—began between the two playwrights, threatening to break up MAT. Chekhov and Gorky were the protagonists, but remained in the shadows, while their wives, Knipper and Andreyeva, MAT's stars, acted it out, each trying to pull the theater in her husband's direction. In a letter to Chekhov on February 16, 1903, Nemirovich-Danchenko informed him that a disgusting "crack, like the ones in walls, needing some repair," had formed in MAT and it is, alas, "growing slowly."[34] Clever Nemirovich-Danchenko told Chekhov (as if the writer didn't already know from his own wife) that two hostile camps had formed at MAT: in one were Stanislavsky with Nemirovich-Danchenko and Knipper, in the other, Andreyeva and Savva Morozov, the Moscow merchant and patron of the arts who was unrequitedly in love with Gorky's wife.

The Moscow merchant class, long ridiculed by the liberal press for its wealth and its bigoted retrograde views, had by the start of the twentieth century nurtured a number of extraordinary figures who mightily increased Russia's cultural prestige. An example was set in the late nine-teenth century by Pavel Tretyakov, who put together the largest collec-tion of Russian art (his younger brother, Sergei, collected French artists almost exclusively, from Géricault to Courbet). Following Sergei Tretyakov's cosmopolitan line, the Moscow merchants Ivan Morozov and Sergei Shchukin bought the avant-garde works of the young Picasso and Matisse, which now are the pride (and source of solid income through loans for exhibitions) of Russia's major museums.

Matisse later said of Shchukin that he always picked his best works. Sometimes Matisse was reluctant to part with a good painting and he would say to Shchukin, "This didn't come off, let me show you some-thing else." Shchukin would look at the canvases long and hard and end up by declaring, "I'll take the one that didn't come off."[35]

Many Moscow merchants were eccentric, but even in their midst, Savva Morozov (of the Morozov clan) stood out. The successful boss of family-owned pig-iron smelters and chemical plants with several thou-sand employees, he was also one of the main sponsors of the Russian Social-Democrats, namely, their most radical part, the Bolsheviks, headed by Lenin.

Morozov was also a generous patron of the arts; he saved MAT from bankruptcy. The brand-new building for MAT, designed by the Art Nou-veau architect Fedor Shekhtel with a revolving stage, rare then even in the West, and state-of-the-art lighting equipment, was built with his money and personal supervision in Kamergersky Pereulok, where it remains one of the architectural landmarks of Moscow.

Morozov became the de facto executive director of MAT. The new tri-umvirate running the famed theater struck a curious picture: the elegant giant of a man Stanislavsky, with gray hair, demonic black eyebrows, and childlike eyes; the stocky, confident, shrewd Nemirovich-Danchenko, the typical Moscow gentleman with well-tended beard; and with them the nervous, grimacing, and extremely unattractive Morozov, with a dark red, Tatar-like face and a crew cut on his round head.

With his newfound power at the theater, Morozov began giving cen-tral roles to his goddess Andreyeva, cutting out MAT's other star, Knip-per. Naturally, Gorky was delighted and wrote to Chekhov: "When I see Morozov backstage, covered in dust and worrying about the success of the play, I am prepared to forgive him all his factories (a forgiveness he does not need)—I like him because he loves the theater altruistically."[36]

Chekhov, upset and informed by his wife that Morozov also loved Andreyeva altruistically but did not care too much for Knipper, tried to keep the patron away from the stage. "He should not be permitted to get too close to the essence of the work. He can judge acting, plays, and actors as a member of the audience, not as the boss or director."[37]

Few people knew that Andreyeva (before MAT she was married to a high tsarist official) had become a committed Marxist. She financed the Bolshevik press; Lenin gave her the party nickname "Phenomenon." Only she could dare let a Bolshevik leader, Nikolai Bauman, hide in her closet while she entertained the Moscow chief of police in the next room. Andreyeva was a welcome guest at the palace of Grand Duke Sergei, whose wife (sister of the empress) painted her portrait, never suspecting her subject was the financial agent of the Bolshevik Party. Andreyeva made both Morozov and Gorky sponsors of the party, introducing them to Lenin.

For the radically inclined Gorky and Andreyeva, their recent idol Chekhov was no longer revolutionary enough. In 1903 when he read *The Cherry Orchard*, Gorky, still smarting from Chekhov's remark two years earlier about his aesthetic backwardness, disparaged the play: "In reading, it does not impress me as a major work. There isn't a single new word."[38]

Chekhov himself was not averse to fame and popularity, and he was worried over *The Cherry Orchard*. He fretted that the "progressive" audience, typical of MAT, would reject the play as apolitical, and therefore old-fashioned. He was not comforted in the least by the raptures of Stanislavsky, who insisted that he had wept like a woman over the play. Stanislavsky's tears, as Chekhov knew too well, did not mean much, since the director, who admitted that he did not understand contemporary literature anyway, considered *The Cherry Orchard* a tragedy, while Chekhov described it as a comedy, even a farce.

Chekhov's apprehensions came to pass. The critics saw nothing in the MAT production, bathed in elegiac tones, but the author's deep pessimism. One wrote: "If this theater needs a motto for the portal, I would recommend the inscription from a medieval bell: *Vivos voco, mortuos plango* [I hail the living, mourn the dead] . . . *Mortuos plango:* Anton Chekhov. *Vivos voco:* Maxim Gorky."[39]

Chekhov blamed Stanislavsky and MAT for the unsuccessful production of his last play; he died soon afterward. Andreyeva felt that she and

Gorky were winning. She had already fought with Nemirovich-Danchenko and Stanislavsky, which is documented in the latter's rather harsh letter to her (February 1902), in which he calls her the nastiest word in his vocabulary: "ham." "I hate the ham actor in you (don't be mad). . . . You start telling lies, you stop being kind and intelligent, you become abrasive, tactless, insincere on stage and in life."[40]

Back then, in 1902, Andreyeva pretended not to take offense. But in 1904, she left MAT, telling Stanislavsky in parting, "I have stopped respecting the work of the Art Theater." Naturally, Gorky broke off relations with MAT, too. The worst blow for the theater was Morozov's announcement that he was quitting the directorship of MAT and stopping his financial support. Stanislavsky was horrified: the theater had suddenly lost two of its major authors, Chekhov and Gorky, a leading actress, and its main sponsor.

Then came the sensational news that Morozov was planning a new theater in St. Petersburg especially for Andreyeva, even more fabulous than the one he built for MAT. The press had a field day, relishing the story that the new enterprise would be a dangerous competitor for MAT, opening in the fall of 1905 with a sensational new play by Gorky. Stanislavsky wrote to his confidant: "Someone is spreading rumors in Moscow and the papers that we have a schism, that everything is collapsing, that I am leaving the Art Theater."[41]

It all ended literally with a bang. On May 13, 1905, Savva Morozov shot himself in his hotel room in Nice. To aim accurately, he circled the heart on his chest with a marking pencil. Nervous breakdowns were not unusual in the Morozov family, but the official version of suicide after a severe depression is now considered suspect. Some suggest the Bolsheviks were involved, and Morozov's family hinted that it was a murder: after all, Morozov had insured his life for one hundred thousand rubles (an enormous sum in those days), and he gave the bearer policy to Andreyeva, who turned the money over to the Bolsheviks immediately after his death.

As it happens, Morozov's sudden death saved MAT. Without a sponsor, the planned competing theater in St. Petersburg did not materialize, Andreyeva quietly returned to MAT, and even Gorky, who had scornfully declared that he could not possibly give his new play to the Art Theater, reconsidered. His drama *Children of the Sun* premiered on October 24, 1904, at MAT, and it is remembered for the mayhem on the opening night.

At the time, the situation in Moscow, as elsewhere in Russia, was extremely tense. In 1904, Nicholas II declared war on Japan, a war intended to be brief and victorious but which ended eighteen months later in a humiliating defeat. Then on Sunday, January 9, 1905, a demonstration of thousands of workers who'd gone to the tsar's palace with a petition of grievances ended when the army and police opened fire and killed many hundreds.

After that Bloody Sunday in St. Petersburg, mass strikes by workers in Moscow and other cities turned into street battles with police and soldiers. Under pressure of his advisors, the tsar reluctantly signed a manifesto on October 17, 1905, granting constitutional rights—freedom of speech, assembly, and political parties—and announced the creation of the first elective Russian parliament, the Duma.

The manifesto did not defuse the situation. The next day, October 18, Bauman, the Bolshevik who had hidden from the police at the apartment of the actress Andreyeva and was now a leader of the rebellion, was killed by a member of the Black Hundred, an ultranationalist right-wing populist organization. His funeral on October 20 turned into a mass demonstration in Moscow, the first in the city's history. Gorky, who attended with Andreyeva, maintained that several hundred thousand people, "all of Moscow," took part in the procession: workers, students, intellectuals, actors, and performers, including Stanislavsky, and the famous bass Fedor Chaliapin. There were more than one hundred fifty wreaths, including one from Gorky and Andreyeva: "To a fallen comrade." When the demonstrators began to disperse, they were attacked by Cossacks and a mob of supporters of the tsar.

The last act of Gorky's *Children of the Sun* at MAT depicted a riot: an infuriated crowd burst on stage, a shot was heard, and the hero, played by audience darling Vassily Kachalov, fell. Stanislavsky apparently had not expected this bit of stagecraft to be the equivalent of shouting "Fire!" in a crowded theater. The audience at the premiere was edgy: they feared all kinds of provocations and even an attempt on the life of the author. The mob scene and shot seemed too real to the spectators, who perceived it as an attack by armed thugs on the actors. As Kachalov recalled: "The noise was incredible. Women had hysterics. Part of the public rushed to the stage, apparently in order to defend us. Others fled to safety. Some rushed to the coatroom, to get guns from their coat pockets. Some shouted:'Curtain!' "[42]

The performance had to be interrupted. This may have been the first time in the history of Russian theater that art and politics became so intertwined that the audience could not tell where one ended and the other began.

Most of the Russian cultural elite was involved one way or another in the revolutionary tumult of 1905, and positions—as always in Russia— were quickly polarized. The poet Zinaida Hippius complained in her article "Choice of Sack" that Russia's cultural figures were "divided in half and tied up in two sacks, one labeled 'conservatives,' the other, 'liberals.' "[43] As soon as one enters the public arena and opens one's mouth, Hippius grumbled, one is instantly thrown into one of the sacks. There is no way out.

Confrontation was not avoided even in music, traditionally the most apolitical of all cultural endeavors. The controversy centered on the composer Nikolai Rimsky-Korsakov, who was Russia's most influential musician after Tchaikovsky's death in 1893.

At the St. Petersburg Conservatory, where Rimsky-Korsakov was an esteemed professor, a deadlock developed after Bloody Sunday. A student in the military band boasted that he had participated in the shooting of the workers. Other students were outraged and demanded his expulsion. The administration balked. When Rimsky-Korsakov, whose political views had taken on a "bright-red shade," as he put it, supported the student demands, the composer was fired from the staff.

This hasty step by the supervising officials once again showed the political shortsightedness typical of Russian cultural bureaucrats. The firing of Rimsky-Korsakov quickly became a newspaper scandal and outraged the public: the composer received piles of letters and telegrams of support from all over the country, even from people who had not heard of him before that. Peasants collected money to aid "the musician who suffered for the people." Rimsky-Korsakov became a national hero.

The influential St. Petersburg newspaper *Novosti*, in an article sarcastically headlined "How We Support Talent," added a composer's name for the first time in Russian history to a list of political victims of the tsarist regime. "We drove Pushkin to a suicidal duel. We sent Lermontov to face bullets. We sentenced Dostoevsky to hard labor. We buried Chernyshevsky alive in a polar grave. We exiled one of our greatest minds, Herzen. We expatriated Turgenev. We excommunicated and denounced Tolstoy. We expelled Rimsky-Korsakov from the conservatory."[44]

The culmination of the confrontation with the regime came with the St. Petersburg premiere of Rimsky-Korsakov's one-act opera *Kashchei the Immortal*, composed in 1902. It was an obvious political allegory, in which Kashchei, the evil sorcerer of Russian folk tales, is vanquished by the power of love. The musical fairy tale was a genre in which Rimsky-Korsakov, a master of national idiom and opulent orchestral writing, had no peers. But *Kashchei* was an unusual experiment for him, where the composer, known for his dislike of the innovations of Debussy and Richard Strauss, unexpectedly embraced musical modernism, adding strange harmonies and impressionistic colors, so strong were his political emotions.

The production of *Kashchei*, performed on March 27, 1905, by the students of the same conservatory from which the composer had been fired, turned into an event that was described by a newspaper as "an unprecedented, colossal, overwhelming public demonstration. The beloved artist was blanketed by flowers, greens, bouquets."[45] The authorities acted foolishly here, too. When shouts from the audience called "Down with autocracy!" the police lowered the fire curtain with such alacrity that it almost squashed sixty-one-year-old Rimsky-Korsakov, who was onstage taking his bows. On orders from the governor general of St. Petersburg, Dmitri Trepov (who would soon order the troops suppressing riots: "No warning shots and don't be stingy with the bullets!"), the audience was chased out of the hall. No wonder that twenty-three-year-old Igor Stravinsky, a student of Rimsky-Korsakov, wrote to his teacher's son in 1905 with uncharacteristic radical fire: "Damned kingdom of mental hooligans and obscurantism! The Devil take them!"[46] and went on in unprintable language.

Stravinsky's outburst reflected a swiftly expanding gap between the

Russian intelligentsia and the autocracy. Nicholas II was losing his credibility. This was an unstoppable development influenced also by cultural giants such as Tolstoy, Chekhov with MAT, Gorky, and Rimsky-Korsakov, each in his way and degree. The Red Wheel, to use Solzhenitsyn's metaphor, started to roll.

Chapter Two

The dizzying events of 1905, and in particular the tsar's manifesto of October 17 granting constitutional freedoms, which encouraged liberals, also brought into the political arena powerful conservative forces that came to be known as the Black Hundred. The term applied to the members of the Union of the Russian People, a party on the extreme right that existed from November 1905 until the revolution of February 1917. In a broader sense, it was henceforth used for all proponents of a rigidly conservative and xenophobic line in Russian public and cultural life.

Over the years, the term "Black Hundred" became strongly pejorative, which is why leading conservatives like Solzhenitsyn disliked it. But the original Black Hundred was proud of it. One of the founders of the movement, Vladimir Gringmut, in his 1906 article "Manual for the Monarchist Black Hundred," explained, "The enemies of autocracy use the term 'Black Hundred' for the simple, black [in Russian, the word also means illiterate, unenlightened] Russian people who during the armed revolt of 1905 stood up to defend the sovereign Tsar. Is it an honorable name, 'black hundred'? Yes, very honorable."[1] Vadim Kozhinov, a leading neoconservative of the late twentieth century, also considered the term appropriate.

According to Kozhinov, the Black Hundred was an "extremist monarchist" movement, which led an uncompromising battle with revolution. Russian Jews, in the views of the Black Hundred, played a disproportionately active or even leading role in the revolutionary movement. This was formulated succinctly by the monarchist Vassily Shulgin: "For me the 'Jewish preponderance' in the Russian intelligentsia class was clear at the turn of the century. The Jews have taken over, besides the universities, the press and through it, control over the intellectual life of the country. The result of this preponderance was the power and virulence of the 'liberation movement' of 1905, of which the Jews were the backbone."[2] In the opinion of Shulgin and other ultraconservatives, by 1905 "Jews had taken over political Russia. . . . The brains of the nation (except for the government and government circles) were in Jewish hands."[3]

The essayist and philosopher Vassily Rozanov, perhaps the most brilliant and most controversial exponent of Russian antiliberal thought, a figure some find attractive and repellent simultaneously, had a somewhat different opinion of the matter. "Kikes, madness, enthusiasm, and the holy purity of Russian boys and girls—that is what wove our revolution, which carried the red banner down Nevsky Prospect the day after the manifesto of October 17 was proclaimed."[4]

Rozanov cut an eccentric figure. Physically quite unattractive (red hair sticking out in all directions, rotted black teeth, mumbled speech with spittle flying), he exaggerated that ugliness in his frank autobiographical writings. He started out his literary career with a thick philosophical treatise of more than seven hundred pages, which he published at his own expense and which went unnoticed. Rozanov gradually developed a quasi-Nietzschean aphoristic style, never seen before in Russian literature.

Ideologically Rozanov was a committed proponent of monarchy and a devout Orthodox Christian. But readers of his best books in the aphoristic genre—*Solitaria* (1912), *Fallen Leaves* (1913 and 1915), and *Apocalypse of Our Times* (1917–1918)—easily fall under Rozanov's spell regardless of their own ideology. The Soviet dissident Andrei Sinyavsky, for whom Rozanov was one of the most important writers, justly noted that *Fallen Leaves* was not simply a book title but a definition of a genre. Or as Rozanov himself put it, "The wind blows at midnight and carries leaves. . . . Life in swift-flowing time tears off from the soul our exclamations, sighs, half-thoughts, half-feelings."

Rozanov was very proud of his innovative literary manner. For all the profundity and perceptiveness of his remarks on literature or religion, it sometimes seems that stylistic originality was more important to him than his ideas. "Not every thought can be written down, only if it is musical." Because he willfully published articles pro and contra the revolution, in support of the monarchy and criticizing it, anti-Semitic pieces and Judophilic ones, Rozanov was labeled unprincipled. He shot back, "Isn't there one hundredth of truth in revolution? And a hundredth in Black Hundred? . . . So, you should all bow down to Rozanov for, let's say, 'cracking the eggs' of various hens—geese, ducks, sparrows—constitutional democrats, Black Hundred, revolutionaries—and then dropping them on a single 'frying pan,' so that you can no longer distinguish 'right' and 'left,' 'black' and 'white.' "[5]

For Rozanov perhaps the central theme was the connection between God and sex. He spoke and wrote about it with disarming frankness, which was shocking in those days (his book *Solitaria* was banned for a while as pornographic). Rozanov's interest in the subject was typical of the Russian intellectual elite of the early twentieth century. One of the seminal thinkers of the period, Nikolai Berdyaev, categorized himself as "a kind of erotic philosopher."

The "sex problem" was a dominant topic in the influential intellectual salon of the St. Petersburg writer and philosopher Dmitri Merezhkovsky and his wife, the poet Zinaida Hippius, a red-haired beauty with the eyes of a mermaid. As Berdyaev noted, "an unhealthy mystical sensuality, which had not existed previously in Russia, was everywhere."

This erotic-religious obsession crystallized into a notorious incident in St. Petersburg. On May 1, 1905, a group gathered at the apartment of the decadent poet Nikolai Minsky, including Berdyaev, the influential Symbolist Vyacheslav Ivanov, the writer Alexei Remizov (all with their wives), Rozanov, Fedor Sologub, soon to be celebrated for his novel, *Petty Demon,* and a certain musician, as an eyewitness recorded, "a blond Jew, handsome, unbaptized." They dimmed the lights and twirled in a dervish-like dance in a mock Dionysian mystery. Then they symbolically crucified the musician, who had volunteered for the part.

The point of the gathering was to perform a blood sacrifice. Ivanov and his wife, Lydia Zinovyeva-Annibal, dressed in red chitons with sleeves rolled up ("just like an executioner," that eyewitness put it) cut the musician's wrist, mixed the blood with wine in a chalice and offered it around the circle. The ritual ended with "fraternal kisses."

Word of the strange ritualistic gathering quickly spread through St. Petersburg, picking up new, spicy details. In the version of the writer Mikhail Prishvin, who had not been there, Rozanov became the main protagonist: "They dined, drank wine, and then took communion with the blood of a Jewess. Rozanov crossed himself and drank. He tried to get her to undress and get under the table, and offered to undress and be on the table."[6]

It was no surprise that Prishvin, who knew Rozanov well, imagined him to be the initiator of such a risqué sexual-religious rite. Rozanov's philosophical writings were always balancing on the edge of erotic provocation, and many suspected that he was prepared to cross the line not only in theory but in practice. The proper Alexandre Benois, the leading art critic of the period, recalled with a shudder another time that Rozanov almost turned an evening into "an outrage."

Rozanov, Merezhkovsky and Zinaida Hippius, Benois, and a few others were debating the symbolic significance of the episode in the New Testament when Jesus washes the feet of his disciples before the Last Supper. The Merezhkovskys hailed that "deed of humiliation and service," and suggested that they enact the ritual then and there. According to Benois, the greatest enthusiast of the idea was Rozanov, who babbled, eyes aglow, "Yes, we must, we must do this and do it now." Benois, who generally had the greatest sympathy for Rozanov and his eccentricities, this time suspected "depraved curiosity," since Rozanov obviously was planning to wash the white, slender legs of the seductive Hippius, and no one could guess where that would lead. The cautious art critic, horrified by the specter of unbridled group sex, stopped the religious ecstasy of his fellow guests in their tracks, for which Rozanov later berated him; Benois, he said, your skepticism scared off an infusion of the Holy Spirit.

Benois recalled that he and the people of his artistic circle "were in those years acutely interested in the mystery of life and sought an answer in religion."[7] To debate these issues, they decided to form The Religious-Philosophical Assembly, which opened in November 1901 in the building of the Imperial Geographical Society on Theater Street, across the way from the famous Imperial Ballet School.

For Russia, which lacked a tradition of regular public religious debates with the participation of the intelligentsia, this was an unprecedented event. They first had to get permission from the Holy Synod, which had only nine months previously excommunicated Leo Tolstoy. The Synod gave its approval. While the intellectuals wanted to break the hold of positivism, which had reigned in the Russian discourse since the 1860s, the church officials were eager to show that they were open to dialogue with the intelligentsia. So a delegation of the founding fathers of the Assembly went for the blessing of Metropolitan Anthony of St. Petersburg at the Alexander Nevsky Monastery.

Benois, who described the trip with a bit of humor, was quite impressed by the white hood with a diamond cross pin of the regal but gentle metropolitan and by the excellent tea in heavy, faceted glasses and the delicious pastries. He was also amused by the fact that the delegation included, besides the Russian Orthodox Merezhkovsky and Hippius, two Jews (Nikolai Minsky and the artist Leon Bakst) and, as the Catholic Benois put it, the "definitely Jew-obsessed" Rozanov. Thus, the delegation had first to discuss whether or not to approach for the metropolitan's personal blessing, and if they did, whether or not to kiss his hand as he made the sign of the cross over them.

These recollections of an avid participant in the Russian religious revival of the early twentieth century are very telling. They evince the extraordinary breadth of the movement's spectrum, which is forgotten now, sometimes intentionally in an attempt to underscore its fundamentalist characteristics. And yet this religious renaissance, which played such an exceptional role in Russia's twentieth-century culture, included both conservatives and innovators—"two of each kind," like Noah's Ark: religious fanatics but also anticlericals like Maxim Gorky, the composers Nikolai Rimsky-Korsakov and Sergei Taneyev, the poet Sergei Esenin; monarchists, populists, and Bolsheviks (the latter represented by Anatoly Lunacharsky and Alexander Bogdanov); realist painters and the founders of abstract art (Vassily Kandinsky); and committed homophobes and some open homosexuals (most famous among the latter, the poets Mikhail Kuzmin and Nikolai Klyuev).

Early exponents of the ideas of the religious renaissance were the painters Viktor Vasnetsov and Mikhail Nesterov (considered today by some nationalists as the best Russian painter of the twentieth century; Nesterov lived to receive the Stalin Prize in 1941), who began painting stunning frescoes at the end of the nineteenth century in monasteries and churches. With them was Mikhail Vrubel, the most formidable personality in Russian Symbolist art, still underappreciated in the West, but now regarded in Russia as a seminal figure of the era.

Vrubel, of Polish descent with an admixture of Russian, German, Danish, and Tatar blood, sometimes called the Russian Cézanne (with Van Gogh's temper, one might add), was notable for his artistic dualism. He began with the creation of an iconostasis for a church and ended with an enormous, mysterious painting *Demon Downcast* (1902), the culmination of almost twenty years of obsession with that theme. (Demonism in a Nietzschean interpretation was fashionable among Russian Symbolists.)

Even Vrubel's prophet Moses (for the frescoes in the church of St. Cyril in Kiev) was endowed with a strangely demonic gaze. The artist felt that his demons were not so much evil as suffering and grieving androgynous spirits. Vrubel's downcast Demon, spread out on a fantastical mountain landscape, had an elongated body, with slender arms behind his head, and a feminine gaze, injured, fragile, but at the same time imperious and winning.

Researchers have found that the same young woman's face served as the model for the twenty-eight-year-old Vrubel's study for an icon of the Virgin and for the first sketches of the Demon's image. The philosophical and artistic antinomy that tore at the artist's mind (as well as bad genes) brought Vrubel in 1902 to a psychiatric hospital, where he died in 1910, at the age of fifty-four, completely blind. The artist Sergei Sudeikin left a description of his visit at the clinic, Vrubel's tiny body, bright pink face with the whites of his eyes a horrible pale blue, and with a blue cast beneath the eyes and around his lips. Sudeikin thought those colors symbolized "frozen madness," but Vrubel astonished him by reciting *The Iliad* in Greek, Virgil in Latin, *Faust* in German, *Hamlet* in English, and Dante in Italian, adding commentary in French.[8] Sudeikin saw a drawing of the head of the Demon in Vrubel's room—the image continued to haunt the artist.

In 1906, Sudeikin attended an exhibition of Russian artists organized by Sergei Diaghilev at the Paris Salon d'Automne. It began with icons and ended with Vrubel. The Vrubel hall included the grand panel, ten by sixteen meters, *Mikula Selyaninovich*, depicting the Russian mythological hero. In 1896 it was presented at the National Russian Industrial Art Exhibition in Nizhny Novgorod. Even though its sketch had been approved by Nicholas II, the panel's unusual modernist manner created a scandal among viewers and in the press (in particular, it was viciously attacked by the young reporter Maxim Gorky). At the insistence of the Academy of Arts, the panel was removed from the official pavilion. It was one of the more infamous artistic-political imbroglios at the turn of the century.

Sudeikin and the refined mystical artist Pavel Kuznetsov, both of whom had their own works in the Diaghilev show, restored Vrubel's panel, which had begun flaking in storage, folded up like a blanket. With his friend, the Futurist artist Mikhail Larionov, Sudeikin wandered around the Autumn Salon every day, and always saw a stocky man in the Vrubel hall, standing for hours in front of *Mikula Selyaninovich*. It was the young Pablo Picasso.[9] This must have been the only case when the tastes of an avant-garde Spanish artist and an extremely conservative Russian monarch coincided.

At Vrubel's funeral on April 3, 1910, in St. Petersburg, the only eulogy at the open grave was given by Alexander Blok, the best-known Russian Symbolist poet in the West and one of the most esteemed twentieth-century poets in Russia. Looking "grim, remote, charred" (in the words of his friend and rival, the writer Andrei Bely), Blok, twenty-nine, his face an enigmatic Apollonic mask, uttered sad words in a monotone about the victory of the night, both in Vrubel's paintings and in life, for "what is darker wins."[10]

Blok's speech was heard in silence by the luminaries of the Russian art world: Benois, Bakst and Diaghilev, Valentin Serov, Nikolai Roerich, Boris Kustodiev, Mstislav Dobuzhinsky, Kuzma Petrov-Vodkin. Did they guess that in eulogizing Vrubel, Blok was also metaphorically mourning the defeat of the revolution of 1905? Like Vrubel's art, Blok's poetry was antinomic: it contains the lofty and base, the altar and the tavern, the Madonna and the heroine of one of his most popular poems, *The Unknown Woman*, a prostitute slowly wending her way through the drunks "with rabbit eyes" in a bar.

Blok's poetry charted the path of Russian Symbolism, which appeared as the native response to the French experiments of Charles Baudelaire, Paul Verlaine, and Arthur Rimbaud. But like everything Russian, this literary movement blossomed with mysticism and heightened philosophical aspirations modeled on Tolstoy and Dostoevsky.

Boris Eikhenbaum, in a speech at a memorial for Blok in 1921, said: "The knight of the Beautiful Lady; Hamlet pondering nonexistence; the wild profligate, nailed to a bar counter and giving himself up to gypsy charms; the grim prophet of chaos and death—all that for us was the unfolding of a single tragedy, and Blok was its hero."[11]

Blok, earlier than others, was pinpointed by Russian literary scholarship (especially by the "formalists" Eikhenbaum and Yuri Tynyanov) as the creator of his own biographical mythos. Tynyanov explained the "Blok phenomenon" thus: "When people speak of his poetry, almost always they unwittingly replace the poetry with the *human face*—and everyone has come to love the *face* and not the *art*."[12]

True, the image Blok created, not only in his poems, but also in his letters, diaries, and notebooks, of a martyr sacrificing himself for art and truth, was an inspiring one. It does not matter that the real Blok in the reminiscences of his contemporaries appeared as an alcoholic, debaucher, misogynist who ruined his wife's life, and anti-Semite (Zinaida Hippius, who shared Blok's Judophobic views, called him an "exceptionally fierce anti-Semite" and noted in her diaries his desire "to hang all the kikes").[13] Yet none of the evidence managed to shake Blok's legend, such was the power of his image: the severity and significance of Blok's looks, ideally confirming the idea of how a "poet" should appear and act; the unfeigned tragic tone and music of his poetry; and his symbolically untimely death. Nor was Blok's image undermined by the attacks of his literary enemies—in particular, the envious parody of Blok in Alexei Tolstoy's novel *Road to Calvary*, where he is depicted as the famous poet Alexei Bessonov, gulping down wine, seducing women right and left, and writing about the fate of Russia, although he knows the country "only from books and pictures."

Tynyanov was the first to place Blok's "literary personality" in a historical, mythos-forming tradition that can be traced to Pushkin and Leo Tolstoy and was continued by Vladimir Mayakovsky and Sergei Esenin, for whom the "Blok mythos" served as an example. (We can now add later writers to the list: Anna Akhmatova, Boris Pasternak, Joseph Brodsky.) Blok modeled himself also on Vrubel (the legend of artist as "sacred madman").

The wing of Vrubel's Demon touched the work and posthumous legend of another famous Nietzschean and occultist of the period, the composer Alexander Scriabin (1872–1915), whose music was met with incomprehension, irritation, and anger, but also with elation and adoration similar to the cult of Blok. Scriabin was a particular favorite of the Russian Symbolists Andrei Bely and Vyacheslav Ivanov and then the younger poets Boris Pasternak and Osip Mandelstam, who in typically grandiloquent fashion proclaimed: "In the fateful hours of cleansing and storm we raised aloft Scriabin, whose heart is a sun burning above us."[14]

Many leading Russian Symbolists followed the German Romantics (Friedrich Schiller) and Dostoevsky in the belief in the great transformative power of art. "From art," said the visionary and mystic Bely, author of the novel *Petersburg,* considered by the finicky Vladimir Nabokov to be on the level of the works of Proust, Joyce, and Kafka as a masterpiece of twentieth-century world literature, "will come a new life and the salvation of humanity."[15]

But Scriabin did not simply talk about the possibility of combining art with ethics and religion: he tried to turn his utopian romantic-symbolist ideas into reality. A small, quick-moving dandy with a neat beard and upward pointing mustache, Scriabin, an extreme solipsist, came to believe that he was a religious prophet ("theurge," in Symbolist jargon). From his adolescent "grumbling at fate and God" (as he admitted), he came to self-divinity and the connected ideas of self-sacrifice, without ceasing to play with Nietzsche's demonism ("Satan is the yeast of the Universe"). Hence, the demonic motifs in some of his best piano works, such as "Poème satanique" (1903) and the Ninth Sonata (1913), which the composer called a Black Mass.

Scriabin's music is exalted, seductive, comparable to Vrubel's infernal canvases and Blok's intoxicating poetry. The peak of the flirtation with the occult came with Scriabin's *Prométhée—Poem of Fire* (1910), a stunning work for a large symphony orchestra and piano, organ, chorus, and special light keyboard. The musical symbolism of this innovative opus was influenced by *The Secret Doctrine* (1888), the fundamental work of Theosophy leader Helene Blavatsky, who interpreted the mythological Prometheus as a theosophist hero, a titan rebelling against God.

Blavatsky's concept of Lucifer as the "bearer of light" (*lux* and *fero*) apparently prompted Scriabin to introduce the part of Luce (light) in the score of *Prométhée:* during the performance, the composer called for multicolored "fiery columns" in the hall. The score was published in 1911 by a fan of the composer, the conductor Sergei Koussevitzky, with a fiery orange cover, as specified by Scriabin, and an androgynous depiction of the demon Lucifer (cf. the androgynous nature of Vrubel's Demon).

Scriabin contemplated a great *Mysterium,* an apocalyptic musical action that, once realized, would lead to the "end of the world," when matter would begin to perish and the spirit would triumph: a Second Coming brought on by the power of art as transformed by Scriabin. Bely and Ivanov could only watch in envy as the rather abstract idea for a mysterium that they had propagated suddenly moved closer to reality: Scriabin was already discussing how he would build a special temple on a lake in India to be the center of this unheard-of ritual, which would in some way involve all of humanity; the composer started raising funds for the temple; he was picking the right spot for it. . . .

It all ended abruptly in the spring of 1915, when Scriabin died from blood poisoning at the age of forty-three. There were only forty pages of sketches for the *Acte préalable* of the *Mysterium*, an introduction of sorts. Others tried to turn those sketches into a completed work; it has even been performed and recorded, but, alas, without the anticipated mystical effect.

The Scriabin case was unique in the speed of his trajectory, which stunned contemporaries compared to a rising line, and composer's exalted image, unheard-of previously in Russia. But it was also a typical part of the new spiritual strivings in Russian culture. The notable musical premieres of 1915, just before the death of Scriabin, included Sergei Taneyev's cantata *Upon Reading the Psalms*, Alexander Gretchaninoff's cantata *Praise God*, and Sergei Rachmaninoff's *All-Night Vigil*. The next year, 1916, saw the performance of the stylish requiem *Fraternal Prayer for the Dead* by Alexander Kastalsky, director of the Synod School and of the Synod Choir, a connoisseur of ancient Russian chorale music and leader of the "new wave" in Russian spiritual music, which sought to purify but also to democratize it.

Compared to Scriabin's works (and bearing in mind that Igor Stravinsky's *Sacre du printemps* had already exploded on the scene), these compositions appear quite conservative, although their archaism is varied. It is curious to note that while Gretchaninoff was undoubtedly a religious man (but a political radical, who wrote "Funeral March" in revolutionary 1905 for the Bolshevik Bauman), church was never central to Rachmaninoff's world view, and Taneyev was openly agnostic and anticlerical. (Kastalsky presents a special case: he started out with a loyal submission of his church music to Nicholas II in 1902 and ended up in 1926 as a member of the Red Professors group at the Moscow Conservatory, writing works about Lenin and the Red Army to the doggerel of the Communist court poets Demyan Bedny and Alexander Bezymensky and creating the officially approved arrangement of the "Internationale," which served as the Soviet Union anthem until 1944.) But all these quite different composers were active in the Russian religious renaissance.

Like Taneyev (head of the Moscow composers), the patriarch of the St. Petersburg school of composition, Rimsky-Korsakov, was openly atheistic, but that did not hinder him, as one of the directors of the Court Capella, from taking part in Orthodox arrangements of the traditional Easter service. Rimsky-Korsakov's reaction to Scriabin's mystical plans was sarcastic: "Could he be losing his mind because of religious-erotic lunacy?"[16]

Rimsky-Korsakov was in no danger of such lunacy. Critics often described the open sensuality of the billowing waves of Scriabin's music, which they felt was exactly what Rimsky-Korsakov's oeuvre lacked. (Scriabin was very amorous, like Blok. The only known extramarital romance of Rimsky-Korsakov, with the singer Nadezhda Zabela, wife of the artist Vrubel, was apparently platonic.)

Quite telling is the reaction of the critic Yevgeny Petrovsky (who had given Rimsky-Korsakov the idea for his antimonarchist opera *Kashchei the Immortal*) to the premiere of his idol's new opera, *The Legend of the Invisible City of Kitezh and the Maiden Fevronia*, in St. Petersburg in 1907. The reviewer noted that Rimsky-Korsakov, who based the opera on the religious legend about the miraculous rescue of Kitezh from the Tatar invasion (according to the story, the city sank underwater and its residents were taken aloft to heaven), expressed in his music not the "elevation of souls upward," but a "measured procession of the cross around and near the church." Another observer agreed: "That walking 'around' rather than 'upward' is characteristic of *Kitezh* as a whole."[17]

This curious Freudian criticism missed the mark: the restraint of *Kitezh* is affecting. Anna Akhmatova once said that she held *Kitezh* higher than Wagner's *Parsifal* because of the purity and chastity of its religious feeling, which she considered typically Russian.[18]

The young Sergei Diaghilev loved *Kitezh* for the same reason. There is a perception of Diaghilev, who created the model for art entrepreneur in haute culture in the last century, as being a Westernizer and cosmopolite. That is a misapprehension: Diaghilev throughout his life was an inveterate Russian nationalist, even a "fanatic" one in Benois's opinion, but he learned in his later years to mask these feelings out of pragmatic considerations.

The personality of Diaghilev, that Rastignac from the Russian provinces (he came to St. Petersburg from remote Perm, pink-cheeked, red-lipped, and blatantly optimistic), managed to combine altruistic adoration of art with charming opportunism, which he was the first to admit. This can be seen in his relations with Rimsky-Korsakov, with whom he claimed to have studied composition (probably just a legend).

But Diaghilev did in fact show his compositions to Rimsky-Korsakov once in 1894, and the master called them "more than foolish." The infuriated twenty-two-year-old Diaghilev told Rimsky-Korsakov: "The future will show which of us history will consider greater!" And left proudly, slamming the door behind him.[19]

This confrontation did not keep Diaghilev, who was gathering a landing party of Russian music to descend upon Paris in 1907 for his now-legendary Russian Historical Concerts, to ask for support and cooperation from Rimsky-Korsakov, whom he now addressed as his "favorite and beloved teacher." Rimsky-Korsakov did not want to appear before "those feuilleton French" who "understand nothing," but Diaghilev was a great arm-twister. An eyewitness reported that Diaghilev "flattered, hypnotized with praise, he berated, he grew heated, gesturing furiously and running around the room."[20] In the end, the austere maestro wrote to Diaghilev, "If we have to go, let's go, said the parrot as the cat pulled him out of the cage," and traveled to Paris, where he and the other Russian composers and performers dragged there by the persistent impresario—Alexander Glazunov, Rachmaninoff, Scriabin, and Chaliapin—were met with great success (despite the ominous rumors that "terrorists with bombs" were seen at the concerts).

In 1897, Diaghilev outlined his ambitions in a letter to Benois: "To polish Russian painting, cleanse it, and most importantly, present it to the West, glorify it in the West."[21] Diaghilev did not manage to realize this program successfully in painting, but ten years later he began implementing it in music (and after that, in ballet), where things went much better.

The Russian Historical Concerts of 1907 (five performances) cost an enormous sum, 180,000 francs, which came not from the tsar's treasury, as rumor had it, but from the businessmen of the Russo-American Rubber Company, who got "a cup of tea" with Diaghilev's patron, Grand Duke Vladimir, in exchange. Diaghilev was an innovator even in the field of finding sponsors; however, the Russian press was quick to dub him a "Gescheftmacher of genius."[22]

But without this dealmaker, it is now clear, one of the cultural milestones of Russia would probably not have existed. This was the journal *Mir Iskusstva* [World of Art], which appeared from 1899 to 1904, published by the association of young artists and literati of the same name, which tried to rejuvenate national culture (Benois even suggested calling the journal *Renaissance*). While striving to overcome the utilitarianism of the previous generation of Russian artists (and condemning the radically populist aesthetics of Leo Tolstoy, considered by the younger crowd "a slap in the face of beauty"), Diaghilev still proclaimed that "art and life are inseparable." This dualism was evident in the Mir Iskusstva attitude toward the West: Diaghilev and Benois professed "love for Europe," but also insisted that that very love helped Russian classics from Pushkin to Tchaikovsky to Tolstoy "to express our *izbas* [cottages], and our *bogatyrs* [mythic heroes], and the unfeigned melancholy of our songs," that is, to be true nationalists.

The editorial board, authors, and friends of *Mir Iskusstva*, which was subsidized at the outset by the Moscow merchant Savva Mamontov (who also started the first private opera company in Russia) and Princess Maria Tenisheva, a wealthy patron of national culture and crafts, quickly fell apart into two camps. One consisted of artists—Benois, Bakst, Serov, and Konstantin Somov—and the other, of writers and philosophers who despised "those stupid and ignorant daubers"—Merezhkovsky, Zinaida Hippius, Rozanov, and the proto-existentialist Lev Shestov, who published one of his most important early works, "Dostoevsky and Nietzsche: The Philosophy of Tragedy," in *Mir Iskusstva*.

Diaghilev, as the editor, tried to avoid excessive "decadence" and to play a mediating centrist role. The first issue carried, to the horror of Benois and his snobbish friends, reproductions of the then-popular religious and historical works of the traditionalist painter Vasnetsov. Diaghilev also promoted not only the subtle Impressionist landscape artist Isaak Levitan and the perceptive portraitist Serov, who tended toward stylization (both were close to *Mir Iskusstva*), but the much more conservative titan of Russian realist painting, Ilya Repin.

To keep the journal afloat, Diaghilev had to perform miracles of political tightrope walking. In 1900, Mamontov, who went broke, and Tenisheva, who was infuriated with showoff Diaghilev, stopped funding the journal, so the quick-witted impresario talked his close friend Serov, who was doing a portrait of Nicholas II, to ask the tsar for help. Nicholas II (according to the artist Kustodiev, who had discussed aesthetic topics with the tsar while doing his own sketch of the sovereign) was not in favor of artistic innovation ("Impressionism and I are two incompatible things")[23] and was skeptical about the "Decadents." Still, trusting Serov, the tsar commanded that a subsidy of fifteen thousand rubles be given to Diaghilev, with another thirty thousand later added: a very impressive sum for those years and a salvation for the journal.

Diaghilev had to maneuver through the shoals of religious issues, too. He was probably more superstitious than devout, but he was proud to publish the "God-seeking" Rozanov and he frequented the meetings of the Religious-Philosophical Assembly. He was strongly influenced by the literary lions on the board of the journal, Merezhkovsky, Hippius, and especially, his cousin Dmitri Filosofov, tall, languid, charismatic, and probably Diaghilev's first lover (who dropped him to spend fifteen years living in a ménage à trois with Merezhkovsky and Hippius).

This did not keep Filosofov from being a moral purist in questions of culture and a religious fundamentalist. We can find echoes of Filosofov's ideas in Diaghilev's letter to Chekhov of December 23, 1902, where recalling a discussion with the writer on "whether a serious religious movement is possible in Russia now," the impresario insists: "It is, in other words, the question: to be or not to be? for all contemporary culture."[24]

Chekhov, who viewed Diaghilev sympathetically, was much more skeptical. When Diaghilev, who worshipped him, asked him to become a coeditor of *Mir Iskusstva*, Chekhov refused: "How could I live under one roof with D. S. Merezhkovsky, who believes definitely, believes like a teacher, while I have long lost my faith and can only look incredulously at any intelligent believer?"[25]

Both Merezhkovsky and Filosofov saw Chekhov as an aesthete, remote from real life, and a social relativist. (Interestingly, Leo Tolstoy was convinced that Merezhkovsky and company used religion "for fun, for a game.") They promoted these views in their own magazine, *Novy Put* [The New Path], which they started with Filosofov as editor in 1904. Zinaida Hippius wrote sarcastically in *Novy Put* that Chekhov was not a teacher of life, as a true writer must be, but "merely a slave who was blessed with ten talents, high trust—and squandered that trust."[26]

A mighty circle of influential religious philosophers (mostly former Marxists) appeared on the pages of *Novy Put*—Berdyaev, Sergei Bulgakov, and Semyon Frank. In 1909 they published the anthology *Vekhi* [Landmarks], accusing the Russian intelligentsia of atheism, nihilism, and sectarianism, which led, in their opinion, to the defeat of the revolution of 1905. *Vekhi* proclaimed philosophical idealism to be the most reliable foundation for all future reforms.

Vekhi turned out to be enormously influential and went through five editions in a single year. Leo Tolstoy found the main idea in the anthology—the priority of self-perfection—to his taste, but the literary style repulsed him as vague and artificial. Gorky called *Vekhi* "the vilest little book in the entire history of Russian literature," and Lenin branded the anthology "the encyclopedia of liberal renegades." (This became the required answer about *Vekhi* on future exams in Soviet colleges.)

By 1909, when *Vekhi* appeared, Diaghilev was not very interested in religious and philosophical disputes. He had begun his celebrated Russian Seasons the previous year, bringing Mussorgsky's *Boris Godunov*, with Fedor Chaliapin in the starring role, to Paris. Rimsky-Korsakov did the instrumentation for the opera, and at Diaghilev's persistent requests, wrote several additions. He died a few days after the final Paris performance of *Boris Godunov*, at the age of sixty-four.

Diaghilev's goal was to astonish Parisians by the opulence of the production. With Benois, he found and bought ancient brocade and expensive silks for the costumes, designed by Ivan Bilibin, an artist of the Mir Iskusstva group. The coronation scene of *Boris Godunov* was produced with maximum lavishness. Parisians were overwhelmed by the spectacle of the tsar accepting the scepter and orb from the patriarch, Boris being showered with gold and silver coins and having an embroidered belt wrapped around him. There was also a solemn procession with icons and gonfalons, impressive boyars in sparkling raiments, grim archers in red caftans bearing aloft enormous banners, and exotic-looking priests with censers regally entering to the deafening ringing of church bells.

But the center of the performance, amid all its color and lushness, was the gigantic figure of Chaliapin in the role of Tsar Boris. The great bass, famous not only for his thunderous voice but his incomparable dramatic interpretations, played the hero of Mussorgsky's proto-Expressionist opera with the full range of emotions. At first his Boris was imperious, but with a sense of foreboding; at the end, he was desperate and exhausted and half-crazed by the knowledge of his doom. The French saw more than a mighty singer on the stage of the Grand Opera; Chaliapin appeared as the hero of some work by Dostoevsky.

This was a turning point in Diaghilev's enterprise and in the Western reputation of Russian music. The picky Parisian critics were amazed by the innovations of Mussorgsky, whom they compared to Shakespeare and Tolstoy (the composer had a strong influence on Debussy, Ravel, and other leading French musicians of the time), and they raved over the production and the performers, Chaliapin in particular, whom they called "actor number one of our age." Chaliapin wrote with justifiable pride to Gorky, "We shook up the flabby souls of contemporary Frenchmen. . . . They'll see where the power is."

The fascination of the French with Chaliapin had a political element. While he was at the Grand Opera he published in the newspaper *Le Matin* a passionate open letter in which he complained that the Russian land, so rich in talent, was constantly oppressed "by someone's heavy boot, trampling everything alive into the snow"—first the Tatars, then the ancient princes, now the police. Chaliapin promised the French audience: "I will give my heart to the citizens of this birthplace of freedom. It will be the heart of Boris Godunov: it will beat beneath the raiments of brocade and pearl, the heart of the criminal Russian tsar, who died tormented by his conscience."[27]

This was a clever and bold move on the part of the singer, a smart mix of political gesture and artistic emotion. (Subsequently, other famous Russian musicians, like Mstislav Rostropovich, tried to emulate Chaliapin.) In the revolutionary year of 1905, Chaliapin sang a protest song, "Dubinushka" [The Club], from the stage of the Imperial Bolshoi Theater, for which the irritated tsar demanded he be punished. Wisely, the management demurred. Then, in 1911, during a performance of *Boris Godunov* at the Maryinsky Theater in St. Petersburg with Nicholas II in the audience, Chaliapin got on his knees with the chorus and sang the national anthem, "God Save the Tsar." Both episodes were widely publicized. The first riled the right, the second, the left, because both sides wanted to have the great singer in their camp.

This continued after the revolution of 1917. In 1918, eight years after Chaliapin was granted the highest title of "His Majesty's Soloist," the Bolsheviks made Chaliapin the first recipient of a new honorific, "People's Artist." But that did not help the Bolsheviks keep Chaliapin.

Although he had hailed the overthrow of the monarchy, Chaliapin saw that " 'liberty' had been turned into tyranny, 'fraternity' into civil war, and 'equality' meant stomping down anyone who dared raise his head above the level of the swamp,"[28] as he put it, and he left Russia in 1922, never to return. Later Stalin, who was a big fan of Chaliapin, made a few attempts (through Maxim Gorky, a close friend of the singer) to get him to return to his homeland. The cautious Chaliapin did not fall into Stalin's trap.

The political zigzags continued even after Chaliapin's death in 1938 in Paris. (He lived to be sixty-four, like Rimsky-Korsakov.) Despite the fact that the Soviet Union had stripped the singer of his People's Artist title in 1927 because he donated a large sum to help the poor children of Russian émigrés in France, the cult of Chaliapin continued to flourish in his former homeland.

The Chaliapin mythos promoted by the press before the revolution was of the poor boy who made it to the top by virtue of his talent (the Gorky model). This legend persisted in the Soviet Union, even after his departure for the West, because Chaliapin was one of the first Russian musicians to make recordings, and they became hugely popular. He sang both the classical repertoire and popular folk songs. The old, hissing records were played for many years at parties all over Russia, where people consumed vodka and pickles and sobbed listening to the magnificent bass singing the heartrending ballad "The sun rises and falls, but it is dark in my prison."

Chaliapin's ambivalent status as émigré also bolstered his reputation. By remaining in the West, like his friend and musical mentor Rachmaninoff, the singer avoided the total appropriation of his image by the Soviet regime. He remained the personification of Russian strength, valor, and flair, unfettered by party discipline or Communist ideology. So the émigré Chaliapin made an unexpected posthumous journey: in 1984, after coming to terms with the singer's heirs, the Soviet government flew his remains from Paris to the prestigious Novodevichy Cemetery in Moscow. This political gesture signaled the rise of a new cultural atmosphere and the advent of perestroika. Chaliapin maintains his position in Russia as the most famous musician of the twentieth century, surpassing not only his mentor Rachmaninoff but every contender even from the world of pop.

. . .

It was not Diaghilev who placed Chaliapin on that pedestal, although he did much to make it happen. But it is hard to deny that Diaghilev played Svengali in the case of Vaslav Nijinsky, turning his short ten years onstage into the longest-lived and most mysterious ballet legend of the twentieth century.

When Nijinsky met Diaghilev in the fall of 1908 in St. Petersburg (and became his lover), the eighteen-year-old dancer was already known to ballet fans: his remarkable performance in the early works of choreographer Mikhail Fokine drew attention. But Diaghilev made Nijinsky an international star.

Diaghilev introduced ballet in his second Russian Season in Paris (1909), and it quickly became the raison d'être of his enterprise. Ironically, this had not been his original intention. Benois always insisted that Diaghilev had never been a rabid ballet fan. Political and socioeconomic circumstances made him a ballet impresario.

In 1909 bureaucratic intrigues stopped the tsar's support for the Russian Seasons and they lost their official status as a cultural manifestation of the Russo-French political alliance. The wealthy Western bourgeoisie became the main sponsor of Diaghilev's enterprise. For that audience, one-act ballets that did not require overcoming linguistic and historical barriers were much more attractive than long, complex, and heavy Russian operas. Plus presenting ballets was much cheaper.

The ambitious Diaghilev had not only wanted to become director of the imperial theaters, he dreamed of an even higher position, as arbiter and manager of all Russian culture. Fate determined otherwise, although the court intrigues and scandals that put an end to Diaghilev's official career cannot be laid at the feet of fate alone: the clashes were predetermined by the entrepreneur's modernist tastes, his independent behavior, and his open homosexuality.

The resulting situation was unique for Russia: a powerful cultural enterprise, independent of the government (and consequently at odds with it), supported by Western capital and audiences, and therefore oriented to them. Its success was due to Diaghilev, the first (and still unsurpassed) global impresario of Russian culture.

There were losses for Russia in this case, as well. In culture, the role of personality is supreme; it is tempting to imagine the flowering of Russian culture if Diaghilev had remained in the country. On the other hand, it is not difficult to assume that he would not have gotten along with the Bolsheviks any more than he had with the tsarist court. Perhaps his role was to build a revolutionary yet workable model for the interaction of Russian and Western cultures under the aegis of a charismatic personality.

In 1927, at the end of the Diaghilev era, Anatoly Lunacharsky, still the first Bolshevik cultural boss (although his comparatively liberal reign was coming to a close), called Diaghilev "amuser of the gilded crowd."[29] Lunacharsky meant the impresario's dependence on a group of wealthy sponsors who were "rootless, feckless, and wandering all over the world in search of amusement"and which could "pay a lot of money, which can grant newspaper fame, but it is greedy. It demands continually new sensations from its'amuser.' "[30]

This was a Marxist critique of the Diaghilev model, perceptive but perhaps not quite fair. For the Communist Lunacharsky hundreds of thousands of Red Army soldiers, workers, and peasants attending an official exhibition of politically correct realistic paintings in Moscow in 1926 were vastly more important than "ten thousand glazed drones" gathering at Diaghilev's opening nights. Lunacharsky recorded his conversation with Diaghilev, who defended his patrons ("thirty or forty Maecenas-connoisseurs") as the progressive cultural elite whom the unwashed masses would follow, in Diaghilev's expression, "like thread behind a needle." It was that elite (the leading patrons, connoisseurs, collectors, influential journalists, dealers) who shaped the modern market for high culture.

Lunacharsky naturally considered Diaghilev's analysis obsolete bourgeois nonsense, and the actual minister of culture condescendingly instructed the would-be minister Diaghilev from the height of his ten-year Soviet experience: "This is the first time in history that art is properly posited as the vital element of people's lives and not as dessert for the gourmands."[31] But now, more than eighty years after that conversation, the world market for haute culture functions more on the Diaghilev model, and Lunacharsky's lecture sounds like old-fashioned social rhetoric. In other words, Diaghilev's ideas turned out to be more practical.

Diaghilev did have his own illusions. He thought he was controlling the tastes of his Western patrons, while in fact it was at least a two-way process. He whetted the artistic appetites of his sponsors, and they urged him on toward ever-greater avant-garde and cosmopolitan offerings.

The provincial from Perm was transformed into the cultural arbiter of Paris, London, and New York, along the way changing from an earnest admirer of Repin, Vasnetsov, and Nesterov into the aesthete who commissioned stage sets from Picasso, Braque, Roualt, and Matisse.

Two productions stand out on Diaghilev's astonishing journey among the milestones in twentieth-century culture: the premieres of Igor Stravinsky's ballets *Pétrouchka* (1911) and *Sacre du printemps* (1913). *Pétrouchka* alone would be enough to immortalize its creators, the composer and designer (Stravinsky and Benois), choreographer (Mikhail Fokine), dancers (Nijinsky and Tamara Karsavina), and producer (Diaghilev).

We can picture them in late May 1911 in the basement of the Teatro Constanzi in Rome, where they rehearsed *Pétrouchka* for the Paris premiere: there was a heat wave (and certainly no air-conditioning), sweaty Fokine dashing around the greasy raspberry red cloth covering the floor, trying to drum into the dancers the extremely complicated rhythmic figures that the composer, in his proper vest but with his shirtsleeves rolled up, banged out on a tinny upright piano that barely covered up the noise of traffic outside.

Occasionally the artist Serov (who also helped with a sketch of one of the costumes) and the religious philosopher Lev Karsavin, the ballerina's elder brother, both living in Rome at the time, would drop by the rehearsals. What a bouquet of talents and what different fates awaited them. The first to die, of angina in 1911 in Moscow, was Serov, forty-six, the highly regarded (by everyone from the tsar to the revolutionaries) maverick of early Russian modern art, whose reputation at home, as opposed to the West, was always high both among connoisseurs and the public.

Benois, stunned by Serov's death, in his obituary placed him in the ranks of Titian, Velázquez, and Franz Hals (in Russia, many agreed). Benois did not overestimate his own potential as an artist; he considered the only work worthy of outliving him his monumental memoirs. In that masterpiece, Benois, who died in 1960 in Paris, just two months short of his ninetieth birthday and without seeing his work published in full, wrote about his constant bickering with Diaghilev, who had died thirty years earlier, in Venice (just as a fortune-teller had once predicted, "on water"). Benois felt Diaghilev was too taken with the avant-garde, even if the impresario had become with Stravinsky one of the most influential artistic figures of Russian descent in the West. Together they radically reshaped the map of world culture, yet in Russia their fame never equaled Serov's.

This happened in part because both Diaghilev and Stravinsky were perceived (and still are) as émigré modernists. Having bid Russia farewell in 1914, Diaghilev never returned. Before his death, he waxed nostalgically about the Volga River, the gentle landscapes of Levitan, and music of Tchaikovsky. Stravinsky visited the Soviet Union in 1962, at the age of eighty, after a hiatus of half a century, and was even received by the country's leader, Nikita Khrushchev. But in response to an invitation to return again, he reportedly muttered, "Enough's enough."[32]

In the West, Nijinsky became the personification of men's dancing, but in the Soviet Union he fell so far off the cultural map that even at the height of perestroika in 1989, when *Pravda,* then still the country's most influential newspaper, decided to mark the centenary of the émigré dancer's birth, it misspelled his name as Nejinsky.

Fokine's *Pétrouchka* and *The Dying Swan* (he basically improvised the latter in 1907 as a sad and charming solo for its incomparable first performer, Anna Pavlova) are now ballet emblems of the twentieth century. But while *The Dying Swan,* which later became the signature piece of another great ballerina, Maya Plisetskaya, is nostalgic and fragile, *Pétrouchka* is all movement and tragic urgency.

The ballet is a puppet drama: pathetic Pétrouchka (a mixture of the British Punch and the Italian-French Pierrot) loses his beloved Ballerina to the arrogant and coarse Moor. The puppets are manipulated by the mysterious and powerful Magician. All around is the spectacle of the Russian Shrovetide carnival, which stunned Parisians with the vividness and energy of the music, the beauty of stylized sets and costumes, and the inventiveness of the choreographer in depicting—almost à la Stanislavsky's Art Theater—the holiday crowds (there were more than one hundred dancers onstage).

Karsavina, who replaced Pavlova as chief star of Diaghilev's company, was the ideal Ballerina in *Pétrouchka,* a sensual and naïve toy. The artistic presentation of that naïveté was informed, however, by Karsavina's fierce intellect. It could be said that both she and her brother were philosophers, only she danced and her brother wrote books.

Of all the members of that carefree and happy Roman group, Lev Karsavin had the most tragic fate. Exiled on Lenin's personal orders from Bolshevik Russia in 1922 (with other leading anti-Soviet intellectuals— Berdyaev, Frank, Ivan Ilyin, Fedor Stepun, and Pitirim Sorokin), Karsavin settled in Paris, lectured on medieval philosophy at the Sorbonne, befriended Matisse and Fernand Léger, and then found himself living once again on Soviet territory after World War II, in Lithuania.

Karsavin was arrested and deported to Siberia, to the Abez camp in Vorkuta, where Nikolai Punin, a prominent theoretician of avant-garde art, was also serving time. There Karsavin and Punin used to lecture fellow prisoners on the fine points of the icon of the Virgin of Vladimir or Malevich's *Black Square*.[33] The camp guards had other forms of amusement: the prisoners were regularly awakened in the middle of the night, lined up and marched to a big pit, and then spread out around its perimeter in preparation to be executed. Each time, the prisoners prepared to die, but they were returned to their barracks.[34] Karsavin died of tuberculosis in 1952 and was buried without a coffin, in nothing but a shirt with his camp number, tossed into a hole dug out of the frozen ground. Punin died there a year later.

Nijinsky's life, while different, was tragic and symbolic in its own way. In *Pétrouchka* he danced himself, as the insiders at the premiere knew full well: a puppet manipulated by the all-powerful Magician Diaghilev. Nijinsky was famous for his phenomenal leaps, in which he seemed to hang in the air for an instant. But for the role of Pétrouchka, Fokine did not create any virtuoso steps. Nevertheless, it was a signature role for Nijinsky, as was the Faun in *L'Après-midi d'un faun*, choreographed by Fokine to music by Debussy.

Fedor Lopukhov, a great choreographer and classmate of Nijinsky's (whom he did not like very much), told me that in ballet school Nijinsky was awkward, to the point of seeming mentally retarded.[35] Benois recalled that Nijinsky had a lot of trouble with the role of Pétrouchka in rehearsals. The artist was astonished by the metamorphosis that occurred when Nijinsky put on Pétrouchka's patchwork costume and tasseled cap and applied the whiteface makeup with round spots of rouge and crookedly drawn eyebrows. Suddenly Benois saw the beseeching eyes "of that horrifying grotesque, half-puppet half-human."[36]

For the first time in the history of the dance, on June 13, 1911, on the stage of the Théâtre Châtelet in Paris appeared a hero who could have come from the pages of a Dostoevsky novel, as the French press noted instantly. But the Parisian critics understandably missed the influence of Alexander Blok's Symbolist drama *The Fair Show Booth*, produced in St. Petersburg in 1906 by the avant-garde director Vsevolod Meyerhold: the characters included an awkward and suffering clown Pierrot (played by Meyerhold himself), who bled cranberry juice instead of blood.

Pétrouchka might have seemed to be a triumph of Mir Iskusstva. And it was, if one takes into account Fokine's production, Benois's design, and Karsavina's interpretation: a nostalgic look at old St. Petersburg by a sophisticated group of Russian Europeans gathered in Paris. But Nijinsky and Stravinsky, encouraged by Diaghilev, boldly leaped beyond the Mir Iskusstva stylized aesthetics toward the avant-garde.

Nijinsky left Diaghilev in 1913, after choreographing the premiere of Stravinsky's *Sacre du printemps*. It was a desperate attempt by Pétrouchka to escape his master, and it led to a nervous breakdown.

Nijinsky's last performance was on September 26, 1917, as Pétrouchka (a joke of fate); he was twenty-seven. Sojourns in expensive clinics treating schizophrenia followed. The most famous dancer of the twentieth century, Nijinsky died in London in 1950, leaving not only his legend but an astonishing document, his diaries of 1919. In those notes, Nijinsky surprises us by his naïve wisdom. Calling himself a crazy clown and "God's fool" ("a fool is good where there is love"), Nijinsky writes about his fascination with the religious teaching of Leo Tolstoy (the dancer was a vegetarian, "meat develops lust"), his bisexuality, his rejection of war, and his love of Russia and dislike of the Bolsheviks. Nijinsky wanted people to stop deforestation and overuse of oil. He also admits his addiction to morphine and masturbation, and he concludes bitterly: "Now I understand Dostoevsky's *Idiot,* for they take me for an idiot."[37]

There is a photograph taken in 1929 with Nijinsky with a terrified smile standing between Karsavina and a pompous Diaghilev in tails: the impresario had brought the "crazy clown" to a performance of *Pétrouchka,* in the hope that watching it might return his sanity. Diaghilev died that year; Nijinsky survived him by almost twenty-one years.

Coming after *Pétrouchka* (but conceived before it), Stravinsky's *Sacre du printemps* is arguably his most successful and organic work. It may well be the greatest score of the twentieth century. The audience at the premiere of *Sacre* on May 23, 1913, in Paris, famously rioted. The French public resisted the overwhelming onslaught of Stravinsky's music, afraid to hear its message, loud and clear: the world was on the brink of catastrophe.[38]

The First World War, which broke out in July 1914, took millions of young lives, destroyed the old European order, and triggered a series of destructive revolutions. European civilization never did rebound from that blow, which was foretold by the turbulent, cruel rhythms of *Sacre du printemps.*

The Russian empire, which entered the war on the side of France and England against Germany and Austro-Hungary, turned out to be a colossus with feet of clay. At first the war was hailed by many leading Russian intellectuals: they thought it "a great blessing" (the Symbolist poet Vyacheslav Ivanov). Berdyaev then also believed that the war had a providential significance: "It punishes, kills, and purifies by fire, reviving the spirit."[39]

The figure of Razumnik Vasilyevich Ivanov, whose pen name was Ivanov-Razumnik (1878–1946), stands apart. An antiwar critic and cultural historian, he had published as early as 1912 a magazine article signed "The Scythian" which proclaimed a rejection of bourgeois civilization as an "alien culture." "The order of such a life inevitably will be destroyed."[40]

That article was the proto-manifesto of an influential Russian cultural movement known as Scythianism, which retains its attraction for many in Russia to this day; from it came the theory of cultural Eurasianism, according to which Russia, as the great state on the border of Europe and Asia, has its own unique path and role in global geopolitics. Herodotus used the term "Scythian" for the semi-mythical nomadic tribes that invaded the Black Sea steppes from Asia in the eighth century BC; in the imagination of the Russian intellectuals they became a symbol of barbarian might and energy. Among adherents of Scythianism, a left-radical ideology with populist roots, were the major Russian poets of the era—Blok, Bely, Esenin, and Klyuev.

The motto chosen by Ivanov-Razumnik and his friends were the words of the nineteenth-century Russian revolutionary Alexander Herzen from his classic work, *My Past and Thoughts:* "I, like a true Scythian, happily see the old world fall apart and think that our calling is to inform it of its imminent death."

Stravinsky, who never formally declared himself a Scythianist, clearly was at that period (and later) influenced by its neonationalist ideas. (Interestingly, Ivanov-Razumnik and Stravinsky had a common friend, the musicologist Andrei Rimsky-Korsakov, one of the composer's sons.) Stravinsky's Scythian outlook can be seen in his conversation with Romain Rolland, who wrote it down in September 1914.

The French writer had come to Stravinsky with a request to join a protest in print against German "barbarism"—a timely topic. But Stravinsky (whom Rolland described as a short man, with a sallow, weary face, and weak-looking—a false impression!), without justifying Germany, did not agree that it was a barbaric country, calling it instead "decrepit and degenerate."[41]

Barbarism, according to Stravinsky, was a feature of a new culture. Stravinsky argued, in the Scythian spirit, that Russia was predestined to play the role of a "beautiful and powerful barbarian country, pregnant with new ideas that will fertilize world thought."[42]

Stravinsky also made a political prediction that was fully in line with the ideas of Ivanov-Razumnik and his friends: that the war would be followed by the revolution that would overthrow the Romanov dynasty and create the Slavic United States.

It is tempting to perceive *Sacre du printemps* as the greatest manifestation of the Scythian spirit in culture. In Russian poetry that spirit was expressed powerfully in Blok's topical poem, "Scythians" (1918):

> *Yes, we are Scythians! Yes, we are Asians,*
> *With slanted and greedy eyes!*

The Blok–Stravinsky parallel was never considered, as far as I know, by their contemporaries (even by the Eurasianist Pierre Souvtchinsky, who knew both men and wrote about both). Blok was not friends with Stravinsky, and judging by his diary and notebooks, had never heard a single note of his music. Still, one might imagine that it was *Sacre du printemps* that the poet had in mind when he called upon the Russian intelligentsia to accept the revolution: "We loved those dissonances, those roars, those ringing sounds, those unexpected transitions ... in the orchestra. But if we *really loved* them instead of merely tickling our nerves in fashionable theater halls after lunch, we must listen and love the same sounds now, when they fly out of the world orchestra."[43]

The ideologist of Scythianism, Ivanov-Razumnik, had in 1915 distributed hectograph copies (the samizdat of the time) of his antiwar article, "Trial by Fire,"in which he maintained that only united democratic forces could stop the monstrous slaughter. Blok liked the article; he subsequently wrote about war: "For a moment, it seemed that it would clear the air; it seemed that way to us, people overly impressionable; in fact it turned out to be a worthy crown to the lies, filth, and vileness into which our homeland had sunk."[44]

Russia suffered one humiliating disaster after another in the war. The economy was falling apart, with long breadlines even in the capital. The three-hundred-year-old autocratic rule of the Romanov dynasty, which had survived the revolutionary upheavals of 1905, was drawing to an end.

On January 1, 1916, Alexander Benois wrote in his diary (which was published only in 2003): "What will the new year bring? If it only brings peace, the rest will fall into place."[45] But for Benois (like Blok, a committed opponent of war), it was clear that Nicholas II (whom Benois was calling "the madman" who was "absolutely incapable" of ruling Russia) and his government did not comprehend "the meaninglessness of this deviltry."It horrified the moderate, cautious Benois: "Human stupidity is limitless, all-powerful, and it is quite possible that we will end up in universal bankruptcy and cataclysm!"

On February 20, 1917, Benois wrote: "Something *must* happen—there is an awful lot of electricity accumulated. But will it be anything decisive?"[46] He did not have long to wait for an answer: the autocracy, which had seemed invincible quite recently, collapsed within a few days that month. Gorky hailed this development enthusiastically. Most probably, Leo Tolstoy and Chekhov, had they lived to see it, would have reacted in the same way. The fall of the Romanov dynasty was not a chance occurrence but the culmination of a process.

Nicholas II abdicated from the throne, a Provisional Government was formed, but it too was unable to end the war and stop the economic decline. Only Lenin, the charismatic leader of the extremist party of Bolsheviks, promised workers and soldiers immediate peace and a good life if a dictatorial socialist regime is created.

Blok, in his 1917 diary, pointedly noted an absence of "genius" in the old ruling class. "Revolution presupposes will,"[47] he wrote. Only Lenin had the focus and iron will at that moment, and following his plan, on October 26, 1917, the Bolsheviks burst into the Winter Palace, arrested the meeting ministers of the Provisional Government, and took over the capital.

The Russian cultural elite on the whole considered this an irrational adventure. Almost all of them were certain that the new regime would fall in a week or two. The Bolshevik culture commissar Lunacharsky hoped that if they managed to hold for a month, events would follow by momentum. In the meantime, the Bolsheviks found themselves isolated in the Winter Palace. Only a very few people from the intelligentsia were willing to make contact with them—of course, they included such notables as Benois, Blok, and Meyerhold.

The astonished Benois thought it all resembled a production by his friend Diaghilev, whom he had compared to Lenin in his diary. With Diaghilev "everything first looked ridiculous and sometimes even nasty," creaking and collapsing until the last moment, and then somehow, he turned it into a beautiful and successful show. Perhaps the Bolsheviks would burn a few things and then calm down and in the end establish sober and reasonable order. "I doubt that they will build anything lasting," concluded the skeptical Benois.[48] He was a cultivated man but certainly no prophet.

Part Two

A TIME OF
CATASTROPHES

Chapter Three

In December 1917, the newly minted Bolshevik Commissar of Education (who in fact dealt with all cultural issues), Anatoly Lunacharsky, had two visitors in his small office in the Winter Palace: Nikolai Punin, twenty-nine, formerly the art critic of the trendy magazine *Apollo,* and experimental composer Arthur Lourié, twenty-six. Lisping but eloquent Punin (who also had a facial tic) and, in contrast, the outwardly calm, ironic, and exquisitely dressed Lourié were part of the innovative milieu in post-revolutionary Petrograd. They had come for permission to use the Hermitage Theater, which adjoined the Winter Palace, for the production of *Death's Mistake* by Velimir Khlebnikov, the mad genius of Russian experimental literature, in the staging of another giant of the Russian avant-garde, the artist Vladimir Tatlin. (Khlebnikov had a reputation in advanced circles as a dervish and prophet, and in 1912 he had predicted the year of the coming revolutions—1917.)

It's quite possible that the planned presentation of Khlebnikov's eccentric play (one of his best works) was merely a pretext for Punin and Lourié to meet with Lunacharsky. In any case, the conversation quickly moved on to more lofty issues—the creation of a new communist culture and the participation in it of the intelligentsia. The situation here was very unfavorable for the Bolsheviks.

The three main directions in Russian arts had formed before the revolution. The traditionalists were in the right wing: the Imperial Academy of Arts and the society of "Wanderers," realistic painters who had once fought against academic art but later joined it, setting up a profitable conveyor belt for producing popular genre paintings "from Russian folk life" and undemanding landscapes.

The center was held by the moderately eclectic and passéist Mir Iskusstva, headed by Benois, the first Russian artistic association to be oriented toward the West but with strong overtones of traditional Russian ideas of "art serving the people." By the time the monarchy fell, Mir Iskusstva, which had criticized academic culture and the Wanderers as being old-fashioned, had itself turned into a respectable brand name, whose leaders were probably the most influential trendsetters for current mainstream tastes.

The new players began to appear in 1910, ambitious groups of so-called left art, which for many years was labeled "Futurist" in Russia: such associations as the Knave of Diamonds, Union of Youth, and Donkey's Tail. Petr Konchalovsky, Ilya Mashkov, Aristarkh Lentulov, Mikhail Larionov, Natalia Goncharova, Vladimir Tatlin, Kazimir Malevich, Pavel Filonov and other innovators and visionaries subsequently became famous in the West as the Russian avant-garde, stunned the world, and today attract the greatest interest among Western art historians.

But in 1917 the artistic merits of their works were rather questionable to the majority of people. Most, even members of the educated intelligentsia, regarded the innovators with a snigger, if not outright hostility. The Bolsheviks were no exception in this case. Their leader Lenin, while a political radical, had extremely conservative tastes in culture.

Lunacharsky's views on art were much more tolerant than Lenin's, but even he could, for example, in 1911 refer to Vassily Kandinsky, a pioneer of abstract art, as a man "obviously in the final stage of psychic degeneration."[1] Contrary to later legends about Lunacharsky as a connoisseur and fervent proponent of avant-garde art, he was sincerely baffled by Kandinsky's work: "He scrawls, he scrawls some lines with the first paints that come to hand and signs them, the wretch—'Moscow,' 'Winter,' and even 'St. George.' Why do they permit him to exhibit, really?"[2]

When the Bolsheviks seized power, they encountered sabotage everywhere. Lunacharsky, arriving at the Ministry of National Education to take over the job, was not met by a single official, only guards and messengers. Recalling how the major cultural figures had reacted to the Soviet regime, Lunacharsky wrote in 1927: "Many of them fled abroad and others felt like fish out of water for quite some time."[3]

The Bolsheviks themselves would have preferred to deal with the established big names. But the luminaries were in no hurry to meet the Bolsheviks halfway. Even the "stormy petrel of the revolution" Gorky, who at one time was a friend of Lenin, attacked him in the opposition newspaper *Novaya Zhizn* [New Life]: "Imagining themselves the Napoleons of socialism, the Leninists rail and roar, completing the destruction of Russia."[4]

Gorky knew very well that the Bolsheviks' plans for culture were rather vague: it was supposed to become "proletarian" and accessible to everyone. But that was for the future, and in the meantime they had to organize the protection of palaces and museums from looting by the revolutionary masses. The Bolsheviks got several important experts from Mir Iskusstva involved, particularly Benois, who found a common language with Lunacharsky, whom he sarcastically called St. Anatoly Chrysostom.

Remaining Commissar of Education until 1929, Lunacharsky played an extraordinary role in the formation of Soviet culture of the Lenin period. He looked like a typical member of the intelligentsia (soft beard and ever-present pince-nez); he had received a doctorate from Zurich University and as a young man had even worked part-time at the Louvre as a guide for Russian tourists. After the revolution he started wearing a military green jacket, but he never lost his geniality and relish for playing the role of the arts patron.

Lunacharsky was a prolific cultural journalist, publishing 122 books with a total of more than a million copies, between 1905 and 1925. Most importantly, Lenin trusted him, assuming that Lunacharsky "knows how to persuade people," as long as you keep him under control. And even though a strict Lenin kept his often over-enthusiastic cultural tsar on a short leash, he did not accept his resignations when Lunacharsky tried to protest some of Lenin's harshest decisions.

However, even that "good-natured child" (as cynically inclined literary critic Kornei Chukovsky called him) grew impatient dealing with the endlessly vacillating Benois and his friends from Mir Iskusstva, who in typical centrist fashion wanted "to retain their innocence and still make money"—obtain cultural power through the Bolsheviks but run things from backstage, taking on no real responsibility. Benois, as can be seen from his diary for 1917–1918, was unpleasantly surprised by the fact that the role of favorite to "Queen Lunacharsky" was suddenly played by the Futurists: the poet Vladimir Mayakovsky and his henchman, Osip Brik.[5]

That should not have been a surprise to Benois: yes, after a brief hesitation (which did take place, even though they tried to deny it later), the Russian avant-gardists decided to collaborate openly and actively with the new regime, since it gave them a unique opportunity to be in charge, and the Bolsheviks, holding their noses, accepted this arrangement out of purely pragmatic considerations. This was a classic marriage of convenience.

As a result, in 1918–1919, the previously marginal avant-garde suddenly was omnipresent. Even without enumerating titles and posts in the ever-changing bureaucratic and cultural structures and institutions that the "left wing" occupied, it was clear that the reins for once belonged to them. Punin and Lourié, after their meeting with Lunacharsky, took leading positions in the cultural departments of the People's Commissariat of Education.

Futurists, being socially engaged in their desire to modernize not only all aspects of culture, but also of everyday life, were the most visible. But other avant-garde sects became involved. Stocky and with a pockmarked face, Kazimir Malevich created the famous *Black Square*, the icon of twentieth-century abstract art and the highest achievement of the non-figurative Suprematist movement he founded, based on fundamental geometric forms. His antagonist and competitor for leadership of the Russian avant-garde, Vladimir Tatlin, the tall, thin, and clumsy Constructivist who assembled objects of art from nontraditional components, also occupied various executive positions in Petrograd and Moscow. Even Kandinsky (despite Lunacharsky's initial dislike of his work), who looked like a real aristocrat compared to Malevich, who resembled a Polish peasant, and Tatlin, whose cloth cap gave him a rather proletarian air, dashed about from meeting to meeting, feverishly participating in the total reorganization and transformation of the old system of art education, while constantly fighting with his fellow avant-gardists.

With the blessing of the Bolsheviks, they did away with the old Academy of Arts in Petrograd and instituted Free State Art Studios—first in Petrograd and then in Moscow and other cities. Their goal was to attract the broad masses to art, preferably of the avant-garde kind. There were no exams or requirements for admission and students could invite anyone they wanted to teach.

An astonished realist painter described the situation: "In Tatlin's studio, instead of easels, palettes, and brushes there were anvils, carpenter's benches, a lathe, and corresponding tools. They built compositions out of various materials: wood, iron, mica, bast, combining them without giving thought to meaning. The works were incongruous but bold."[6]

According to him, Tatlin would say, "Who needs anatomy, who needs perspective?"[7]

The walls of the Free Studio in Moscow (the former Stroganov School) were covered with Malevich's slogans: "The downfall of the old world of art is in your hands," "Let's burn Raphael." Raphaels were not burned, but valuable plaster casts that generations of young artists had used in their study of the craft were thrown out on Punin's orders. A huge canvas by Mir Iskusstva artist Nikolai Roerich, *The Taking of Kazan'*, was removed from the storeroom of the Academy and cut up into pieces for students to use as they saw fit "in class work."

At that moment, both the regime and the avant-garde gained by their symbiosis. Living conditions after the revolution had become much harsher, with destruction and hunger at a peak. The Bolsheviks tried to control the situation using the policies of "War Communism": they nationalized industry, monopolized trade, and introduced a barter system of food parcels and coupons.

Serving the Soviet system gave the avant-garde artists not only a chance to survive but to promote their radical views in official media and to publish books, a great luxury in those days. Kandinsky managed to print his monograph "Steps: An Artist's Text" under the aegis of the People's Commissariat of Education in early 1919, when the catastrophic paper shortage (it was available only for Communist propaganda) and shrinking printing capacities had brought about the "café period" in literature: writers and poets unable to publish their works gave readings in various seedy, semi-underground establishments proudly dubbed "cafés." This was how they earned their keep and managed to reach an audience.

The Soviet government was the dominant sponsor of culture. It gave Kandinsky, Malevich, Tatlin, and other recent outsiders the opportunity to head commissions that bought paintings for the new museums of contemporary art (the first of the kind in the world) and selected works for exhibitions that were now free both for participating artists and viewers. For the Soviet regime this was a way of warning off the sabotage of eminent traditionalists; in fact, the Bolsheviks used the energetic radicals as effective strike-breakers.

The avant-garde artists were also brought in to do propaganda for the new regime, and the most visible projects were statues of famous revolutionaries of the past (this was the personal pet idea of Lenin) and the decoration of cities for revolutionary holidays. The artist Natan Alt-man did the most radical work (which subsequently found its way into every anthology of avant-garde design): he remodeled the symbols of the tsarist regime in Petrograd—the Winter Palace and the square in front of it. In October 1918 the Winter Palace and the other buildings that made up the famous classical architectural ensemble were covered in gigantic propaganda panels depicting workers and peasants in a Futurist manner.

The tireless Punin urged the revolutionary designers to obliterate the historic buildings and monuments, not merely ornament them. "Blow up, destroy, and wipe the old artistic forms from the face of the earth—how could the new artist, the proletarian artist, the new man not dream of this?"[8] In realizing Punin's ideas as much as the cautious Bolsheviks would permit, Altman placed a tribune made up of red and orange sections in the center of the square by the Roman-style Alexander Column, creating a visual metaphor: the column was burning in revolutionary flames.

I'll never forget Altman's reply to my question in 1966: where did they find the apparently substantial funds needed to transform the Winter Palace, Hermitage, Admiralty and the many other palaces of the city in the lean year of 1918? "They weren't stingy then,"[9] the old artist replied enigmatically, the thin line of his Parisian mustache twisting in a smile.

One of the notable events in the celebration of the first anniversary of the Bolshevik revolution was the premiere of *Mystery Bouffe,* a play by the twenty-five-year-old leader of literary Futurism, Mayakovsky. The actress Andreyeva, the politically involved wife of Maxim Gorky, had become a cultural big shot under the Bolsheviks. She gave the young poet the idea of writing a topical satirical review. On October 27, 1918, at 8 p.m., at the Petrograd apartment of his mistress Lili Brik, Mayakovsky gave the first reading of the play to an elite group that included Lunacharsky, Altman, Punin, Lourié, Levky Zheverzheyev, and most importantly, the director Vsevolod Meyerhold, at the time in charge of all theaters in Petrograd. (Mayakovsky had invited the poet Alexander Blok, but it was a rainy night and Blok did not go, writing in his notebook: "No will, no me.")[10]

The tall and handsome Mayakovsky read impressively in his lush bass voice (Andreyeva believed he would make a brilliant actor). *Mystery Bouffe*—an avant-garde and ironic retelling of the story of the Flood and Noah's Ark from the Old Testament, in which the flood becomes the metaphor for world revolution—made a profound impression on the audience and the very next day a delighted review by Lunacharsky appeared in the press, announcing that Meyerhold would stage a production as part of the anniversary celebrations. Malevich, who had proclaimed the triumph of Suprematism (a term he invented for his austere concept of abstract art) over "the ugliness of real forms" back in 1915, took on the design. He defined Suprematism as the "purely painterly art."[11]

For Malevich, Mayakovsky's Futurist play looked too conservative. Later he would explain, "I perceived the staging as the frame of a painting and the actors as contrasting elements . . . the actors' movements had to complement rhythmically the elements of the sets."[12] Mayakovsky was trying to present an avant-garde propaganda play, but the visionary Malevich wanted more: "I considered it my task not to reproduce the existing reality but to craft a new reality."[13]

No designs by Malevich for *Mystery Bouffe,* which was performed only twice, nor have any photographs of the performance survived. According to members of the audience, Malevich construed Hell as red and green "Gothic" stalactite caves; the devils' costumes were in two halves, red and black. The Promised Land that the ark reaches at the end of the play looked like a large Suprematist canvas. The audience did not comprehend the scenic design, and Mayakovsky himself was not very pleased with Malevich's work, as Zheverzheyev (who later became the father-in-law of George Balanchine, a great admirer of Mayakovsky) remembered.[14]

Mayakovsky was a jack-of-all-trades for the November 7 premiere: some of the actors, frightened by the play's apparent blasphemy, skipped the performance, and the playwright had to appear as Methuselah and even as one of the devils (in a red and black leotard). The influential critic André Levinson, who later as an émigré in Paris berated both Diaghilev and Balanchine for their break with tradition, declared that Mayakovsky, Malevich, and Meyerhold "need to please the new master, which is why they are so crude and vehement."[15]

Surprisingly thin-skinned, the ruffian Mayakovsky immediately demanded that Levinson be condemned "for filthy slander and insulting my revolutionary feelings."[16] Punin and other Futurists also denounced the hapless critic in the press for "covert sabotage."

For Meyerhold, meeting Mayakovsky was a blessing; as the director recalled, "We immediately found a common ground in politics, and in 1918 that was the most important thing: for us both, the October revolution had been a way out of the intellectual dead end."[17] At that point, Meyerhold was forty-four, one of the most prominent people in Russian theater, reaching dizzying heights via a very zigzagged path. The son of a provincial Lutheran vodka distillery owner and a convert to Russian Orthodoxy, he had become one of the stars of the Moscow Art Theater from the moment Stanislavsky and Nemirovich-Danchenko founded it in 1898. But after an argument with Stanislavsky he left to become a notorious leader of Symbolist theater and in 1908 was offered the position, to everyone's surprise, of director of the Imperial theaters—the Alexandrinsky and Maryinsky—only to perform an even more unexpected somersault in 1918, when he joined the Bolshevik party.

Like all geniuses, Meyerhold was a complex and contradictory personality. With all the qualities of a theater leader—self-confidence, independence, persistence, and unflagging energy—Meyerhold, paradoxically, always sought a powerful ally, an authority figure on whom he could depend. Chekhov was such a surrogate father for Meyerhold, who was fourteen years his junior. They began a correspondence in 1899, when he was an actor at the Art Theater, and some eighteen months later he wrote to Chekhov: "I think of you always. When I read you, when I perform your plays, when I ponder the meaning of life, when I am at odds with my surroundings and myself, when I am suffering loneliness. . . . I am irritable, picky, and suspicious, and everyone considers me an unpleasant man. But I suffer and contemplate suicide."[18]

In that same, extremely frank letter to Chekhov dated April 18, 1901, Meyerhold expressed outrage over the police suppression of a student demonstration by the Cathedral of Kazan in St. Petersburg, which he had witnessed on March 4, when "on the square and in the church, those young people were beaten with whips and sabers, ruthlessly, cynically." Meyerhold complained to the playwright that he could not "engage calmly in artistic matters when my blood is boiling and everything calls for struggle," and yet exclaimed, "Yes, the theater can play a tremendous role in the reshaping of everything that exists!"[19] (A curious detail: Meyerhold's correspondence—or was it Chekhov's?—was read by the tsarist police and an extract from the seditious letter by the future director was placed in the "File of the Police Department on Actor of the Art Theater Vsevolod Meyerhold.")

Later, Meyerhold would insist: "Chekhov loved me. That is the pride of my life, one of my most treasured memories."[20] He claimed that it was Chekhov who had raised doubts in him about the validity of Stanislavsky's "realistic" Method and encouraged him to search for new Symbolist ways in theater.

In any case, after Chekhov's death in 1904, Meyerhold found a new guiding star, the poet Alexander Blok. In 1906 in St. Petersburg, he staged the twenty-six-year-old's *Balaganchik* [Fair Show Booth], which brilliantly combined a declaration of mystical Symbolism and a vicious parody of it. Preceding the Stravinsky-Benois-Fokine *Pétrouchka* by five years, Meyerhold appeared onstage in *Fair Show Booth* as a suffering Pierrot, at the end of the performance crying to the audience: "Help me! I'm bleeding cranberry juice!"

The following apt description of the scandal provoked by the premiere of *Fair Show Booth* can be compared to the similar reaction to *Sacre du printemps* in 1913: "The fierce whistling down of the foes and the thunder of friendly applause mixed with shouts and cries. That was fame."[21] Blok and Meyerhold came out together for bows, a contrasting couple—the stony poet, whose Apollonic ashen mask of restraint hid the gloom in his steel-gray eyes, and the Dionysian director and actor, moving and swaying as if boneless, waving the long sleeves of his white Pierrot costume.

This was a memorable moment for both. Meyerhold always considered the premiere of *Fair Show Booth* the real start of his life as a director. Four years before his death, Blok described *Fair Show Booth* enigmatically as "a work that came out of the depths of the police department of my own soul."[22]

Unlike Chekhov's mysteriously missing letters to Meyerhold, Blok's diary notes about the director have survived; they serve as a guide to the "very difficult" (in Meyerhold's words) relationship. In the archives of the Institute of Russian Literature in St. Petersburg, there is a photograph of the young Meyerhold—dandified hat, his famous aquiline nose, the meaty lips—with an inscription to the poet: "I came to love Alexander

Alexandrovich Blok before I ever met him. When we part, I will take away a steady love for him forever. I love his poetry, I love his eyes. Yet he does not know me."[23]

Blok admitted that Meyerhold's production of *Fair Show Booth* was ideal, but by 1913 he referred to another of Meyerhold's stagings as "Mediocre Hue and Cry."[24] The director would come to the poet for advice on whether or not to get a divorce, while Blok noted in his diary his "distrust for Meyerhold."[25] The director later recalled Blok: "We argued rarely. Blok did not know how to argue. He would say his piece, which had been building up, and then be quiet. But he had a marvelous ability to listen—a rare trait."[26]

With the other founders of the Art Theater, Meyerhold was at the source of the defining interpretations of Chekhov's plays using the Stanislavsky Method. Another person might have exploited this for the rest of his life. But just four years later, Meyerhold made a sharp turn to Symbolist theater with his production of Blok's *Fair Show Booth*. Then followed a period of extravagantly lavish productions in the Imperial theaters, which many contemporaries considered opulent requiems for the fading tsarist regime: Molière's *Don Juan,* Richard Strauss's *Elektra,* and Mikhail Lermontov's *Masquerade.*

They called Meyerhold's *Masquerade* the "last play of tsarist Russia." This is apt both metaphorically and factually: the premiere took place in the Imperial Alexandrinsky Theater on February 25, 1917, and the Romanov dynasty fell a day later. By 1918, Meyerhold was doing the first production of the first truly Soviet play, Mayakovsky's *Mystery Bouffe.*

Unceasingly inventive and experimental, in 1920 Meyerhold proclaimed "October for the theater," a revolutionary slogan: "No pauses, psychology, or 'emotions' on stage. . . . The public should be involved in the stage action and create the play collectively—that is our theatrical program."[27]

In realizing this manifesto, Meyerhold staged the play *The Dawn,* by the Belgian Symbolist poet Emile Verhaeren, as a mass rally. Ramps connected the stage with the hall, where the lights were left on for the performance. The actors, without makeup or wigs, spoke directly to the audience, which had plants who provoked viewers into discussion with the actors.

The most memorable example of this new approach was seen on November 18, 1920, when during a performance a telegram was delivered to Meyerhold about a decisive victory in the Civil War: the advancing Red Army forced the broken remains of the White Army to flee to Turkey. Meyerhold had the actor playing The Messenger read the historic telegram from the stage. An eyewitness described the audience reaction: "I had never heard such an explosion of shouts, cries, and clapping, such a fierce howl within theater walls. . . . I never saw a greater merging of art and reality either before that performance or afterward."[28]

Inspired by this experiment, Meyerhold decided to stage a new adaptation of *Hamlet*, with the graveyard scene an up-to-date political review, the text to be written by Mayakovsky. Marina Tsvetaeva was commissioned to render the verse translation of the tragedy, but this project fell through: Tsvetaeva fled to Berlin in May 1922.

Meyerhold continued bursting with innovations that changed the landscape of theater: he got rid of the curtain; he used constructions by the avant-garde artist Lubov Popova instead of traditional sets; he introduced a new system of training actors that he called "biomechanics"—a complex mixture of gymnastics and acrobatics that helped the actor control his body's movements precisely and naturally, an "anti-Stanislavsky Method" of sorts.

In the 1920s, Meyerhold's fame reached its peak: he was adored by progressive youth, he was copied, envied, showered with awards (after the then-rare title of People's Artist, which he received even before Stanislavsky, Meyerhold became honorary Red Soldier of the Moscow Garrison, honorary Red Sailor, Miner, and so on), and—the truest sign of popularity—parodied. Mikhail Bulgakov predicted acidly that Meyerhold would die when the trapezes with naked boyars in an "experimental" production of Pushkin's *Boris Godunov* collapsed and fell on him. (Even clairvoyant Bulgakov could not have imagined Meyerhold's cruel death at the hands of Stalin's henchmen.) At that time, "Meyerhold" and "stage director" were synonymous.

Meyerhold's influence extended to the fledgling Soviet film world, where one of his students was the up-and-coming Sergei Eisenstein, whose revolutionary masterpiece *Battleship Potemkin* appeared in 1926. Iconoclastic Eisenstein nevertheless called Meyerhold "incomparable"

and "divine." In his memoirs, published in Russia only after Gorbachev's perestroika, Eisenstein bitterly recalled the period in 1921 when
Meyerhold, still a famous and revered director, was being harassed out
of positions of responsibility by the authorities.[29]

Meyerhold's radicalism seemed excessive in the new political landscape, which had changed noticeably. In 1921, after winning the Civil
War against the White Army, the Communists once again faced the
threat of counterrevolutionary revolt from within. The severe revolutionary order they had instituted was not working. The country lay in ruins.

The Soviet regime kept clinging to the disastrous market-free economy. The cultural avant-garde wholeheartedly supported this policy, for
it suited their artistic ideals. But the workers and peasants grumbled.
More than 20,000 seamen rebelled in March 1921 at Russia's largest naval
base, Kronstadt near Petrograd, bringing the city to a siege situation.
Anti-Bolshevik peasant riots spread in the provinces.

Gathering their last strength, the Bolsheviks cruelly suppressed the
Kronstadt Rebellion and the peasant Vendée. Switching to carrot-and-
stick policies, Lenin decided to make some concessions. In May 1921,
overcoming the resistance of the majority of his party comrades, he proclaimed the New Economic Policy (NEP). Small private trade was permitted again, small private factories and crafts shops opened, kiosks
selling trifles appeared on the corners and intersections of Moscow and
Petrograd, and were gradually joined by shops, cafés, delis, patisseries,
and bakeries. Workmen tore down old boards from the windows of
closed shops and installed new panes, and soon displays showed luxurious still lifes forgotten over the hungry years of revolution and war:
bread, cheese, pastry, bagels and rolls of every size and shape, heavy
hams, a variety of sausages and cheese, and even such exotic fruit as
grapes, oranges, and bananas.

Private initiative created the economic miracle that had eluded the
Bolsheviks, and collapse was averted. Hunger and misery dissipated, and
so did the dreams of the avant-garde artists for hegemony in culture. Not
so long ago, they had been instituting utopian projects on a planetary
scale: Meyerhold intended to open the Theater of International Proletarian Culture in Moscow in 1920, and Kandinsky wanted to convene
an International Congress of Art. But once "normal" life was reestab-
lished, it turned out that the masses did not need avant-garde art.

The innovators were being replaced in their executive cultural posts by traditionalists, who had previously taken a wait-and-see position regarding the Bolsheviks. The Soviet leaders were eager to form an alliance with the "realists," because the majority of the Bolsheviks had very conservative tastes. And so, the patriarch of the Art Theater, Nemirovich-Danchenko, came out of an audience at the Kremlin and announced with pleasure that "the attitude toward theaters has changed strongly: Meyerholdism has lost not only its prestige, but all interest."[30]

With growing confidence, the Bolsheviks were pushing aside the Futurists, especially their loudest representative, the loyal Mayakovsky, whom Lenin viewed "with suspicion and even irritation," according to Maxim Gorky. "He yells, he makes up these crooked words."[31] Lenin's patience broke when Mayakovsky published his new narrative poem *150,000,000* at a state printing house without the author's name but under the seal "Russian Socialist Federative Soviet Republic," which made the Futurist poem appear to be an example of sanctioned, official literature.

A note sent by Lenin to Lunacharsky during a government meeting on May 6, 1921, has been preserved: "Aren't you ashamed to vote for publishing Mayakovsky's *150,000,000* in 5,000 copies? It's nonsense, stupidity, idiotic and pretentious. I think only 1 out of 10 such things should be published and *no more than 1,500* copies for libraries and eccentrics. And Lunacharsky should be horse-whipped for Futurism."[32]

With Lenin's support and even direct participation, an attack began on the avant-garde in the state art education system, where they had previously held command positions. In an appeal addressed to Lenin on June 13, 1921, the adherents of realism expressed their indignation that for the last three and a half years the "Futurists ruthlessly suppressed all the other movements in art, creating a privileged financial situation for themselves and placing artists of a different creed into a hopeless situation."[33] The traditionalists presented a long list of grievances against the avant-garde: "They strive via pure force to cultivate Futurist and abstract art. . . . They shamelessly turn students into grimacing 'innovators.' . . . The country is in danger of being left without seriously trained artists."[34]

The Bolsheviks continued to play cultural games with the administrative dexterity they had demonstrated from the first days of the revolution, but there was only one aim of all those complicated bureaucratic maneuvers, the endless denunciations, counterdenunciations, government and party resolutions, decrees, and ukases (many of which were Lenin's): to disavow the avant-garde as the official cultural course.

The avant-garde artists were the first to realize it. They fought back desperately, calling their aesthetic opponents anti-Soviet and swearing fealty to the authorities at every step. But some of them, under various pretexts, began drifting to the West. Kandinsky, who had been, among other things, vice-president of the Russian Academy of Artistic Studies, went to Germany in 1921, ostensibly to create an international branch of the Academy. He became one of the leaders of the avant-garde Bauhaus school of art and design and found world recognition as the father of abstract painting and predecessor of the American Abstract Expressionists of the late twentieth century.

The colorful Jewish primitivist Marc Chagall, who had been "plenipotentiary in charge of art affairs of the city of Vitebsk" in Russia and who had festooned the city for the first anniversary of the Bolshevik revolution, moved to Moscow (pushed out of Vitebsk by the more radical Malevich), and from there in the summer of 1922 to Berlin, and then to Paris. (Many critics believe that the best works of both Chagall and Kandinsky belong to their early period.) The Constructivist sculptors Naum Gabo and Natan Pevsner (who were brothers) had worked actively in Moscow but also ended up in Western Europe. One of the "Amazons of the Russian avant-garde," Alexandra Exter, left for Venice in 1924 to take part in the organization of the Soviet pavilion for the international art exhibition; like Chagall, she settled in Paris. These people lived through the most difficult years in Russia. Their emigration signaled the beginning of the end of the Russian avant-garde as a national phenomenon.

Exter's departure in particular meant the complete collapse of the unofficial group of "Amazons" that had formed in Russian innovative culture before the revolution. They were called Amazons by friends and foes— the latter mockingly, the former with delight and awe, stressing their uniqueness not only for Russia but for the world. In fact, it is impossible to name another similar group of such powerful, vivid, and innovative women artists.

Outwardly, the status of women in prerevolutionary Russia, even among the educated urban strata, was low—they had not won the right to vote nor did they have equal rights with men for education and labor. But within the elite and bohemian groups of Moscow and St. Petersburg the situation was different: the participation of gifted women in the cultural discourse was keenly welcome.

A veteran of the prerevolutionary Futurist movement, Benedikt Livshits, later recalled in his book, *The One-and-a-Half-Eyed Archer* (1933), remarkable for its density, the role played by Exter and her friends Olga Rozanova and Natalya Goncharova: "Those three amazing women were always in the front lines of Russian painting and brought a warlike ardor into their milieu, without which our further success would have been impossible. These true Amazons, those Scythian riders, got an immunity to Western 'poison' from an injection of French culture."[35]

The great tragic actress Alisa Koonen (a star of Alexander Tairov's expressionist theater) maintained: "Goncharova did not look like an Amazon at all. She attracted people with her femininity, gentleness, and pure Russian beauty. Her hair was combed back, she had a thin face with big black eyes."[36] And art critic Abram Efros described Rozanova this way: "Her image was distinguished by total alertness and noiseless restlessness. Truly she resembled a mouse, housewifely and anxious. Exhibitions and paintings were her murine kingdom."[37]

Another deviation from the feminist stereotype was that most of the Russian Amazons were apparently happy in their heterosexual relationships. The most famous couple was, of course, Goncharova and her comrade-in-arms of many years, Mikhail Larionov, the royal couple of the Russian avant-garde, who moved to Paris in 1917 and created some of Diaghilev's most famous productions, such as Prokofiev's *Chout* [Jester] (Larionov) and Stravinsky's *Les Noces* (Goncharova). Stravinsky valued Larionov's talent highly, but thought, nevertheless, that sometimes Goncharova did his work for him. "He made a vocation of laziness, like Oblomov."[38]

The relationships of the other Amazons were legendary, too: Varvara Stepanova and one of the leaders of the Russian avant-garde, Alexander Rodchenko, Nadezhda Udaltsova and the artist Alexander Drevin. Rodchenko, who was a friend of Udaltsova's, later recalled that she "spoke of Cubism softly and ingratiatingly. As if a living confirmation of Cubism, she had a very interesting face of a nun with close-set eyes, looking with two completely different expressions, a slightly deformed Cubist nose and thin, nunnish lips."[39] According to the severe Rodchenko, Udaltsova "understood Cubism more than the rest and worked more seriously than the rest."[40]

The fate of Udaltsova and her husband was tragic: Drevin was arrested on the night of February 16, 1938, and he was executed ten years later in a Stalinist prison. Udaltsova was not told of her husband's death, and she continued submitting appeals for his pardon for almost twenty years, until she learned the horrible truth in 1956. But before her death in 1961, taking advantage of the Khrushchev "Thaw," Udaltsova managed to have an exhibition of her own works (1958) and to show her husband's paintings after a gap of a quarter century. It was only then that Udaltsova and Drevin were talked about again, only to be soon forgotten for another thirty years, until their full canonization after Gorbachev's perestroika.

Chapter Four

From the beginning of their rule, the Bolsheviks were reluctant to allow leading cultural figures to travel abroad. They were more lenient with the avant-garde: first, because they were mostly lefties themselves, and therefore more trustworthy; second, the authorities did not consider them very important—even if they did not return to Russia, it would be no great loss.

It was another thing when the major mainstream writers and poets, respected and popular even before the revolution, started heading west: Bunin, Alexander Kuprin, Konstantin Balmont, Merezhkovsky and his wife, Hippius. This became embarrassing for the Soviets, especially when they received the following memorandum in June 1921 from the head of the foreign department of the Cheka, or secret police, who handled requests for travel abroad. "Taking into account that the writers who have gone abroad are waging an active campaign against Soviet Russia and some of them, such as Balmont, Kuprin, and Bunin, stoop to the vilest lies, the All-Russian Cheka does not consider it possible to satisfy such requests."[1]

Now it was the Politburo, headed by Lenin, that discussed every candidate who asked to travel to the West. The case involving Alexander Blok, the forty-year-old leader of Russian Symbolism who was perhaps the most beloved poet in Russia at the time, was most troubling.

Blok, who considered the old Russia a "horrible world," had welcomed the Bolshevik revolution and supported it with two of its arguably most impressive poetic manifestoes: the dense and intensely lyrical narrative poem *The Twelve,* in which a squad of Red Army soldiers patrolling revolutionary Petrograd is compared to the twelve apostles and Christ miraculously appears to lead them, and the passionate and prophetic poem *The Scythians,* inspired by the nationalist ideas of his ideological mentor Ivanov-Razumnik. These masterpieces, quickly translated into all the major languages (in France they were illustrated by Larionov and Goncharova), were read in the West as the most profound artistic interpretation of the seismic revolutionary cataclysms in Russia.

But the Bolsheviks still did not trust Blok, even arresting him—albeit briefly—in 1919 on suspicion of conspiracy. In 1921, Blok, exhausted and malnourished, developed septic endocarditis (inflammation of the inner lining of the heart) and inflammation of the brain (meningial encephalitis). Gorky and Lunacharsky appealed to Lenin to let the poet go to Finland for treatment. At first the Politburo refused. Then Lenin and his comrades relented, but too late: on August 7, Blok died, mourned as a victim of the Bolshevik regime by many. As Lunacharsky bitterly commented in his secret letter to the Central Committee of the Bolshevik Party: "There will be no doubt and no refutation of the fact that we killed Russia's most talented poet."[2] Thus Blok, a fellow traveler, became the first widely acknowledged great martyr of Soviet cultural policies. The second major figure to appear on that list was the poet Nikolai Gumilev, thirty-five, who was executed on August 25, 1921, with sixty other "counterrevolutionaries," accused of supporting the recently routed anti-Soviet Kronstadt uprising.

Before the revolution, Gumilev became well known as leader of the Acmeist movement in poetry, which he founded with his wife, Anna Akhmatova, and Osip Mandelstam, to bring "beautiful clarity" in opposition to the fogs of poetic Symbolism. An adventurer and conquistador by nature, but awkward looking with long limbs and crossed eyes, Gumilev was transformed by action, being a born leader. As a young man he had gone on three dangerous expeditions to Africa (as it has recently been revealed, most probably on assignment from Russian intelligence agencies)[3] and at the very start of World War I, where he had volunteered, he was twice awarded the highest medal for valor, the St. George Cross.

In 1917, Gumilev was in Paris, where he befriended Larionov and Goncharova. She drew an expressive portrait of the poet as a sleek dandy in her favorite colorful neoprimitivist manner. He returned to Bolshevik Petrograd, where he embarked on a dangerous and still somewhat mysterious game with the authorities: he participated energetically in various educational endeavors promoting the new regime yet behaved provocatively, giving public readings of his pro-monarchist poetry and announcing, "The Bolsheviks won't dare touch me."

Well, they did, executing Gumilev on flimsy evidence and despite

Lenin's promise to release the poet, which he allegedly gave to Gorky, who was constantly intervening on behalf of the persecuted Russian intelligentsia. It seems that Gumilev used himself as a guinea pig to see if the Soviet regime would allow major cultural figures a certain degree of intellectual freedom. The answer, which the poet paid with his life to get, was "No."

Entering NEP, the Bolsheviks in effect told the intelligentsia: as long as we were unable to feed you, you had the right to a small bit of independence; now take your hunk of bread and salami and serve the new regime without murmur. This period saw a lessening role for Lunacharsky, arguably the most educated and tolerant of Soviet leaders, whom Lenin, the wily political tactician, made mediator between the authorities and the intellectuals whenever the situation was critical for the Bolsheviks.

Lenin once admitted to the German Communist Klara Zetkin: "I am incapable of considering the works of Expressionism, Futurism, Cubism and other 'isms' the highest manifestation of artistic genius. I do not understand them."[4] When Lenin (whom Gorky later described as a "bald, solid, sturdy man who could not pronounce the letter R" with "amazingly lively eyes") was asked to express his opinion about a work of art, he usually replied, "I don't understand anything here, ask Lunacharsky."[5]

Still, Lenin was obviously annoyed by Lunacharsky's fondness for high culture, especially the theater (Lunacharsky wrote plays, too), over the elementary education of the masses. Lenin rebuked Lunacharsky on August 26, 1921, the day after Gumilev was shot, with a harsh remark: "I suggest piling all theaters into the grave. The People's Commissar of Education should be teaching grammar, not dealing with the theater."[6] According to Lunacharsky's memoirs, Lenin tried to shut down the Bolshoi and the Maryinsky theaters several times, reasoning that the opera and ballet "were a piece of purely bourgeois culture, and no one can argue with that!"[7] Fortunately, Lunacharsky, with figures in hand, could show that shutting down these great cultural palaces would bring tiny economic profit and enormous propaganda loss, thereby fighting off Lenin's attacks (with the quiet support of Stalin, a fan of opera and ballet).

In the second half of 1921, Lenin became seriously ill, and in May 1922, a stroke paralyzed his right side. In the gap before the next stroke, in December, Lenin initiated the expulsion abroad of 160 "of the most active bourgeois ideologues," including the crème de la crème of Russian philosophy—Lev Karsavin (at the time, the elected rector of Petrograd University), Sergei Bulgakov, Berdyaev, Frank, Ivan Ilyin, and Stepun.

The final list of banished philosophers was sanctioned personally by Lenin. It was his last anti-intellectual shot before his third stroke, which in March 1923 ended his involvement in state affairs.

Lenin died January 21, 1924, but the Party's cultural policy had been supervised for some time by Leon Trotsky, the Bolshevik military leader, and Nikolai Bukharin, the prominent ideologue. Both were much more authoritative figures than Lunacharsky, but they dealt with culture more as a hobby, even while writing about it frequently enough.

Their later struggle against Stalin and their deaths at his hand has created a myth of their cultural tolerance. But both Trotsky and Bukharin, while comparatively educated men who spoke several languages, remained Marxist doctrinaires all their lives and ruthlessly criticized philosophers, writers, and poets for any sort of ideological deviation.

For example, in a *Pravda* article published in September 1922, Trotsky belittled the expelled leaders of the Russian religious renaissance—Berdyaev, Karsavin, Frank, and others: "There aren't many takers to shake up the neoreligious liquid distilled before the war in the little apothecaries of Berdyaev and others."[8]

In Trotsky's opinion, the influence of the "new religious consciousness" on Russian literature had "dwindled to nothing." Contradicting himself, Trotsky petulantly scoffed at the religious motifs in the poetry of Akhmatova and Tsvetaeva, especially mocking their constant appeals to God: "Now there's truly a place where you can't get to the door without God. . . . It is a very convenient and portable third person, completely house trained, a friend of the family, who sometimes performs the duties of doctor for female dysfunctions. How this elderly personage, burdened by the personal and often very labor-intensive errands of Akhmatova, Tsvetaeva, and others, manages in his spare time to handle the fate of the universe is incomprehensible."[9]

Bukharin, who held more moderate positions politically than the extreme left Trotsky, could be just as unbridled in his attacks on cultural figures who displeased him: he called Berdyaev's work "nonsense"[10] in

1924 and in 1925 a "brain eclipse."[11] But Bukharin and Trotsky united to push through the Politburo a famously benign resolution "On the Party's policy in the sphere of literature"of June 18, 1925 (the draft had been prepared by Bukharin). This resolution not only defended mainstream authors who were attacked brutally by the Communist dogmatists in the Russian Association of Proletarian Writers (RAPP), but also proclaimed that the Party "cannot insist on a preference for any particular literary form" and even called for free competition among various cultural groups and tendencies.

Naturally, even in 1925 the Communists were not as liberal in deed as they were in word. NEP, which started in 1921, forced them to loosen the ideological reins a little (in Moscow alone in 1922 there were 220 small private publishing houses), but by 1922 the authorities restored tight control over printed product by establishing a special censor's office—The Main Directorate on Literary Affairs and Publishing (Glavlit).

The ruling party supported "proletarian"writers, of whom, according to RAPP data, there were several thousand in 1925. They were given priority financing, organizational help, and access to state publishing houses. Peasant writers were treated much more suspiciously, even though officially the Soviet state was one of united workers and peasants.

In a letter to Bukharin dated July 13, 1925, Maxim Gorky endorsed the wariness of the Bolsheviks toward the peasantry. "The Central Committee resolution 'On the Party's policy in the sphere of literature' is a marvelous and wise thing, dear Nikolai Ivanovich! There is no doubt that this smart smack on the head will push our belles-lettres forward."And after that dubious compliment, Gorky moved on to his point: "Dear comrade, either you or Trotsky should point out to worker writers that the work of *peasant* writers is appearing next to their oeuvre and there is the possibility, I would say, inevitability, of conflict between these two 'directions.' Any censorship here would only be a hindrance and would exacerbate the ideology of muzhik-worshipers and village-lovers, but criticism—ruthless criticism—of that ideology must be aired right now."[12]

Gorky—unlike Leo Tolstoy, who idealized the Russian muzhik—always considered the peasantry a dark, uncontrollable force, simultaneously lazy and cruel and permanently anti-intellectual. He felt that Count Tolstoy did not know the real countryside, while he, Gorky, who had come out of the people and had walked all over Russia, understood it completely. Like the leading Bolsheviks, Gorky disliked and feared the peasants, pointing out: "I have always been distressed by the fact that in Russia the illiterate village dominates the city and also by the zoological individualism of the peasantry and the almost total absence of social emotions in it. The dictatorship of politically literate workers, in close alliance with the scientific and technical intelligentsia, was, in my opinion, the only possible way out of this impossible situation."[13]

In a country where at the start of the revolution, the mostly illiterate peasants constituted 82 percent of the population, the Bolsheviks, who considered themselves the avant-garde "proletarian" squad, shuddered when assessing the economic and cultural threat coming from the gloomy and distant peasant ocean. Many urban intellectuals felt the same way; Gorky was no exception here.

In this unsettled context, the suicide of Sergei Esenin was no less symbolic than the death of Blok and execution of Gumilev in 1921. Esenin, thirty, was the leader of the so-called New Peasant poets. On the night of December 27, 1925, Esenin hanged himself in a room at the Hotel Angleterre in Leningrad. That morning, he had attempted to write down a farewell poem, but there was no ink in the room; he cut a vein in his left wrist and wrote in blood:

> *Farewell, my friend, without a hand, without a word,*
> *Do not sorrow or furrow your brow—*
> *In this world, dying is nothing new,*
> *But living, of course, is no newer.*

The appeal of Esenin's tender, crooning poems (he wrote mostly of love, nature, and animals) was greatly enhanced by his tragic fate. This made him the most universally popular twentieth-century poet in Russia. Still, the Esenin phenomenon remained local, and even in Russia some connoisseurs (for example, Akhmatova) regarded his poetry skeptically.

Prince Dmitri Svyatopolk-Mirsky (perhaps the finest Russian literary critic of the twentieth century, writing as D. S. Mirsky in English after he emigrated), while noting in 1926 that Esenin "had many bad poems and almost no perfect ones,"[14] nevertheless lauded his poetry's special charm and touching appeal and also his specifically national longing, for which unsophisticated (but also many quite sophisticated) readers in Russia still adore Esenin.

Foreigners who wish to peek into the soul of eternal Mother Russia must read Esenin in the original, since the translations fail to convey his essential Russianness. For all the seeming simplicity of his most famous poems, some of which have become folk songs, Esenin remains a mysterious figure. His political, aesthetic, and religious views form a tangle of unresolved contradictions.

One can find statements by Esenin for and against the old Russia, the Soviet regime, the Bolsheviks, the West, and America. He has poems that are tender, misogynistic, sad, brutish, imbued with religious feeling, and blasphemous. His admirers included the last Russian empress, Maria Fedorovna, and the militant Bolshevik Trotsky. The empress told Esenin that his poetry was "beautiful but very sad." Esenin replied that so was all of Russia.[15]

Gorky recalled the first time he saw Esenin in Petrograd in 1915: "Curly-haired and blond, in a light blue shirt, a long coat with a fitted waist and soft boots that gathered at the ankles, he was very much like a saccharine postcard."[16] Ten years later Esenin looked very different: the blond hair had faded, his heavy drinking muddied his once bright blue eyes, and the angelic face had turned ashen gray. He had had countless brief affairs and three notorious marriages.

His first wife was Zinaida Raikh, who later married Meyerhold and was brutally murdered in her apartment in 1939, soon after the director's arrest; the murder—there were seventeen knife wounds in her body—was never solved. His second wife was a granddaughter of Leo Tolstoy, and the third, the great American dancer Isadora Duncan, who came in 1921 to revolutionary Moscow to start a school of "free dance." Duncan was eighteen years older than Esenin and obviously madly in love with him, always cuddling up to him in public, which embarrassed the poet. He would curse at her and even hit her, but nevertheless, he was proud of his marriage.

Esenin traveled through Europe with Duncan and even came to the United States. Upon his return in 1923, Esenin, deeply offended by the Americans' total lack of interest in his poetry, wrote: "The supremacy of the dollar has destroyed any striving in them for complicated issues. The American is totally involved in *beeznis* and wants to know nothing else. Art in America is on the lowest level of development."[17]

But the achievements in "art of manufacture," as Esenin called it—the Brooklyn Bridge, the neon lights on Broadway, the radio broadcasting Tchaikovsky—made a strong impression on him (as it had on Mayakovsky, who first came to the United States in 1925): "When you see or hear all that, you are amazed by the possibilities of mankind and you are ashamed that back in Russia people still believe in an old man with a beard and pray for his mercy."[18] In 1923, electricity was more important than God for Esenin. In that respect, at that moment he was closer to Chekhov and Gorky than to Leo Tolstoy.

Esenin's death in 1925 stunned Russia; a wave of copycat suicides swept the country. The Communists were worried. Their culture arbiter Bukharin was not thrilled by Esenin: "Ideologically Esenin represents the most negative traits of the Russian countryside and the so-called national character: brawls, an enormous inner lack of discipline, and an idolization of the most backward form of social life."[19]

But the poet's undisputed popularity made Bukharin panicky: "How does Esenin capture the youth? Why are there 'Esenin's widows' clubs among the young people? Why do Young Communist League members often have a copy of Esenin's poems under their *Communist Guide*? Because we and our ideologists have not touched the strings in young people that Sergei Esenin did."

As to be expected, the Soviet state fought Esenin's influence, which they called Eseninism, with repressive measures: lovers of Esenin's poetry were expelled from college and the Komsomol and in the years before World War II and even later, you could get a sentence in the prison camps for having and distributing handwritten copies of Esenin's "hooligan" works.

The Soviets "purged" the circle of Esenin's friends; one of the poet's mentors, the "Scythian" Ivanov-Razumnik, was first banned from publication and then arrested. He survived purely by accident. Ivanov-Razumnik, citing a private conversation with Esenin in 1924, explained that the poet's suicide was "the result of his inability to write and breathe in the oppressive atmosphere of the Soviet paradise."[20]

· · ·

The other New Peasant poets, close comrades-in-arms of Esenin, suffered a dramatic fate as well. Stalin's antipeasant policy was detailed in 1929 (the year he declared The Great Watershed), soon after the national celebrations of his fiftieth birthday, which cemented the cult of personality of the new Soviet leader.

Stalin announced the end of NEP and the start of the first industrial Five-Year Plan, with mass collectivization of agriculture. The millions of peasants who refused to join *kolkhozes* (collective farms) were branded *kulaks* and were subject to mass deportation. Disavowing the compromising policies of the past, Stalin put the question this way: "Either *backward* to capitalism, or *forward* to socialism. There is no and can be no third path."[21]

It was obvious which path was chosen; a violent change was imposed on the Russian peasantry—in the words of Solzhenitsyn, "an ethnic catastrophe." Stalin's "liquidation of kulaks as a class" brought indescribable suffering and led to a famine. The ruthless policy also destroyed the cultural ideologues of the peasantry, the poets Nikolai Klyuev, Sergei Klychkov, Petr Oreshin, and their younger follower, the talented Pavel Vasilyev, who was touted as the new Esenin. Charged with "counterrevolutionary" sympathy for kulaks, they all perished.

In the declassified transcripts of Klyuev's interrogation after his arrest in February 1934, the poet describes collectivization as "the state's violence against the people, spurting blood and fiery pain. . . . I regard collectivization with mystical horror, as an invasion of demons."[22] Klyuev also declared stubbornly: "My opinion is that the October revolution sent the country into a vale of suffering and disasters and made it the most miserable in the world, and I expressed that in my poem, 'There are demons of plague, leprosy, and cholera.' "[23]

Many literati (including Akhmatova and Joseph Brodsky) considered Klyuev a better poet than Esenin. Like him, Klyuev was a maddeningly complicated figure, at once a firm traditionalist and a bold innovator. Like Esenin, even before the revolution he began to mourn the wasting away of the traditional peasant way of life in Russia, doing so in complex verse weighted down by clusters of modernist metaphors. Like Esenin, Klyuev dressed as a stylized *paysan*—in a side-buttoned collarless shirt and a woolen jacket known as *armyak,* low boots, a large pectoral cross, and brilliantined hair—and did not hide his homosexuality, which was rather unusual in Russian literary life then. (Another exception to this rule was his contemporary, the prominent modernist poet Mikhail Kuzmin.)

In 1918, Klyuev joined the Bolshevik Party, only to be expelled two years later because "his religious convictions are in complete contradiction to the party's materialistic ideology."[24] Klyuev left behind a powerful cycle of poems in honor of Lenin (1919) and *Pogorelshchina* [Burned Out], in Brodsky's opinion the most brutal poetic exposé of the Soviet antipeasant policy.

Sadly, there were not many works written about those horrible years, despite the fact that Russia was predominantly a peasant country with a powerful tradition of idolizing the peasantry in literature, culminating in the works of Leo Tolstoy. It is telling that for Chekhov peasant life was no longer a central theme and that Gorky treated peasants with undisguised contempt. This reflected the growing cultural gap between the peasantry and the intelligentsia.

The liberal author and critic Kornei Chukovsky ventured in his diary on June 1, 1930, at the height of the destruction of the Russian peasantry, that "the kolkhoz is the only salvation for Russia, the only solution to the peasant question in the country!"[25]

The diaries also record a presumably unfeigned appreciation of Stalin as destroyer of the kulaks, expressed in a private conversation with Chukovsky by the literary theoretician Yuri Tynyanov: "As author of the kolkhoz, Stalin is the greatest genius restructuring the world."[26]

Isaak Babel, the master of the Soviet short story, attempted to write about collectivization. In 1931 he published a fragment of a planned novel in the journal *Novy Mir*, but it was not very successful and he dropped the project, because, as Babel admitted, "that grandiose process was torn into disjointed shreds in my consciousness."[27]

Stocky, bespectacled, and ironic, Babel did not condemn collectivization publicly, but he did not become its singer, either, even though the nationalist critic Vadim Kozhinov and his colleagues in the postperestroika period accused the late writer of participating in the forced collectivization of farms in the Caucasus and Ukraine. In his youth, Babel, a man with an extremely checkered past, had—by his own admission—worked for the Cheka, and later considered as close friends some of the highest-ranking officials of the Soviet secret police (this fact was noted with disapproval by Solzhenitsyn in 2002), but that still did not make Babel an apologist for the security apparatus.

As early as 1925 the émigré D. S. Mirsky noted that the magic of Babel was "to sharpen" a tragic anecdote artfully as in Pushkin's novellas and maintained that even in his most "realistic" works, like the short-story cycle *Red Army* about the Civil War, the writer remained politically unengaged: "Ideology for him is just a helpful device."[28]

In fact, Babel cannot be called the bard of the criminal world, either, but his colorful stories about Odessa's exotic bandits and muggers belong to the highest achievements of Russian prose. His ability to preserve a distance between author and character is comparable to Chekhov's.

Next to Babel, Osip Mandelstam, a famously difficult poet, seems, strangely enough, much more politicized. Born just three and a half years before Babel, in 1891, Mandelstam had won a serious literary reputation even before the revolution, unlike Babel. Mandelstam, with Gumilev and Akhmatova, belonged to the Acmeists, the St. Petersburg group of poets opposed to Symbolism. Scrawny but scrappy, Mandelstam saw a "longing for world culture" in Acmeism, and even in his early poems, collected in 1913 in *The Stone,* he created an original style—hieratic, solemn, filling intentional ellipses in meaning with numerous historical, literary, and political allusions. Mandelstam declaimed his poetry to everyone he met, wailing and lisping, according to a contemporary, "insinuating and at the same time arrogant, even satanically arrogant."[29]

Even sympathetic contemporaries mistakenly took him for a self-centered eccentric remote from real life. The social theme was a natural component in Mandelstam's work from his youth. His artistic response to every political situation was always sincere, significant, and original— for instance, his 1918 poem "Twilight of Freedom," a substantial ode to Lenin, whom the poet, according to Mirsky, "praised for something that I think no one else ever did: for the courage of responsibility. . . . Here we are very far from the *Scythians* and Mayakovsky. The Bolshevism in Mandelstam is combined with courageous and positive Christianity."[30]

It was Mandelstam, with his reputation as sophisticated master and bookish aesthete and seemingly infinitely far from the New Peasant poets (even though he rated Klyuev's work very highly and liked some lines in Esenin), who was one of the few to respond to the famine that befell the peasant regions of the Soviet Union as a result of Stalin's collectivization in the early 1930s.

Mandelstam's "Fourth Prose,"a stunning example of the Russian confessional genre (comparable to Dostoevsky's *Notes from the Underground*), describing the animal fear engulfing Soviet society, the fear that "writes denunciations, beats people when they are down, and demands execution for the prisoner,"reveals the author's revulsion for such anti-peasant slogans of the Stalin regime as "The muzhik has hidden rye in his storeroom—kill him!"

This growing horror and anger ("The authorities are as revolting as a barber's hands") burst out in May 1933, when Mandelstam poured out several political poems, the most biting of which was the openly anti-Stalin satire "We live, not feeling the country beneath us."It has become perhaps his most famous poem.

The irony is that this work, which lacks complex associative images, is not at all typical of Mandelstam's work: Akhmatova observed that Stalin's portrait in it resembles the primitive folk style known as *lubok*:

> *His fat fingers are as flabby as worms,*
> *His words are as accurate as pound weights,*
> *His cockroach eyes mock*
> *And his boots are shiny.*

Boris Pasternak refused to recognize these lampoon lines as poetry when Mandelstam rushed to declaim them to him: Pasternak was horrified not only by the poem's unheard-of political daring but its provocatively direct, almost caricature-like style: "This is not a literary fact but an act of suicide, of which I do not approve and in which I do not want to take part."[31]

Mandelstam saw his anti-Stalin lampoon in a different light, according to his friend Emma Gershtein: "The Young Communists will sing it in the streets! At the Bolshoi Theater . . . at congresses . . . from every row." He knew what he was risking: "If they find out, I could be . . . EXECUTED!"[32]

Even though Mandelstam was not executed for this work, he had been essentially right: the poem started a spiral of events that led to his death on December 27, 1938, at a transit camp in the Far East. Mandelstam was first arrested in Moscow in 1934 for anti-Stalin and anti-kolkhoz poetry, after one of his listeners informed on him. The poems were characterized by the investigators as a "terrorist act against the leader," but Stalin, in response to a plea for mercy from Bukharin, unexpectedly ordered: "Isolate but preserve."[33]

Mandelstam was then forty-three, but he looks like a very old man in photographs of the period. The arrest and interrogations broke him. In prison he slit both wrists, and in exile, where he was sent, he threw himself out of the second-story window of the local hospital. He was saved each time (Stalin's orders!), but the inner logic of the situation inexorably pushed Mandelstam to the position of outcast despite his attempts to make peace with Soviet reality and Stalin himself.

It all ended predictably: a repeated arrest (on the denunciations of zealous colleagues) and a martyr's demise in the camps, where the crazed Mandelstam, dressed in rags and plagued by lice, offered to read his anti-Stalinist poetry to prisoners for a hunk of bread.

Mandelstam did not live long enough to create his own mythos. His posthumous legend in Soviet times was the work of two completely different people—his widow, Nadezhda, an independent and ambitious writer herself, and the influential journalist and novelist of current events, Ilya Ehrenburg. He managed to push through a long essay about the poet, after a twenty-year hiatus, as part of the publication of his memoirs, *People, Years, Life,* which the journal *Novy Mir* began serializing in 1960. Ehrenburg was the first to talk about Mandelstam's tragic death publicly and with an emotional tone that was not typical of the old cynic: "Who could have been bothered by that poet with his puny body and that music of verse that fills the nights?"

Ehrenburg's memoirs are not a masterpiece, but I remember the powerful impression they made on the Soviet intelligentsia with their massive erudition, unusual European tone, and effort to revive the half-forgotten or still-banned names of persecuted writers and artists. Those qualities made it very difficult for the book to pass the censor's eyes.

Nadezhda Mandelstam's monumental memoir about her late husband, written in the 1960s, could not get into print at all. But the manuscript was circulated widely in *samizdat.* I remember that this upset the envious Akhmatova, who had expended a lot of effort on the creation of her own version of the posthumous mythos of Mandelstam (with her by his side) and who quipped acidly about Nadezhda that "talent is not transmitted by rubbing."

Brodsky, on the contrary and perhaps to spite Akhmatova, always considered Nadezhda Mandelstam's prose (which in its stylistic sharpness is comparable with other masterpieces of twentieth-century Russian nonfiction—Benois's memoirs, Andrei Bely's autobiographical trilogy, and Vladimir Nabokov's *Other Shores,* in its English version called *Speak, Memory*) on par with the works of Andrei Platonov, whom he admired greatly.

Nadezhda Mandelstam's memoirs were eventually published in the West, where they unexpectedly became a sensation in the 1970s, for many years being the only source of detailed, albeit not always objective, information and opinion about Mandelstam and also perhaps the most vivid description of the fate of the nonconformist artist in the Stalin era.

Another great urban poet whose fate took a sharp turn after writing about the Stalin collectivization was Nikolai Zabolotsky, a follower of the refined literary experimenter Velimir Khlebnikov and one of the leaders of the Dadaist group OBERIU (Association of Real Art).

The son of an agronomist, Zabolotsky spent his childhood in the country. A solid bespectacled man who did not look like the highly original and eccentric absurdist poet he was (he was frequently taken for an accountant) and whose hobby was pondering philosophical issues, Zabolotsky wrote the utopian poem *Triumph of Agriculture,* which could have had as its motto, the author said, Khlebnikov's lines: "I see the horses' freedom / and the equality of cows." It was published in 1933, during the famine caused by collectivization, and it was immediately targeted for attack by the official critics.

Pravda and other newspapers derided Zabolotsky's poem as a "lampoon on collectivization." "This is not simply abstruse nonsense but politically reactionary priest-loving rubbish which is in solidarity with the kulak and in literature with the Klyuevs and Klychkovs."[34] Zabolotsky was thus included in the doomed circle of New Peasant poets, with whom he had little in common, both in his avant-garde style and his world view.

Zabolotsky's "crime" from the orthodox point of view was that the poet did not want and did not know how to praise the creation of the kolkhozes: "He presented the greatest struggle in the world as a pointless and mad pastime. He danced, grimaced, stuck out his tongue, and made scabrous jokes when talking about work led by the Leninist Party and by a steel Bolshevik with a name of steel [Stalin]."[35]

In a situation when, as Stalin had pointed out, the class struggle in the Soviet Union had become more acute, "jesters" were superfluous. On March 19, 1938, Zabolotsky was arrested and then put through the "conveyor," when investigators took turns interrogating and beating prisoners day and night until they got the confessions they wanted.

Zabolotsky, in his appeal in 1944, described the effect of the conveyor this way: "Without food or sleep, under an endless barrage of threats and humiliation, on the fourth day I lost clarity of thought, forgot my name, stopped understanding what was going on around me, and gradually reached the state of numbness when a man cannot be responsible for his actions. I remember that I gathered my remaining spiritual strength to keep from signing lies about myself and others."[36]

But the investigators were not worried that Zabolotsky, despite the beatings, did not admit his guilt in writing "anti-Soviet works used by the Trotskyite organization in their counterrevolutionary agitation." The poet was sent to a labor camp in the Far East. When Zabolotsky was transported there in a frozen freight car filled with dozens of prisoners, Mandelstam, the other poet also sentenced to five years in the camps, had already died.

At the camp, Zabolotsky was sent to fell trees, where exhausted men (dinner was 30 grams of bread and a ladle of thin gruel) were expected to work until they dropped, and, as the poet recalled, "If you sat down for a moment, they set dogs on you."[37]

He learned about the cruel jokes of the Stalin regime. The investigators in Leningrad tried to beat an admission out of him that the leader of the counterrevolutionary organization to which he allegedly belonged was the noted poet Nikolai Tikhonov, who was a member of the Serapion Brothers, an avant-garde literary group. Zabolotsky denied it categorically, but was certain that they would arrest Tikhonov anyway.

In the camps, Zabolotsky heard that Tikhonov was not only not arrested but given the highest Soviet award, the Order of Lenin, in early

1939. That happened, apparently, because in 1937 at a meeting at the Bolshoi Theater dedicated to the centenary of Pushkin's death, attended by Stalin, Tikhonov (dubbed "little wooden soldier" by some) made a fiery speech that "spoke about Pushkin but praised Stalin,"[38] as contemporaries recalled. Stalin liked the speech and that became a good shield for the little soldier, who moved from one official honor to the next.

The irony was that at the very same time, the Leningrad secret police continued concocting the mythical "case of the counterrevolutionary organization headed by Tikhonov." People arrested in the case were beaten to get compromising material on Tikhonov, and some of them were shot in 1938, including the poets Benedikt Livshits and Boris Kornilov. In 1959, I was a teenager passionate about poetry, and I tried to get the gray-haired and pompous Tikhonov to talk about the fate of Livshits and Kornilov, who had been posthumously rehabilitated a few years earlier, but he condescendingly evaded an answer.

By this time, Tikhonov was a very big shot. However, his poetry, which even a demanding critic like Tynyanov once considered worthy of Pasternak, became ever blander, until he turned into a purely ceremonial figure. It was said that right until his death at eighty-two in 1979, he kept a portrait of Stalin over his desk.

Zabolotsky survived the camps. His friends from OBERIU were not as lucky. The great absurdist poets Daniil Kharms and Alexander Vvedensky died in prison, and another Dadaist, the handsome Nikolai Oleinikov, who had also been fitted up in the "Tikhonov group" case, was executed.

Chapter Five

Present-day neo-Slavophiles are convinced that Stalin, being irrationally hostile toward the Russian peasantry, dealt with the peasant poets and writers with particular cruelty. In fact Stalin, the politician par excellence, always ruthlessly attacked whatever social stratum seemed most dangerous to him at the moment. Along with that group, its cultural leaders were usually repressed as well. At one moment, they could have been the peasant poets Klyuev, Klychkov, and Vasilyev, but at another, the urbanists Mandelstam, Zabolotsky, Vvedensky, and Kharms.

Even though Stalin's formal education ended when he was expelled from the Tiflis Seminary in 1899 for revolutionary notions, he read a lot (some recall his reading 400 pages a day, both fiction and nonfiction) and had a lively interest in cultural issues. But as with other Bolshevik leaders, this interest was colored strongly by political considerations. And as Stalin's political views evolved, his cultural positions changed. After Lenin's death, Stalin (whose Russian was literate but with a marked Georgian accent that increased when he was agitated) addressed cultural matters more frequently, and gradually his soft, muffled voice grew more confident.

Recently declassified documents of the early meetings of the Politburo of the Bolshevik Party show that Stalin apparently did not participate actively in writing the relatively liberal Politburo 1925 resolution "On the Party's policy in the sphere of literature"—it was Bukharin, Trotsky, and Lunacharsky—but by 1925 Stalin was airing his ideas on cultural affairs at Politburo meetings.

When in 1926 the Politburo discussed the possible return to the Soviet Union of the émigré artist Ilya Repin, the patriarch of the realist movement who had settled in Finland, Kliment Voroshilov, the culture-loving military leader who had recently replaced the outcast Trotsky, felt it necessary to speak with Stalin first before writing a memo. "Knowing your opinion on this matter will make it be resolved more easily and quickly at the Politburo." The leader approved of loyal Voroshilov's initiative.

"Klim! I think that the Soviet regime must support Repin in every way. Greetings. J. Stalin."[1] Still, the elderly artist was afraid to return to the Soviet Union and died in 1930 in Finland.

Stalin's role was crucial in a series of extraordinary and often ambivalent decisions made by the Politburo in 1927–1929 about permitting or closing Mikhail Bulgakov's plays *Days of the Turbins, Zoyka's Apartment,* and *Flight.* The leader's hand was also obvious in the vicious attacks that began in 1929 on the major writers Yevgeny Zamyatin and Boris Pilnyak: the former dared to publish his dystopian novel *We* in a Prague émigré journal and the latter his novella *The Red Tree* in a Berlin émigré publishing house; both works were deemed hostile to the Soviet regime.

The short and pockmarked Stalin came out on the stage of cultural life rather cautiously (a quality that was a hallmark of his political style) and weighed every word. In that sense, the turning point came in 1929, when the leader stepped forward as cultural arbiter for the first time, writing two letters that were immediately disseminated in party circles: one was addressed to the leaders of the Russian Association of Proletarian Writers (RAPP), the most powerful literary pro-Communist organization of that period, with great state support, and the second was a reply to the complaint of the "proletarian" playwright Vladimir Bill-Belotserkovsky about RAPP.

In both letters, Stalin tries to find a middle way, calling for restraint on the "literary front," seemingly endorsing the liberal Politburo resolution of 1925, which RAPP wanted disavowed. Stalin expressed his displeasure with the excessively aggressive tactics of RAPP: "Who now needs a 'polemic' which resembles an empty squabble: 'Oh, you bastard!' 'Look who's talking!' . . . That is no way to unite people of the Soviet camp. That is the way to scatter them and confuse them, pleasing the 'class enemy.' "[2] Tellingly, in sending copies of these letters to Maxim Gorky, Stalin still felt it necessary to say that it was merely "personal correspondence." When his henchmen obligingly asked Stalin to publish his letter to Bill-Belotserkovsky, "since it, in essence, is the only expression of your thoughts on our policy in art" and therefore "has found rather widespread distribution in party circles,"[3] Stalin refused—he was not fully confident of such a move yet. (Stalin published that letter only twenty years later, in the eleventh volume of his collected works.)

But he had already formulated his opinion about the need and wisdom of his personal supervision of Soviet culture in that letter to RAPP quite firmly: "It is necessary. It is beneficial. It is, after all, my duty." It was no accident that Stalin made Lunacharsky retire as cultural commissar in September 1929.

This move signaled the transition from one era to another, when the strengthened and solidly placed Soviet regime no longer felt it necessary even to pretend to play up to the intelligentsia to attract it to its side. Now, on the contrary, the intelligentsia was expected to prove its loyalty. This new hard line was sarcastically formulated by Ilya Ilf and Yevgeny Petrov, coauthors of the two funniest Soviet novels, *The Twelve Chairs* and *The Golden Calf*. "No point in hiding it, comrades, we all love the Soviet regime. But loving the Soviet regime is not a profession. You must also work. It is not enough to love the Soviet regime, you must make it love *you*. The love must be reciprocal."

Lunacharsky was a confirmed Communist, but he spoke out often against the personal tastes of the leaders defining the state's cultural policies. Stalin was of a different opinion. It did not crystallize immediately, but through trial and error. By 1929, after his fiftieth birthday, Stalin was ready to manage Soviet culture more or less single-handedly (which did not exclude calling in expert opinion from time to time).

His most important expert, who for a time was truly Stalin's viceroy in culture, was Maxim Gorky, even though neither man publicized it and many of their meetings were private.

The well-informed émigré journal *Sotsialisticheskii Vestnik* reported as early as 1933 (and it is thought now that their source was Babel) that Gorky "is considered the second-most important person in the Union, by weight following Stalin. It must be said that the friendship of the latter with Gorky has taken on planetary scale: Gorky is the only man whom Stalin not only takes into account but courts."[4]

A friendship like this between ruler and writer is unique in Russian culture, and not only for the twentieth century. Neither before nor after did a cultural figure have such access to Russia's leader. Both sides had a lot to gain, which is why both Stalin and Gorky were willing to make significant compromises to retain the friendship.

Stalin had "inherited" Gorky from Lenin, who had rated the writer very highly as a "European celebrity." Gorky certainly was the most major cultural figure whom Lenin knew personally, and one with a marked pro-Bolshevik orientation even before the revolution. Lenin used Gorky's popularity in the interests of his party, including pumping enormous sums of money out of Gorky himself and with his help from others to support the illegal Bolshevik activities.

Before the revolution the fame and influence of Gorky and Lenin were incomparable: one was an international cultural superstar, the other a marginal political radical. Naturally, Lenin was not an authority for Gorky, and after the overthrow of Nicholas II in 1917, their paths diverged sharply, since Gorky considered the Bolshevik seizure of power from the Provisional Government not only premature but dangerous— "the Russian people will pay for this with lakes of blood."[5]

Immediately following the October 1917 revolution, Gorky was very negative about Lenin, even though he had already noted Lenin's extraordinary abilities as a political figure: "A talented man, he has all the qualities of a 'leader,' and also the requisite lack of morals and a pure landowner's ruthless attitude toward the lives of the masses."[6] In response, in 1918, Lenin shut down the newspaper *Novaya Zhizn'*, where the writer regularly printed similar and even harsher attacks on the Bolshevik government.

For a few more years Gorky got on Lenin's nerves, constantly pestering him about the misery of the impoverished Russian intelligentsia and with pleas on behalf of many who were arrested. Lenin, himself from the intellectual class, felt nothing but contempt for the intelligentsia, expressing his opinion in a notorious letter to Gorky dated September 15, 1919: "The intellectual forces of the workers and peasants are growing stronger in the struggle to overthrow the bourgeoisie and its helpers, the petty intellectuals, the lackeys of capital, who consider themselves the brains of the nation. In fact, they're not the brain, they're shit."[7]

Gorky's innumerable appeals on behalf of persecuted intellectuals finally made Lenin lose his temper (in one letter to Gorky he called him "irresponsible") and push the writer abroad using the excuse that he needed "to recuperate and rest."

Gorky did not want to end his activities in defense of Russian culture from Bolshevik excesses, but Lenin added, "If you don't go, we'll exile you." So when Gorky finally left Soviet Russia in 1921, his relationship with Lenin was badly soured. In 1922, Lenin had a stroke and in January 1924, he died.

Living in Germany and later Italy, Gorky through the second half of the 1920s gradually strengthened his relations with the new Soviet leadership, particularly Bukharin and Stalin. Ironically, it was Stalin (at Lenin's urging, certainly) who had attacked Gorky viciously in the newspaper *Rabochii Put'* in 1917, when Gorky vainly called on the Bolsheviks not to take power into their hands. Stalin lectured the famous author and recent ally: "The Russian revolution has overthrown quite a few authorities. Its power is expressed, incidentally, by how it does not bow to 'famous names,' but takes them into its service or throws them into oblivion."[8] Stalin warned Gorky that if he did not climb out of the "swamp of the intelligentsia's confusion," he would find himself in the "archives" of history.

The criticism of Gorky was not signed: this was typical of Stalin as a party columnist and a method he would use later (cf. his article "Muddle Instead of Music," aimed at Shostakovich in *Pravda* in 1936). In 1951, when the writer had been dead for fifteen years, Stalin included this anti-Gorky pamphlet in the third volume of his collected works, revealing his authorship. But Gorky must have been informed at the time who had attacked him in 1917.

Stalin could have assumed that Gorky, who did not forgive easily, would hold that insult against him. Gorky, on the other hand, had learned early and personally that if you got Stalin angry, he did not care how famous the opponent was. As Stalin wrote: "The revolution does not know how to pity or how to bury its dead."[9]

Undoubtedly, Gorky remembered Leo Tolstoy as he created his own relationship with the authorities. Tolstoy was an example of the Olympian heights a Russian writer could reach as a public figure. From an early age, when his ambition could have appeared unseemly and therefore was carefully hidden even from his friends, Gorky was already aiming at Tolstoy's fame and influence.

The prose writer Konstantin Fedin, who knew Gorky well, noted a curious passage in the latter's reminiscences of Tolstoy: "He was the devil and I was still an infant, and he should not have touched me." Fedin commented: "I jumped up in delight, reading that 'still'—'and I was still an infant!' What pride, I laughed, running around the room in my unbuttoned army coat, and look where it revealed itself! *Still* an infant!"[10]

Gorky had neither Tolstoy's literary might nor his Yasnaya Polyana estate. But he started early to create a public forum for himself: at the age of thirty-two in 1900, the year he met Tolstoy, Gorky formed the Znanie Publishing House and began by printing his own works in huge numbers, followed by forty collections of works by writers of the realistic and progressive camp, usually edited by Gorky and instantly becoming best sellers.

The aesthete critics attacked the Znanie publications: "Everyone who loves Russian literature and the Russian language should fight the influence of these collections."[11] Interestingly, in 1907 these books, quite uneven in quality but immensely popular, in their distinctive green covers (where you could find Chekhov's *The Cherry Orchard,* Kuprin's *The Duel,* a sensational work about army life, and the latest by Bunin, but also a dreary naturalistic hodgepodge by someone like Yevgeny Chirikov), were defended by none other than the demanding poet Blok. His article supporting Gorky (albeit with many reservations) drew such indignation from Symbolist circles that Blok almost had a duel with his former best friend, Andrei Bely.

Blok had always considered Leo Tolstoy "the only genius of contemporary Europe." But when they feted Gorky in starving 1919 Petrograd, it was Blok, famous for his directness and honesty, who essentially declared Gorky Tolstoy's successor in social and political spheres: "Fate has placed a great burden on Maxim Gorky, as the greatest artist of our day. It has made him the intermediary between the people and the intelligentsia, between two countries which neither yet understand themselves or each other."[12]

Even while praising Gorky, Blok still underestimated his ambitions. For Gorky, like Tolstoy, felt being the intermediary between the people and the intelligentsia was not nearly enough. Tolstoy, for all his proclaimed reverence for the people's initiative, so vividly reflected in *War and Peace,* still understood that without the direct involvement of the regime, nothing gets done in Russia—thus his appeals by letter to Alexander III and Nicholas II.

Gorky, unlike Tolstoy, did not idealize the Russian people. He characterized them thus: "The most sinful and filthy people on earth, stupid about good and evil, intoxicated by vodka, disfigured by the cynicism of violence, hideously cruel and, at the same time, inexplicably good-natured—and at the end, this is a talented people."[13] So for Gorky, effective dialogue with higher-ups played an even more important role than for Tolstoy.

The émigré poet Vladislav Khodasevich, who knew Gorky well, recalled that "in the depths of Gorky's soul there always lived awe of power, authority, with its external attributes, which Lenin despised. (You should have heard Gorky's raptures when describing the visit of Emperor Alexander III to Nizhny Novgorod.)"[14] (In 1932, Stalin renamed Nizhny Novgorod as Gorky in the writer's honor; it became notorious in the 1980s as the closed city where Academician Andrei Sakharov was exiled. It is Nizhny Novgorod now once more. Sic transit gloria mundi.)

Understandably, the former tramp was much more fascinated by power than Count Tolstoy. But Gorky was also a greater realist and in particular realized that Tolstoy's practical influence on reforms had been limited by the count's intentional stance as political outsider. It must have seemed a mistake to Gorky.

So, as soon as the February 1917 revolution that overthrew the tsar gave him the opportunity, Gorky enthusiastically plunged into organizational affairs, becoming for a while the de facto minister of culture. The former Imperial Academy of Sciences, which twenty years earlier under pressure from Nicholas II had rescinded its decision electing Gorky an honorary academician, hurriedly crowned him with the title again. Gorky headed countless commissions and committees, composed appeals and resolutions, signed letters. He was in his element, the man of a thousand and one projects.

Gorky's life motto could have been his declaration: "Knowledge must be democratized, it must be made accessible to the entire nation." Gorky's god was culture: "I know of nothing else that can save our country from disaster." Unlike Tolstoy, a great cultural skeptic, he worshipped this god his whole life: headlong, without a second thought.

Gorky never tired of saying that "ignorance and lack of culture are characteristic of the entire Russian nation. Out of that multimillion mass of unenlightened people, devoid of the concept of life value, we can distinguish just a few thousand of the so-called intelligentsia. . . . These people, despite all their flaws, are the greatest achievement of Russia throughout its difficult and ugly history, these people were and are the true brains and heart of our country."[15] (Lenin, as we know, did not share this view.)

Gorky devoted the last twenty years of his life to nurturing the "brains and heart" of Russia and defended it tirelessly from danger from above and from below, from the real possibility of being wiped out by rebel peasants or being thrown onto the dustbin of history by the Communist regime. He perceived this as his historical mission. Gorky was unable to come to terms with Lenin and his anti-intelligentsia attitude. Now he was pinning his hopes on the new strong ruler of Russia—Stalin.

The interests and plans of dictator and writer coincided in many aspects, which cemented their relationship. Tsarist cultural policy had been conservative and protective; Nicholas II had no radical plans to enlighten the Russian people. Lenin had embarked on a grand economic and cultural experiment, which Stalin considered his task to bring to a successful conclusion: the building of a completely new society and the creation of the new Soviet man. For Stalin, a necessary part of that unprecedented plan was a forced modernization of Russian society: collectivization, industrialization, and what was particularly close to Gorky's heart, a planned "acculturation" of the masses.

In letters to Gorky in Italy, Stalin laid out his ambitious program: "The USSR will be a first-class country with the largest, technologically equipped industrial and agricultural production. Socialism is invincible. There will be no more 'pathetic' Russia. It's over! There will be a mighty and abundant progressive Russia."[16] Replying to the leader, Gorky not only supported Stalin's plans but gave them a cultural footing: "You destroy the way of life that has existed for millennia, a way of life that created a man who is extremely ugly and capable of horrifying bestial conservatism."[17]

Stalin apparently found this interesting. In his youth, he had written poetry, and he was a lifelong avid reader of varied nonfiction (history, economics, and so on) and fiction, including foreign and naturally Russian classics as well as contemporary Soviet literature, which Stalin read in real time, as it appeared in periodicals.

He was a great lover of film and classical music, especially Russian opera (Glinka, Borodin, Mussorgsky, Tchaikovsky, and Rimsky-Korsakov). He was frequently seen at the theater. Less educated than

Lenin, Stalin was more of a consumer and connoisseur of high culture. Therefore his plans for the overall "civilizing"of the Soviet public gave an important role to literature and art.

Stalin revealed his ideas in 1929 during a three-hour meeting at the Central Committee with party-member Ukrainian writers. It was a frank discussion "among friends"; when one of the participants published a few fragments of Stalin's speech, he was severely chastised by his bosses. Stalin's unedited remarks were only recently declassified. He explains that without making the entire population literate and "cultured" they will not be able to raise the level of agriculture, industry, or defense.

The peasants and workers must learn to use more complex machinery, soldiers must learn to use maps, explained Stalin to the Communist writers, and therefore "culture is the oxygen without which we cannot take a step forward." Echoing Gorky, Stalin juxtaposed the backward peasant "who lives sloppy and dirty"to the progressive laborer who "has picked up some knowledge, reads books, wants to manage agriculture in a new way."[18]

For such readers there should be new quality works of literature and art: "An awful lot depends on the form, without it there can be no content."[19] (Here too Stalin's position is similar to that of Gorky, who made constant appeals to writers to raise their craftsmanship, to work on language and form.)

There was one more important issue where they were of one mind then: both felt that Soviet culture needed "consolidation,"and that varying and not necessarily strictly orthodox approaches could coexist under a single Communist umbrella. When overly zealous party writers demanded an implacable class approach to literature, Stalin put them in their place: "Then we'd have to get rid of all the non-Party writers."And Stalin did not want that in the least.

Apparently, this cultural umbrella under which all writers loyal to the Soviet regime could gather was socialist realism, as invented by Stalin, Gorky, and a few others. Socialist realism was proclaimed the official cultural doctrine in late August 1934 in Moscow at the First All-Union Congress of Soviet Writers, a very showy and solemn event, widely covered in the Soviet press, which became the culminating point in Gorky's work as Stalin's cultural advisor.

Gorky achieved a number of important goals. During the preparations for the congress, which took several years, the Politburo issued a special resolution on April 23, 1932, liquidating the super-orthodox "proletarian" cultural associations, foremost of them RAPP, which were an obstacle, Gorky felt (and Stalin agreed) to a successful consolidation of the most productive forces in Soviet culture. The chairman of the new literary megastructure, the Union of Soviet Writers, completely formed in 1934, was Gorky.

His dream of state support for cultural workers came to pass, too. A special system was created—first for writers and then for other members of the "creative" intelligentsia—to guarantee members of the unions of writers, artists, architects, cinematographers, composers, and so on, a multitude of privileges that included state commissions for new works, large printings, high fees, more comfortable living conditions, special food parcels, special vacation resorts, and hospitals.

This system of privileges lasted unchanged for almost sixty years, until the Soviet Union collapsed in 1991. It was complex, extremely detailed, and strictly hierarchical, which I discovered in 1972 when I became a member of the Union of Soviet Composers (musicologists could be members, just as literary critics could be members of the Writers' Union). Naïvely assuming that now I could have a free vacation in one of the tempting resorts that I had heard so much about from my older colleagues, I went to the Moscow Composers' Union (where I was listed as senior editor of *Sovetskaya Muzyka* magazine) with an application. They treated me as a loony: there wasn't a space to be had in any of the resorts, they had all been reserved by more honored comrades.

I had to vacation as I had in years past, visiting my parents in Riga, on the shores of the Baltic Sea. This was my first lesson in how the hidden mechanisms of the Soviet "creative" unions worked. I soon discovered that other privileges written into the bylaws remained empty promises for many of the members: only the nomenklatura elites got to use all the announced perks. But even the crumbs from their table were very tempting in a society of shortages in everything.

Gorky kept coming up with new publishing ideas, which he brought to Stalin. He wanted to bring out several monumental book series: *The History of the Village*, *The History of Factories and Plants*, and *The History of the Civil War*. At first Stalin supported the writer's initiatives, even joining the editorial board for the *History of the Civil War*, and not just as a figurehead, but making corrections and insertions on literally every page of manuscript. When the first volume of the series came out in 1936 in an edition of 300,000 copies and sold out completely, Gorky asked Stalin for a second edition of another 100,000, and Stalin complied with his wish. (After Gorky's death, the project was dropped.)

Gorky's plan for *The History of Factories and Plants* was unusual—each book in the enormous series would be devoted to a single industrial enterprise. It was an innovative idea, a precursor to today's cross-discipline approach to the history of production as part of cultural development. At the time, Stalin approved of this project, too (even though it was never fully implemented): it supported his ambitious plans for industrializing the Soviet Union.

Interestingly, in 1924 Stalin declared that the main character trait to be developed by a true Leninist and the new Soviet man was "the combination of Russian revolutionary sweep and American businesslike approach."[20] Stalin suggested in a cycle of lectures he gave in Moscow soon after Lenin's death, "American business character is that irrepressible force that knows no bounds, that washes away all obstacles with its business persistence. But American business has every chance of degenerating into a narrow and unprincipled small-time hustle if it is not combined with Russian revolutionary sweep."[21]

This curious position had unexpected consequences for culture. Positioning himself as a cultural pragmatist, the leader tried to involve various artists in his plans for industrialization—not only the traditionalists dear to his heart, but also the Russian avant-garde, which he considered repulsive.

By the early 1920s some Russian innovators considered that experimentation in painting had exhausted itself (where could one go after Malevich's *Black Square* or Alexander Rodchenko's 1921 triptych called *Smooth Color: Pure Blue, Pure Red,* and *Pure Yellow*?) and moved on to so-called industrial art. The Constructivists came to the fore, with their leader and constant opponent of Malevich, Vladimir Tatlin, who had declared: "Not the old, not the new, but the necessary!"

Tatlin's most famous project was his two-meter wooden model called *Monument of the Third International,* intended in imitation of the Eiffel Tower as a planned construction for the propaganda apparatus of the Soviet state. The idea was utopian, eventually erecting a glass building 400 meters tall and consisting of three segments revolving at different speeds: a cube below, for the legislative organs, in the middle a pyramid, for administrative and executive agencies, and the top cylinder was to house media, "all the various means of mass information for the international proletariat." As Punin, a leading theoretician of the avant-garde, commented in 1920, "Implementing this form would mean embodying the dynamic with the same unexcelled majesty as the static is embodied by the pyramids."[22]

Tatlin's bold project remained unfulfilled, as did another idea close to his heart, on which he worked for almost twenty years—an engineless flying machine that would be operated by the occupant's muscle power, a kind of winged aerial bicycle, which the artist dubbed "Letatlin" (short for Letayushchii Tatlin, Flying Tatlin).

Tatlin's fantastic aviation model was developed with the help of Soviet military specialists and test pilots and in the early 1930s was demonstrated and discussed in quasi-governmental defense organizations like Osoaviakhim (Volunteer Association for Helping Aviation and the Navy).

Some of Tatlin's ideas were used in the construction of the latest Soviet planes of the times, and Tatlin was even rewarded financially.[23] Along with his students, he also designed furniture, dishes, sanitary and other coats from rubberized fabric, wooden sleighs of a new design, and even an environmentally improved stove that gave more heat using less wood. Tatlin now called himself "lifestyle organizer" and all these works "material culture." They could also be used in the defense industry.

The desire to do the "necessary" was equally felt by another leading avant-garde artist, Alexander Rodchenko. He set out with Mayakovsky in the 1920s to create the new Soviet advertising: Rodchenko's vivid drawings and Mayakovsky's brief and catchy slogans were extremely popular. As Rodchenko recalled: "All of Moscow was covered with our advertisements. All the kiosks of Mosselprom, all the signs, all the posters, all the newspapers and magazines were filled with them."[24]

Rodchenko was taken by photography and photomontage, becoming one of its leading innovators with the influential El Lissitzky. Rodchenko's first works in that medium were phantasmagoric illustrations for Mayakovsky's poem About That. Having developed his easily recognizable bold photographic style—dynamic composition and unusual angles—the former abstract artist turned into a dominant Soviet photographer and worked with the magazine *USSR on the Construction Site* (the magazine was yet another of Gorky's ideas, implemented by Stalin).

Rodchenko went north on assignment for the magazine in 1933 to photograph the construction of the Stalin Belomor-Baltic Canal, built by thousands of convicts. A heavy tome edited by Gorky was published after a highly publicized trip of one hundred twenty writers to the construction site, which took the lives of so many people. A number of major names appeared among the writers of the anthology: Alexei Tolstoy, Shklovsky, Nikolai Tikhonov, Valentin Katayev, D. S. Mirsky; one chapter, about an international thief who turned into a model construction worker at the canal, was written by the popular Soviet satirist, Mikhail Zoshchenko, a favorite of Gorky, which later prompted Solzhenitsyn's wrath in his *Gulag Archipelago:* "Oh, humanologist! Have you ever pushed a canal wheelbarrow while on punitive rations?"

Present-day commentators ponder why outstanding writers agreed to participate in an anthology in praise of forced labor and wonder if it was sincere misapprehension? Blindness? Hypocrisy? Fear of repressions? It was probably a complex mix of them all.

Gorky's moral guilt (he gave his blessing to the volume and wrote the foreword) is obvious, even though it is unlikely that he could have done anything to change Stalin's plans to use gulag prisoners in Soviet construction projects. On his desk in the luxurious mansion Stalin gave Gorky in Moscow, he kept a netsuke, a small Japanese ivory carving, depicting three monkeys, one covering its eyes, one its ears, and the third its mouth: see no evil, hear no evil, speak no evil. It was a startling symbol of Gorky's position in that period, and not only his.

Many of Rodchenko's photographs were used in that ill-starred book, and he tried to explain his emotions in 1935. "I was confused, stunned. I was caught up in the enthusiasm. It all seemed close, everything became clear . . . Man came and conquered, conquered and rebuilt himself."[25] But his photographs, which at the time probably played the propaganda role expected of them, today tell a completely different story. Intended to be in an optimistic key, they make a devastating impression, serving as one of the great photographic exposés of the Stalinist era.

An outstanding figure among the avant-garde artists Stalin wanted to press into service for his policy of collectivization and industrialization was the crafty favorite of the world film elite, Sergei Eisenstein, sybarite and eccentric. Highly pleased with his influential revolutionary film *Battleship Potemkin,* Stalin commissioned Eisenstein in 1926 to make a propaganda film about the benefits of collective agriculture, under the grandiloquent title *The General Line.* The production schedule dragged and the film did not appear until 1929, as *Old and New* (another title supplied by Stalin).

The pampered gentleman filmmaker did not know or care for the countryside. He created a film that was fantasy, pure and simple: a story about how a peasant woman (played by a real country girl, Marfa Lapkina) joins an agricultural cooperative and becomes a tractor driver. The problem was that the real Marfa never did learn to drive a tractor (which was imported from America), and so they used a double, Eisenstein's assistant, Grigory Alexandrov, who dressed as a woman and drove the tractor past amazed crowds of peasants.[26] It all took place against backdrops of plywood farms built for the film in a village near Moscow from designs by the talented Constructivist architect Andrei Burov, a friend of Le Corbusier.

This Potemkin village served as a backdrop and excuse for Eisenstein to demonstrate his usual cascade of formal experiments, such as the "overtone montage," which he invented while working on *Old and New.* According to the director, in this form of editing, the "central stimulus" in a shot is accompanied by "secondary stimuli." As an example, he gave the episode from *Old and New* where a scene of harvesting is followed by shots of rain: "the tonal dominant—movement as light oscillation—is accompanied here by the second dominant, a rhythmic one, that is, movement as transference."[27]

The dazzling film documentaries of Dziga Vertov were filled with such experimentation in the 1920s—*Forward, Soviet!, One Sixth of the World, The Eleventh,* and *Man with a Movie Camera.* Meant to be propaganda for collectivization and industrialization, these Vertov films were not popular among the very masses for whom they were allegedly intended (*Old and New* was a bomb, too), but along with the works of Eisenstein, Vsevolod Pudovkin, and other Soviet avant-garde filmmakers, they became a veritable encyclopedia of virtuoso technical and artistic techniques later widely employed by many Western directors, cameramen, and editors.

· · ·

It is difficult to judge the sincerity of the great Soviet avant-garde artists when they still insisted in the late 1920s and early 1930s that the mass audience could and would learn to love their art. In the more than ten years since the revolution, they should have seen that they were unlikely to achieve popular recognition. But almost all of them, as it befits true prophets and utopians, continued to fool themselves and others by trying to prove that they could still be useful to the Soviet regime.

Vladimir Mayakovsky, who today is esteemed most as an intensely lyric poet of great imagination and expressiveness, made superhuman efforts in that regard, insisting publicly, in a speech in Moscow on October 15, 1927, "I don't give a damn that I'm a poet. I'm not a poet, but first and foremost someone who has placed his pen at the service—note, service—of the current moment, the true reality and its guide—the Soviet government and the party."[28]

We can guess that these relentlessly repeated statements were a painful pose, in light of Mayakovsky's final, tragic act. On April 14, 1930, the poet, thirty-six, shot himself: he was tired of "stepping on the throat of my own song," as he put it.

The bitter irony was that when Esenin hanged himself in 1925, Mayakovsky condemned the suicide unflinchingly in the name of all the poets loyal to the Soviet regime, "who have organically welded themselves with the revolution, with the class, and see before them the big and optimistic path."[29] At that time, Mayakovsky fulfilled the "civic commission" of the state, writing the poem "To Sergei Esenin," which was supposed to counteract the effect of the last lines of Esenin's farewell poem that had prompted so many suicides:

> In this life dying is nothing new,
> But living, of course, is no newer.

Mayakovsky's reply to that was:

> In this life dying is not hard,
> Making a life is significantly harder.

And now, Mayakovsky repeated Esenin's move, when dying was obviously easier than living, and chose the "false beauty of death" (as he had condemned Esenin's suicide) to "making life" in a socialist society.

Mayakovsky's fans were profoundly shocked. Boris Pasternak later recalled, "I think that Mayakovsky shot himself out of pride, over something in himself or around him that his pride could not accept."[30] For the authorities, his suicide must have been an unforgivable weakness. That made all the more inexplicable Stalin's cultural and political gesture some five years later when he declared (via *Pravda*) that Mayakovsky was "the best, the most talented poet of our Soviet era."[31]

This totally unexpected statement by the country's supreme cultural arbiter, which immediately elevated Mayakovsky to join Gorky as patron saint of Soviet literature, stunned many: why aggrandize a patently avant-garde poet? It seemed to counter Stalin's general preference for realism in literature and art.

Stalin must have been pleased, for with one brief declaration he had achieved several goals. First, he created a kind of counterbalance to Gorky's overly saintly reputation as the highest Soviet literary authority. Then, he demonstrated a certain independence from the cultural tastes of his mentor, Lenin, who disliked Mayakovsky's poetry. And last, in a growing atmosphere of pushing the avant-garde artists out, even from "industrial art," where they had been allowed for some time to frolic with their utopian projects, Stalin tossed a bone to the comparatively small but very active (and therefore politically important) stratum of revolutionary urban youth, who idolized Mayakovsky with his propagandistic "temperament of the prophet Elijah," in Gorky's envious observation.

People forget now that in his time even Lenin had to take that into account. When on February 21, 1921, he met with a group of Moscow art students and asked, "What do you read? Do you read Pushkin?" the reply was, "Oh, no, he was bourgeois. We read Mayakovsky."[32] Lenin's widow, Nadezhda Krupskaya, who left a record of this episode, recalled that after that meeting Lenin "grew a bit kinder" to Mayakovsky: he saw that the poet had a following, as she put it, of "young people, full of life and joy, ready to die for the Soviet regime, not finding words in the contemporary language to express themselves and seeking that expression in the hard-to-understand poems of Mayakovsky."[33]

Stalin was even more pragmatic than Lenin in his attitude toward the political aspects of culture. In 1935 he was preparing to destroy his political opponents, including Grigory Zinoviev, Lev Kamenev, and Nikolai Bukharin. Each had his own followers. They could be scared off by terror, which was Stalin's plan. But Stalin also wanted to win some of them over to his side—after all, they were fanatically loyal to communist ideals, honest, energetic, hardworking, and optimistic. Many of them adored Mayakovsky's poetry.

For that part of the urban youth, as the playwright Alexander Gladkov, himself a great fan of Mayakovsky's, later recalled, typical character traits were "spiritual fastidiousness and disdain for chauvinism, bribetaking, and false erudition."[34] Those were the people Stalin had in mind when he spoke of combining American business spirit with Russian revolutionary sweep as a model for the progressive Soviet workers. His approving words about Mayakovsky seemed like an important signal to them. For Stalin it was just one of many moves in his lengthy and ingenious political and cultural chess game.

Chapter Six

December 5, 1935, the day *Pravda* published Stalin's definitive assessment of Mayakovsky as "the best, the most talented poet of our Soviet era," was the culminating point in the political history of Russian left art. No other avant-garde artist was ever—before or after—heralded on such a high state level as a model for national culture. No other oeuvre of a committed Futurist ever became the object, even in a distorted and truncated form, of such intense inculcation into the masses from above. The result was a half-century cult of Mayakovsky's personality and work that the poet could have only dreamed about. The paradox is that this canonization also marked the end of any real participation of actual avant-garde art in the country's cultural development.

As Stalin had undoubtedly planned, a frontal attack on "formalism" in culture was initiated in 1936. Formalism was defined by the authoritative Soviet Short Literary Encyclopedia as "an aesthetic tendency expressed in a disparity between form and content and the absolutization of the role of form."[1] In practice, the word was used as a political label to suppress the slightest deviation from the current party line in culture, both in Stalin's lifetime and for many years after his death.

It would be hard to find an outstanding Soviet writer, poet, artist, director, or composer who at some point, somewhere, was not accused by someone at least once of the sin of formalism. They repented of the sin just as ritually, almost mechanically.

The antiformalist campaign of 1936 began with the infamous editorial whose title, "Muddle Instead of Music," has become a symbol of the state's diktat in the cultural sphere. It appeared in *Pravda*, the country's main newspaper, on January 28 and was most probably written or dictated by Stalin.[2] The editorial brutally criticized the opera *Lady Macbeth of Mtsensk District*, based on a story by Nikolai Leskov, which was written by the young composer Dmitri Shostakovich and had been running with great success for two years in Leningrad, before Stalin heard it on January 26, 1936, at a performance of the Bolshoi Theater's annex in Moscow.

Stalin left the theater enraged by this "tragedy-satire," as the composer named it, about a provincial merchant's wife, Katerina Izmailova, who kills her husband and father-in-law to be with her lover and commits suicide on the way to a prison camp in Siberia. He expressed his indignation in the *Pravda* editorial: "The listener from the very first minute is stunned by the opera's intentionally unharmonious muddled flow of sounds. Snatches of melody, embryos of musical phrases drown, escape, and once again vanish in rumbling, creaking, and squealing. To follow this 'music' is difficult, to remember it impossible."

But Stalin would not have been the effective politician he was if he had not used a concrete excuse (in this case, his real irritation with Shostakovich's expressionist music and macabre plot) to let the urban intelligentsia know that the time of comparative tolerance of avant-garde culture, which could be called the "Lunacharsky era," was over once and for all. "The danger of this tendency in Soviet music is clear. Leftist ugliness in opera is growing from the same source as leftist ugliness in painting, poetry, pedagogy, and science. Petty bourgeois 'innovation' is leading to a gap away from true art, science, from true literature." For those who were slow on the uptake, Stalin warned quite unambiguously: "This is playing at esoteric things, which can end very badly."[3]

First to hand, Shostakovich got battered two more times by *Pravda:* in an editorial on February 6, "Ballet Falsehood" (aimed at his colossally successful comic ballet at the Bolshoi Theater about kolkhoz life, *The Limpid Stream*) and on February 13 in another unsigned article ("Clear and Simple Language in Art"), which once again attacked Shostakovich's opera and ballet: "Both these works are equally far from the clear, simple, and truthful language in which Soviet art must speak."[4]

At the same time, *Pravda* fired an entire antiformalist volley, printing another four editorials between February 13 and March 9 with threatening headlines: "A Crude Scheme Instead of Historical Truth" (about film), "Cacophony in Architecture," "About Blotting Artists," and "External Glitter and False Contents" (about dramatic theater). Stalin's ideas on the fate of the avant-garde were coming to pass; back in 1932, in a conversation with a culture functionary, Ivan Gronsky, he said, "The nonsense with these fashionable tendencies in art has to be ended."

Unexpectedly for Stalin, Maxim Gorky, whom he had elevated so high, came out against the antiformalist attack. The dictator had expected Gorky to be his ally in this matter: the idea, after all, was "to banish crudity and savagery from every corner of Soviet life," as it was put in "Muddle Instead of Music." Stalin and Gorky both believed that Russia, that backward agrarian country with a population that was mostly illiterate, had to be made *kulturny* in the shortest time possible. The achievement of collectivization and industrialization, a top priority for Bolsheviks, was impossible without such forced "acculturation."

The fate of the hapless Russian peasantry, caught in these catastrophic developments, did not worry Gorky as much as the vicissitudes of the "leading proletariat" and the urban intelligentsia. He also needed to maintain his reputation as the "great humanist" in Europe, where Gorky's influential friends, like Romain Rolland and André Malraux, were voicing alarm about the treatment of Shostakovich and other "formalists" (the peasants were of much less concern for the French as well).

That is why Gorky reacted quite nervously to Stalin's antiformalist pogrom. In the middle of March 1936, Gorky wrote a terse letter to Stalin, which was basically a demand that he disavow the attacks on Shostakovich in *Pravda*. The secret police also reported to Stalin that "Gorky is very displeased by discussions of formalism."

Despite the prevalent view in our day of Stalin as a one-track tyrant, he knew how to maneuver when it suited him. He cut off the attack on Shostakovich and supported his 1937 Fifth Symphony, characterizing it (anonymously, again) as a "businesslike creative response of a Soviet artist to just criticism."[5] For Stalin this was a tactical (and rather humiliating) retreat, which he avenged more than a decade later.

S talin came to power bolstered by many qualities needed by a successful politician: inhuman energy and capacity to work; the ability to comprehend and formulate the essence of a social problem, to understand the emotion of the masses and direct it as needed; the knack for maneuvering, biding his time, pitting his opponents against one another, and coolly choosing the right moment for getting rid of them and destroying them.

Yet there was one quality that is quite desirable in the leader of an influential European state with planetary ambitions, as the Russian empire had traditionally been (and also was in its incarnation as the Soviet Union), that Stalin lacked: international experience. Unlike Lenin and his comrades-in-arms, much less the high officials of tsarist Russia,

Stalin had never spent much time abroad and was not acquainted with the Western political and cultural elite.

Trotsky maintained that when Stalin met with Westerners, he demonstrated the "insecurity and shyness of a provincial who does not speak foreign languages and is lost when dealing with people he cannot order about and who do not fear him."[6] We know of a private remark by Maxim Litvinov, Commissar of Foreign Affairs, about Stalin's foreign policy: "He doesn't know the West. . . . If our enemies were a few shahs or sheiks, he would outsmart them."[7] Litvinov underestimated his boss. Tricked by Hitler, Stalin won in the end, and in dealing with such giants as Churchill and Roosevelt, he showed himself to be at least their equal in international maneuvering. The road to this intellectual parity was not an easy one for Stalin, but he was a good student, mastering the lessons and advice of people with a wider worldview, knowledge of languages, and European connections, such as Lenin and other old party leaders with émigré experience.

It is also obvious that Gorky was an excellent advisor for Stalin. Lenin had told Gorky: "It is always stimulating speaking with you, since you have a more varied and wider set of impressions." It was through Gorky that Stalin made personal contact with the luminaries of European culture. Here is an interesting chronology: June 29, 1931, Stalin met George Bernard Shaw; December 13, Emil Ludwig, a popular German writer at the time; August 4, 1933, the French writer and Communist Henri Barbusse; July 23, 1934, H. G. Wells; and June 28, 1935, Romain Rolland. They all came away charmed by Stalin.

After Gorky's death in 1936 Stalin had only one more meeting with a prominent foreign writer (Lion Feuchtwanger, January 8, 1937). It was the last such dialogue in Stalin's life. Without Gorky's helpful hints on how to deal with people like that, Stalin apparently decided not to risk it. And he must have been tired of playing the role of the "great humanitarian" and controlling himself.

Nobel laureate Rolland's impressions of Stalin were typical: "Absolute simplicity, straightforwardness, truthfulness. He does not impose his viewpoint. He says, 'Perhaps we were mistaken.' "[8] One can imagine Stalin's hidden laughter when he told Rolland: "It is very unpleasant for us to condemn and execute. It is dirty work. It would be better to remain above politics and keep our hands clean."[9]

Gorky seems to have been sincere in believing that his influence could "humanize" Stalin. Their correspondence, declassified in the late 1990s, shows that the writer showered Stalin with requests (as he had earlier done to Lenin) to help countless cultural figures. This had to have annoyed Stalin at some point, as it had Lenin. Moreover, Gorky had lost some of his aura as world luminary in Stalin's eyes. This happened when the writer, despite enormous support from the Soviets, did not win the Nobel Prize for Literature.

In the early 1930s a serious battle broke out among the Western literati over which Russian writer would be the first to win the Nobel Prize. Neither Leo Tolstoy nor Chekhov had become Nobel laureates (Chekhov had died too soon, and Tolstoy irritated the Swedish Academy with his radical political views and "hostility toward culture"). The prize had grown to be the most prestigious literary award in the world. Inevitably, political considerations as well as aesthetics went into the decision-making process. One of the polarizing political issues was the division of Russian culture after 1917 into two parts: the mainland—that is, Soviet—and the diaspora—émigré.

More than two million former citizens of the Russian empire were tossed outside the country's borders by the Bolshevik revolution. These émigrés settled in dozens of countries, literally all over the world, but the biggest centers of the diaspora were first Berlin (where more than half a million former Russians lived in the early 1920s) and then Paris.

The intelligentsia formed the majority of the immigrants, which was rather an exception for such mass resettlements. This explains the extraordinary cultural activity of the Russian diaspora. In Berlin alone there were dozens of Russian-language newspapers and magazines and close to seventy publishing houses.

Understandably, most of the immigrants were hostile to the Soviet regime. It repaid them in kind, having good reason to fear that the intellectual potential of these people would be used in the struggle with Bolshevism. This is exactly what happened. The Western states tried to create a "cordon sanitaire" around Soviet Russia, using the scattered elements of the White Army that had lost the Civil War to the Bolsheviks. The Russian cultural émigrés gave ideological support for the military. In Paris, Dmitri Merezhkovsky and his wife, Zinaida Hippius, formerly prominent Russian Symbolists, were active in "White" circles.

Gorky had tense relations with these people. In 1906, Merezhkovsky had written: "Gorky deserves his fame: he opened new, unknown countries, a new continent of the spiritual world; he is the first and the only, in all likelihood, unique in his field."[10] But just two years later Merezhkovsky grumbled: "Once Gorky had seemed a great artist—and has stopped being one."[11] It went downhill from there.

With some émigrés Gorky was more friendly; he valued Vladislav Khodasevich, a truly great poet who wrote a precious few refined and profoundly pessimistic poems. Early on, Gorky considered him "the best poet of contemporary Russia"and raved: "Khodasevich for me is immeasurably higher than Pasternak."[12] But later, in a letter to Stalin (1931), Gorky changed his mind: "He is a typical decadent, a man both physically and spiritually flabby, filled with misanthropy and hatred for all people."[13]

Particularly complex were relations between Gorky and Ivan Bunin, the leading figure of the Russian literary diaspora. Introduced in 1899 on the Yalta boardwalk by Chekhov, they became fast friends, and Gorky published a lot of Bunin (especially his fine poetry) in the popular collections of his Znanie Publishing House.

Gorky was always impressed by Bunin's craftsmanship, but he was more skeptical of his human qualities: "A talented artist, marvelous connoisseur of every word, he is a dried-up, unkind man, who is ridiculously careful of himself. He knows his own value, even somewhat exaggerates it, and he is demanding and vain, capricious to the people close to him, and tends to use them cruelly."[14]

Gorky the tramp and Bunin the aristocrat had similarly unsentimental views of the Russian *muzhik*, which Bunin expressed most vividly in his novella (which he considered a novel), *The Village* (1910). Gorky wrote to Bunin in delight: "In every phrase there are compressed three, four objects, every page is a museum!"[15] Gorky considered Bunin among the major figures of the Znanie circle (along with Leonid Andreyev and Alexander Kuprin). After the revolution, which the conservative Bunin abhorred, he distanced himself from Gorky, declaring that he considered their relationship "ended forever."

In emigration, Bunin continually attacked Gorky's pro-Soviet position, his work and even his image, mocking Gorky's "crude fairy tales about his allegedly miserable childhood, sprinkled with thousands of adventures, his laughably innumerable travels and encounters, and his imaginary life as a tramp."[16]

Bunin was jealous of Gorky's bond with Tolstoy. He had met Tolstoy, whom he idolized, only a few times. Tolstoy had no interest in Bunin, either as a writer or a human being, and once made a very disparaging remark about him. His attitude toward Gorky was very different, he was curious about him, this vibrant person from a different world. (The perceptive Marina Tsvetaeva sensed this intuitively; she considered Gorky "bigger, and more human, and more exceptional, and more needed" than Bunin: "Gorky is an era, while Bunin is the end of an era.")[17]

In his reminiscences of Tolstoy, Gorky's descriptions of the great elder are sometimes barbed, and Tolstoy could appear, as Eikhenbaum noted, as "a devious old man, a wizard, listlessly speaking of God, an obscenity-spewing mischief maker."[18] Gorky never felt himself to be Tolstoy's devout ideological follower, so different were their cultural positions. At the end of his life, Tolstoy became a cultural anarchist in his rejection of high art for its pretense and falsehood. Gorky, on the contrary, adulated culture.

> *Gentlemen! If the world*
> *Cannot find the way to holy truth,*
> *Glory to the madman*
> *Who can instill the golden dream in mankind.*

Those simplistic verses from his play *Lower Depths* contain "Gorky's motto that determined his entire life, as a writer, social figure, and personally,"[19] observed Khodasevich. For Bunin, who was a Tolstoyan in his youth and in the 1930s wrote a book filled with the greatest piety, *The Liberation of Tolstoy,* in which he compared the writer to Jesus Christ and Buddha, Gorky's position was alien. Now, their political and aesthetic disagreements were intensified by the ever-growing rivalry between Gorky and Bunin in the international cultural arena, centering on the Nobel Prize.

The prize was first awarded in 1901 in Stockholm in accordance with the will of the Swedish industrialist and inventor of dynamite Alfred Nobel, who had died five years earlier. Given every fall by the Swedish Academy on the recommendations of the Nobel Committee, it soon became internationally authoritative. It aroused nationalistic and political passions. A ritual developed that continues to this day: the world press begins its guessing game in September and October, publicizing various lists of potential winners and creating an atmosphere of tense anticipation.

Because of the secrecy surrounding the selection, the press is more often wrong than right in its predictions. The lucky winner is hailed and derided and all this adds to the mystic aura of the Nobel.

Much has been written about Alfred Nobel and his family, but the Russian connection is not often remembered. Ludwig, Alfred's older brother, turned the steel mill founded by their father in St. Petersburg in 1862 into one of Europe's largest diesel manufacturing enterprises. (It still exists under the name Russkii Dizel.)

The innovative diesel engines ran on oil, so the Nobels built an oil refinery in Baku in the Caucasus. Ludwig's son, Emmanuel Nobel (1859–1932), ran the family business in Russia for almost thirty years, until the revolution of 1917. His sister, Marta, married a Russian journalist, Oleinikov, her senior by seventeen years. Thus the scene was set for the intrigue around the Nobel Prize that pitted Gorky against Bunin.

Romain Rolland played a direct role in this intrigue from the start. In the early 1920s, Rolland, enraptured by Bunin's short story "The Gentleman from San Francisco," agreed to support his bid for the award ("He is zealously, biliously antirevolutionary, antidemocratic, antipopulist, almost antihumanitarian, a pessimist to the marrow of his bones. But an artist of genius!"),[20] but with one proviso: "If Gorky were to be nominated, I would vote for him."[21] However, in 1928, when Gorky was one of the finalists, the prize went to the Norwegian writer Sigrid Undset.

During the NEP period (1921–1927), the Soviet government permitted some cultural contacts with the émigrés, and works by Bunin—of course, without his permission and without any royalties—were printed in Russia even by state publishing houses. At that time, in an attempt to divide and neutralize the emigration, the Soviet regime was playing complicated games with some intellectual diaspora groups, such as the Eurasianists.

This ambivalent picture changed sharply after 1928, when books by Bunin and other leading émigré writers were banned and even expunged from libraries. (The remarkable writer Varlam Shalamov, sent to Siberian labor camps in 1943, got an additional ten-year sentence for carelessly characterizing Bunin as a "great Russian author"in a conversation.) That was when the real iron curtain fell between Moscow and the diaspora, for a long sixty years (with a brief hiatus in the early postwar years, when the Soviet poet Konstantin Simonov was sent to Paris by Stalin to meet with Bunin).

This explains why it was so politically important which Russian writer would first receive the Nobel Prize. Giving it to Gorky could be interpreted as support from the world cultural community for the revolutionary changes in Russia. Awarding it to Bunin or another émigré (the names of Merezhkovsky, Kuprin, Balmont, and Ivan Shmelev were circulating as possible candidates) would send exactly the opposite message.

The prize would also show whom Europe considered the true heir to Leo Tolstoy in Russian literature. Before the very first Nobel Prize was announced in 1901, the general expectation was that the recipient would be Tolstoy. When instead it was given to the minor French poet Sully-Prudhomme, a group of indignant Swedish writers and artists, including August Strindberg, Selma Lagerlöf, and Andreas Zorn, sent Tolstoy a letter that also appeared in the Russian press: "Everyone is outraged by the fact that the Academy out of political and religious considerations that have nothing to do with literature demonstratively ignored the achievements of Tolstoy."[22]

Both sides used all their behind-the-scenes resources. Bunin's most powerful ally may have been Emmanuel Ludwigovich (as the Bunin family called him) Nobel. This is apparent from a close reading of the diaries of Bunin and his wife (and also of Galina Kuznetsova, then Bunin's mistress) of the early 1930s, when the question of the "Russian Nobel"leaped back on the agenda.

Emmanuel Nobel even sent his Russian brother-in-law, Oleinikov, as an emissary to Bunin in France to discuss the ticklish details—after all, officially Nobel had no right to influence the members of the academy. (Kuznetsova recorded in her diary that Nobel sent a letter in 1931 "where he writes that he is for Bunin: he had read five or six of his books and is delighted by them.")[23] That is why when Oleinikov let them know that his brother-in-law had a brain hemorrhage (he died the following year), Bunin took this as a catastrophe.[24]

Another important figure who supported Bunin in his quest for the

Nobel was Thomas Masaryk, president of Czechoslovakia, an influential patron of the Russian diaspora culture. The Soviet government went on the counterattack, pressuring the Swedes through diplomatic channels: as Bunin was informed, "the Bolsheviks are agitating against an 'émigré prize,' and spreading rumors that if it happens they will break the agreement"[25] (the Soviet Union and Sweden were close to announcing telephone communications between the two countries).

The Soviet candidate for the Nobel Prize was Gorky, naturally. According to information given to Bunin, the Bolsheviks had support from Germany. The democratic West, especially France, backed Bunin. The Soviet strategy did not succeed: after two unsuccessful attempts, Bunin finally got the Nobel Prize in 1933, thereby beating not only Gorky, but Stalin as well (which was gleefully noted in the international press). The fact that Bunin stayed at the Nobel house in Stockholm instead of a hotel like the other laureates who had come for the ceremonies was not reported widely.

Bunin's speech, which he delivered in French, after accepting the Nobel medal (and a check for 80,000 francs) from King Gustav V in Stockholm on December 10, 1933, was broadcast all over the world. The thin, gray author, looking like a Roman patrician, was restrained—undoubtedly by previous arrangement with the Nobel family. He did not say a single word about the Bolsheviks, but did stress that this was the first time in the prize's history that it was given to an exile and that the gesture, politically significant, "proved once more that in Sweden the love of liberty is truly a national cult." As Kuznetsova wrote in her diary, "the word 'exile' created a stir" among the VIPs attending the ceremony, "but everything turned out all right."[26]

But once Bunin returned to France, he no longer felt constrained by diplomatic protocol and he spoke out about Bolshevism without euphemisms: "I am personally completely certain that nothing more despicable, lying, evil, and despotic than this regime ever existed in human history, even in the most depraved and bloody times."[27]

The presentation of the Nobel Prize to Bunin had to be perceived by Stalin not only as a serious blow to the international authority (and therefore, to his potential usefulness on the international scene) of his most trusted cultural advisor, but also as an unforgivable cultural humiliation for the entire country. And so the extraordinary political mystique of the Nobel Prize for Literature for twentieth-century Russian culture was born. Here is an intriguing note. In Bunin's published diary for October 1, 1933, that is, almost six weeks before the official announcement of his award, a laconic and somewhat mysterious reference appears to a postcard that he allegedly received from Stalin.[28] What could the Communist dictator have had to say to the great White émigré author?

The coolness that arose between Stalin and Gorky, noticed by many observers, affected the result of a notable international cultural and political event: suggested by Ilya Ehrenburg and formulated by Gorky and Stalin, the International Writers' Congress "in defense of culture from fascism" took place in Paris in June 1935.

At the time, some European intellectuals perceived the Soviet Union as the most reliable anti-Hitler force. They considered the barbaric Nazi ideas a grave threat to the traditional values of European humanism. So-called Popular Fronts uniting liberals and communists were organized in France and Spain to combat fascism. The writers' congress in Paris was intended to cement this union on a world scale.

Stalin allocated major expenditures for the congress. He wanted superstars like George Bernard Shaw, H. G. Wells, Romain Rolland, Thomas Mann, Theodore Dreiser, and Ernest Hemingway to come to Paris and to support the USSR's leadership in the antifascist coalition. Soviet backstage ideologue Ehrenburg and the journalist Mikhail Koltsov, Stalin's favorite, dealt with the practical side. But the central role had been assigned to Gorky from the start, and his presence would have guaranteed the congress both gravitas and the "correct" political line.

However, Gorky suddenly refused to go to Paris, blaming his health in a letter to Stalin and adding that the congress "does not seem particularly important to me."[29] In Gorky's absence, the situation in Paris quickly spun out of control. In Thomas Mann's stead came his brother, Heinrich, not nearly as important; instead of Shaw and Wells, there was Aldous Huxley. André Gide and André Malraux, representing France, were no match for Romain Rolland, who pointedly went to Moscow to be with Gorky. Besides, Gide and Malraux demanded that Babel and Pasternak, who were not in the original list of the Soviet delegation, attend the congress, and they permitted French Trotskyites to be heard at the congress, criticizing Soviet policy. The latter, from Stalin's point of view, was an open challenge. Pathologically suspicious, Stalin must have wondered whether Malraux and Gide were sabotaging his policies intentionally and who was helping them on the Soviet side.

Still, Stalin permitted both writers to visit the Soviet Union as honored guests. This was done on the insistent recommendation of Gorky and Koltsov. Malraux had already been to Moscow before the congress, and now came to spend time with Gorky at his Crimean dacha, after a meeting in Moscow with Meyerhold to discuss a planned Moscow production of a play based on his novel *La Condition humaine* [*Man's Fate*]. At the time, Malraux was secretary of the leftist international Association of Writers in the Defense of Culture, founded under the aegis of the congress and intended to actively participate in world politics. He was full of ambitious projects, including a new journal and a large-scale *Encyclopedia of the Twentieth Century*, modeled after the famous *Encyclopédie* of eighteenth-century French philosopher Denis Diderot.

According to his plan, this new *Encyclopédie* would be published simultaneously in four languages—French, English, Spanish, and Russian. Malraux suggested Bukharin as head of the Soviet editorial board. The encyclopedia would be funded, of course, by the Soviets.

Gorky, who adored all kinds of grandiose epochal projects, was in full agreement with Malraux's plan and personnel suggestions. He informed Stalin of them right away, in March 1936. Citing the opinions of Babel (who "understands people very well and is the wisest of our literary figures") and Koltsov, Gorky endorsed Malraux's idea that "by organizing the intelligentsia of Europe against Hitler and his philosophy, against Japanese warmongering, we are instilling the idea of the inevitability of world social revolution."[30]

The Frenchman's crazy projects paradoxically fit the Soviet political and cultural intrigues at the highest level. We now know that Gorky and Bukharin were nurturing the idea of creating a political association that would be an alternative to the communists—the "party of nonparty members," or "union of intellectuals." Gorky was to head the organization.

Interestingly, Stalin at first toyed with this idea, for he was thinking about uniting all the strata of Soviet society while at the same time positioning himself as leader of the international antifascist forces. A cultural "party of nonparty members," controlled by Stalin, could be a useful tool. That is why Malraux's propositions were for a moment taken so seriously in the Soviet Union. All this was crushed with Gorky's death and led to calamity.

Gorky died on June 18, 1936. It is still hotly debated whether people in Gorky's inner circle, infiltrated with informers and secret agents, had hastened his end on Stalin's orders. (The old writer annoyed the dictator with his unpredictability and whims.) In any case, it is clear that Gorky was seriously ill: the autopsy revealed that his lungs were almost totally calcified (as a result of many years of tuberculosis); when the pathologist tossed them into a basin they made a clanking noise, a witness recalled.

Moscow radio announced the death of a "great Russian writer, a genius of verbal art, the selfless friend of the working man, and fighter for the victory of communism." More than a half million paid their respects to Gorky on his bier in the Hall of Columns in the House of Unions, on June 19; and about one hundred thousand people were let in by special pass to the funeral on Red Square. Standing atop Lenin's mausoleum, Stalin listened to the Chairman of the Soviet of People's Commissars, Vyacheslav Molotov, opening the ceremony: "After Lenin, the death of Gorky is the greatest loss for our country and for humanity."

One of the speakers was André Gide, who had arrived in Moscow on the eve of Gorky's death. He spoke on behalf of the Association of Writers in the Defense of Culture that was headed by Malraux. His interpreter was Koltsov, who later told his brother that Stalin had asked him: "Comrade Koltsov, what, does this André Gide have great authority in the West?" When Koltsov answered affirmatively, Stalin regarded him suspiciously and said, skeptically: "Well, please God. Please God he is."[31] He did not like being led around by the nose.

Stalin's grave doubts were quickly confirmed; as Ehrenburg wrote in his memoirs, in the Soviet Union, André Gide "was wholeheartedly delighted by everything but when he got back to Paris, he condemned everything just as wholeheartedly. I don't know what happened to him: another person's soul is a mystery."[32] Even toward the end of his life, Ehrenburg maintained the fiction of being surprised, not mentioning the fact that the last days of Gide's sojourn in the USSR coincided with the open Moscow trial of the "anti-Soviet united center" (Grigory Zinoviev, Lev Kamenev, and other old Bolsheviks who were opposed to Stalin), which signaled the beginning of the Great Terror.

All sixteen defendants were executed on August 24, 1936, a little more than two months after Gorky's death. Such brutality was a shock not only to Gide; even the experienced cynic Babel had been certain that they would be pardoned. Stalin did not allow Gide to attend the trial, despite his requests; he did not grant the writer a meeting, either.

The somersault in Gide's attitude toward the Soviets was now seen by Stalin as a planned act of sabotage ("the enemy's calculation is evident here"). Stalin decided that Malraux was also a spy and saboteur. In 1938–1939, the Soviet intellectuals in contact with the two French writers—Koltsov, Babel, and Meyerhold—were arrested on Stalin's personal orders. Only Ehrenburg was spared.

The causes, sources, aims, and consequences (including the total number of victims) of the Great Terror (its parameters usually defined as the summer of 1936 to the end of 1938) are still not fully understood and measured, and it is unlikely that much-needed clarity will come in the near future, despite the research being done.

The differences of opinion on the Great Terror in contemporary Russia are astonishing, especially within the conservative wing. Solzhenitsyn characterized this period as a frontal "attack of the Law on the People," when innocents were delivered a "crushing blow," while the ultranationalist historian Oleg Platonov in his 2004 book, *State Treason: The Conspiracy Against Russia,* stated that "the majority of people repressed in 1937 and later were enemies of the Russian people. In destroying the Bolshevik guard, Stalin not only dealt with his rivals for power but to some degree expiated his guilt before the Russian people, for whom the execution of the revolutionary pogrom attackers was an act of historical vengeance."[33]

There is a certain smugness in the writings of some Russian conservative historians when it comes to the repressions during the Great Terror against the urban intelligentsia, which, they feel, did not come to the defense of the peasantry in time. The Russian intelligentsia may be guilty of many sins, but it did not deserve the blow that befell it in those years. Behind every person arrested and sucked into the funnel of the Stalin repressions came the family and relatives, followed by distant relatives, coworkers, subordinates, and mere acquaintances. As a historian noted: "It seemed as if the flywheel of repression slipped out of the hands of those who were turning it: the resulting purges shattered the system of management of the economy, beheaded the army, and demoralized the party."[34] It also frayed the fabric of the culture.

At least six hundred published authors were arrested during the Great Terror, that is, almost a third of the members of the Union of Soviet Writers. They are all to be pitied as human beings. There weren't all that many major writers among them; many of the figures were party workers first and foremost, "moonlighting" as writers. The cultural damage, however, cannot be calculated only by the number of arrested and executed geniuses; the corrosive atmosphere of omnipresent fear, suspicion, uncertainty, and epidemic levels of informing and self-censorship of the Great Terror fatally poisoned the moral climate.

As historians now believe, Stalin began the Great Terror with several political goals: to cement his personal rule, to quash real and imaginary opposition and the Fifth Column, to intimidate the populace, and as an economic bonus, to guarantee cheap slave labor for his industrial efforts. Once he thought he had achieved those ends and saw that society was on the verge of total destabilization, Stalin started curtailing the terror in 1939, admitting that it had been accompanied by "numerous errors."

But it was that moment when the demoralized elites tried to catch their breath that Stalin sent another terrifying signal to the intelligentsia: Koltsov, Babel, and Meyerhold were arrested in late 1938 and early 1939 and shot, after an unusual delay, probably caused by Stalin's deliberations, in early 1940.

All three had been accused of being part of an "anti-Soviet Trotskyite group" and of participating in a "conspiratorial terrorist organization" as agents of French and other foreign intelligence services. They were blamed for their contacts with Malraux, who at that moment in Stalin's imagination had turned into a major Western spy and provocateur, responsible for many failures in Stalin's foreign policy. (A prominent Soviet writer told me that in the 1960s, when he began traveling to the West, the KGB tried to recruit him, using Malraux as an example and model: for some reason the recruiter thought that an irresistible argument.)

Koltsov, Babel, and Meyerhold were forced to confess their "guilt" and inform on the crème de la crème of Soviet culture—Pasternak,

Shostakovich, Eisenstein, Alexei Tolstoy, and Yuri Olesha, author of the fine short novels *Envy* and *Three Fat Men*. We know the methods used from the statements (to the prosecutor and also to the Chairman of the Soviet of People's Commissars Molotov) by Meyerhold, who had renounced his statements, as had Babel. "I was beaten—a sick sixty-year-old man, they made me lie face down on the floor, beating me with a rubber hose on the soles of my feet and back, when I was seated in a chair, they used the rubber to hit my feet (from above, with great force) and along the legs from the knee to the top of the feet. And in subsequent days, when those parts of my legs were covered with large internal bruises, they beat me again on those red-blue-yellow spots with the hose, and the pain was so strong that it felt as if they were pouring boiling water on those painful, sensitive spots (I screamed and wept with pain). They beat my back with that hose, they beat my face with big swings from above . . . the investigator kept repeating and threatening me: 'If you don't sign (that is, make it up?), we will keep beating you leaving only your head and right hand untouched, the rest we'll turn into a piece of formless bloody chopped meat.' And I signed everything."[35]

The fate of major figures like Meyerhold was decided by Stalin personally: when he put two vertical lines next to the name of the accused, it meant a ten-year sentence; one line meant execution. Stalin put one line on Meyerhold's file.

It is often said that he did it because he did not like Meyerhold's avant-garde theater productions. That is hard to believe. Stalin, a politician through and through, was capable of overcoming aesthetic and personal dislike if it served his cause. He praised the avant-garde poet Mayakovsky and he did not touch Tatlin or Rodchenko. Andrei Platonov, whose prose he hated, was never arrested. On the other hand, Stalin never had a more loyal cultural functionary than Koltsov, whom he had killed.

The answer to this riddle may lie in the fact that for Stalin the removal of an important opponent was just a winning move in a political chess game. Did Stalin ever make mistakes, even from his own extremely cynical and ruthless, often cannibalistic, point of view? Of course, more than once. One such grave error within Stalin's political paradigm was killing Koltsov, Meyerhold, and Babel.

Stalin was obviously basing his thinking on the situation at hand. In 1939, the Soviet leader unexpectedly changed his foreign policy, entering into an alliance with Hitler and thus giving up his antifascist pretense. Consequently, he dropped all his carefully developed plans for uniting the international anti-Hitlerite and liberal intellectuals under the aegis of the Soviet Union.

Stalin now considered all that effort and expense an abject failure. A particularly painful event was the loss of the Soviet-supported republican government of Spain in the civil war begun by General Francisco Franco in 1936. Franco was helped by Germany and fascist Italy, and antifascists from all over the world came to help the republicans, including Ernest Hemingway and Malraux. Stalin's political emissary in Spain was Koltsov, whose attempts to bond the pro-Soviet elements in Spain failed. Someone had to pay for that and other international fiascoes.

Stalin always found "traitors" and "saboteurs" to be useful lightning rods and scapegoats. In this case, the part was given to a group of leading Soviet cultural figures who in his view had been mere puppets in the hands of Gide and Malraux and through them served their "real masters,"the European imperialists and plutocrats from France and England.

This explanation fit both Stalin's worldview and the current needs for his policy. But he still hesitated. Meyerhold's heartbreaking appeal, as we know, did not weaken Stalin's resolve. But it is telling that the information obtained under duress during interrogations was never used to arrest other celebrities like Shostakovich, Pasternak, or Eisenstein: apparently, Stalin reconsidered his plan to hold a sensational show trial of major cultural figures.

Nevertheless, the execution of Koltsov, Meyerhold, and Babel, which was not reported in the press at the time, poisoned the relationship between Stalin and the intelligentsia. Their ruthless dispatch showed that nothing—not talent, not achievements on behalf of the Soviet regime, not personal loyalty and closeness to Stalin (everyone knew that Koltsov, the de facto editor-in-chief of *Pravda*, was his favorite)—could save you from the dictator's wrath. In his own way an extremely pragmatic man, Stalin suddenly took on terrifying irrational traits in the eyes of the cultural elite. Perhaps that is what he wanted. In that case, he had made another mistake.

Yet another signal, loud and clear, was sent by Stalin: all contact with the West was fatally dangerous. In culture, the iron curtain fell then, in early 1940—only to be lifted a bit during the war, when relations had to be mended with the British and American allies. Stalin had expended a lot of effort in order to establish cordial personal ties with Soviet intellectuals. At some point, he decided that crude intimidation would be more effective. It was: the intellectuals were frightened, but the honeymoon with Stalin—and therefore, with the Soviet regime—was over.

Part Three

RENDEZVOUS
WITH STALIN

Chapter Seven

What is socialist realism? Ask five specialists and you will get five different answers. Should it interest us in the least? I believe so: socialist realism reigned in Soviet culture from the early 1930s for an entire half century, and after World War II it was declared to be the dominant force in culture for all countries of the Soviet bloc, that is, on the territory of over a dozen countries in Europe and Asia with a total population of almost a billion people.

For Russia, the significance of socialist realism cannot be overestimated. It is an inalienable and important part of its cultural heritage. Russian culture of the twentieth century was created in large part before our eyes, yet its history contains many mysterious "black holes," as if it were a long-vanished civilization. The doctrine of socialist realism is one of those mysteries.

Soviet people of a certain age still remember the time when the words "socialist realism" were used as frequently as "Soviet rule" or "Communist Party," that is, constantly. But unlike the other two terms, which stood for something concrete and had more or less clearly defined features, the true meaning of socialist realism, despite the thousands of articles and books attempting to explain it, remained quite elusive.

This vagueness was built into the original definition of socialist realism from 1934, of which Stalin was a coauthor, as "the basic method of Soviet literature and art," which "demands of the artist a truthful, historically concrete depiction of reality in its revolutionary development."[1]

Like Lenin before him, Stalin preferred slogans that were simple and clear and easily understood by the masses. According to Stalin's confidant Ivan Gronsky, the ruler chose the label "socialist realism" because of "its brevity (just two words), second, perspicuity, and third, its connection with tradition."[2] (Stalin was referring to the label's link with the great literature of "critical realism," that is, Dostoevsky, Leo Tolstoy, and Chekhov.)

The sought-after clarity was illusory, however. An animated discussion of the meaning of socialist realism continues to this day. Is it a method or only a style, or both? Can only works with a strongly expressed Communist ideology be considered socialist realist? Mayakovsky's narrative poems *Vladimir Ilyich Lenin* and *Good!* come to mind, but their style is rather more expressionist than realist. But if we accept that these works are examples of socialist realism, in accordance with Soviet doctrine, then why not use the same criteria for the poems of Pablo Neruda and Paul Eluard? (This was done in 1972 in the Moscow *Short Literary Encyclopedia*, which also made Romain Rolland and Bertolt Brecht socialist realist writers, an absurd proposition.)

But if you consider German and Chilean Expressionists and a French Surrealist as socialist realists, then why deny the appellation to Boris Pasternak's revolutionary narrative poems *Nineteen Hundred Five* and *Lieutenant Schmidt*? Contemporary Russian literary criticism tends to leave Pasternak and Andrei Platonov, who also wrote quasi-Communist works, outside the limits of socialist realism: they, you see, are "good" writers, and today only "bad" ones are considered socialist realists. (In the Soviet Union, in their time Pasternak and Platonov were also not regarded as socialist realists, but precisely because they were viewed as "bad"writers.)

One way to deal with this confusion would be an attempt to place the problem in a historical context. Let us try to put ourselves in the shoes of the man who was personally responsible for the appearance and later wide usage of the term "socialist realism,"Joseph Stalin. We can understand better what he himself considered real socialist art and literature, worthy of state support, if we open *Pravda* for March 16, 1941. This issue of the country's main newspaper was full of materials on the first winners of the Stalin Prize, instituted in 1939, when he was celebrating his sixtieth birthday.

Stalin's idea was to recognize the most outstanding works of Soviet art and literature. A special multilevel bureaucratic system was set up for the selection process, which was topped by the Stalin Prize Committee chaired by the artistic lion Vladimir Nemirovich-Danchenko, who had founded the Moscow Art Theater with Stanislavsky. But the last word always belonged to Stalin, who personally wrote in or crossed out names and who was impressively enthusiastic and informed. At the beginning, the prize was awarded in the first and second degrees (respectively

100,000 and 50,000 rubles), but a third degree (25,000 rubles) was added in 1948.

Stalin was particularly attentive and demanding when it came to the very first winners of the prize named for him. Subsequent awards were given for works that appeared the previous year, but the first ones were given, as the Resolution of the Council of People's Commissars of March 15, 1941, stated, "for outstanding works in art and literature for the period of the last 6–7 years," that is, since 1935.

The editorial of the "laureate" issue of *Pravda* formulated the current cultural priorities: "Soviet art must inspire the masses in their struggle for a full and final victory of socialism, it must help them in this struggle. In the great competition of two systems—the system of capitalism and the system of socialism—Soviet art must also serve as a weapon in this struggle, glorifying socialism. The era of the struggle for Communism must become the era of Socialist Renaissance in art, for only socialism creates the conditions for a complete flourishing of all national talents."[3]

The characteristically catechistic style of this lecture, with its tautology and fixation on the words "socialism" and "struggle," suggests that the author is Stalin. I've argued (in my book *Shostakovich and Stalin*) that the ruler was not only an attentive reader of *Pravda* but one of its main authors, and often the texts that he wrote or dictated appeared without his signature. No one but Stalin could have dared propose the unexpected parallel with the Italian Renaissance, for that would inevitably lead to a rather ambivalent comparison of him as a patron of the arts with the violent Medici family and the willful Roman popes of that period.

Without a doubt it was Stalin's decision to publish the photos of the six winners on page one. The "magnificent six" appeared in an order that surely was meaningful for Stalin: Dmitri Shostakovich, Alexander Gerasimov, Vera Mukhina, Valeria Barsova, Sergei Eisenstein, and Mikhail Sholokhov. Four men, two women (Stalin was apparently not a misogynist), some of whom are geniuses known to the entire world, and others who today are known even in Russia only to specialists. But Stalin saw them as the most representative examples of his cultural renaissance.

Valeria Barsova (1892–1967), a lyric coloratura soprano and soloist of the Bolshoi Theater, is rarely remembered today, but in the 1930s and 1940s she was one of the most popular and beloved Soviet singers. She was called the "Soviet nightingale" and shone in the Verdi roles of Gilda and Violetta, but Stalin liked her best in her nuanced performance (she consulted with Stanislavsky) as Antonida, daughter of the Russian peasant patriot Ivan Susanin in Mikhail Glinka's *A Life for the Tsar,* the first mature Russian opera. Stalin loved Glinka's work, which had been banned after the revolution for its monarchism; he returned it to the repertoire in 1939, with a new title, *Ivan Susanin,* purged of pro-tsarist sentiments (the revisions were quite skillful).

As always with Stalin's cultural gestures, politics mattered. A fan of Russian classical opera (he would interrupt a meeting of the Politburo to get to the Bolshoi in time for his favorite aria in *Susanin*), Stalin also used Glinka's majestic work to legitimize, on the eve of the war with Hitler, the nationalistic emotions that had been downplayed by the internationalist Lenin.

It's quite possible that Stalin chose Barsova not only for her talent and high professionalism (on the plump side, she tortured herself with exercises to stay trim enough even after fifty to leap around the stage as Rosina in *The Barber of Seville;* on vacation, she swam far out into the sea and sang voice exercises out there), but also for her civic activities—Barsova was a deputy of the Supreme Soviet of the RSFSR and then of the Moscow Soviet. Of the "magnificent six," she and Sholokhov were the only card-carrying Party members at the time of the award.

Rumor had the beautiful Barsova as Stalin's mistress, but even if we discount that, we can see why her picture graced *Pravda*'s page one. Barsova was the personification of the new type of music theater artist—a sphere Stalin loved and considered important and where there had been superstars before the revolution, too: the bass Chaliapin, the tenor Leonid Sobinov, the sopranos Antonina Nezhdanova and Nadezhda Obukhova, and ballet dancer Anna Pavlova.

The ruler wanted to show that the new generation of stars of opera and ballet were as good as the prerevolutionary masters, so that is why the early winners of the Stalin Prize included the great performers of the Soviet era—basses Maxim Mikhailov and Mark Reizen, tenors Ivan Kozlovsky and Sergei Lemeshev, and the ballet dancer Galina Ulanova (the only one in this list to become a legendary figure in the West, as well).

Although the name of sculptor Vera Mukhina, the second woman among the first round of Stalin Prize winners, is not well known outside Russia, her most famous work, *The Laborer and the Farm Worker*, a twenty-five-meter composition of stainless steel, weighing seventy-four tons and erected above the Soviet pavilion at the Paris World's Fair in 1937 (the task was to visually block the nearby German pavilion), is still widely reproduced in countless posters and book covers.

Many people (including Romain Rolland) considered this dynamic depiction of two gigantic, semi-nude figures striving forward (she brandishing a sickle and he a hammer) the most eloquent symbol of Soviet art and even of the Soviet state. (There are some who insist that honor belongs to El Lissitzky's poster for the Soviet exhibition in Zurich in 1929, which elaborates a theme similar to Mukhina's, of the ecstatic unity of the male and female in the name of the socialist idea in a more avant-garde key.)

The beloved daughter of a wealthy merchant, the mannish Mukhina studied in Paris and with her friends Nadezhda Udaltsova and Lubov Popova was one of the "Amazons" of the Russian avant-garde. Mukhina was particularly close to one of the leading Amazons, Alexandra Exter; together they designed the modernist plays of the influential Moscow Chamber Theater, under the direction of Alexander Tairov, and also extravagant hats for the capital's fashion plates in the early 1920s.

In 1930, Mukhina was arrested and exiled for a year for an attempt to escape abroad, but that did not keep her from becoming one of Stalin's favorite sculptors just a few years later. Highly admiring her *Laborer and Farm Worker*, he protected Mukhina from potentially lethal accusations of maliciously hiding an image of Trotsky in the billowing folds of the couple's drapes.

In her lifetime, Mukhina received five Stalin Prizes (she outlived Stalin by seven months, dying in 1953), but she never did produce the obligatory portrait of the country's leader. When she was asked to do so, she played the principled realist and set one condition: Stalin had to pose for her personally. (They say that the artist Petr Konchalovsky used the same ruse to avoid having to paint Stalin.)

It would be hard to find a greater opposite to the severe and principled Mukhina than the painter Alexander Gerasimov, who received the Stalin Prize for his painting *Stalin and Voroshilov at the Kremlin;* most memoirists depict him as a cynical opportunist. Gerasimov always underscored his birth to a peasant family of former serfs: this gave him substantive preeminence in Soviet society over the "socially alien" merchant's daughter Mukhina. In his youth an epigone of the French Impressionists, Gerasimov began denouncing them publicly as decadent and formalist as soon as the Party directive was announced.

A stocky, curly-haired man who swore freely and sported a foppish, thin mustache, Gerasimov privately enjoyed painting nudes, while millions of reproductions circulated around the country of his formal portraits of Lenin, Stalin, and Marshal Kliment Voroshilov, patron and friend of Gerasimov (who often stopped by the artist's studio to see the latest depiction of a plump nude beauty).

As president of the Academy of Arts of the USSR, created in 1947 in imitation of the prerevolutionary one, Gerasimov became "chief artist" of the land and a symbol of socialist realism in art, paid fantastic sums by the state for the huge, multifigured official canvases churned out in his studio. Yet to demonstrate his unbreakable bonds with his folksy past, he had his chauffeur pile hay in the backseat of his state-supplied limousine, and he rode up front.

Gerasimov was a colorful figure, but his paintings, recipients of many awards (including four Stalin Prizes and gold medals at the World's Fairs in Paris and Brussels), are now considered artistically uninteresting: anemic in composition and technically inept. Critics are as dismissive of other idols of socialist realism, even though there were true painterly virtuosi among them: Isaak Brodsky, one of Repin's favorite students, Vassily Efanov, and Alexander Laktionov.

But is it even possible to judge the work of Gerasimov and his socialist realist colleagues using purely artistic criteria that are based on the aesthetic of the Western avant-garde of the last hundred years while ignoring their social function in Stalin's society?

Such asocial methods of evaluation until recently were applied to the cultural artifacts of non-European traditions—the sculptures and masks of Asia, Africa, and Oceania. They were ritual objects, valued by their peoples and tribes for their social utility rather than their artistic merit. In the West the artifacts were viewed through the prism of the prevalent modernist aesthetic—what resembled it got high marks, the rest was considered less "interesting," and therefore, less artistically valuable. Now, this approach is being reconsidered.

The art of Stalin's era apparently must be treated as ritual to a high degree. In that sense, we can discover intriguing roots of socialist realism (which Western and Russian art historians have recently been examining). At the source of socialist realism stood Gorky and Lunacharsky, who before the revolution toyed with quasi-religious cultural ideas (for which they were berated by Lenin), and the slogan of socialist realism was introduced by Stalin, a former Orthodox seminarian. Both Lunacharsky and Gorky spoke often of the shamanistic influence of art on human behavior. Stalin did not speak of that aloud, but he undoubtedly sensed the magical powers of art as something real; this was noted by Osip Mandelstam: "That is a superstition with him [Stalin]. He thinks we poets are shamans."[4]

Gorky considered socialist realism a tool to "arouse a revolutionary attitude toward reality, an attitude that will practically change the world."[5] Here, Gorky is apparently referring to the ritual, magical role of socialist realism. Lunacharsky was even more frank: "Soviet art is in no essential way different from religious art."[6]

As befitted a professional politician, Stalin avoided frank declarations but persistently pushed Soviet culture to perform quasi-religious functions: novels had to play the part of lives of the saints, plays and films of religious mysteries, and paintings of icons. The cult of the late Lenin portrayed him as God the Father, with Stalin as the son. Lenin, and after his death, Stalin, were displayed in a mausoleum on Moscow's Red Square, embalmed as the relics of Communist saints.

The architecture of the Stalin period served the same goal. Even the subway, which in Western cities had strictly utilitarian purposes, in Moscow was used as a showcase, the stations secular temples that were part of the obligatory tour for foreigners and meant to inspire ritual awe in them as well as in Soviet citizens. The anticlerical skeptic Malraux is said to have responded to the underground miracle with a bon mot: "Un peu trop de métro."[7]

The monumental socialist realist paintings and sculptures of the Stalin period that depicted the rulers and their meetings with the people, the exploits of heroes, and mass demonstrations and festivities should also be viewed as ritual objects, even if they are in museums. Only by situating these works in a historical and social context can we appreciate the craft of their creators, crowned by Stalin Prizes, and to see that the awards were not given without good reason.

Probably the most controversial figure of the first group of Stalin Prize winners was Mikhail Sholokhov, who later became the third Russian Nobel laureate. The range of opinions about Sholokhov is astounding even for the contentious twentieth century—from recognition of him as a great writer, one of the world classics of our time, to Solzhenitsyn's disdainful remarks: "With Sholokhov, one shouldn't even speak of whether he's educated or not, but if he is literate or not."[8] This about the man who in 1939 became a member of the Academy of Sciences of the USSR.

Stalin gave Sholokhov the prize for his epic novel *The Quiet Don* (also known in the West as *And Quiet Flows the Don*), depicting the tragic trajectory of the Don Cossack Grigory Melekhov in the years of World War I and the Civil War, against the background of the period's tectonic social shifts. Even Solzhenitsyn has high regard for the novel; what then was the cause for his dismissive attitude toward Sholokhov?

As soon as the twenty-three-year-old Sholokhov published the novel in 1928, rumors began circulating that he was not the real author, but had plagiarized the manuscript (or diaries) of another writer, Fedor Kryukov, who died in 1920; other sources were also mentioned. With time the search for the person behind *The Quiet Don* turned into a small industry, with thick volumes written pro and contra.

This problem, considering that Sholokhov's archives for the 1920s and 1930s are missing (allegedly burned during World War II), is unlikely to be resolved in the near future. So in this case, following Mikhail Bakhtin and Roland Barthes, we can treat the question of "authorship" as a conditional one. Sholokhov, contrary to the opinion of his numerous foes, was a major figure and an ambivalent one, and he remains inseparable from the dramatic fate of *The Quiet Don*.

The legend that the Soviet regime embraced *Don* from the beginning has become entrenched. But in reality it was not the case. Sholokhov did not come from a proletarian background, growing up in a wealthy family, and the "proletarian" critics immediately dismissed the novel as "an idealization of the kulaks and White Guards." When it came to the publication of the third and final volume, Sholokhov encountered stiff resistance: influential literary bureaucrats, all-powerful Fadeyev among them, felt that the publication of this book "would give great satisfaction to our enemies, the White Guards, who emigrated."[9] It was held up for more than two years.

Sholokhov turned to his patron Gorky for support and in July 1931 the young writer met at Gorky's apartment with the country's main censor, Stalin. He already knew the first two volumes and read the third in manuscript before the meeting, and at Gorky's (who, as Sholokhov recalled, kept quiet, smoked, and burned matches over the ashtray) he interrogated Sholokhov: why were the Whites shown "in a soft way" in *The Quiet Don*? On what documents was the novel based? (Knowing about the plagiarism charges, Stalin must have been checking Sholokhov's historical erudition.)

In self-defense, Sholokhov argued that General Lavr Kornilov, who fought against the Bolsheviks on the Don River, was "subjectively an honest man." The writer later recalled that Stalin's "yellow eyes narrowed like a tiger's before it leaps," but the ruler continued the argument with restraint, in his favorite catechistic manner: "A subjectively honest man is one who is with the people, who fights for the good of the people." Kornilov had gone against the people, had spilled a "sea of blood." How could he be an honest man?

Sholokhov was forced to agree. Stalin must have been pleased with his conversation with the short and boyishly thin twenty-six-year-old with a shock of curls over his large forehead. His resolution was: "The depiction of the course of events in the third book of *The Quiet Don* works in our favor, for the Revolution. We will publish it!"[10]

But Sholokhov's foes did not lay down their weapons. The discussion of *The Quiet Don* at the Stalin Prize Committee was a battlefield. The great filmmaker Alexander Dovzhenko, who created one of the masterpieces of Soviet silent film, *Earth* (1930), and who was one of Stalin's favorites (he got the Stalin Prize for his film *Shchors*, about Ukraine during the Civil War), rose to an emotional speech. "I read the book *The Quiet Don* with a feeling of great inner dissatisfaction. . . . I can summarize my impressions this way: for centuries the quiet Don lived, Cossack men and women rode horses, drank, and sang . . . their life was juicy, aromatic, stable, and warm. The Revolution came, Soviet rule and the Bolsheviks destroyed the quiet Don, chased people away, pitted brother against brother, father against son, husband against wife, impoverished the country . . . infected it with gonorrhea and syphilis, sowed filth, anger, and pushed the strong men with character into banditry. . . . And so it ended. That is an enormous mistake in the author's concept."[11]

Other members of the Committee also spoke out against *The Quiet Don*, but the most damning conclusion about the novel came from Fadeyev, head of the Writers' Union of the USSR then (and known as Stalin's trusted person): "My personal opinion is that it does not show the victory of the Stalinist idea." Fadeyev later admitted to Sholokhov that he had voted against him. But Sholokhov, as we know, received the prize and appeared on the front page of *Pravda*. Why?

The answer lies in part in the fact that Stalin apparently encouraged the writer not only for *The Quiet Don* but also for the first part of his second novel, which had been published by then. *Virgin Soil Upturned* was about collectivization, that is, a very important topic for the country and for Stalin personally. Stalin's opinion of the book is reflected in a letter to his henchman Lazar Kaganovich, dated June 7, 1932: "An interesting work! You can see that Sholokhov studied the kolkhozes on the Don. Sholokhov, I believe, has a great creative gift. Besides which, he is a very conscientious writer: he writes about things he knows well."[12] (That is, Stalin had further confirmation that Sholokhov was not a plagiarist.)

But that is not all. It seems that Stalin was rewarding Sholokhov's actions, about which very few people knew then. They remained a secret for many years and even though they were first mentioned by Nikita Khrushchev in 1963, the details of the story did not surface until the 1990s, after the collapse of the Soviet empire, when the correspondence between Sholokhov and Stalin was declassified.

Fifteen letters and notes from Sholokhov to Stalin, and a letter and two telegrams from Stalin to Sholokhov read like a riveting novel, with the difference that this is the true (albeit not complete) story of the interactions of the ruler and the writer over the most tragic events of that era, collectivization and the Great Terror.

Sholokhov, not yet thirty, sent the first letters to Stalin in 1931–1933, during the throes of an agricultural crisis caused by the forced collectivization. In order to supply the cities with food, the government confiscated all the grain the kolkhoz farmers had. Sholokhov depicted the situation straightforwardly, with rare candor and directness: "Right now kolkhoz farmers and individual farmers are starving to death; adults and

children are swelling and eating everything that humans are not supposed to eat, starting with carrion and ending with oak bark and all
kinds of swamp roots."[13] In another letter he wrote, "It is so bitter, Comrade Stalin! Your heart bleeds when you see it with your own eyes."

Sholokhov describes the "disgusting 'methods' of torture, beatings,
and humiliations" used to find out where peasants are hiding their grain:
"At the Vashchaevsk kolkhoz, they poured kerosene on the women's legs
and hems of their skirts, set them on fire, and then put them out: 'Will
you tell me where the pit is? I'll light it again if you don't.' "

There are many stark examples of torture, threats, and violence in
Sholokhov's letters to Stalin; he piles them up, like an experienced
writer, and remarkably, dares to pressure him by threatening to
denounce the Soviet regime in his new book: "I decided that it was better to write to you than to use this material for the last volume of *Virgin
Soil Upturned.*" (You have to be certain of your own genius to write like
this to Stalin; it's unlikely that an ordinary plagiarist would be so bold.)

How did Stalin react? Khrushchev recalled later that Stalin, whenever
he was told about something wrong, would usually grow irritable, even if
he knew the situation had to be corrected: he would agree but be angry.
This complex brew of contradictory emotions can be seen in Stalin's
reply to Sholokhov (dated May 6, 1933), in which he thanks the writer for
his alarmist letters, "since they lift the scab from our party-Soviet work,
reveal that sometimes our workers, wanting to shackle the enemy, accidentally strike our friends and even become sadistic."

But Stalin also points out to Sholokhov that the peasants the writer
wanted to protect (Stalin mockingly refers to them as the "esteemed
grain-harvesters") were in his view saboteurs who were trying to deny
bread to the workers and the Red Army and that those "esteemed grain-
harvesters were in fact waging a 'quiet' war against Soviet rule. A war of
starvation, dear Comrade Sholokhov." At the same time, Stalin gave
orders to send food to Sholokhov's starving fellow countrymen. That was
a typical move for Stalin, making temporary and small concessions while
basically pressing on with his plans.

Sholokhov appealed to Stalin with another long letter on February 16,
1938, at the peak of the Great Terror. The writer was threatened with
arrest as an enemy of the people (a detained member of a Cossack choir
testified under duress that Sholokhov ordered him to assassinate a government official during the choir's performance in Moscow), but

Sholokhov spends most of the letter defending his friends who were in prison and being tortured: "Comrade Stalin! This method of investigation in which the prisoner is given into the hands of the investigators without any control is profoundly corrupt. . . . We must put an end to the shameful system of torture used on prisoners."

Sholokhov was called into the Kremlin to see Stalin and there, in the presence of the much-feared head of the NKVD, Nikolai Yezhov, he told a joke making the rounds. A hare making a headlong dash is asked why he's running.

"I'm afraid they'll shoe me!"

"They don't shoe hares, they shoe camels!"

"Once they catch you and put shoes on you, go prove that you're not a camel!"

Telling the dictator a political joke was really working without a net. As Sholokhov recalled later, Yezhov laughed out loud; Stalin, not so much, and said sarcastically, "They say you drink a lot, Comrade Sholokhov?" Sholokhov continued in the same jesting tone, "A life like this, Comrade Stalin, will drive you to drink."

There was no point in denying it: the writer had been brought to the Kremlin from a Moscow restaurant where he had been drinking heavily with Fadeyev, who also had a weakness for booze. Stalin forgave both of them. His personal secretary, Alexander Poskrebyshev, had a much more severe reaction to the drunken writer's appearance in the Kremlin. "Blotto, you motley fool?" Before Sholokhov's audience with Stalin, the secretary threw him into a hot shower, gave him a fresh shirt with a white celluloid collar, and sprayed him with cologne, to disguise the vodka reek.

Stalin, who generally disliked so-called immoral behavior, overlooked more than Sholokhov's drinking. At the time of that conversation, he knew—and he knew that Yezhov also knew—that the NKVD chief's beautiful wife, thirty-four-year-old Yevgenia ("Zhenya") Khayutina-Yezhova, had been Sholokhov's mistress for several months.

The boldest novelist might have hesitated over a plot like this, but its reality was confirmed by secret documents declassified in 2001. Dubbed the Iron Commissar by friends and the Bloody Dwarf by enemies, Yezhov was put in charge at age forty-one of the Great Terror, a policy that became known as *yezhovshchina.* He was remembered as a sadist and monster, but Nadezhda Mandelstam and Lili Brik, who knew him personally in more "vegetarian" times, thought him a "rather pleasant" man.[14] He was also bisexual, and his marriage to Yevgenia Khayutina, an independent, energetic, and amorous woman (her numerous lovers included the writer Babel) was rather open.[15]

The matchmaker—intentionally or not—in this relationship was the omnipresent Fadeyev, in whose company Sholokhov, who had come to Moscow, went to visit Khayutina in August 1938. The three had lunch at the National Hotel, where Sholokhov was staying. The next day Khayutina came back to see Sholokhov at the National, but alone. The transcripts of the recording made by the secret police in Sholokhov's bugged room notes not only the conversation ("We have a difficult love, Zhenya," "I am afraid") but sounds as well ("go into the bathroom," "kiss," "lie down").[16]

Khayutina had good reason to be afraid. It is strange that the wife of the head of the secret police did not realize that the rooms at the National, one of Moscow's most choice hotels, would be bugged. In any case, the transcript was on Yezhov's desk the next day; he took it home to the dacha that night and slapped his wife in the face with it (a female friend was a witness), but did not go further. The recently omnipotent commissar (Babel used to say, "When Yezhov calls in members of the Central Committee, they dump into their pants") was beginning to feel the ground beneath his feet slipping away.

Stalin had apparently decided that the Great Terror had achieved its aim and that the pressure could be eased. That is why he appeared to agree with Sholokhov's emotional protest against the lawlessness of the secret police. A special resolution of the Council of People's Commissars and the Central Committee appeared on November 17, 1938, "On arrests, procuratorial supervision, and investigative procedures," which read like a direct reply to Sholokhov's complaints: "The mass operations of destroying and rooting out hostile elements implemented by the organs of the NKVD in 1937–1938, with a simplified investigation and trial, could not have avoided leading to a number of major flaws and perversions in the work of the organs of the NKVD and the Procurator's Office."

Now Stalin would make Yezhov the scapegoat. Khayutina took a fatal dose of sleeping medication on November 21, 1938, and two days later, Yezhov handed Stalin his resignation as head of the NKVD. When the Bloody Dwarf was arrested six weeks later, the charges were "treasonous and espionage ties"with Poland, Germany, England, and Japan, but they also included poisoning his wife: the investigators fabricated a theory thatYezhov, Khayutina, and her lover Babel had planned to assassinate Stalin and thatYezhov killed his wife to cover up traces of the conspiracy.

Yezhov was executed on February 4, 1940, eight days after Babel and two days after the execution of Khayutina's other lover, Koltsov. Her third lover, Sholokhov, had another fate in store: a little over a year later, he became the Stalin Prize winner—not only as a writer (for two novels simultaneously) but as a public figure in the traditional Russian cultural role of "defender of the people"as well (Stalin had told him, "Your letters are not literary writing, they're nothing but politics"), and even as a colorful personality.

If Sholokhov was walking a tightrope in his relations with Stalin, so was Sergei Eisenstein, who won the Stalin Prize for his famous 1938 film *Alexander Nevsky.*

Eisenstein was of medium height and rounded (some described him as being boneless), with stubby legs, thinning hair that stuck out around his bald spot, and a constant ironic smile playing on his lips. At first glance he created an impression of coziness, but that was misleading: the sexually ambivalent Eisenstein had been a tormented personality since adolescence with an interest in sadism and torture, as well as an "abnormal" (in the words of his friend, the filmmaker Mikhail Romm) habit "of drawing lewd pictures in front of ladies."[17] But Eisenstein, who had a heart condition, led an exceptionally moderate and orderly life and did not drink or smoke; his only known vice was a childish love of sweets.

Alexander Nevsky is a formally brilliant but cold work. Done at Stalin's personal request, it had to be completed as speedily as possible, so the central scene of the battle between the thirteenth-century Prince Alexander Nevsky and the Teutonic knights on frozen Lake Peipus had to be filmed in the summer, on a back lot of Mosfilm, the asphalt covered with a thick layer of liquid glass and sprinkled with crushed chalk to create a winter landscape.

In that landscape Eisenstein played out his film as if it were a smart chess game with the end required by Stalin, Alexander Nevsky intoning: "And if anyone comes to us with a sword, then he shall die by the sword, that is the foundation of the Russian land." (Eisenstein had planned to end the film with Nevsky's death on his return from the Golden Horde, but Stalin rejected it: "Such a good prince cannot die.")

The film was basically conceived for the sake of its final slogan, but when in 1939 Stalin signed a nonaggression pact with Hitler and the Nazis became "sworn friends," *Nevsky* vanished from movie screens. That made even more significant the fact that Eisenstein and also Nikolai Cherkasov, who played Nevsky in the film, and two members of the crew were awarded prizes for the film in March 1941, when the pact was formally still in place.

Interestingly, at a private screening of *Alexander Nevsky* in Moscow for visitors from America—the writer Erskine Caldwell and the photographer Margaret Bourke-White—in mid-June, a week before the Nazis attacked the Soviet Union, Eisenstein confidently predicted that the film would be in wide distribution again very soon.

The director's political intuition was highly tuned. But apparently not Stalin's, because the neo-Teutonic attack, vividly foretold in Eisenstein's film, came as a total surprise in reality. The consequences of Stalin's miscalculation were catastrophic: the German army that attacked on June 22, 1941, rolled through the Soviet Union and reached Moscow by October.

Along with the rest of the country, the workers of the "cultural front" were mobilized against the enemy, thereby proving their usefulness to the Fatherland. The patriotic anthem Sergei Prokofiev wrote for *Alexander Nevsky* was played everywhere: "Arise, Russian people, for the glorious battle, the mortal battle!" The composer himself liked the anthem, and justly so. But in 1941, Stalin did not recognize Prokofiev's work with a prize. At the time (and today, too) it looked like a punishment for something, especially since Prokofiev's main rival, Shostakovich (who was fifteen years younger), not only got the Stalin Prize for his Piano Quintet, composed in 1940, but his photograph was placed first, clearly not alphabetically, in the display of the six "main" laureates on the front page of *Pravda*.

The story of Shostakovich's prize is puzzling. We remember that in 1936 the young composer and his opera *Lady Macbeth of Mtsensk District* became central scapegoats in Stalin's antiformalist campaign, which intended to define the parameters of Soviet art. Essentially, Stalin purged Shostakovich's work from the confines of socialist realism. But in late 1937, the composer was rehabilitated for his Fifth Symphony.

The Fifth can be described as a symphony-novel (just as *Alexander Nevsky* can be described as a film-opera). A comparison to *The Quiet Don* seems appropriate. Both works are profoundly ambivalent and were at different times perceived as being Soviet and anti-Soviet. The very nature of symphonic music permits a wide variety of interpretations. Shostakovich's opus is a magical vessel: each listener fills it in his imagination as he wishes. That is why the Fifth Symphony will remain for many people the most shattering reflection on the Great Terror, while *The Quiet Don* will compete with Pasternak's *Doctor Zhivago* for the most vivid depiction of Russia during World War I and the Civil War.

Strangely, while giving the award to Sholokhov for *The Quiet Don,* Stalin singled out in Shostakovich's oeuvre not the Fifth Symphony, of which he had obviously approved, but the Piano Quintet, which did not fit at all even in the fairly broad spectrum of socialist realist works (from *The Quiet Don* to *Alexander Nevsky,* with Mukhina's and Gerasimov's creations in the middle) that he presented as "models."

Symphonies, while not as high in the official genre hierarchy as Stalin's beloved opera and not in the approved category of program music, were still epic works, which as a lover of the Russian classical tradition, Stalin preferred. Instead, the Piano Quintet was a refined chamber work in a neoclassical style, with a definite nod to Western tradition, which as we now know, was pointed out to Stalin by Shostakovich's detractors among the Soviet musical bureaucrats.[18]

In literature, an analogous work to Shostakovich's Piano Quintet would be a late poem by Khodasevich or a short story by Nabokov, in art—a drawing by Tatlin. Nothing of the sort could possibly be glorified on the front page of *Pravda*—not then, not later.

What had attracted Stalin in the Quintet? Its political and "civic"value must have seemed like zero to him then. Could he have been charmed by its neo-Bachian restraint, spiritual profundity, and impeccable craftsmanship? We can only guess.

But we can presume that Stalin did not regret his generous advance to Shostakovich when he was informed at the end of 1941 that the composer had completed his Seventh Symphony, dedicated to Leningrad, which was under Nazi siege. The composition's fate is unprecedented.

Hurriedly performed in March 1942 (first in Kuibyshev and then Moscow, with the composer attending both premieres, after he was brought out of besieged Leningrad on a special plane on Stalin's orders), the Seventh took on instant political relevance, unheard-of in the history of symphonic music.

Like the Fifth, this symphony-novel is semantically ambiguous. The forceful finale of the Fifth can be perceived as a straightforward tableau of mass rejoicing or as an attempt at an ironic depiction of the forced gaiety and imposed "carnival"-like (to use the word in Bakhtin's sense) enthusiasm typical of the Stalin era. The first movement of the Seventh provides the same opportunity for polar interpretations: is the vicious march theme with eleven variations, performed with an inexorable, avalanche-like crescendo (the "invasion episode"), a depiction of the Nazi attack on the Soviet Union, as the world press instantly announced, or is it a reflection of the insidious expansion of Stalin's repression apparatus, as the composer himself hinted in conversation with close friends?[19]

The polysemantic nature of the Seventh Symphony is intensified by the religious motif that is in the subtext: originally Shostakovich (influenced by Stravinsky's Symphony of Psalms, which he admired so fervently that when he was flown out of Leningrad, the piano score he made of this great work was one of the few belongings he took with him) intended to use a chorus that would intone excerpts from David's Psalms.

Russian audiences were extremely sensitive to these religious overtones and they wept at every performance in the Soviet Union: in the difficult war years Shostakovich's music had a cathartic effect, and the concert hall substituted for the church, proscribed in socialist life. An important symbolic event that promoted the transformation of the symphony into a quasi-religious work was its performance in Leningrad. It was organized on Stalin's orders with great efficiency, like a real military operation, and played on August 9, 1942, by the starved musicians of Leningrad, which by then was already considered a martyr-city.

For the democratic West, which for the sake of victory over Hitler had given up its anti-Bolshevik prejudices while entering into an "unholy" alliance with Stalin, the high point in the Seventh's political status came with the national broadcast of its New York radio premiere on July 19, 1942, conducted by Arturo Toscanini; hundreds of North American performances followed, and after his picture appeared on the cover of *Time* magazine, Shostakovich, thirty-six, became the most popular contemporary "serious" composer in the Unites States and in the Soviet Union.

The Seventh Symphony was the second work by Shostakovich to receive the Stalin Prize, and once again, of the first degree. That was on April 11, 1942, a little over a month after its premiere, an unprecedented haste in the annals of the Stalin Prize. Of course, the geopolitical situation was extraordinary then, too. Behind lay the battle for Moscow, ahead, the fateful battle of Stalingrad. Washington announced that Allied troops were prepared to open a second front in Europe against Hitler.

Stalin had little faith that these promises would come to pass soon. But he cared about every cultural bridge that brought closer the two sides so far apart socially and politically. Shostakovich's Seventh Symphony was such an opportunity. That is why Shostakovich was probably Stalin's most valued composer at that moment. But we cannot blame Shostakovich for that. It was the way the political cards fell then.

Chapter Eight

O n August 31, 1941 (while Shostakovich was completing the first movement of his Seventh Symphony in besieged Leningrad), Marina Tsvetaeva, forty-eight, who had been evacuated to the small town of Elabuga in Tatarstan, hanged herself. This was the third suicide of a great Russian poet in the twentieth century, after Esenin in 1925 and Mayakovsky in 1930. Mourning these deaths later, Pasternak wrote: "Once they reach the idea of suicide, they give up on themselves, they condemn their past, declaring themselves bankrupt and their memories nonexistent."[1] Pasternak speculated that Tsvetaeva, "not knowing where to hide from the horror, hastily hid in death, shoving her head into a noose as if under a pillow."[2]

In fact, Tsvetaeva's fatal decision had not been spontaneous. A year earlier her fifteen-year-old son, Georgy ("Mur"), wrote in his unusually frank diary: "Mother is living in an atmosphere of suicide and keeps talking about it. She keeps crying all the time and talking about the humiliations she must endure. . . . We sent a telegram to the Kremlin, to Stalin: 'Help me, I am in dire straits. The writer Marina Tsvetaeva.' "[3]

The figure of the outsider is common in twentieth-century Russian culture. Among them, Tsvetaeva was perhaps the most extreme case. She positioned herself early on as "the last romantic" in her work and life, and resembling an exotic bird, with piercing eyes peeking out beneath her bangs, the bisexual Tsvetaeva always made clear her rejection of the established order, whatever it may be. Joseph Brodsky, who insisted that she was the greatest twentieth-century poet in any language, described her viewpoint as Calvinist, with the poet feeling guilt for all human suffering.

Tsvetaeva was among the first to be repulsed by the mass chauvinist passions of World War I; while living in Bolshevik Moscow she openly sang the praises of the counterrevolutionary White Guards (her husband Sergei Efron had fought on their side), and when she immigrated in 1922 to the West, she took an intransigently antibourgeois position, which isolated her from the émigrés.

Tsvetaeva's loneliness in the West increased as her husband's political views radicalized: Efron evolved from a fierce opponent of the Bolsheviks to an equally staunch supporter. He joined a small but ideologically influential émigré movement, the Eurasianists, which included some of the greatest minds of the Russian diaspora, the linguist and philosopher Prince Nikolai Trubetskoy, the theologian Georgy Florovsky, the literary critic D. S. Mirsky, the music critic Pierre Souvtchinsky, and the philosopher Lev Karsavin.

The central idea of the Eurasianists was Russia's special geopolitical place and destiny as the bridge between Europe and Asia (Eurasia). They were the successors of the Scythian group in Russia, with right and left wings: the right (Trubetskoy, Florovsky) tending toward Christian Orthodoxy while the left (Mirsky, Efron) drifted to the side of the Soviet Union, which the Eurasianists considered the true heir to the Russian empire and the force to be reckoned with. The Kremlin took a keen interest in this movement, gradually bringing the left Eurasianists under the control of the Soviet secret services.

Son of the tsarist minister of internal affairs, Mirsky, whom Edmund Wilson affectionately called "comrade prince," joined the British Communist Party in 1931. By then he had published the best—then and now—history of Russian literature in English, but in 1932, craving Gorky's patronage, he returned to Moscow from England. It was a fatal mistake: in 1937, twelve months after Gorky died, "comrade prince" was arrested and expired in a Siberian prison camp.

Efron, together with Mirsky and Souvtchinsky, published the literary almanac *Versty* (Mileposts), which printed Tsvetaeva, Pasternak, and colorful Alexei Remizov. In 1931, Efron became an agent of the NKVD in France. On orders from Moscow, he helped Spanish antifascists, kept surveillance on Trotsky's son, and procured new agents. He had a flair for it, recruiting twenty-four people for Soviet intelligence.

Tsvetaeva, who considered Efron "the most noble and selfless man in the world," explained that "he had seen Russia's salvation and the truth" in the White movement, and "when he discovered otherwise, he left it completely and wholly and never looked back."[4]

In 1937, after a notorious "wet" operation (killing former Soviet agent Ignace Reiss, who defected to the West), Efron and a few comrades fled

France to the Soviet Union, where Ariadna ("Alya"), Efron and Tsvetaeva's twenty-five-year-old daughter, had been living for the last six
months. Tsvetaeva was called in for questioning by the Paris prefec-
ture but released when she started reciting poetry in French, her own
and other writers': they thought her mad. The less-kind Russian émigrés, who had already been suspicious of Tsvetaeva, now rejected her
completely.

Through Soviet diplomatic channels, Efron pleaded with Tsvetaeva to
join him in Russia, and in June 1939 she and Mur came to Moscow. Soon
after, her husband and daughter were arrested as part of a purge of the
NKVD and particularly its foreign agents initiated by Lavrenti Beria, who
replaced Yezhov.

Alya later recalled her predeparture conversation in Paris with Nobel
laureate Bunin: "Where are you going, you little fool? What for? What's
pushing you? They'll arrest you."

"Me? For what?"

"You'll see. They'll find a reason."[5]

Tsvetaeva's strong, passionate, highly emotional, even occasionally
overwrought (some said hysterical) poetic voice and her image as a willful, independent, and proud Amazon made her a favorite in gender
studies. But the attempts by her admirers to prove that she had no idea
of her husband's secret work are absurd and belittle her intelligence.
Tsvetaeva herself claimed to have had nothing to do with underground
pro-Soviet work "and not only out of total inability but out of a profound
revulsion toward politics, *all* of which—with the rarest of exceptions—I
consider *filth*."[6]

She was not being sincere. Her hatred of Nazism (so clearly expressed
in her great cycle of angry poems on Hitler's annexation of Czechoslovakia in 1939) and her sympathy for the Spanish republicans are well documented. Even émigré poet and essayist Georgy Adamovich, who was
rather skeptical of Tsvetaeva, noted her "innate awareness that everything in the world—politics, love, religion, poetry, history, absolutely
everything—converges."[7]

Much of Tsvetaeva's work (especially the poetry and prose relating to
public figures and events—Nicholas I, Nicholas II, the White movement,
Mayakovsky) is clearly political. She raised her children, Alya and Mur, as

Soviet patriots (Alya even becoming a Soviet agent in France). Her lover and later close friend in Paris, Konstantin Rodzevich, to whom she dedicated two of her masterpieces, *Poem of the Mountain* and *Poem of the End,* was also a Soviet spy, recruited by Efron.

Tsvetaeva herself apparently did not participate in her husband's underground activities. Still, she used the apolitical mask mainly as a survival tactic. It helped her to endure interrogations by the French police, but it did not work in Moscow, where she wrote on September 5, 1940: "Everyone considers me brave. I don't know a more fearful person than I. I'm afraid of everything. Eyes, blackness, steps, and most of all—myself." And on the same day: "I do not want to die. I want not to be."[8]

In other circumstances the ambitious Efron could have become a big shot in Soviet intelligence. But he was executed on October 16, 1941, in the Moscow Butyrka Prison on the ridiculous charges of espionage for France.

On that day the Butyrka Prison was being "cleansed" of prisoners: the Germans were at the gate of Moscow. Knowing nothing of the execution of his father, Mur wrote in his diary, which was first published in 2004: "An enormous number of people are running away, loaded up with sacks and trunks. . . . The Academy of Sciences, the institutes, the Bolshoi Theater—they've all vanished like smoke. . . . Some say that the Germans are expected in Moscow tonight."[9]

Mur did not know he was all alone. (His sister, Alya, had been sent to a northern prison camp the year before.) The sixteen-year-old's political views were changing quickly now that he was experiencing Soviet reality: "When I lived in Paris, I was definitely a Communist. I attended hundreds of rallies, frequently took part in demonstrations . . . André Gide, Hemingway, Dos Passos were very close to the Communists. Then they grew disillusioned, for various reasons. . . . So am I, and how!"[10]

In 1944, when Tsvetaeva's son was nineteen, he was sent to the front, where he was killed; the whereabouts of his grave—and of his father's and mother's—are unknown. They say that when Mirsky was dying in the Soviet prison camp he laughed bitterly at his Communist illusions. Probably Tsvetaeva had profound regrets about returning to the Soviet Union. But there is also an example of a great master hounded by the Soviet regime who remained true until his dying breath to communist ideals, the dictatorship of the proletariat, and atheism.

Count Leo Tolstoy in his
favorite photograph, 1908

Anton Chekhov (left) with
Maxim Gorky, Crimea, 1900

The great bass Fedor
Chaliapin in the role
of Tsar Boris Godunov,
Bolshoi Theater, 1918

Sergei Rachmaninoff,
in a portrait by
Konstantin Somov, 1925

Impresario Sergei Diaghilev, in
a portrait by Valentin Serov, 1908

Igor Stravinsky, 1928

Vaslav Nijinsky, 1906

An avant-garde exhibition in Petrograd in 1913, with *Black Square*, the icon of twentieth-century abstract art, by Kazimir Malevich, hanging high up in the corner of the gallery

Anna Akhmatova with her husband,
poet Nikolai Gumilev, and their son,
Lev, 1916

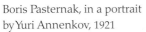

Boris Pasternak, in a portrait
by Yuri Annenkov, 1921

The first Soviet Commissar of Education
(who dealt with all cultural issues),
Anatoly Lunacharsky, in a portrait by
Yuri Annenkov, 1920

Four pillars of the Soviet avant-garde: the composer Dmitri Shostakovich (far left) with the theater director Vsevolod Meyerhold (seated), the poet Vladimir Mayakovsky (behind them), and the artist Alexander Rodchenko (standing, far right), 1929

Konstantin Stanislavsky, 1928

Sergei Prokofiev (at the piano, left) with Sergei Eisenstein, working on the film *Alexander Nevsky*

George Balanchine

Photo by Marianna Volkov

Vladimir Horowitz

Photo by Marianna Volkov

Vladimir Ashkenazy

Photo by Marianna Volkov

The theater director Yuri
Lyubimov (left) with the
sculptor Ernst Neizvestny

Photo by Marianna Volkov

Yevgeny Yevtushenko

Photo by Marianna Volkov

Vassily Aksyonov

Photo by Marianna Volkov

The poet and singer Bulat Okudzhava

Photo by Marianna Volkov

The actor, singer, and poet Vladimir Vysotsky

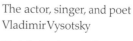

Photo by Marianna Volkov

Solomon Volkov (left) interviewing Joseph Brodsky in the poet's New York residence

Photo by Marianna Volkov

The composer Alfred Schnittke at his Moscow apartment

Photo by Marianna Volkov

The movie director Andrei Tarkovsky at work

Courtesy of the Ivanovo Museum, Russia

Maya Plisetskaya

Photo by Marianna Volkov

Rudolf Nureyev

Photo by Marianna Volkov

Mikhail Baryshnikov

Photo by Marianna Volkov

The dissident writer
Andrei Sinyavsky

Photo by Marianna Volkov

The émigré writer
Sergei Dovlatov

Photo by Marianna Volkov

The artists Emilia and
Ilya Kabakov, Oleg
Vassiliev, and Grisha
Bruskin (left to right)

Photo by Marianna Volkov

The poet and artist
Dmitri Prigov

Photo by Marianna Volkov

The violinist and
conductor
Vladimir Spivakov

Photo by Marianna Volkov

The conductor
Valery Gergiev

Photo by Marianna Volkov

The movie director Nikita Mikhalkov

Photo by Marianna Volkov

The rock musician Yuri Shevchuk

Photo by Marianna Volkov

Aleksandr Solzhenitsyn

Courtesy of Ignat Solzhenitsyn

That is the case of the artist Pavel Filonov, one of the leaders of the Russian avant-garde before the revolution, who moved from his early works, influenced by German Expressionism, to meticulously crafted kaleidoscopic paintings where the eye slowly discovers outlines of people and objects. He called these works "formulas"—*Formula of the Petrograd Proletariat* (1920), *Formula of a Komsomol Member* (1924), *Formula of Imperialism* (1925).

Filonov is much less known in the West than Kandinsky, Chagall, Malevich, Tatlin, Rodchenko, and other Russian avant-garde artists. Filonov's manifestos are even more mangled than Malevich's coarse and clumsy statements. He never traveled to the West and sold practically nothing, hoping that all his works would one day be displayed in a special museum in Leningrad.

Filonov wanted, as he wrote in his diary, first published almost sixty years after his death, "to give all my works to the state, the party, the proletariat."[11] But the Party replied that "Filonov is a bourgeois artist. A ruthless struggle is being waged against him, and filonovism will be uprooted."[12] Even Filonov's portrait of Stalin, vastly superior to Picasso's famous likeness of the ruler, remained unwanted.

Filonov modeled his life after revolutionary artists of the past, like Van Gogh. Tall, pale, and ascetic, with a biblical prophet's fanaticism, Filonov was surrounded, in the tradition of the Russian avant-garde, by loyal students whom he taught for free. There were not many commissions and the artist was often hungry. His diary entry of August 30, 1935, is typical: "Seeing that my money was coming to an end, I used the last to buy tea, sugar, shag tobacco, and matches and began, not having money for bread, to bake pancakes from the white flour I still had. On the 29th, having economized on the flour, I baked my last pancake, preparing to follow the example of many, many other times—to live, not knowing for how long, without eating."[13]

When the Germans began the 900-day siege of Leningrad in September 1941, no one even thought of evacuating Filonov, unlike Shostakovich, Akhmatova, and Zoshchenko (whom Stalin considered valuable cultural cadres then). Tending to his paralyzed wife, who was twenty years his senior, Filonov, fifty-eight, was among the first to die in early December, as soon as the famine began in Leningrad. As survivors of the siege explained, "The men died first, because they are muscular and have little fat. Women, even small ones, have more subcutaneous fat."[14] Filonov's wife died in 1942. Between December 1941 and February 1942, more than a quarter million Leningraders died of starvation.

One of Filonov's students recalled: "When Filonov died, I was dystrophic myself, but could still move, so I dragged myself to his house. He lay on a table in the cold room, majestic among his paintings, which still hung on the walls."[15] There are now precious few works by Filonov available on the art market (the great majority are in St. Petersburg at the Russian Museum), but when one appears, it is valued in the millions of dollars.

Tsvetaeva's suicide in evacuation and Filonov's hungry death in besieged Leningrad, depriving Russian culture of two of its geniuses, went practically unnoticed in the war years that plunged the country into a sea of despair and suffering and took tens of millions of lives. These were tense times. Still, Ilya Ehrenburg, whose numerous propaganda articles in the army newspaper *Krasnaya Zvezda* [Red Star] made him perhaps the most popular writer in the Soviet Union at the time, noted an important paradox in his memoirs: "Usually war brings with it the censor's scissors; but here in the first year and a half of the war, writers felt much freer than before."[16]

The loosening of the ideological noose that Stalin had sanctioned was intended to unite the country in the face of mortal danger. Stalin also made an alliance with the Orthodox Church: as a former seminarian, he understood the enormous spiritual potential of a religious appeal.

Among those for whom, in the words of Pasternak, "the war was a cleansing storm, a breath of fresh air, a portent of deliverance," was Andrei Platonov, considered by many today as the greatest twentieth-century Russian prose writer after Leo Tolstoy and Chekhov. (Joseph Brodsky felt that Platonov was on the level of Joyce and Kafka; sometimes he would add, "and maybe, higher.")[17]

Filonov and Platonov could be considered twins in art, although there was little physical similarity. Filonov was tall and had eyes that his friend the poet Khlebnikov described as "cherry-like," and his voice was beautiful, deep and rich. Platonov had childlike blue eyes, was short, and spoke in a muffled voice. Both had high foreheads and piercing eyes, but fanaticism dominated in Filonov's charismatic appearance, while broad-faced Platonov, who could be sarcastic in his youth (especially when drunk), became withdrawn over time, more and more resembling his favorite character, the Russian "hidden man."

In his works, Platonov often depicted frenzied and inarticulate "non-Party Bolsheviks" like Filonov, while the writer himself, with his sullen proletarian looks (as a friend once put it, Platonov could easily be taken for a drunkard waiting outside a liquor store for someone to split the price of a bottle), would have fit into any of Filonov's expressionist urbanist drawings.

Platonov was born to the family of a locomotive engineer in 1919, and at the age of twenty he volunteered for the railroad Unit of Special Assignments (ChON), the notorious Bolshevik punitive corps. He began publishing his work early, and in 1927 his novella "The Sluices of Epiphany" (a parable about Russian folk wisdom and the willfulness of the authorities) caught Gorky's attention. Encouraged, Platonov sent Gorky the manuscript of his masterpiece, *Chevengur*, a novel about a bizarre attempt to build "separate communism" in a provincial Russian town.

Gorky's sympathetic response makes Platonov's dilemma clear: "For all the indisputable high qualities of your work, I do not believe that it will be published. That will be prevented by your anarchic mindset, apparently a trait of your 'spirit.' Whether you wanted it or not—you have given your depiction of reality a lyrical satirical character, which, naturally, is unacceptable for our censorship. For all your tenderness toward people, they are colored ironically, and appear before the reader not so much revolutionary as 'eccentric' and 'half-witted.' "[18]

Gorky's prediction came true: *Chevengur* was not printed in Platonov's lifetime, and in the USSR it was published only at the height of perestroika, sixty years after it was written. But when Platonov's works did break through the censorship of Stalinist Russia, the consequences for the writer were often catastrophic.

In 1931, Stalin, who followed the Soviet literary magazines closely, read Platonov's novella "Benefit" in *Krasnaya Nov'*. His remarks in the margins (the issue is in the archives) make the dictator's reaction clear: "This is not Russian, but some gobbledygook language," "Fool,"

"Scoundrel," "Bastard," and so on. Stalin's resolution is on the first page: "A story by an agent of our enemies, written with the goal of sabotaging the kolkhoz movement."[19]

One of the literary bosses of those years, Vladimir Sutyrin, later recalled how he and Fadeyev, then editor-in-chief of *Krasnaya Nov'*, were brought late one evening in June 1931 to the Kremlin, to a Politburo meeting. Stalin, puffing on his pipe and holding a copy of *Krasnaya Nov'*, paced around the table, where Molotov, Voroshilov, Mikhail Kalinin, and other leaders of the country were seated. Stalin attacked Fadeyev when he was still in the door: "It was you who printed Platonov's kulak anti-Soviet story?" Pale, Fadeyev replied that the issue had been prepared by the previous editor. That editor was brought to the Kremlin within a half hour, during which total silence reigned.

The former editor, face to face with Stalin, could barely stand up and babbled something incoherent in self-justification. Sweat poured down his face. Turning to his secretary, Poskrebyshev, Stalin said disdainfully: "Take him away. . . . Someone like that manages Soviet literature. . . . And you, comrade Sutyrin and comrade Fadeyev, take this magazine, it has my comments, and write an article that will expose the anti-Soviet meaning of Platonov's story. You may go."[20]

A car brought Fadeyev and Sutyrin to the latter's apartment, where they immediately wrote a strong anti-Platonov article, hastily published in the official newspaper *Izvestiya* and signed by Fadeyev. At the same time an entire series of brutal attacks against Platonov appeared in the press with such characteristic titles as "Lampoon on a Kolkhoz Village" and "More Attention to the Tactics of a Class Enemy." They were also, without a doubt, instigated by Stalin. The authorities stopped publishing Platonov completely.

Yet Stalin did not execute Platonov. When he attended the famous meeting with writers at Gorky's apartment on October 26, 1932 (it was then that Stalin called Soviet writers "engineers of the human soul"), his first question was "Is Platonov here?" No one had ever intended to invite "class enemy" Platonov to the literary summit, but after the ruler expressed interest in him, the writer's life grew a little easier: they knew that Stalin did not pose random questions.

In 1933 a report from the secret police was placed on Stalin's desk, with an account by an informer of how Platonov reacted to Stalin's criticism of "Benefit." "I don't care what others will say. I wrote that novella for one man (for Comrade Stalin), that man read it and responded substantively. The rest does not interest me." The same memorandum said that Platonov's works were "characterized by a satiric and essentially counterrevolutionary approach to the basic problems of socialist construction," but also noted that Platonov was "popular among writers and highly esteemed as a master," and that he himself felt that his work "helps the Party see all the mold on some things better than the Worker-Peasant Inspection."[21]

In literary circles, where many people knew Stalin's wrathful reaction in 1931, Platonov was treated like a doomed man. But disaster befell Platonov from an unexpected side: on May 4, 1938, his son, Anton, barely sixteen, was arrested on the denunciation of a classmate (they were both in love with the same girl), and sentenced as a member of an "anti-Soviet youth terrorist organization" to exile in Siberia.

Sholokhov, an admirer of Platonov, offered to help the boy. According to Platonov, Sholokhov reached Stalin, who immediately asked for information by phone about Anton. The youth was returned to Moscow, his case was reviewed, his explanation that he confessed to terrorism "under threats of the prosecutor who said that if I did not sign my parents would be arrested" was accepted.[22] Platonov's son was one of the very few people for whom Stalinist justice went into reverse: on the eve of the war he was released. But Anton had contracted tuberculosis in prison and died on January 4, 1943, in the arms of his grief-stricken parents.

Despite all his misfortunes, Platonov was patriotic during the years of the war with Hitler. Lev Gumilevsky, a writer friend, recalled meeting Platonov in the fall of 1941 in one of the ubiquitous Moscow lines (this was for cigarettes), and Platonov expressed his firm conviction that Russia would win. "But how?" asked bewildered Gumilevsky. "How? . . . With their guts!" Platonov replied.[23]

Although official historiography would like to convince us otherwise, such optimism was not shared by all in those tragic days. The literary scholar Leonid Timofeyev recorded in his secret diary (published only in 2002), the same day, October 16, 1941, that Tsvetaeva's husband, Sergei Efron, was executed: "Apparently, it's all over. . . . A defeat that will be hard to recover from. I can't believe that they will manage to organize resistance somewhere. Thus, the world, apparently, will be united under the aegis of Hitler. . . . In the lines and in town there is a sharply hostile attitude regarding the *ancien régime:* they betrayed us, abandoned us, left us. The populace has started burning portraits of the leaders and the works of the church fathers."[24] (Timofeyev meant the classics of Marxism.)

Platonov, moving through chaotic Moscow that day, noticed with his acute writer's eye a collection of the works of Karl Marx left on the street by a frightened resident, neatly stacked on a clean cloth, and commented wryly to his companion, Gumilevsky: "Done by a decent man."[25]

The writer Vassily Grossman, later to write the great epic novel about the war and Stalin's camps, *Life and Fate,* but during the war years in Stalin's good favor, recommended Platonov as a war correspondent to the army newspaper *Krasnaya Zvezda.* That was quite risky: Stalin read the paper every day, very attentively, often calling the editor with comments and criticism about the contents—he considered *Krasnaya Zvezda* an important instrument for the army's political education. But Grossman's plan worked: Platonov's essays and stories began appearing regularly in the newspaper, to be followed by collections of his articles.

As the army newspaper's editor recalled, he was very nervous: "I expected Stalin's call every minute: who gave you permission to hire that 'agent of the class enemy' at *Krasnaya Zvezda?*" But the call never came, even though Stalin occasionally was vexed by Platonov's "holy fool" style, and then *Pravda* would print irritated reviews that characterized his works as being "a heap of oddities."[26]

When the war ended in victory in May 1945, the tactical need to be tolerant of such talented but suspicious writers as Platonov disappeared. The final blow against Platonov came on January 4, 1947, when *Literaturnaya Gazeta* ran a big piece by one of the most vicious critics of those years, Vladimir Ermilov, titled "A. Platonov's Slanderous Story," with a categorical conclusion: "We are tired of the whole manner of 'holy fool for Christ' that characterizes A. Platonov's writing. . . . The ugly and impure little world of A. Platonov is repulsive and alien to the Soviet people."[27]

Platonov was ill in bed, the tuberculosis he had contracted from his son flaring up. He said bitterly to a friend who had come to visit him: "He knows I'm in bed, he's kicking me when I'm down!" And as the newspaper with the merciless review fell from Platonov's hands, "he shut his eyes, tears glistened."[28]

From that day, editors and publishers steadily rejected all of Platonov's essays, stories, film scripts, and plays. We know that Sholokhov tried to help him even in those years; he got him scarce imported medicines. When Platonov died on January 5, 1951, he was fifty-one. In the history of modern Russian culture, full of warped lives and premature deaths, this was one of the greatest losses.

Chapter Nine

The war with Hitler, which brought the Soviet Union to the brink of collapse, demanded huge sacrifices from the entire country. Stalin, who was among the first political leaders of the century to appreciate the propaganda potential of culture, constructing a highly effective cultural apparatus even before the war, now turned it to the service of the war effort.

Propaganda material was devised for varying audiences. For the masses there were pop songs, patriotic films, and plain army broadsheets. For the intelligentsia and Western allies, there were novels, symphonies, and operas like Vassily Grossman's novel *For the Just Cause,* Shostakovich's Seventh and Eighth symphonies, and Prokofiev's Fifth Symphony and his opera *War and Peace,* based on the Tolstoy novel, but also the sophisticated historical film *Ivan the Terrible,* on which Eisenstein worked starting in 1941, when he was evacuated from Moscow to Alma-Ata in Kazakhstan at the start of the war.

The film was commissioned by Stalin, and he spared no expense. Even though it was made during the war, *Ivan the Terrible,* with its meticulously constructed historical sets, opulent boyar costumes, and multitudes of extras, looked much more expensive than Eisenstein's prewar film *Alexander Nevsky.* The director shot so much material that he planned to make it in three parts (the music was written by Prokofiev, who had also done the score for *Nevsky*).

But while the first part (in which the sixteenth-century tyrant Ivan, who deals ruthlessly with his enemies, was played by Nikolai Cherkasov as a tall, long-haired, and handsome man whose nostrils flared dramatically) was approved by Stalin, the second, in which Eisenstein, almost in a Dostoevskian manner, showed Tsar Ivan contorted in spiritual torment, infuriated the Soviet leader. The historical allusions were too obvious: Eisenstein was clearly suggesting that Stalin should repent.

Eisenstein and Cherkasov were called to the Kremlin to be chastised,

Stalin banned part 2 of *Ivan the Terrible* ("abominable!"), and the film did not appear on the Soviet screen until 1958, ten years after the director's death and five after Stalin's. Eisenstein's planned third part was never made.

The mass movie audience in the Soviet Union never shared Stalin's interest in Eisenstein, and even he often found the director's "formalist" mannerisms irritating. During the war years less sophisticated movies played a much more important propaganda role, particularly *Chapaev* (1934), a film about the Civil War made by Georgy and Sergei Vasilyev, who were not related—they used "the brothers Vasilyev" as a *nom de camera*.

According to the notes made by Boris Shumyatsky, head of the film industry then (he was shot in 1938 as a saboteur and "enemy of the people"), between November 1934 and March 1936, Stalin watched *Chapaev* in his private screening room at the Kremlin (usually with several members of the Politburo) thirty-eight times.[1] He considered it the best Soviet film, and many Russians agree even today: an entertaining plot, sure direction, and solid acting make this "brothers Vasilyev" work a landmark. Even though the Red commander Chapaev dies at the end, his screen exploits never failed to inspire Soviet soldiers in the war.

The literary work that played a similar role was Alexander Tvardovsky's narrative poem *Vassily Terkin*. The young poet came from a peasant family that had suffered under Stalin's forced collectivization. The poem's protagonist, an ordinary soldier, became a new quasi-folkloric Soviet hero with traditional roots, who goes through the war with jokes and a wink, without looking like a propaganda cartoon.

Tvardovsky's *Terkin* won the admiration not only of millions of grateful readers at the front and back home, but of Bunin, who lived in exile in France, and who like many other White émigrés became patriotic during the war with Hitler. The picky Bunin, who criticized Gorky and even Dostoevsky, proclaimed *Terkin,* apparently quite sincerely, a great work. "This is a truly rare book: what freedom, what marvelous boldness, what precision and accuracy in everything, and what an extraordinary folksy soldier's language—free flowing, without a single false, ready-made, that is, literary-clichéd, word!"[2] *Vassily Terkin* (like *Chapaev* earlier) received a Stalin Prize First Degree, even though Stalin was not even mentioned in either work. They performed their propaganda function all the better for it.

Of the celebrated émigrés who radically revised their attitude toward the Soviet Union because of the war, like composer Rachmaninoff and conductor Serge Koussevitzky, the most unusual is the story of chansonnier Alexander Vertinsky (1889–1957). He was the first in the group of great poet singers who would hold an important place in twentieth-century Russian culture, like Bulat Okudzhava and Vladimir Vysotsky. He created the "Vertinsky style," which retains its popularity almost a century after his first songs appeared—simultaneously overwrought and ironic micronovellas (they were called "Les Vertinettes") about exotic people and places: "The Purple Negro," "God's Ball," "Little Creole Boy."

Tall, slender, and elegant, Vertinsky had a slight but distinctive voice, augmented by the singer's expressive gestures. He began his career in prerevolutionary Moscow, appearing in crowded nightclubs and cabarets, costumed and made up like a contemporary Pierrot. Vertinsky captured the spirit of that decadent era with songs of religion-tinged erotica (from the arsenal of the early Akhmatova) and cocaine, but his work miraculously retains its charms even today. Vertinsky's secret, as one of his fans put it, is that "the sad seems funny in his art, and vice versa, therefore the banal becomes original."[3] His oeuvre could be regarded as high kitsch, or in Susan Sontag's term, camp, and in that quality, along with the best examples of Gypsy ballads, continue to be appealing.

Curiously, one of Vertinsky's fans was Stalin, who would privately play his records, issued in huge numbers in the West where the singer had fled after the revolution, and banned in the Soviet Union, because the music was considered harmful for the masses as émigré and "decadent." (In 1924 the secret police compiled a long list of banned recordings, and these lists were updated regularly.) Stalin's sympathy for Vertinsky remained through the years, and the singer, who had become a Soviet patriot, was permitted to return home in 1943. His appearance created a small sensation and generated intense gossip.

An entry dated February 12, 1944, in Leonid Timofeyev's secret diary is typical: "The singer Vertinsky is in Moscow. He came from China. Before his arrival he had to spend seven years singing the Soviet repertoire. Besides that, he donated three million to the Red Army. In Moscow, as usual, he became rationed through passes for special audiences. Today

there is a rumor that he died of a stroke."[4] Vertinsky, fifty-five then, continued performing widely for another thirteen years, giving more than
three thousand concerts. For all the external signs of success (tickets sold
out instantly), it was a strangely spectral existence, without reviews in
the press, without radio broadcasts, and most importantly, without mass
distribution of his recordings, to which he had grown accustomed in the
West.

For his niche audience (Vertinsky often performed in closed officers'
clubs and before the elite) the singer, now in elegant white tie and tails,
was a mirage of sorts from the émigré Western world, mysteriously
materializing in the drab Soviet reality. Yes, he sang of the émigrés' longing for home. But Vertinsky's public, living behind the Iron Curtain, also
learned (in tango, foxtrot, or shimmy rhythms) about the "dives of San
Francisco," the Piccadilly bar, and the singer's affair with Marlene Die-
trich in Hollywood.

Denunciations of Vertinsky constantly arrived at the Kremlin. Vigilant
Bolsheviks wrote to Stalin that his repertoire must be Sovietized quickly.
According to the recollections of the singer's widow, Stalin's reaction was
unexpected: "Why should the artist Vertinsky create a new repertoire? He
has his repertoire. The people who don't like it don't have to listen."[5]

The ruler's fondness for Vertinsky went as far as giving him the Stalin
Prize in 1951, not for little songs about the dives of San Francisco, but for
his part in *Conspiracy of the Doomed,* an anti-American propaganda film
by Mikhail Kalatozov (later director of the famous war film *The Cranes
Are Flying*), in which Vertinsky played a plotting cardinal in a characteristically grotesque style. Yet, even after this, his records were not made
available. The first Vertinsky LPs appeared only in the early 1970s and
became instant best sellers.

Stalin, who personally rated Russian classical music—Glinka, Tchaikovsky, Mussorgsky, and Rimsky-Korsakov—as the highest form, understood the need for popular entertainment: "One likes the accordion with
Gypsy songs. We have that. Another likes restaurant songs. We have
that, too."[6] At the turn of the century, gramophone records made popular numerous Gypsy and pseudo-Gypsy songs about unrequited love,
mad passions, and wild drinking sprees ("Black Eyes," "The Autumn
Wind Moans Piteously," "The Night Breathed with the Delight of Lust")

and created the first stars of the Russian entertainment industry—the Gypsy Varya Panina, who sang in a low, almost masculine voice (her admirers included Leo Tolstoy, Chekhov, and Blok), the "incomparable" Anastasia Vyaltseva, and sprightly Nadezhda Plevitskaya, who performed her quasi folksongs for Nicholas II himself.

After the revolution the star system went underground for twenty years, but began a cautious revival before the war, when the first Soviet celebrities of pop music began to appear, including the composer Isaak Dunaevsky and the singers Leonid Utesov and Klavdia Shulzhenko. They performed at the front throughout the war years with patriotic and entertainment programs, trying to make up for the severely reduced production of records.

The war situation, which had paradoxically created more liberal conditions for all of Soviet culture, gave rise to an unprecedented number of great songs that have retained their appeal to this day: "Dark Night" by Nikita Bogoslovsky, "Dug Out" by Konstantin Listov, "The Cherished Stone" by Boris Mokrousov, "Evening on the Road" and "Nightingales" by Vassily Solovyov-Sedoy, and a series of songs by Matvei Blanter with lyrics by Mikhail Isakovsky—"In the Woods by the Front," "Under the Balkan Stars," and "The Enemy Burned Down His House," the last about a soldier who returns home from the war:

> The enemy burned down his house,
> Killed his entire family.
> Where can the soldier go now,
> Who will listen to his sorrow?

The tragedy of a country that lost tens of millions of lives in the war was expressed in that song with such power and simplicity that it became one of the best epitaphs for the period. But the song was not played then; it waited fifteen years on the shelf. Stalin attributed the victory over Hitler to his own military genius and did not want any reminders of the horrible price the people paid for it.

Stalin's superman attitude toward his citizens was reflected in a strange episode described by former Yugoslav communist Milovan Djilas. In the spring of 1945, after a dinner at the Kremlin in honor of visiting leader of Yugoslavia Marshal Tito, Stalin screened a 1938 film by Efim Dzigan, *If Tomorrow There Is War*, which was awarded one of the early Stalin Prizes.

If Tomorrow There Is War, described in the opening credits as a "battle film on newsreel materials," painted a fairy-tale picture of a swift, easy, and bloodless victory in the then-hypothetical clash with the Nazis. In the film, the war that the Germans try to win with poison gases ends with them crushed in just a few days, and the German proletariat rises to support the Soviet Union.

Djilas wrote in astonishment that, after the screening, Stalin said to his Yugoslav guests, "It's not too different from what really happened, except there was no poison gas and the German proletariat did not rebel."[7]

In that period, Stalin, a gifted actor, deftly projected the image of a powerful, calm, and wise politician to Western leaders at their meetings. But behind the façade, he hid a growing irritation and anxiety. He might have considered two pivotal events in Russian history: the Decembrist antimonarchical uprising in 1825 and the fall of the Romanov dynasty in February 1917. In both cases the Russian army picked up "harmful" liberal ideas during campaigns in Europe and involved itself in the country's political life.

In 1825, Nicholas I dealt decisively with the rebels, "chilled" Russia, and reigned for thirty years. His ideological formula "Orthodoxy, Autocracy, and Nationality" was strong enough to create a comparatively stable foundation for the monarchy a half century after his death, that is, at least until 1905. A weak Nicholas II did not bother to assert the ruling ideology, and he let loose the cultural reins. The army, the intelligentsia, and the populace united and swept away the monarchy.

The similarities in 1946 had to have made Stalin, knowledgeable in historical parallels, quite wary. Soviet intellectuals had been talking for a while about the probability that Russia's Anglo-Saxon Allies in the anti-Hitler coalition would pressure him into making democratic concessions after the war.

Reports were placed on Stalin's desk by the secret police on the malcontent statements of notable Soviet cultural figures, such as the popular critic and children's poet Kornei Chukovsky: "Soon we must expect some more decisions to please our masters (Allies), our fate is in their hands. I am glad that a new, rational era is beginning. They will teach us culture."[8] Here is what the poet Iosif Utkin said in a private conversation, according to the report: "We must save Russia, not conquer the world. . . . Now we have the hope that we will live in a free democratic Russia, for without the Allies we will not manage to save Russia, and that means making concessions, which will lead to internal changes."[9]

The multimillion-man Soviet army crossed Europe in 1944–1945 and came face to face with the Western way of life, so clearly superior, even in wartime, that this "visual-aid propaganda" threatened to overcome years of Soviet ideological indoctrination. An unstable mass of bewildered soldiers and an intelligentsia looking hopefully to the West—Russian history teaches that this combination could be explosive. That is why Stalin chose to repeat what he had done in 1936, making a series of strikes that would guarantee him ideological control.

In 1946–1948, he attacked outstanding cultural figures, followed by mass brainwashing. The victims included Eisenstein, a group of leading Soviet composers (Shostakovich, Prokofiev, Nikolai Myaskovsky, Aram Khachaturian, Vissarion Shebalin, and Gavriil Popov), and in literature, the poet Akhmatova and the popular satirical writer Zoshchenko.

Anna Akhmatova's "life scenario" is impressive: she began as a young and "cheerful sinner" (as she called herself), slender and graceful, a bohemian poet with a memorable profile (a bump on her nose) and signature bangs, whose early collections of love lyrics *Evening* (1912) and *Rosary* (1914) brought her scandalous protofeminist fame; she became the author of the anti-Stalinist *Requiem* in 1940, and she proclaimed her voice to express the suppressed scream of the "one hundred million nation"; and later, in her old age, she was the heavyset, gray-haired, majestic empress who considered her "personal life as the national life, the historical life"[10] (according to Eikhenbaum).

Akhmatova was the master par excellence of self-fashioning. Back before the revolution she wove a legend into her poems about a love affair with the most popular Russian poet of the time, Blok, and about her allegedly masochistic relationship with her first husband, the poet Lev Gumilev, whom she divorced in August 1918. When both Blok and Gumilev died in August 1921 (the former of exhaustion, the latter executed by Bolshevik firing squad), Akhmatova was accepted by the Russian elite as the spiritual widow of both poets (even though they both left real widows).

Akhmatova did not serve the Soviets, nor did she leave for the West, remaining in what was called "internal emigration." After 1922, her books of poetry were no longer published and she lived in proud isolation. But in 1935, when her husband, Punin, and her son, Lev Gumilev, were arrested, Akhmatova wrote to Stalin: "Iosif Vissarionovich, I do not know of what they are accused, but I give you my word of honor that they are not fascists, or spies, or members of counterrevolutionary societies. I have lived in the USSR since the start of the Revolution, I have never wanted to leave the country to which I am tied by mind and heart. Despite the fact that my poetry is not published and reviews by critics cause me many bitter minutes, I have not given in to despair; I continued to work in very difficult moral and material conditions . . . In Leningrad I live in great isolation and am frequently ill for long periods. The arrest of the only two people close to me is a blow that I will not be able to survive. I ask you, Iosif Vissarionovich, to return my husband and son to me, certain that no one will ever regret it."[11]

Stalin wrote his resolution on the letter: "Free both Punin and Gumilev from arrest and report on the implementation." From that moment, Akhmatova felt that she was in dialogue with the ruler. She had good reason. There is a story that in 1939 Stalin saw his young daughter, Svetlana, copying Akhmatova's poetry from somebody's notebook into her own, and asked her: "Why don't you just use the book?" Learning from her that there were no easily available books of Akhmatova, Stalin, as the poet later wrote, "was bitterly stunned."[12]

Akhmatova also maintained that in early 1939, "Stalin asked about me at a banquet for writers."[13] The fact remains that on November 11, 1939, the Presidium of the Union of Writers met urgently for a closed session where they voted on the resolution proposed by Union Secretary Fadeyev, Stalin's tried and true henchman, on aid for Akhmatova— "bearing in mind Akhmatova's great contributions to Russian poetry."[14]

Who was behind the abrupt change in the official organization's formerly hostile and scornful attitude toward Akhmatova can be guessed from Fadeyev's letter to then Deputy Chairman of the Council of People's Commissars Andrei Vyshinsky: Fadeyev asked him to find Akhmatova a room in Leningrad, since she "was and remains the most major poet of the prerevolutionary period."[15] This definition, strikingly similar to Stalin's famous evaluation of Mayakovsky (who "was and remains the best, the most talented poet of our Soviet era"), must have been a quote

from Stalin's verbal order, since Vyshinsky, an infamously ruthless Stalinist butcher, supported Fadeyev's request with extraordinary readiness.

Akhmatova was also given "a one-time grant of 3,000 rubles" and a
monthly pension. (Fadeyev's argument was charming: "After all, she
doesn't have that long to live." As it happens, Akhmatova lived another
twenty-seven years, outliving Fadeyev, who shot himself in 1956, by
eleven years.)

The publishing house Sovetskii Pisatel (according to Akhmatova, on
orders from Stalin "to publish my poetry"[16]) speedily printed her collection *Iz shesti knig* [From Six Books], in fact, her selected works. There is a
story that Sholokhov had asked Stalin to do this.[17] Most interestingly,
the book came up in May 1940, just at the peak of the feverish intrigues
in preparation for the first series of Stalin Prizes; it was instantly nominated for the prize by the most influential writers of the time—
Sholokhov, Fadeyev, and Alexei Tolstoy. They were supported by
Nemirovich-Danchenko, chairman of the Committee on Stalin Prizes.

However, Akhmatova did not get the Stalin Prize (neither did Pasternak, who had been nominated for his translation of *Hamlet*): someone
reversed. Was it Stalin himself? We have only Zhdanov's resolution:
"How could this 'depravity with prayer in the praise of god' of Akhmatova's ever appear? Who promoted it?"[18]

A special decree of the Secretariat of the Central Committee of the
Party banned the Akhmatova collection as being "ideologically harmful"
and required it to be removed from sale—an empty gesture, since the
entire printing had sold out long before. All this was a tremendous blow
for Akhmatova then, but later it helped cement her anti-Stalinist image
(while, for example, Prokofiev and Shostakovich are often blamed nowadays for their numerous Stalin Prizes).

In 1941, along with other leading cultural figures of Leningrad like
Shostakovich and Zoshchenko, Akhmatova was evacuated on Stalin's
orders. She landed in Tashkent in Central Asia, where on February 23,
1942, she wrote her famous patriotic poem "Courage." It was published
two weeks later in *Pravda*, the central Party newspaper.

> *We are not afraid of dying beneath bullets,*
> *We will not be bitter left without shelter—*

We will preserve you, Russian speech,
The mighty Russian word.

One of the somewhat mysterious episodes in Akhmatova's biography took place that same year. A military base located near Tashkent was the training site for a Polish anti-Hitler army under the command of General Wladislaw Anders. Stalin had these forces under his personal control and often summoned Anders to the Kremlin.

Anders was playing a complicated game with Stalin. His goal was to bring his men, Polish soldiers and officers who were interned in the Soviet Union, to Iran, where he would join up with the British (which he managed to do eventually). In order to lull Stalin's suspicions, Anders had to keep sending him signals of his loyalty. With that in mind, he invited the famous writer and Stalin favorite, the Red Count Alexei Tolstoy, author of the historical novel *Peter the First*, to visit his headquarters. The visit was organized by Count Jozef Czapski, a cavalry officer who handled cultural issues for Anders and also, as Brodsky told me (having learned it from Akhmatova), counterintelligence.[19]

In response, Tolstoy invited the count to lunch. There, forty-six-year-old Czapski, an artist and writer in peacetime, met Akhmatova, who was fifty-three. In his memoirs, Czapski described her as a woman with vestiges of former beauty and big gray eyes. Her confidante, Lydia Chukovskaya, asserts that the poet began meeting the Polish officer secretly, trying to escape his Soviet surveillance. Akhmatova later wrote a poem about their meetings, which begins clearly enough: "That night we drove each other mad."

Did Akhmatova really think that she and Czapski managed to hide from the vigilant eyes of Stalin's spies? Brodsky expressed his doubts: "How could you even consider that, especially in those times? In Tashkent, I believe, a whole multitude followed their every step."[20]

You couldn't call Akhmatova naïve; she was a tough nut. We know that she wrote down her anti-Stalinist poems (including *Requiem*, about the Great Terror) for her closest friends, let them read the lines, and then burned the paper on the spot. She feared—and properly so—that her rooms were bugged. (Remember careless Sholokhov in the National Hotel.) Why was Akhmatova not punished for her forbidden liaison with a Polish officer? Another girlfriend of Czapski's in Tashkent was arrested by the Soviet authorities, as he wrote in his memoirs.[21]

Akhmatova might have begun to think that she was indeed under "higher protection," as Czapski put it. That certainty played her false in late November 1945, when she was back in Leningrad and spent a night talking with Isaiah Berlin, a thirty-six-year-old British diplomat of Russian descent. This was her second contact with a foreigner in the Soviet Union, and this time Stalin was furious, as Akhmatova learned soon enough.

Akhmatova was condemned in a special Resolution of the Central Committee of the Party on August 21, 1946, which proclaimed that her poetry "brings harm to bringing up our youth and therefore cannot be tolerated in Soviet literature," and the Stalinist spokesman Zhdanov announced that Akhmatova "is either a nun or a whore, or rather a whore and nun who combines depravity with prayer."[22]

Zhdanov's pogrom-like denunciations of Akhmatova (and Zoshchenko, who was subjected to state ostracism at the same time) became touchstones for Soviet cultural policy for the next eight years, and they were not disavowed formally until 1988, in Gorbachev's time. Those of us who studied in the Stalin years were obligated to quote them by heart in school and university, intoning, for instance, that Zoshchenko in his works depicts "people and himself as vile lascivious animals, who have neither shame nor conscience."[23]

Stalin, who considered himself master of half the world (and actually was that in the postwar years, for once China joined the Soviet bloc in 1949, the "socialist camp" was almost a billion people), apparently pictured the ideal Soviet Union as a permanent military camp, where he would keep tightening the loosened cultural screws. For Stalin, Zoshchenko and Akhmatova themselves meant absolutely zero: all they were just pawns in a global ideological game. But for Akhmatova and Zoshchenko these persecutions (even though they were not arrested) skewed their lives. They both fought it, using different behavioral strategies.

Zoshchenko, a former tsarist officer with awards for valor, tried to defend his dignity, writing to Stalin: "It is very difficult for me to appear in your eyes as a literary rascal, a base person, or a man who worked for landowners and bankers. That is a mistake. I assure you."[24] Akhmatova in 1952 was forced to publish a pro-Stalin cycle of poems in an attempt to lessen the burden of her son, arrested yet again. No one blamed her for it, then or now.

Akhmatova, who died on March 5, 1966 (thirteen years to the day after Stalin), managed to create an image of herself for future generations as a fierce and uncompromising opponent of Stalin—the ancient Greek prophet Cassandra, through whom spoke History itself. Her image as "empress in exile," extraordinary for the times, was obviously calculated and honed in the smallest details.

Shostakovich in his later years took an anti-Stalinist position similar to Akhmatova's, although he did not project as imposing a presence in person (and who else could?). Neurotic and twitchy, looking like a frightened schoolboy with his round eyeglasses and cowlick, Shostakovich nevertheless had unparalleled inner discipline and enormous confidence in his creative power, which helped him to withstand Stalin's personal attacks in 1936 and later in 1948.

Shostakovich's Fifth Symphony can be read as a coded narrative about the years of the Great Terror, parallel to Akhmatova's *Requiem,* and his Seventh Symphony echoes Akhmatova's patriotic and memorial poems of the war years. It is no accident that she felt great affinity for him. She had wanted Shostakovich to set her *Requiem* to music.[25]

Akhmatova and Shostakovich had no illusions about the nature of the Stalinist regime, they simply rendered unto Caesar what was Caesar's when it was demanded. Prokofiev, Shostakovich's senior colleague and rival, was also attacked by the party in 1948, but his reaction to Zhdanov's rebukes for "formalism" and music that was "anti-people" was more like Zoshchenko's in an attempt to maintain personal dignity and decorum.

Prokofiev tried with utmost seriousness to explain to his Communist vilifiers the difficulties of writing easily accessible music: "You need particular care in composing a simple melody not to turn it into something cheap, saccharine, or imitative."[26] Zhdanov demanded a complete break with the West, while the former émigré Prokofiev, who still had many friends and admirers in the West, responded with explanations of the subtleties of his aesthetic differences with Wagner or Arnold Schoenberg.

The resemblance of Prokofiev and Zoshchenko could be gleaned in the parallel arc of their creative development (from stylistic excesses of the early oeuvre to the rather forced, pallid simplicity of the late works) and similarities of their personal problems. Beneath their impenetrable "business" mask, both hid an eternal infantilism and profound insecurity; both were tormented by neuroses and weak hearts, which they tried to cure with self-treatment. They both wanted to deal with their organism "scientifically" and it turned into an idée fixe: Zoshchenko wrote an autobiographical book of Freudian self-analysis, which he wanted to call *The Keys of Happiness* and considered the most important work of his life; Prokofiev, as it became known after his diaries were published for the first time in 2002, turned to Christian Science, which he had joined in Paris in 1924.

Christian Science teaches that illness must be overcome not through medication but spiritual influence. There is an entry in the composer's diary when he was reading *Science and Health,* by the sect's founder, Mary Baker Eddy: "If I refuse medications but wear eyeglasses, that is a contradiction and lack of conscientiousness. I've decided to take them off. My glasses are not strong and I can manage without them anyway."[27]

After the Bolshevik revolution, the ambitious Prokofiev left Petrograd for the United States, to have a world career as a composer and pianist, even though Cultural Commissar Lunacharsky, who admired him, tried to talk him out of emigrating when he signed permission for him to leave. At first things went well in the West for Prokofiev, but by the early 1930s he sensed that he would not beat Stravinsky as a composer or Rachmaninoff as a pianist. They were the musical pillars of Russian émigrés. And therefore Prokofiev, assuming that he had no rivals back home (he did not consider young Shostakovich a real threat), decided to return to the Soviet Union in 1936, at the height of the Great Terror.

We will never know how much the principles of Christian Science helped Prokofiev adjust to the realities of Soviet life, but in 1936–1938 he composed some of his greatest works: the operas *War and Peace* (after Tolstoy) and *Betrothal in a Monastery* (after Sheridan's *The Duenna*), the ballet *Cinderella,* the Fifth and Sixth Symphonies, and his three best piano sonatas, the Sixth, Seventh, and Eighth. Other works, overtly tied to the Stalin era, are also masterpieces: the *Cantata for the Twentieth Anniversary of October* (with texts by Marx, Lenin, and Stalin), the *Alexander Nevsky* Cantata (from the score for Eisenstein's film), *Hail* for Stalin's sixtieth birthday, and the opera *Semyon Kotko.* It is no accident that of all the Soviet composers, Prokofiev received the most Stalin Prizes—six

(Myaskovsky and Shostakovich got five each, Khachaturian four, and the popular songwriter Isaak Dunaevsky two).

Some of Prokofiev's later works are unjustly dismissed as compromised and primitive by some today: the *Winter Bonfire* Suite (1949), the *On Guard for Peace* Oratorio (1950), and the Seventh Symphony, which was completed and performed in 1952. It may be that my perception of this music is influenced by the peculiar atmosphere of the last years of Stalin's rule.

I was in school in Riga, the capital of Soviet Latvia, but even in that most "Western" part of the Soviet Union, the cultural situation was palpably stagnant and oppressive. Prokofiev's late music seemed like a gulp of pure and fresh water. I had started reading early, at four, and I had skipped picture books and devoured almost immediately the daily newspapers and mainstream Soviet literature, often in the cheap mass editions of Roman-Gazeta.

Many of those books, popular with adults and teenagers alike, were based on true stories: *Chapaev* (1923) by Dmitri Furmanov, on which the famous film was based, was about the legendary Red commander who died in the Civil War; *How the Steel Was Tempered* (1932–1934) was the autobiographical novel of the blind and paralyzed Nikolai Ostrovsky about his exploits in battles with the White Army and in the early Soviet construction sites; *Tale of a Real Man* (1946) by Boris Polevoy was in the same key, about a military pilot who continued to fly after his legs were amputated; and *The Young Guard* (1945) by Alexander Fadeyev described heroic deeds of young guerrillas executed by the Germans during World War II.

Tellingly, these propaganda works, written in a very entertaining way and therefore consumed as adventure stories by many, were primarily about martyr heroes or war cripples. This was a topical issue for the devastated country, where it would be hard to find a family without a loss. My father returned from the front with an amputated leg, and so I was particularly moved by Polevoy's description of the amputee pilot's struggle to return to aviation.

This story also touched the outwardly cynical Prokofiev, who used Polevoy's book as the basis for his last opera, *Tale of a Real Man* (1948). Though simple and sincere, the Soviet musical bureaucrats, intimidated by the incessant noise about Prokofiev's "formalism," did not dare produce it. It was not performed publicly until 1960.

Stalin regarded Soviet culture as a huge hose for brainwashing his subjects before what he considered the inevitable Third World War, in the course of which Communism would at last conquer the whole world. He was a firm believer in the Communist idea and moved toward its final implementation disregarding all losses, while making only occasional tactical concessions.

The Russian cultural elite had already grown weary of Stalin's ruthless and inhumane methods by the late 1930s. The war against Hitler, even though at some point it put the very existence of the Soviet state at risk, added nationalist fire to the cooling boiler of Communist ideals. But the endless circumstance of combat readiness, hysterical vigilance, and ridiculously exaggerated xenophobia could not continue. In that corrosive atmosphere, any unexpected quiet or lyrical work, like Prokofiev's Seventh Symphony, seemed like manna from heaven.

Stalin continued pulling on the ideological levers, provoking new campaigns and drives. He seemed to be trying things out—should he use anti-Semitism as a weapon? Or the tried-and-true espionage and sabotage scare? Or a truly strange method—a national discussion on linguistics? All these actions were actually implemented and added to an already surreal situation.

Where would it have led—to yet another bloodbath in the Soviet Union? A global nuclear catastrophe? Or did Stalin, as some historians now contend, not want either but was simply trying to outmaneuver his real and imaginary opponents inside and outside the country?

It is doubtful that we will be able to ever reach final conclusions on this, because when Stalin died on March 5, 1953 (officially, of brain hemorrhage), he left no political will and had not shared his plans with any of his comrades—apparently he did not trust any of them.

I remember the fear and horror I felt when on the dark and damp morning of March 6 as I was getting ready for school I heard the radio announcer speak slowly and with bathos: "Last night, at nine twenty p.m., our dear and beloved leader passed away without regaining consciousness." I did not know then that on the same day, and also from brain hemorrhage, Prokofiev had died. The composer was weak and the tension that was in the air in the last days of Stalin's life had apparently hastened his end.

In those chaotic days the significance of the deaths of the ruler and the composer seemed incomparable; no one thought of Prokofiev except his closest friends, and it was difficult to scrape up flowers for his coffin because all the flowers and wreaths in Moscow had been requisitioned for Stalin's funeral. But in 1963, on the tenth anniversary of Prokofiev's demise, marked after the official condemnation of the "cult of personality" of Stalin, there were jokes circulating that apparently Stalin was an insignificant political figure in the era of Prokofiev.

The following decades altered that value balance, too, as it turned out to be equally politically motivated. Apparently that balance will be continually shifting, reflecting the inevitable changes and vacillations in the comparative evaluation of Stalin and Prokofiev. It reminds us of the dialectical intertwining of politics and culture.

Part Four

THAWS AND FREEZES

Chapter Ten

Before Stalin's funeral, which took place in Moscow on March 9, 1953, the coffin with his body went on display at the Hall of Columns in the House of Unions. For several days, in relays, the best Soviet symphonic orchestras and soloists played during the viewing. The musicians included David Oistrakh, the violinist, and Sviatoslav Richter—the pianist was flown in from Tbilisi by special plane, and he was the only passenger, the rest of the plane filled with flowers sent to the capital for the funeral.

Richter later maintained that he had hated Stalin even then. There is no reason to doubt him: his father, a Russian German, was executed in June 1941 on charges of espionage for the Nazis. In 1941, his teacher Genrikh Neihaus (another of his students was Emil Gilels) was arrested as anti-Soviet and a "defeatist" (he was also of German descent) and kept almost nine months in solitary confinement in the notorious Lubyanka Prison. But in 1950, the thirty-five-year-old Richter accepted the Stalin Prize, as had other recipients—Oistrakh (he received it in 1943), Gilels (1946), conductor Yevgeny Mravinsky (1946), and twenty-four-year-old cellist Mstislav Rostropovich (1951).

The prizes for these artists, which reflected Stalin's belief that classical music was an effective propaganda tool, symbolized the importance of musical performers in official Soviet culture. As Stalin saw it, classical composers in the interpretation of these talented musicians were mobilized to serve Marxist ideology, and the performers were turned into ideal representatives of the socialist camp: they possessed formidable musical technique (paralleling Stalin's policy of industrialization of the USSR), were optimistic, and civic-minded (as they were depicted in the media), and were happy to travel at the beck and call of the Party and state to the farthest reaches of Central Asia, the Far East, or Siberia to play for the worker and peasant masses there thirsting for high culture (as the media reports trumpeted).

The real picture was rather different. Yes, the state gave its best musicians significant privileges, but saw them as no better than celebrity slaves, obliged to service any official occasion, be it a performance in a regional election campaign headquarters, a factory lunch break (concerts by symphony orchestras, those mobile Potemkin villages, were particularly awkward for the musicians and the forced audience of weary laborers), before and after various political speeches, or at funerals, like Stalin's, where Richter and Oistrakh and the other musicians were not allowed to leave the Hall of Columns for several days and nights, kept there on dry rations.

While the musicians were under lock and key at the Hall of Columns, in their breaks watching the endless procession of Muscovites come to pay their final respects to the leader, the last bloody drama of the Stalin era played out in the streets. Thousands of people tried to make their way to the bier. The young poet Yevgeny Yevtushenko found himself in that crowd and later recalled, "It was a horrific, fantastic sight. The people who poured into that flow from behind kept pushing and pushing. The crowd turned into a terrifying vortex."[1]

The tragedy that had occurred in Moscow fifty-seven years earlier was repeated. In 1896, during the coronation of the last Russian tsar, Nicholas II, several thousand people were crushed to death in the crowds. The difference was that this time the catastrophe was not in suburban Khodynka field, but in the center of Moscow, and yet the tragedy was hushed up completely. Still, some witnesses paradoxically sensed that "even in that terrible, tragic surge of Muscovites there was some passion of nascent freedom."[2]

Yevtushenko also maintained that at that moment he "thought of the man we were burying for the first time with hatred." That must have been a seismic shift for the poet who just the previous year in his first book of poetry, *Scouts of the Future,* called Stalin "my best friend in the world," and had responded to the anti-Semitic campaign of 1953 against the "killer doctors" this way: "None of the killers will be forgotten. They will not leave without paying. Gorky may have been killed by others, I think, it's the same ones now."[3]

(In 1989, a wiser Yevtushenko included that troubling episode in his perestroika-era film, *Stalin's Funeral,* adding the commonsense advice that he himself had followed rarely: "Let future poets be more careful when they start writing 'civic poetry.' "

The impetus for the shift in the mindset of the capital's intelligentsia is usually considered to be the Moscow International Festival of Youth and Students in 1957 (which the pianist Maria Yudina dubbed "mass derailment") and the sensationally successful American Exhibition at Sokolniki in 1958. But there is reason to suppose that the ideological crack in postwar Soviet society, which had seemed fairly monolithic to the majority of Western observers, appeared earlier, somewhere in the late 1940s or early 1950s. Stalin used his endless brainwashing in an attempt to patch the holes that appeared in the Soviet ideological space after World War II and the return of the Red Army from Europe. In terms of the Soviet masses, Stalin succeeded rather well, but the Western virus lay hidden but alive, at—of all places—the very top of Soviet society.

The writer Vassily Aksyonov described a youth party in 1952 at the home of an important Soviet diplomat that he, a nineteen-year-old provincial student, was lucky enough to attend. The American Victrola played jazz records by Louis Armstrong, Woody Herman, and Nat King Cole. The young *stilyagi* (as the over-the-top admirers of American fashion and pop culture were called in the hostile press articles; they called themselves *shtatniki*, from *shtaty*, "the States"), in fashionable Western-made jackets with huge padded shoulders, pegged black trousers, and thick-soled shoes, sipped whiskey and smoked Camels. The daughter of a big KGB boss danced with Aksyonov and stunned him straight off: "I hate the Soviet Union and love the United States of America!" Aksyonov observed, "The *stilyagi* could be called the first Soviet dissidents."[4]

Such luxuries as American cigarettes, whiskey, and records in postwar Soviet Union were available only to the super elite. But even in that period of tight self-isolation, when in Churchill's memorable phrase an iron curtain fell across Europe, dividing the Soviet and American spheres of influence, American culture managed to infiltrate the Soviet masses, too. Most strangely, that American cultural intervention came about from Stalin's initiative permitting mass exhibition of Western films from the "trophy fund," that is, films that were wartime booty or were gifts from the Allies.

This was intended to make money and also entertain the people: after the war domestic production of films diminished rapidly—seventeen films were made in 1948 and only five in 1952. So, thanks to Stalin's permission, Soviet audiences could see, among other films, John Ford's *Stagecoach* (renamed *The Trip Will Be Dangerous*) and under the title *A Soldier's Fate in America,* William Wyler's *The Best Years of Our Lives.* A special Politburo resolution called for "necessary editorial corrections" to be made in each film and anti-American introductory texts and commentaries were added.

It is amazing that Stalin took this step. He knew better than most the propaganda value of film. Back in 1928, he had spoken of it in a conversation with Eisenstein: "Abroad there are very few books with Communist content. Our books are almost not read at all there, because they do not know Russian. But Soviet films are watched with interest by everyone and they understand everything."[5]

Stalin always bore in mind the influence on progressive Western intellectuals of the films of Eisenstein, Vsevolod Pudovkin, Alexander Dovzhenko, and Dziga Vertov—that is why he respected these directors. Then why did he not consider the possible results of showing "trophy films" in the USSR? Perhaps he had overestimated the sanitizing effect of Soviet censorship. The consequences were quite significant.

Joseph Brodsky described the liberating effect of the American films: "They were presented to us as entertaining stories, but we perceived them as a sermon on individualism."[6] Aksyonov confirms that: "For us it was a window into the outside world from Stalin's smelly den."[7]

I knew people who watched *The Roaring Twenties* thirty or more times, eagerly memorizing every detail of the American way of life: clothing, hairstyles, manners. The greatest popularity was enjoyed by four films of the Tarzan series in the early 1950s; Brodsky's paradoxical opinion is that they promoted de-Stalinization more than Khrushchev's subsequent anti-Stalin speech at the Twentieth Communist Party Congress or even the publication of Solzhenitsyn's *One Day in the Life of Ivan Denisovich.* "It was the first film in which we saw natural life. And long hair."[8]

Rebels throughout the Soviet Union grew their hair long like Tarzan, and his famous cry was heard in backyards and even school corridors. Teachers, obeying orders, tried to quell this and other enthusiasms for "American fashion" by what means they could, including expulsion from college, which could ruin a person's permanent record forever. Along with the media campaign against the *stilyagi* (they were denounced in films, radio, and newspapers and mocked in nasty cartoons in satirical magazines), this created tension among young people.

Could Stalin's miscalculation with the Western films be explained partially by the dictator's desire to prepare Soviet people for the decisive battle with the Americans? The films would have served as an inoculation against the Western "contagion." Privately, Stalin spoke frankly: "Our propaganda is badly done, it's a mush instead of propaganda. . . . The Americans refute Marxism, they slander us, they try to debunk us. . . . We must expose them. We must familiarize the people with the ideology of the enemies, criticize that ideology, and that will arm our cadres."[9]

Trying to tighten the screws again, Stalin started a xenophobic cultural campaign. But at the same time, he understood that the Soviet Union now had to compete with the United States on the international cultural arena: "We are now dealing not only with domestic policy but world policy. Americans want to subordinate everything to themselves. But Americans are not respected in any capital. We must expand the worldview of our people in *Pravda* and Party magazines, we must have a broader horizon, we are a world power."[10]

The Communists had always relied heavily on international ideological propaganda. The role played by the Communist International (Comintern), created on Lenin's initiative in 1919, and its cultural emissary in Europe and the United States, Willy Münzenberg, is well known today. It was Münzenberg who used his international network of pro-Soviet film clubs to promote *Battleship Potemkin* and other revolutionary films in the West. Stalin used technical innovations for these goals: on his orders in 1929, Moscow International Radio was created, the first state broadcast of its kind in the world, which with time became a powerful propaganda center.

Americans had a traditional aversion to the use of state-sponsored propaganda abroad, even though during World War I, President Woodrow Wilson established the Committee for Public Information. That experience was used later for organizing the Voice of America after the Japanese attack on Pearl Harbor. When the war was over, some congressmen wondered why American taxpayers had to continue to pay for international radio.

Those doubts vanished with the onset of the Cold War. On May 6, 1948, John Foster Dulles expressed the feelings of the American political elite faced with the world expansion of Communist ideas: "For the first time since the threat of Islam a thousand years ago, Western civilization is on the defensive."[11] Two years later, President Harry Truman stressed the importance of the propaganda aspect in standing up to the Soviet Union: "This is a struggle, above all else, for the minds of men. Propaganda is one of the most powerful weapons the Communists have in this struggle."[12]

The doctrine of "containment," elaborated by George F. Kennan, was adopted as the instrument of American policy toward the Communist bloc. Kennan later stressed that he had meant political and ideological containment of Soviet expansion. Projected into the sphere of cultural counterpropaganda, this doctrine was quite successful.

Jazz, one of the most important manifestations of American culture, was used right away as a propaganda weapon. Charles Bohlen, the American ambassador to the Soviet Union, had noticed the popularity of Voice of America jazz programs in Moscow and at his suggestion in 1955 the station began a special project, Music USA, devoted to jazz. The theme music of the show, hosted in a soothing baritone by Buffalo native Willis Conover, who became the idol of several generations of *shtatniki,* was Duke Ellington's "Take the A Train."

By that time, production of radios that could receive shortwave transmissions from the United States and other Western countries was banned in the Soviet Union, but many homes still had prewar or trophy radios; besides which, Conover's shows were in English, so they were jammed less than the Russian-language news on Voice of America. (The jamming of Western radio transmissions, which involved building powerful stations all over the USSR, cost the Soviet government a pretty penny.)

Conover's programs gave audiences their first taste of the music of Thelonious Monk, John Coltrane, and Ornette Coleman and became an underground encyclopedia of jazz for Soviet youth. The business of recording "music on bones" was born: X-ray films were used as recording material and these homemade records of jazz and later of rock and roll were sold on the black market, inspiring budding jazz musicians all over the Soviet Union.

The Americans did not forget about "high" culture, either. Knowing the Russians' penchant for classical music (Stalin began sponsoring participation of Soviet musicians in international competitions in the 1930s), the best American symphony orchestras were sent to the USSR—the Boston in 1956, the Philadelphia in 1958. The twenty-five-year-old Canadian pianist Glenn Gould appeared in Moscow and Leningrad in 1957 with eye-opening programs (besides Bach, he played the modernist works of Paul Hindemith and Anton von Webern, banned in the USSR then), and for many stunned professionals, as one of them put it, life was divided into pre-Gould and post-Gould.[13]

The culmination of the musical duel between the two superpowers (the violinist Oistrakh and the pianist Gilels made triumphant debuts at Carnegie Hall in 1955 and the pianist Richter in 1960) was the sensational victory by Van Cliburn, twenty-three, at the Tchaikovsky Piano Competition in Moscow in 1958. Tall, gawky, with a dreamy gaze, the infinitely charming pianist whom Muscovites dubbed with a loving diminutive, "Vanechka," instantly won over the audiences (women in particular). More importantly, Cliburn also won over the competition jury, chaired by Gilels, which consisted of such authoritative Russian musicians as the great interpreter of Scriabin, Vladimir Sofronitsky, who sensed a fellow romantic in Cliburn, and the musical patriarch Alexander Goldenveizer, favorite musician and chess partner of Leo Tolstoy. Goldenveizer compared Cliburn to the young Rachmaninoff.

When the prizes were decided, the Soviet members of the jury had to get Nikita Khrushchev's secret approval before crowning Van Cliburn.[14] The young American's victory at the competition, which had been covered on a daily basis by *The New York Times,* was front-page news all over the world. Being a political sensation, the victory also had a major impact on Russian cultural life.

For the first time, Russian musical émigrés were acknowledged: after all, Cliburn's teacher at the Juilliard School in New York was Rosina Lhevinne, a graduate of the Moscow Conservatory. Cliburn popularized the émigré composer Rachmaninoff's Third Piano Concerto. This paved the way for the triumphant tours of the USSR by Igor Stravinsky and George Balanchine's New York City Ballet in 1962, when the Soviet establishment had to welcome and hail the former émigrés, by now trendsetters of international high modernism.

Another important American program that expanded the cultural horizons and influenced the worldview of the Soviet elite was the publication of books in Russian. Several American publishing houses were established for that purpose with subsidies from government and private sources; among them, Chekhov Press in New York, which printed Russian-language volumes by Bunin, Remizov, Zamyatin, Tsvetaeva, and Nabokov, and had a Ford Foundation grant of $523,000.[15] According to *The New York Times,* at least a thousand titles were sponsored,[16] covering a wide range from translations of poetry and essays by T. S. Eliot, to the collected oeuvres of Gumilev and Mandelstam, and works by Pasternak, Akhmatova, Zabolotsky, and Klyuev.

The absence of ideological preference is remarkable. The most varied movements are represented: traditional and experimental prose, Acmeism, Dadaism, neo-peasant poetry. Anti-Sovietism was not the main criterion, as might be expected (for example, Zabolotsky's neoprimitivist poems would be hard to call "anti-Soviet"); rather, the predominant desire was to return into circulation within the Soviet Union the works of authors who were banned for one reason or another.

Books by Russian authors that were published in the West were called *tamizdat* ("published there"; like *samizdat,* "self-published") in the Soviet Union. In Russia (brought by foreign tourists, Soviet seamen, and Soviet citizens who traveled abroad in official delegations), these books were worth their weight in gold. They were copied by typewriter or hand (there were no accessible copying machines in the USSR in those days); this expanded the range of *samizdat,* for many years one of the main reservoirs of intellectual opposition.

Gradually the cultural space inside the Soviet Union, especially in big cities, was filled with books in Russian published in the West. You could come across them in the most unexpected places, belonging to the most unexpected people.

I remember being at a birthday party for the daughter of an important cultural bureaucrat in Moscow in the early 1970s; taking a furtive look at his impressive home library, I reached for a volume, accidentally bringing down an avalanche of books that revealed, tucked behind them, a recent Western edition of Gorky's *Untimely Thoughts,* a collection of his anti-Bolshevik articles, which had not been reprinted in Russia since 1918 and was well hidden in Soviet libraries in "special archives." I quickly started putting back the books, simultaneously feverishly flipping through the precious volume of Gorky. I read as much as I could and it changed my perceptions of the writer.

In 1972, Yevtushenko tried to bring in a large number of *tamizdat* books when returning to Moscow from a trip to the United States. Since Soviet customs agents were most interested in cultural contraband, every attempt to bring it in was a risky undertaking, punishable by the full extent of the law. There were times when Yevtushenko (like many other, less famous travelers) got away with it, but this time the poet was caught.

The confiscated books included works by the Bolshevik leaders Trotsky and Bukharin, killed by Stalin; poetry by Gumilev, shot by the Bolsheviks, and Mandelstam, who died in the camps; philosophical studies by members of the Russian "religious renaissance," Berdyaev and Shestov; the prose of the émigré Nabokov and *Cursed Days*, the anti-Bolshevik diary of the first Russian Nobel laureate, Bunin. Along with the books, they confiscated Yevtushenko's photographs taken with Richard Nixon and Henry Kissinger.

The poet was required to write an explanation, in which, describing himself later as a "clever and rather nimble Mowgli of the Soviet jungles," he declared: "During my trips abroad with the goal of propagandizing the ideas of our Homeland, I sometimes feel myself ideologically unarmed in the struggle with our enemies, for I am not familiar with the primary sources on which they base their shameless hatred. It is impossible to get many of these primary sources in the USSR, even in the special archives of the Lenin Library. That is why I brought in these books—not for distribution but in order to raise my ideological vigilance."[17]

Amazingly, after such a demarche and after an audience with General Filipp Bobkov, head of the KGB's Fifth Directorate, in charge of cultural exchange with the West, the poet got back almost all of the confiscated books.

The KGB was harder on less famous and less connected Soviet intellectuals. The Criminal Code had, in Solzhenitsyn's sarcastic definition, "the majestic, mighty, fruitful, multibranched, variegated, all-encompassing article Fifty-Eight," which threatened harsh punishment for so-called "counterrevolutionary, anti-Soviet activity." Paragraph 10 of this article called for severe punishment for "propaganda or agitation containing a call for the overthrow, undermining, or weakening of the Soviet regime . . . and equally for the distribution or preparation or possession of literature of such content."

This paragraph was interpreted extremely expansively: according to Solzhenitsyn, almost any idea, spoken or written, could in the Soviet years fall under the notorious article 58. Everyone knew of some person or other who ended up in the camps for books and manuscripts of an "anti-Soviet"content found during a search. Tragic curiosities abounded. In Riga, in the early 1950s, a friend of my father's was sent to seven years in the camps for possession of the books *The Turbulent Life of Lazik Roitshvanets* and *In Protochny Alley*, published in the 1920s. The sentence described both books as anti-Soviet, but did not name the author, with good reason: he was Ilya Ehrenburg, winner of two Stalin Prizes, who at that time represented Riga as deputy to the Supreme Soviet of the USSR.

During all the years of the Soviet regime, even under Gorbachev, a book of suspicious content, especially if published in the West, found during a search could ruin a person's life. That is why people who lent each other *tamizdat* and *samizdat* literature (often these books were borrowed overnight and read by the whole family and close friends as well) had to use conspiracy methods, often quite clumsy, like the following telephone conversation: "Have you eaten the pie I gave you yesterday?" "Yes." "And your wife, too?" "Yes, she has." "Well then, pass the pie to Nikolai, he wants to taste it, too."

That the Soviet secret police took stopping the flow of undesirable books from the West seriously and how widely it opened its nets to do so can be seen from a recently declassified report from Yuri Andropov, then head of the KGB, to Leonid Brezhnev on May 6, 1968, where he proudly reported that in a year "in the international mail channels more than 114 thousand letters and packages with anti-Soviet and politically harmful literature were confiscated."[18]

That enormous flow of "politically harmful" materials included quite a few copies of the secret speech made by Nikita Khrushchev at the Twentieth Party Congress on February 25, 1956. The speech, "On the Cult of Personality and Its Consequences," was the first exposé of Stalin's crimes coming from the ruling party, and therefore it was a sensational event both in the Soviet Union and in the West, reported by *The New York Times* and other newspapers. Inside the Soviet Union, Khrushchev's anti-Stalin speech was read to party members at first, then classified until 1989.

Stocky, round-headed, and bald, Khrushchev was a politician to the core, hard to pin down, sly, stubborn, and most importantly, inordinately energetic. Compared to Lenin and Stalin, he was uneducated.[19] Khrushchev's numerous and often very long speeches were chaotic improvisations, as he would get carried away. Like a poet, he was borne on the wings of his own eloquence. At the end of his life, Khrushchev dictated memoirs that were meant to fix the author's progressive image in the minds of posterity. (Later the poet Andrei Voznesensky would note dryly: "Khrushchev delights me as a stylist.")[20]

The peak of Khrushchev's career was his anti-Stalin speech, prepared as usual by a group of advisors. But there are quite a few vivid details in that oration that were obviously introduced by Khrushchev himself. It was Khrushchev who first quoted some of Stalin's memorable phrases, for example, Stalin's statement on how he would deal with the rebellious leader of Yugoslavia, Marshal Tito: "Here, I wiggle my pinky and there is no Tito." In his "secret" speech, Khrushchev sarcastically added: "Those 'pinky wiggles' cost us a lot."[21]

Khrushchev generated some truly poetic ideas. On his orders, Stalin's mummy was removed from the mausoleum on Red Square, the virgin soil in Kazakhstan was plowed up, and the first man was sent into space. Khrushchev's political slogans were also of a literary bent, straight out of science fiction: "Today's generation of Soviet people will live under Communism!" "Catch up to and surpass the U.S.A. in production of meat, butter, and milk per capita!" and the infamous remark addressed to the Unites States—"We will bury you."

No contemporary writer could ever compete with such proclamations, which literally made the world freeze in fear. But a group of young Russian poets nevertheless managed to rise above the political clutter. Yevtushenko, Voznesensky, Bella Akhmadulina, and Bulat Okudzhava became widely popular.

The most famous of them was the tall, rangy, loud, and inexhaustible Yevtushenko; according to his own calculations, he has appeared in ninety-four countries, and his poetry has been translated into seventy-two languages. People everywhere—in Russia, France, the United States, Israel—knew that in 1961 Yevtushenko published the poem "Babi Yar," about Jews killed by the Nazis in Ukraine during World War II. This poem was also perceived as a condemnation of Soviet anti-Semitism.

Yevtushenko became the poetic chronicler of political change in the Soviet Union, sometimes running ahead (which would make the government crack down on him, inevitably leading to a surge in his popularity at home and in the West), sometimes falling behind (which made just the opposite happen). Khrushchev was an unpredictable captain, and on his ship people were thrown left and then right, their heads spinning. Yevtushenko had the gift for simple, accessible, and effective poetic slogans expressing the essence of the bewildering changes.

Voznesensky once said that Yevtushenko had created a special genre—"poetic journalism."[22] Thousands of people attended his readings, and with his comrades Yevtushenko filled enormous soccer stadiums with standing-room crowds of admirers. The old Bolshevik and Politburo member Anastas Mikoyan said in amazement that it was the first time he ever saw people standing in line not for meat or sugar but for poetry.

Alexander Tvardovsky often said that real poems were ones memorized by people who were not interested in poetry. If we accept Tvardovsky's criterion, then any anthology of twentieth-century Russian poetry, however selective, will include a dozen or so poems by Yevtushenko and Voznesensky.

Voznesensky was the more experimental, resembling his idol Pasternak and also the early Mayakovsky, with striking, often shocking imagery and elaborate rhyme schemes. He became the most easily translatable modern Russian poet because his poetic approach was largely visual, with a strong surrealistic bent, and thus more accessible to Western intellectuals.

Yevtushenko's self-fashioning followed the long Russian literary tradition from Blok through Esenin and Mayakovsky down to Akhmatova, the great master of self-creation. In the very first line of his official Soviet biography—"Yevgeny Yevtushenko was born July 18, 1933, at Zima Junction, Irkutsk Region"[23]—there are at least three deviations from the facts. Yevtushenko's father's surname was Gangnus, he was born a year earlier, in 1932, and not at Zima Junction, but at a different Siberian village, Nizhneudinsk.

On the disparity in the date Yevtushenko's explanations are rather vague, but the rest is not hard to figure out. A famous Russian poet, as Yevtushenko expected to be from an early age, could not have a German-sounding surname or be born in a place with an unpoetic name. He used his mother's surname, and he squeezed everything possible out of the romantic-sounding Zima (Winter) Junction, including a very long poem.

Yevtushenko paraded around in shiny imported suits, multicolored caps, and bright ties, while the more stylish Voznesensky wore white ascots, coquettishly tied in a knot. And red-haired Akhmadulina astonished her audiences with her exotic looks: a delicate oval face "from Botticelli's brush" and slanted eyes of a "Siamese cat," as her first husband, Yevtushenko, described her.

Akhmadulina read her polished poems in a flirtatious and rather mannered way, never failing to impress her public, not as big as those of her friends, since her works were more refined and distanced from current events. Not everyone was enchanted, as evinced in a bitter entry in the diary of her second husband, the writer Yuri Nagibin: "Akhmadulina is cruel, devious, vengeful, and not at all sentimental, even though she is brilliant at playing touching helplessness. . . . Bella is as cold as ice, she loves no one but—not even herself—but the impression she makes."[24]

Akhmadulina and her friends were not anti-Soviet poets (her mother, according to Yevtushenko, was high up in the KGB).[25] As Yevtushenko recalled, in the early 1950s among student friends, someone said, "The revolution is dead and its corpse stinks." Young Akhmadulina, her eyes sparkling angrily, exclaimed, "You should be ashamed of yourself! The revolution is not dead. The revolution is sick. We have to help the revolution."[26]

Yevtushenko admitted that even after he came to hate Stalin, he continued to idealize Lenin, who was an idol for him until the start of perestroika. He gladly glorified Castro's Cuba in his poetry (and wrote the screenplay for Mikhail Kalatozov's propaganda film I Am Cuba) and had no difficulty writing sloganeering poems on any propagandistic topic. Robert Rozhdestvensky and many other young writers worked in the same vein in the mid-1950s, when the period known as the Thaw became a time for them of a brief but turbulent affair with the regime.

It may seem that at first, Khrushchev had to sympathize with the idealistic young poets, for he needed potent allies in the intelligentsia in his tightrope walk of de-Stalinization. His support, followed by sudden violent attacks, helped to make them world famous. Still, in Russia, not everyone was impressed.

Akhmatova had a skeptical attitude toward the "stadium poets." In private conversation she called Yevtushenko Mayakovsky's epigone "but without his genius"; she compared Voznesensky with Igor Severyanin, a popular turn-of-the-century poet ("the same tastelessness and cheap blasphemy"); and in connection with Akhmadulina unexpectedly cited the mannered poems of Mikhail Kuzmin, who died forgotten in 1936.[27]

Khrushchev tried to form his own cultural elite. Fadeyev, the once talented writer made into the overseer of Soviet literature by Stalin, he removed from power. Now, after the publication of Fadeyev's panicky letters to Khrushchev in 1953, it is clear that it was the new ruler's markedly cold attitude toward the writer, and not at all Fadeyev's pangs of conscience over his role in the Stalinist repressions of his colleagues, as was previously thought, that pushed Fadeyev to his unexpected suicide in 1956 at the age of fifty-four.

Khrushchev also got rid of another Stalin favorite, Fadeyev's deputy Konstantin Simonov, six-time winner of the Stalin Prize and author of the celebrated wartime poem "Wait for Me." The new Soviet leader had been infuriated by Simonov's directive that appeared in *Literaturnaya Gazeta* shortly after Stalin's death: "The most important, the loftiest goal placed before Soviet literature is to capture in all its majesty and in all fullness for contemporaries and future generations the image of the greatest genius of all times and all nations—the immortal Stalin."[28] (Much later, the mortally ill Simonov would dictate perhaps the best memoirs of meetings with Stalin.)

Khrushchev interrupted the career of yet another Stalin protégé, Alexander Gerasimov, president of the Academy of Arts of the USSR and four-time laureate of the Stalin Prize. Gerasimov's audience with Khrushchev, during which the artist tried to persuade him that de-Stalinization was a mistake, ended in a scandal: the temperamental Gerasimov stalked out of Khrushchev's office and slammed the door. Gerasimov was ordered to submit his resignation; that night he drank a whole bottle of vodka and almost died of a heart attack.

The ubiquitous paintings of Stalin were sent into museum warehouses; but on others, especially those where the ruler was depicted next to Lenin, artists painted over Stalin with other figures and the works continued to be exhibited and reproduced, eliciting knowing smirks.

Under Khrushchev's aegis, an adventurous theater was founded in Moscow—the Sovremennik [Contemporary], headed by the young and gifted Oleg Efremov. The actors of the theater, whose productions were always sold out, especially after the premiere of Yevgeny Shvarts's slyly satiric *The Naked King,* called themselves "children of 1956," that is, the momentous year of the anti-Stalinist Twentieth Party Congress and also of their theater's birth. Khrushchev's benevolence was in contrast to Stalin, who shut down the experimental Chamber Theater of the great Alexander Tairov in 1949.

The cultural policy of the Soviet state changed in another important area, too. In 1951, only three feature films—*Unforgettable 1919, Admiral Ushakov,* and *The Composer Glinka*—were in production at Mosfilm, the country's main studio.[29] This was the result of the elderly Stalin's crazy idea that if he made only a few movies but with the best cadres and under his own supervision, they would all be masterpieces. When all three directors calamitously fell sick at the same time, work at Mosfilm came to a complete halt; bats moved into the dark pavilions.

By contrast, by 1960 annual production had grown to more than a hundred feature films. They included two movies about World War II that won prizes at the Cannes Film Festival: Kalatozov's lyrical *The Cranes Are Flying,* starring the unforgettable Tatyana Samoilova and Alexei Batalov, and the moving *Ballad of a Soldier* by Grigory Chukhrai, for many years the calling card of new Soviet cinema in the West. For the first time since the classic era of the avant-garde—Eisenstein et al.—authoritative Western critics were writing about Soviet films with respect.

Akhmatova liked to say, "I'm a Khrushchevian."[30] She was grateful to Khrushchev for the return of millions from the camps, including her son, Lev Gumilev, who had spent almost fourteen years there. Yet Khrushchev never did allow the publication of Akhmatova's anti-Stalin poem *Requiem,* which had to wait until 1987 to appear.

Khrushchev disliked Akhmatova, although for different reasons than Fadeyev or Simonov: for him she was a representative of the prerevolutionary "reactionary literary swamp" (in Zhdanov's term). Instead, Khrushchev placed Alexander Tvardovsky in the role of the country's first poet. Mayakovsky was too "futurist" for Khrushchev, while Tvardovsky, basking in the fame of his wartime narrative poem about the exploits of the soldier Terkin and with his Party membership and position as deputy of the Supreme Soviet, seemed like a dependable ally. Even his "peasant" looks—Tvardovsky was tall, broad-shouldered, blue-eyed, with dignified but plain manners and speech—suited Khrushchev.

The poet could not get *Terkin in the Other World* (a satirical sequel) into print for many years, but after Tvardovsky read it to Khrushchev at his dacha at Pitsunda on the Black Sea (and the author recalled that Khrushchev "sometimes laughed out loud, peasant-style"),[31] the Soviet leader gave personal permission for publication. In 1958, Khrushchev made Tvardovsky head of the important literary journal *Novy Mir,* which under his direction gradually turned into the most liberal publication in the land.

But over the course of his years in power (1953–1964), Khrushchev never did learn how to handle the artistic intelligentsia. Even Stalin, much better read than Khrushchev and a better psychologist, took years to start understanding how to talk to the creative elite and still died in doubt: which worked better—carrot or stick?

Certainly Stalin was ruthless toward his own people and other nations. He did not spare his intelligentsia as a class, but his attitude toward the cultural elite was outwardly friendlier than that of Lenin, which is sometimes explained by the fact that Stalin, a less educated man than Lenin, felt more respect for people of culture. According to reminiscences, Stalin (despite later ideas of him to the contrary) almost never shouted at cultural figures, and when he was angry, he actually lowered his voice. Simonov, who had heard many stories of how cruel and coarse Stalin could be, say, with military men, stressed that the ruler "was never once boorish" to writers.[32]

Having dethroned Stalin politically, Khrushchev liked to state, right up to the moment he was deposed, that in culture he remained a Stalinist (even though that was not quite true). So why did Khrushchev not emulate Stalin's outward caution and respect for the cultural elite? Because he had decided that the best way to rein in people in the arts was to threaten them publicly, humiliating them and shouting at them? Apparently, Khrushchev tried to hide his lack of confidence, and this led to his continual showing off and constant reminder that he—and he alone—was the leader of the Communist Party and the state, and therefore entitled to be the top expert in all fields, including culture.

The list of spectacular failures that were rooted in Khrushchev's inferiority complex is long—from his attempt to make corn the monoculture, which caused him to be a laughingstock all over the country, to his provocative placement of Soviet missiles in Cuba that put the world on the brink of nuclear catastrophe. In culture, one of Khrushchev's greatest disasters came in the wake of the Nobel Prize for Literature for Boris Pasternak in 1958.

Chapter Eleven

As discussed, the Nobel Prize in Literature became an idée fixe of the Soviet leadership in 1933, when the prize went to the émigré Bunin instead of Maxim Gorky, Stalin's close friend. Bunin's prize made such an impression on Stalin that he considered inviting the hard-line anti-Soviet writer to come back to the Soviet Union permanently. He sent Simonov to Paris in the summer of 1946 to feel out seventy-five-year-old Bunin about the possibility. With his characteristic independence and unpredictability, Bunin made a harsh anti-Soviet speech soon afterward, and the question of the laureate's return to Moscow was taken off the agenda.

When they learned in 1946 that Pasternak was a nominee for the prize, the Soviet leadership became agitated. The news from Stockholm could have been worse. For example, the émigré philosopher Nikolai Berdyaev appeared on the list of candidates both before and after the war. The Nobel going for a second time to an émigré would have seemed like a catastrophe in Moscow.

Still, the Soviet favorite was Sholokhov, not Pasternak. *Literaturnaya Gazeta* hastened to print the premature news of Sholokhov's nomination in 1946. In the absence of Gorky and Alexei Tolstoy, who died in 1945, Sholokhov was Stalin's number one Soviet writer.

On the contrary, Pasternak, often a hermetic, elliptical, baroque poet, was at the time an inconvenient candidate, even though back in the 1920s, he wrote well-received long narrative poems about the revolution, *Nineteen Five* and *Lieutenant Schmidt*. Pasternak was also among the first to sing the praises of Lenin and Stalin in verse, and the poems were actually very good. That is why the Bolshevik Bukharin, in his speech at the First Congress of the Writers' Union in 1934, praised Pasternak as "one of the most remarkable masters of verse of our times, stringing onto his creativity not only an entire line of lyrical pearls but also a series of profoundly sincere revolutionary works."[1]

At the same congress, which was supervised by Stalin, Pasternak was seated at the presidium in the Hall of Columns next to Gorky, and he was selected for an important symbolic gesture—to receive in the name of all Soviet writers a gift from the workers' delegation—a large portrait of Stalin. At the time Stalin even considered making Pasternak one of the leaders of the Writers' Union. Debates continue to this day whether or not Pasternak had actually met Stalin, and if so, how many times. A voluminous secondary literature resulted from Stalin's famous telephone call to Pasternak in response to his efforts in defense of the poet Mandelstam, who was arrested in 1934.[2] Stalin met Pasternak's concerns halfway that time (even though in the end it did not save Mandelstam). Pasternak also intervened on behalf of other prisoners: his letter to Stalin helped secure the release in 1935 of Akhmatova's husband, Punin, and her son, Lev Gumilev.

In 2000, the transcript was published of Pasternak's talk at a discussion after *Pravda's* denunciations of "formalism" in 1936, with notes in Stalin's hand; the many passages Stalin underlined suggest that the poet's unusually independent statements (in particular, Pasternak said, to general laughter and applause: "If it is absolutely necessary to shout in newspaper articles, can they at least shout in different voices? That will make things more understandable, because when they shout in one voice, nothing is clear. Perhaps, it is possible not to shout at all—that would be quite wonderful")[3] may have influenced Stalin's reluctant decision to end the pogrom of the "formalists," including Shostakovich.

Bearing in mind that Pasternak's overly complex poetry and early prose were hardly to Stalin's literary tastes, which were primarily (although not exclusively, lest we forget the Futurist Mayakovsky) for the Russian classics, these were quite significant signs of attention from the ruler, all the more surprising in view of Pasternak's moodiness and seeming "lack of discipline." One would think that Stalin, who valued total obedience and predictability, would have found Pasternak rather irritating. Obviously, that was not the case.

Akhmatova observed with irony-tinged admiration that Pasternak "is endowed with a kind of eternal childhood." For all his preference for discipline, perhaps Stalin was also attracted by Pasternak's "infantile" behavior, since his exotic appearance—dusky Bedouin face, burning eyes, impulsive movements—corresponded to the traditional image of a

poet. Imitating his idols, Scriabin and Blok, Pasternak consciously cultivated the image of an artist "not of this world" (even though he was a
very practical person who knew not only how to get his fees, but also
how to mound potatoes in his garden) and probably sensed which but-
tons to push in his relationship with Stalin.

This is evident in Pasternak's letter to Stalin written in late 1935, soon
after the ruler disappointed his expectations and proclaimed that the
"best, the most talented poet of our Soviet era" was Mayakovsky, not
Pasternak. Paradoxically, Pasternak *thanked* Stalin for the verdict: "In
recent times, under the influence of the West, I have been made too
much of, given exaggerated significance (I even grew ill as a result): they
began to suppose I had a serious artistic power. Now, after you have put
Mayakovsky in first place, this suspicion is removed from me and with a
light heart I can live and work as before, in modest quiet, with the unexpected and mysterious moments without which I would not love life."[4]

This epistolary move was quite bold (what if Stalin suspected he was
being meek out of pride and punished him?), but in this case the poet
calculated correctly, and the ruler appreciated his modesty. That Stalin
approved of the letter is evident from his written notation to put it in his
personal archive, where only what he considered the most valuable and
historically important papers were kept.

The letter is in the style of an enamored flirtatious high school girl: "I
am tormented that I did not follow my first desire. . . . Should I have
been bolder and without thinking too long, followed my first
impulse? . . . I wrote to you the first time . . . obeying something secret
that, beyond all that is understandable and shared by everyone, ties me
to you." And in conclusion: "In the name of that mystery, your fervently
loving and devoted B. Pasternak."[5]

Just as personal was his poem dedicated to Stalin and first published
in the New Year's 1936 issue of the government newspaper *Izvestiya*, in
which Pasternak described Stalin as the "genius of action." It wasn't an
act of servility, for Pasternak eschewed servility all his life. He was apparently truly fascinated by Stalin.

Commenting on this enchantment, the clear-headed Lydia Ginzburg
drew a parallel with young Hegel, who declared upon seeing Napoleon
that an absolute spirit had ridden into the city on a white horse. Ginzburg
stated that a certain part of the Soviet (and Western) cultural elite perceived Stalin in that Hegelian key as "world and historical genius."[6]

Pasternak, for one, retained this attitude toward Stalin even after the ruler's death, as can be seen in his letter to Fadeyev dated March 14, 1953. In it, Pasternak gives Stalin his due as one of the elect who "travel to the end past all forms of petty pity for individual reasons to a common goal"—the establishment of a new social order in which world evil "would be unthinkable."[7]

Because of Pasternak's romantic "cult of personality" of Stalin (as Sholokhov, Pasternak's rival in the competition for the Nobel Prize, later observed, "Yes, there was a cult, but there was also a personality"), the poet never became an ardent admirer of Khrushchev the way Akhmatova did.

Pasternak had been circling prose for a while, and in late 1945 he began work on *Doctor Zhivago,* an epic novel about the path of the Russian intelligentsia in the twentieth century, which he completed ten years later. He understood from the beginning that the novel was "not intended for current publication."[8]

Pasternak meant the Soviet censors, who clearly would not accept an untrammeled narrative, without regard to Party demands, about the causes and meaning of the Russian revolution and the horrors of the Civil War, a narrative imbued with the author's openly Christian philosophy.

He considered *Doctor Zhivago* his most important work. He tried to achieve, in his own words, "unheard-of simplicity." Here Pasternak's ideal was, of course, Leo Tolstoy, in parallel to whom Pasternak renounced his own early complex and modernist works. Sometimes the connection between Pasternak and Tolstoy is denied since *Doctor Zhivago* is not a "realistic" novel as Tolstoy understood it. That is true, but the overall ideological influence of the late Tolstoy on Pasternak is indisputable.

Pasternak's father, a well-known artist, worked with Tolstoy in 1898 on illustrations for his novel *Resurrection.* Tolstoy considered Leonid Pasternak's portraits of him the most successful. The Pasternak house revered Tolstoy and that left a profound mark on the poet. In order to bring himself closer to the great writer, Pasternak in his later years even made up a story about seeing Tolstoy when he was four.

Following the late Tolstoy, Pasternak rejected the innovations of modern art and sought to write *Doctor Zhivago* in the manner of a Christian parable "understood in a new way," as he put it. Pasternak probably envisioned some kind of Christian revival similar to what happened under Tolstoy's influence at the turn of the century. This was noted in the West, and Czeslaw Milosz considered the novel a rare example of truly Christian literature.[9]

Tolstoy's departure from Yasnaya Polyana in 1910 and his dramatic death made him a model for Pasternak of a great person who went beyond cultural frontiers to produce an example of Jesus-like sacrifice. Of course, Pasternak was not an equal of Tolstoy's nor did he have his position and authority in Russia or abroad; still, in writing *Doctor Zhivago* he took a rather bold step that could be compared to Tolstoy's struggle against censorship in tsarist Russia.

Pasternak not only wrote a wholly independent novel, but he sent it to the West for publication, bypassing official channels—an act that required more personal courage than Tolstoy's behavior. The count was protected by his world fame and his social position from physical repression. Pasternak could not have felt insured against such danger: too many of his close friends had been destroyed by the Soviet regime, and in 1949 his mistress, Olga Ivinskaya (the prototype for Lara in *Doctor Zhivago*), was arrested and given a five-year sentence in the camps. During her interrogation, the investigator told Ivinskaya that Pasternak "has been a British spy for a long time."[10]

Pasternak's decision to smuggle *Doctor Zhivago* abroad broke the rules of permitted behavior set by the state for a Soviet writer. His confrontation with the Soviet authorities turned into an international scandal in 1958, when two years after its publication in the West, Pasternak was given the Nobel Prize "for his important achievements both in contemporary lyrical poetry and in the field of the great Russian epic tradition."

The Swedish Academy clearly signaled that it was anointing Pasternak as a successor of Leo Tolstoy (correcting once again, as in the case with Bunin, its injustice toward the author of *War and Peace*). The mention of Pasternak the poet was in this case a fig leaf, and it fooled no one. In the old days, the tsarist government created censorship barriers for Tolstoy, and the Holy Synod excommunicated him from the Church. Now the Soviet authorities swiftly orchestrated Pasternak's expulsion from the Writers' Union.

On the wave of the worldwide publicity surrounding the publication of *Doctor Zhivago* in the West and the Nobel Prize, the anti-Pasternak actions in the Soviet Union outraged intellectuals in democratic countries. But the Soviet regime had almost no choice. Giving the most prestigious cultural prize to a comparatively little-known author, and for a novel that was still not published in the Soviet Union, could only be seen as a hostile anti-Soviet move, which one official compared to a "literary atom bomb."[11]

Khrushchev added heat to the campaign against Pasternak in his inimitable way. There was nothing personal in his relationship with Pasternak, unlike Stalin. For him, Pasternak did not have the authority of Sholokhov, Tvardovsky, or even Alexander Korneichuk, a mediocre playwright but a Khrushchev favorite. It goes without saying that Khrushchev had not read Pasternak's poetry, much less his novel, and who would expect an extremely busy leader of a superpower to have the time to do so?

Stalin might have read *Doctor Zhivago,* as he did dozens of other novels by Soviet writers; there are reliable sources confirming his interest in current literature. As stated Simonov, who attended many discussions of literary works nominated for the Stalin Prize at which Stalin was present, "everything that was in the least bit controversial and caused disagreement, he had read. It was quite obvious each time I attended these meetings."[12]

Khrushchev was briefed on the matter (as world leaders usually are) with a few typed pages with selected quotations from *Doctor Zhivago;* for him, they just proved the novel's presumed anti-Soviet attitude. That was quite enough for Khrushchev. He used Pasternak in his attempt to scare Russian writers who might see the smuggling of *Doctor Zhivago* into the West and its subsequent triumph as a tempting precedent.

The anti-Pasternak campaign was organized in the worst Stalin traditions: denunciations in *Pravda* and other newspapers; publication of angry letters from "ordinary Soviet workers,"who had not read the book; hastily convened meetings of Pasternak's colleagues, at which fine poets like Vladimir Soloukhin, Leonid Martynov, and Boris Slutsky were forced to censure an author they respected. Slutsky, who in his brutal, prose-like poems had created an image for himself of courageous soldier and truth-lover, was so tormented by his anti-Pasternak speech that he later lost his mind.

On October 29, 1958, at the plenum of the Central Committee of the Young Communist League, dedicated to the Komsomol's fortieth anniversary, its head, Vladimir Semichastny, attacked Pasternak before an audience of 14,000 people, including Khrushchev and other Party leaders. Semichastny first called Pasternak a "mangy sheep" who pleased the enemies of the Soviet Union with "his slanderous so-called work." Then Semichastny (who became head of the KGB in 1961) added that "this man went and spat in the face of the people." And he concluded with "If you compare Pasternak to a pig, a pig would not do what he did" because a pig "never shits where it eats."[13] Khrushchev applauded demonstratively.

News of that speech drove Pasternak to the brink of suicide. It has recently come to light that the real author of Semichastny's insults was Khrushchev, who had called in the Komsomol leader the night before and dictated the lines about the mangy sheep and the pig, which Semichastny described as a "typically Khrushchevian, deliberately crude, unceremonious scolding."[14]

Pasternak responded to the state insult with a poem in which he wrote that he could not stand seeing those "porcine mugs" in the newspapers anymore. This was an obvious attack on Khrushchev, with more in the poem:

> The cult of personality is stripped of its majesty,
> But the cult of noisy phrases is in force
> And the cult of pettiness and impersonality
> Has increased perhaps a hundredfold.

This poem was not published then, but *Pravda* ran two tortured letters of repentance, one of them addressed to Khrushchev, in which Pasternak announced his "voluntary refusal" of the Nobel Prize and admitted the mistake of *Doctor Zhivago*.[15] I remember the depressing impact of the letters even though they were clearly written under duress.

In the meantime, pressure on Pasternak kept increasing. Public humiliation was not enough for Khrushchev, he wanted the writer on his knees. The excuse for a new push was the publication in *The Daily Mail* of a translation of Pasternak's poem "The Nobel Prize," smuggled out by a British journalist:

> *Like a beast in a pen, I'm cut off*
> *From my friends, freedom, the sun,*
> *But the hunters are gaining ground.*
> *I've nowhere else to run.*

Pasternak was called in for questioning at the office of the General Prosecutor of the USSR, where he was threatened with arrest for "activity, consciously and deliberately intended to harm Soviet society." This was qualified by the General Prosecutor as a "particularly dangerous state crime," which, by law, could be punishable by death.

It's unlikely that Khrushchev intended to have Pasternak executed, but he did think it acceptable to terrorize the sixty-eight-year-old poet without even replying to his letters. This total failure of communication with the new ruler dispirited Pasternak, who complained bitterly, "Even the terrible and cruel Stalin did not think it beneath him to grant my requests about prisoners and on his own initiative called me to discuss them."[16]

For Pasternak, the only escape from the horror he so powerfully expressed in the poem "The Nobel Prize" was, it seems, death, which came on May 30, 1960. But even his funeral on June 2 in Peredelkino, a writers' colony near Moscow, was turned into yet another political confrontation. As Veniamin Kaverin noted, "I had read Briusov on Tolstoy's funeral, and I was amazed by the similarity with Pasternak's burial. The same sense of the total breach between government and people."[17]

Valery Briusov wrote in 1910 that the tsarist authorities, in trying to avoid antigovernment demonstrations, had done everything possible to strip the farewell to Tolstoy of its national significance. Several thousand people accompanied Tolstoy's coffin in Yasnaya Polyana to its final resting place—in Briusov's opinion, "an infinitesimal number." Fifty years later, around two thousand came to Pasternak's grave, but in the present conditions that number seemed huge and unprecedented—this became the first mass unofficial funeral ceremony in Soviet history.

Tolstoy's death was the main topic for the Russian press then, but this time, besides a minuscule notice about the death of "Literary Fund member" Pasternak, nothing seeped into the Soviet newspapers. But word of mouth went into action, and the solemn and worshipful crowd in Peredelkino symbolized the birth of public opinion and the rudiments of civil society in the Soviet Union.

For the first time the intelligentsia was not afraid of either the secret police or the foreign correspondents: both groups photographed and filmed the event, each for its own goals, and that was symbolic, too. Pasternak's funeral, like Tolstoy's, had turned into a media show, but this time it happened—also a first in Soviet history—thanks to the efforts of the Western side, which eagerly sought and magnified the tiniest signs of dissidence in the Soviet monolith.

As the former KGB chief Semichastny complained in 2002: "This was an attempt of the Western intelligence services to publicize one of our first dissidents. . . . The seed took. Several years passed and the 'baton' was picked up by such laureates of the Nobel Prize as Aleksandr Solzhenitsyn, Andrei Sakharov, and Joseph Brodsky."[18]

The Central Committee of the Communist Party received intelligence information that copies of *Doctor Zhivago,* published in Russian in the West, "will be offered to Soviet tourists, various experts and seamen traveling abroad, and will be smuggled into the Soviet Union via 'existing channels.' "[19] When the Soviet delegation arrived in Vienna for the pro-Communist World Festival of Youth and Students in 1959, they had been instructed about possible "provocations" and were panicked to discover their tour bus literally stuffed with paperback copies of the novel. Their experienced KGB sitters gave them practical advice: "Take them, read them, but don't even try to bring them home."[20]

Doctor Zhivago was not published in the Soviet Union until Gorbachev's glasnost; in 1988, *Novy Mir* printed it in two million copies, giving rise to a small industry of scholarly studies. But it did not become a truly popular work, even though Pasternak had intended it to be accessible to unsophisticated readers. In survey after survey, the Russian public names *Master and Margarita* by Bulgakov and *The Quiet Don* by Sholokhov as the best Russian novels of the century, not *Doctor Zhivago.*

In 1965, Sholokhov at last received the Nobel Prize, seven years after

Doctor Zhivago. Many years of political maneuvering preceded the award. The first time Sholokhov was actually nominated was in 1947, but the committee then rejected his candidacy, because while *The Quiet Don* was "juicy and colorful," it wanted to wait for the publication of Sholokhov's announced work-in-progress on the war, *They Fought for the Homeland* (which was never completed).

Sholokhov was a favorite of Stalin and then of Khrushchev, and the leadership continued lobbying on his behalf. In the meantime, Sholokhov made a move to strengthen his reputation in Stockholm. When he went to France in 1959, Sholokhov, once again displaying his independence of character, supported the publication of *Doctor Zhivago* in the USSR, even though he called it an "unpolished, shapeless" work (an opinion shared, among others, by Akhmatova and Nabokov). That unorthodox statement caused an almost apoplectic reaction in the corridors of the Kremlin as "contradicting our interests."[21]

In October 1965, when Sholokhov, then sixty, got the news that he had been selected, he was hunting deep in the woods of the Urals. His first phone call was not home, but to Moscow, to the Central Committee, for permission to accept the award. Only after he received the official word did Sholokhov send a telegram to Stockholm to confirm that he would appear at the awards ceremony. There is a memorandum in the Central Committee archives about giving Sholokhov a subsidy of $3,000 for the purchase of a tailcoat and "to equip the persons accompanying him,"[22] the loan to be repaid from his Nobel Prize winnings.

It is hard to imagine the other longtime Russian pretender to the Nobel Prize, the elegant, restrained, and proud Vladimir Nabokov, in a similar humiliating situation. The aristocratically punctilious Nabokov, in the 1960s considered the preeminent contemporary writer by many in the West, where he lived, never did receive that highest literary accolade, joining Chekhov, Proust, Joyce, Kafka, and Platonov among the overlooked. For many years the Nobel committee was scandalized by Nabokov's most famous work, *Lolita* (1958), about the forbidden love of Humbert Humbert, a forty-year-old professor, for the twelve-year-old "nymphet" (a word invented by Nabokov). Despite his ironic attitude toward fame, Nabokov was deeply hurt by this. He had positioned him-

self as the most innovative Russian prose writer since Bely, busily exper-
imenting with narrative, while combining precise, acutely observed,
details with a markedly phantasmagoric and parodic form.

Nabokov's surrealism increased gradually, from his Russian-language
novel *The Gift* (1937–38, arguably his best work), which shocked the émigré community with its mockery of nineteenth-century liberal icon
Nikolai Chernyshevsky, to his late pyrotechnical English-language
works *Pale Fire* (1962) and *Ada* (1969). All that time, Nabokov was eyeing
the Nobel.

His Western biographers tend to underestimate the symbolic value of
the Nobel Prize for a Russian émigré. The fact that the first Russian to get
the prize in 1933 was his fellow émigré Bunin, with whom he had a complex relationship of master and ambitious younger colleague, must have
encouraged Nabokov, because it evinced the pull of stylistically refined
prose for the international literary arbiters.

Both Lenin and Stalin had been well informed about Nabokov's
father, a prominent prerevolutionary politician of a liberal bent (he was
assassinated in Berlin in 1921 by an extremist monarchist). Nabokov *fils*
came to the attention of Lenin and other Politburo members in 1923 in
the Soviet censors' "secret bulletin" with the firm conclusion: "Hostile to
the Soviet regime."[23] Since that first notice, Nabokov's works published
in the West were included on the Soviet blacklists, as was most of Russian émigré literature.

Nabokov remained hostile to the Soviet regime throughout his life,
both in his writing and his teaching at Cornell University. This unwaver-
ing hostility (unlike that of some other émigré luminaries, like Rachmaninoff or Bunin) was one of the reasons that kept him from
appreciating Pasternak's *Doctor Zhivago,* where the Bolshevik revolution
and its leader, Lenin, were depicted as a legitimate phenomenon: a position unacceptable for Nabokov. He dismissed *Doctor Zhivago* as "a sorry
thing, clumsy, trivial, and melodramatic, with stock situations, volup-
tuous lawyers, unbelievable girls, and trite coincidences."[24]

Nabokov had started out as a poet and continued writing poetry (it
was nice, but in Brodsky's stern opinion, "second-rate") all his life, and
Pasternak's baroque poetic style was alien to him. He ridiculed Pasternak
even in 1927: "His verse is fleshy, goitrous, with bulging eyes: as if his
muse suffered from exothalmic goiter. . . . And even his syntax is per-

verted."[25] That is, Nabokov disdained the early Pasternak for excessive avant-gardism and the later writing, on the contrary, for primitivism.

Pasternak's ode addressed to Stalin and published in *Izvestiya* in 1936, his prominent role in the First Congress of Soviet Writers in 1934, and his subsequent appearance at the pro-Soviet International Writers' Congress in Paris, would hardly have disposed the anti-Communist Nabokov toward the poet. This was at the root of the bizarre theory Nabokov shared privately, that the scandal surrounding the publication of *Doctor Zhivago* in the West was planned by the Soviets for a single goal: to guarantee the commercial success of the novel so that the hard currency earnings could be used to finance Communist propaganda abroad.

Nabokov's ideological and stylistic disagreements with Pasternak were amplified by personal motives. Interestingly, Pasternak knew or guessed that it was so: in 1956 he told a visitor from Great Britain that Nabokov envied him.[26] Scholars who deny the very possibility of envy ("And what was there to envy?") forget how marginalized culturally the émigré Nabokov must have felt in comparison to Pasternak, who was declared the country's leading poet in 1934 by the Bolshevik Bukharin.

And what could Nabokov have felt in 1958, when *Lolita*, which had at last reached the top of American best-seller lists, was knocked from its perch by *Doctor Zhivago,* which he hated so much (and which he felt was supported by the Soviet government) and which was propelled to the top of the list by the news of the Nobel Prize? In addition, Nabokov knew that many critics watching this unprecedented battle between two novels by Russian authors in the Western arena preferred *Doctor Zhivago* as the more worthy, "noble" work with Christian values.

This was not only the opinion in Russian émigré circles, which Nabokov quite understandably felt should be supporting a fellow exile, but to his great dismay, his best American friend, the influential critic Edmund Wilson, had ignored *Lolita* but praised *Doctor Zhivago* to the skies in his notable review in *The New Yorker.*

The Communist leadership always considered the Swedish Academy an anti-Soviet institution. However, there is no doubt that it was Nabokov's uncompromising anticommunism (which extended not only to Stalin but Lenin, which in those years was considered extremist by many Western intellectuals), together with his vulnerable position as an émigré, that made his candidacy "inconvenient" for the Nobel Prize. The semipornographic reputation of *Lolita* was a mere excuse for the Swedish academicians.

That is why they were not moved even by the passionate letter supporting Nabokov's candidacy from Moscow, sent by Solzhenitsyn, who had just received the Nobel Prize in 1970. The letter, in which Solzhenitsyn hails Nabokov as a writer with a "blinding literary gift, precisely the kind we call genius,"[27] is very curious. Solzhenitsyn praised Nabokov's novels, written both in Russian and in English, for their refined wordplay and brilliant composition while feeling little sympathy for high modernism, whose great representative Nabokov was.

Solzhenitsyn was sour about the Nobel Prize going to *The Quiet Don* (ironically, a work that was much closer to him stylistically): "It was a very dreary and hurt feeling in our community when we saw that Sholokhov won the prize for that very book"[28]—yet another example of how aesthetic judgment is subjugated to politics.

Even classic modernism, a milestone of which was Bely's *Petersburg* (1914), a phantasmagoric novel much admired by Nabokov, is still not considered mainstream literature in Russia. That may be one of the reasons that Nabokov's surrealistic novels (eight in Russian, including the tour de force *The Gift* and *Invitation to a Beheading,* and eight in English) have not entered the popular canon, even after they were finally published in Russia. (The first step came in 1987, when an excerpt from the "chess" novel *Luzhin's Defense* appeared in the weekly *Chess in the USSR.*)

The Nabokovian tradition is still little absorbed in Russia. Exceptions are Andrei Bitov's novel *Pushkin House* (even though the author always insisted that he wrote this book before reading Nabokov) and the works of Sasha Sokolov, whose *A School for Fools* was hailed by Nabokov as "an enchanting, tragic, and touching book."[29]

Khrushchev, who was one of Stalin's henchmen in repression, no longer desired to—or perhaps no longer could—act as his ruthless boss once did. Hence his anti-Stalinist speech and attempts at a Thaw. But he still wanted to maintain strict discipline. Any whiff of liberalism made Khrushchev nervous. He feared it would weaken the country in its struggle with the West, and suspected that the main sources of dangerous liberal ideas were the writers, poets, composers, and artists.

Unlike Stalin, Khrushchev was no fan of high culture, and his relationship with these people was colored by the inferiority complex of a poorly educated man. These prejudices, multiplied by Khrushchev's growing high-handedness, as he gradually freed himself of Stalin's humiliating superiority and became more comfortable as leader of the Communist world, were an emotional powder keg, ready to explode at any moment. All it needed was a match.

Many historians continue to assert that the match was always lit by others, that every time Khrushchev exploded (and there were many), it was the result of the sinister intrigues of his advisors, conservative writers and artists. Khrushchev, like all leaders of the Soviet state, including Stalin before him and Brezhnev after, was first of all a professional politician who did not trust anyone fully besides himself and who made all final decisions personally. It is doubtful that anyone could manipulate Khrushchev. But he skillfully simulated spontaneity and impulsiveness in his skirmishes with the intelligentsia.

The first time Khrushchev "lost it" publicly was during a meeting with writers at the Central Committee on May 13, 1957, when after a two-hour rambling speech he shouted at an elderly literary grande dame, Marietta Shaginyan, whose dogged questions about why meat was not available in the stores set him off (he was planning to announce in ten days' time his intention to surpass America in the production of meat, butter, and milk). At the second meeting with the cultural elite, on May 19, 1957, at a state dacha near Moscow, Khrushchev picked another woman as his main target, the poet Margarita Aliger.

Eyewitnesses describe him attacking the tiny, frail Aliger "with all the fire of an enraged drunk muzhik," yelling that she was a traitor. "When Aliger meekly disagreed, Khrushchev howled that she couldn't be an enemy, she was just a little bump in the road that he spat on, stomped on, and it was gone. Aliger burst into tears."[30]

Those present at this humiliating scene were terrified and sure that Aliger and the other writers Khrushchev had attacked that day would be arrested the very next morning. Even though arrests did not follow, we can assume that fear was exactly the effect the wily leader had wanted.

Khrushchev consciously built his political and cultural strategy in imitation of Stalin as a series of unpredictable zigzags: that was his brand tactics. He kept announcing that he was a Stalinist in cultural policy, then he would complain about the Stalinists who could not tolerate his struggle against Stalin's cult of personality, and then he would attack anti-Stalinist literature. The intelligentsia had to keep guessing what his intentions were. From time to time, he would produce some disorienting surprises.

One such mind-boggling bombshell was the highly publicized publication in November 1962 in *Novy Mir* (editor-in-chief, Alexander Tvardovsky) of *One Day in the Life of Ivan Denisovich*, the stunning novella about the Stalin concentration camps by a forty-four-year-old math schoolteacher from provincial Ryazan and a former prisoner, Aleksandr Solzhenitsyn. It was the first work on this banned topic printed in a Soviet magazine, and it would not have appeared without Khrushchev's personal approval. At the urging of Tvardovsky, whom he respected, Khrushchev decided to allow this novella to be published as the final chord of his anti-Stalin campaign, which had climaxed on October 31, 1961, with the removal of Stalin's embalmed body from the mausoleum on Red Square in Moscow, where it had been placed with Lenin's mummy in 1953.

Solzhenitsyn's story had been read aloud to Khrushchev by his aide in September 1962 while he was on vacation, and he liked it very much—it suited his current political plans. Khrushchev's unexpected verdict was: "This is a life-affirming work. I'll say even more—it's a Party work." And he added significantly that at the moment Solzhenitsyn's novella could be "useful."[31]

A few days after the magazine came out, there was a scheduled plenary session of the Central Committee, which brought the Party elite from all over the country. The Kremlin requested over two thousand copies of the magazine with *One Day in the Life of Ivan Denisovich* for the delegates. Tvardovsky, who participated in the plenum's work, recalled that when he saw the light blue cover of the magazine all over the auditorium of the Kremlin Palace of Congresses, his heart beat wildly.[32]

For Tvardovsky this was the high point of his sixteen-year tenure as head of *Novy Mir*, which in the Khrushchev era had become the center of the liberal forces in Russian literature. Three-time winner of the Stalin Prize (and under Khrushchev, the Lenin Prize), Tvardovsky underwent a remarkable evolution from loyal believer to protector of oppositionist voices, like Vladimir Voinovich and Georgy Vladimov. Tvardovsky was most proud of his discovery of Solzhenitsyn, especially dear to him because of his strong Russian roots, keen understanding of peasant psychology, traditional writing style, and stern character.

I was eighteen then, and I remember the general shock caused by *One Day in the Life of Ivan Denisovich*, both because it had been published at all and for its enormous artistic power. Its first readers encountered narrative mastery, amazing in a literary debut: without melodrama or stress, with deliberate restraint it told the story of just "one day," and far from the worst, in the life of one of the millions of Soviet prisoners, the peasant Ivan Shukhov, depicted through his peasant perceptions, his colorful but natural language, which elicited associations with Tolstoy's prose. This publication created in the intelligentsia a sense of unprecedented euphoria, which lasted, alas, just over a week.

On December 1, 1962, Khrushchev with his retinue of associates and sycophants made an unexpected visit to an exhibition at the Manege near Red Square that was dedicated to the thirtieth anniversary of the Moscow Artists' Union. Khrushchev was expected at the moment to support liberal trends in art, but instead he attacked the paintings he saw there by the patriarchs of Russian modernism, like Pavel Kuznetsov and Robert Falk, calling them "dog shit." He was particularly infuriated by the works of young Moscow avant-garde painters, mostly pupils of Eli Belyutin, which had been hastily delivered to the Manege the night before his visit, which later gave rise to completely understandable suppositions that Khrushchev's allegedly spontaneous reaction had been planned.

Just before that, in October, Khrushchev had had to back down in a confrontation with John F. Kennedy, removing the Soviet missiles in Cuba that were aimed at the Unites States. He was concerned that his reputation as a strong leader had suffered, and he wanted to show that he had the reins of power firmly in hand. The attack at the Manege was to be one of the proofs of his strength.

It became the stage for his famous discussion with Ernst Neizvestny, whose expressionistic sculpture of a woman prompted the Soviet leader to shout that if Neizvestny depicted women this way, he was a "fag," and "we give ten years for that." In response the stocky thirty-seven-year-old sculptor, a brave former soldier, demanded that they bring him a girl so he could prove otherwise. Khrushchev burst out laughing, but the KGB person who accompanied him threatened Neizvestny that rude talk with the boss could land him in a uranium mine.

Neizvestny tried arguing with Khrushchev, mentioning that Pablo Picasso was Communist, but the premier interrupted him: "I am Communist number one in the world, and I don't like your works," adding, "Don't you understand that all foreigners are enemies?"[33]

Neizvestny seemed like such a convenient target that Khrushchev continued mocking him two weeks later, on December 17, at a meeting of the Soviet leadership with the cultural elite at the House of Receptions in Lenin Hills, where he said publicly to the sculptor: "Here's what your art looks like: now if a man got into a toilet, got inside the bowl, and then looked up at what was above him if someone sat down on the seat, that would be your work!"[34]

It might be considered an irony of fate that when Khrushchev died in 1971, his headstone at the prestigious Novodevichy Cemetery was made by none other than Neizvestny. Even though the sculptor maintained that the commission had been in Khrushchev's will, in fact it was not: the decision was made by the Khrushchev family, and it hesitated between Neizvestny and Zurab Tsereteli, another rising star of the period in monumental sculpture. But Tsereteli got cold feet over the politically hazardous project.[35]

Now Neizvestny's most famous work, the headstone—a bronze head of Khrushchev on a background of intersecting chunks of white marble and black granite—symbolized in the sculptor's mind the struggle between the progressive and the reactionary in the Soviet leader's personality and work. It is possible that later generations will see one or the other as dominant.

Khrushchev's effectiveness was severely undermined in his last years in the Kremlin, and that was due in great part to his conflicts with the cultural elite: it set the tone, gradually inculcating the idea that Khrushchev was too unstable and unpredictable—in short, dangerous. This is clear from the reminiscences of filmmaker Mikhail Romm, in many ways a typical figure in Soviet culture. Romm was among the first laureates of the Stalin Prize for two of his quality films about Lenin, and then Stalin gave him three more awards for his anti-American propaganda films, also not badly done. In 1962, Romm made the classic Thaw film about a young scientist, *Nine Days of One Year*, and later, *Ordinary Fascism*, a documentary based on Nazi newsreels, whose hidden anti-

Stalinist parallels were eagerly read by Soviet intellectuals adept at understanding Aesopian language.

Romm started out as an ardent Khrushchevian. Even the young avant-garde poet Voznesensky admitted that then he considered Khrushchev "our hope."[36] The faith of Romm, Voznesensky, and many other cultural liberals was finally shattered on March 7, 1963, at another meeting of the Soviet leader with cultural figures, this time at the Kremlin. The irate premier created a scene that stunned everyone there. Khrushchev swore, yelled that for the enemy "we don't have a thaw but a fierce frost," "I'm for war in art," and "Mister Voznesensky, get out of our country, get out!"[37]

Voznesensky recalled that when Khrushchev screamed at him: "Agent! Agent!" he thought, "Well, he's calling in the agents, they'll take me away." Ilya Ehrenburg, who was in the audience and had been yelled at by Khrushchev, too, later asked the young poet, "How did you bear it? Anyone in your place could have had a heart attack. . . . You could have begged for mercy, fallen to your knees, and that would have been understandable."[38]

Yevtushenko, whose anti-Stalinist poem "The Heirs of Stalin" had appeared in *Pravda* some four months earlier, with Khrushchev's personal sanction, also admitted later, "It was pretty scary." As Romm remembered, Khrushchev frightened everyone when he suddenly asked menacingly, "What, do you think we've forgotten how to arrest people?"[39]

According to Romm, "After that surrealistic shouting, everything was topsy-turvy" for the guests at the Kremlin; many members of the elite who had previously been loyal to Khrushchev began to wonder whether this man could lead such an enormous country: "At some point his brakes failed, he went off the rails. . . . You could easily destroy all of Russia that way."[40]

Chapter Twelve

Khrushchev was ousted in October 1964 by his former acolytes inside the Party and replaced as leader of the country by Leonid Brezhnev, heavy-browed, tall, and friendly. He had a reputation as an experienced and reliable apparatchik, unlikely to improvise or heat up passions, and the news was greeted with relief and hope by many intellectuals. Even people who owed Khrushchev a lot personally, like Tvardovsky, Yevtushenko, and Solzhenitsyn, had grown weary of his policy zigzags.

In that sense Yuri Lyubimov's position was typical. A famous actor who was in the signal film of the Stalin era, *Cossacks of the Kuban* (1950, directed by Ivan Pyryev), Lyubimov received the Stalin Prize in 1952, and in 1964 unexpectedly (for everyone, probably himself included) became head of the experimental, politically bold Theater on the Taganka. Lyubimov admitted to me, "Well, without Khrushchev there wouldn't be a Taganka."[1] But the debut production, Bertolt Brecht's *Good Person of Szechwan,* already had a sarcastic poke at Khrushchev—the characters mispronounced "principles" in imitation of the Soviet leader.

Lyubimov went on: "Someone snitched that we were making fun of the leader. I was called in. That was my first explanation before the authorities, by the way. I was just starting out, and so I was very arrogant. So I said, 'Do you know who talks like that? Pretty illiterate people, that's who. . . . Let him learn to speak Russian properly!' "[2] Lyubimov, with his amazing sensitivity to political currents and flair for publicity (he liked to say that "If there's no scandal around the theater, it's no theater"), staked everything and won: while the authorities mulled over the proper punishment for the suddenly obstinate director, Khrushchev was replaced by Brezhnev, who remained well disposed toward the Taganka.

Lyubimov was always balancing on the edge between allowed and forbidden, often crossing the line. Using the long-suppressed and almost forgotten devices of the Russian avant-garde theater, Lyubimov created a politically charged theater with wide appeal. His enemies kept saying that he was merely an imitator of Yevgeny Vakhtangov, Tairov, and

Meyerhold: "We've been through that." Lyubimov's ready reply was: "Been through! You mean, you walked past it! You're stuck in the swamp of realism!"

Lyubimov was always something of an enigma, his jovial mask of a "wastrel" hiding a will of iron and endless ambition. For many years, he was considered an orthodox Communist (he even worked for a while as master of ceremonies in the dance ensemble of the NKVD, whose patron was the chief of secret police Lavrenti Beria) and a loyal follower of the Stanislavsky Method, and at the age of forty-five he suddenly threw off all that baggage. How did it happen? Lyubimov never bothered to explain.

His productions at the Taganka combined into one motley but effective whole Meyerhold's biomechanics, Vakhtangov's expressionist mise-en-scene, and Tairov's songs and pantomime meshed with circus, shadow theater, moving sets, and snatches of avant-garde music. The complex theatrical score that Lyubimov had in his head like an inspired conductor unfolded before astounded audiences, unused to such art, helping to deliver the dissident subtext that existed in almost every work he produced, be it a staging of John Reed's reportage about the Russian revolution, *Ten Days That Shook the World,* a montage of poems dear to Lyubimov's heart (by Voznesensky, Mayakovsky, or Yevtushenko), or an unorthodox *Hamlet* in Pasternak's translation.

The audiences took delight in unearthing all the director's hints. The authorities also understood that Lyubimov was playing cat and mouse with them, but how could they catch him out? They certainly tried. For instance, at the deliberations by the Moscow Culture Administration's acceptance committee over Lyubimov's production about Mayakovsky, the cultural bureaucrats were outraged that in the play Lenin "criticized the poet. And Lenin's text is disrespectfully pronounced through a window above which hangs the letter M, like over a toilet."[3]

Whenever the threat of a ban for "incorrect associations" hung over a production, Lyubimov managed to get through to the top, including Brezhnev and Yuri Andropov, and often they supported the director—to some extent. Since open political discussion was impossible, Lyubimov's theater had turned into an influential public forum, comparable to the early Moscow Art Theater of Stanislavsky and Nemirovich-Danchenko or Meyerhold's revolutionary theater.

The play *Anti-Worlds* was based on the poetry of Voznesensky and was performed almost a thousand times at the Taganka. The poet recalled that he had looked around at one of Lyubimov's premieres and saw "sitting in close proximity the out-of-favor Academician Sakharov, dissidents, Politburo member Dmitri Polyansky, a cosmonaut, an underground millionaire, a liberal Party apparatchik, social lionesses, and students rustling pages of samizdat."[4] Voznesensky maintained that many of the ideas of perestroika were born at Lyubimov's theater. It may be an exaggeration, but not a wild one.

The Taganka Theater's influence on a mass audience was increased many times over by the enormous popularity of its young leading actor, Vladimir Vysotsky. His fame, comparable only to Chaliapin's before the revolution, was not for his theater roles (even though he was an impressive Hamlet) but his songs, which he performed to his own guitar accompaniment, and of which there were several hundred.

Vysotsky, with his older contemporaries Bulat Okudzhava and Alexander Galich, created the phenomenon of *magnitizdat* (bootleg copies of banned music, on the analogy of *samizdat*) when the USSR began manufacturing tape recorders in the 1960s. The domestic unofficial chansonniers, who had no records and were not played on radio, much less television, and were only berated in the newspapers, were known as "bards," and hundreds of thousands of copies of their songs circulated throughout the Soviet Union. Some of them had more in common with their French brethren, for instance, the delicate and slightly sentimental Okudzhava, who continued the old tradition of Russian Gypsy romance and the best of Vertinsky on contemporary material, while Vysotsky was much more of a Soviet phenomenon.

Okudzhava had served in the front lines and he sang of war and love like a true Russian officer, with a shade of aristocratic nostalgia (even though he had joined the Party in 1956, in the period of Thaw hopes). Despite his dandyish mustache, he was no fop, nor did he drink much, unlike Galich and Vysotsky, who were alcoholics and drug users. But Galich was distinguished by a noble mien, unlike Okudzhava and Vysotsky, who seemed quite ordinary when not performing in their jackets with upturned collars, sometimes resembling sparrows with their feathers fluffed.

But once they had a guitar in their hands, Okudzhava and Vysotsky were instantly transformed. I heard both frequently, and every time I marveled at the metamorphosis: quiet Okudzhava, seemingly created for intimate singing in small cellars, held large audiences in sway with his sorrowful ballads; Vysotsky turned into a hoarsely shouting rock star with twisted mouth, sweaty brow, and taut neck tendons who could conquer the most reluctant audience.

The incredible fame of Vysotsky, Okudzhava, Galich, and a few other Russian bards never crossed beyond the borders of the Russian-language world. I remember persuading the *New York Times* rock critic to attend a Vysotsky concert in New York—he was baffled, finding the music and the performance primitive and the energy affected.

Okudzhava, with his refined balance between the slightly surreal lyrics and lilting melodies, made a better impression on the Western audiences. Still, he and the more political Galich remained purely Russian phenomena, and in the nation's collective consciousness, their best songs continue to resonate powerfully. Like Vertinsky's chansons, they are the diary of the twentieth-century Russian soul.

In the last third of the century Vysotsky was more popular in Russia than the Beatles and Elvis Presley combined. His songs were about athletes, soldiers, and criminals, and because of that many of his fans wrongly believed that Vysotsky had fought in a penal battalion and served time in a prison camp. He avoided openly political themes, unlike Galich, who was forced out of the country for his anti-Sovietism.

Galich's songs about winos, waitresses, prostitutes, and minor clerks continued the satirical tradition of Zoshchenko's stories, his characters having a lower social status and vocabulary than those in Okudzhava's songs. Vysotsky descended even lower, into the criminal underworld.

Prison-camp songs were popular in Russia back at the turn of the century. The new impulse for their dissemination came, paradoxically, from the lofty stage of the Moscow Art Theater's 1902 production of Gorky's *Lower Depths*, where a prison song, "The Sun Rises and Sets," was performed; afterward, thousands of gramophone records of this ballad were played in every corner of the empire.

In the Soviet period, the folklore of the criminal milieu went underground until the post-Stalin amnesties that freed huge numbers of inmates who injected prison camp culture into daily life. Vysotsky moved it to the center of the national discourse, even though officially it did not exist. He did it with the utmost conviction and seriousness, without a hint of condescension or commercialization, and that brought him wide-spread admiration, even as his songs made *The Lower Depths* look like nursery school.

Vysotsky, Okudzhava, and Galich outraged and delighted people on the left and the right. I remember the composer Vassily Solovyov-Sedoy, whose many hits include the ever-popular "Moscow Nights," frothing at the mouth as he denounced Vysotsky as an immoral author who cor-rupted Soviet youth. Okudzhava was also seen by the authorities as an individualist, dangerous for Soviet morality, and Galich as openly anti-Soviet, but Vysotsky's message bordered on anarchy. The official poet Yevgeny Dolmatovsky was direct: "Make no mistake: that's not a guitar in his hands but a terrible weapon."[5]

That is why the death and funeral of Vysotsky at age forty-two in 1980—he was destroyed by alcohol and drugs—turned into a political event on a national scale, comparable to the funerals of Leo Tolstoy, Esenin, and Pasternak. Despite the total information vacuum, tens of thousands of people bearing flowers and guitars and playing the singer's tapes came to the Taganka Theater, where the coffin was arranged for a viewing. People wept. The theater canceled the performance of *Hamlet,* starring Vysotsky, and offered money back to ticket-holders; no one returned a single ticket. Busloads of police pulled up to the square in front of the theater. Tension ran high. It is a miracle that there was no fatal crush like the one during Stalin's funeral.

July 28, 1980, will be one of those milestones in Russian history mark-ing the division, mutual lack of understanding, and deeply rooted dis-trust between the masses and the Soviet regime in the post-Khrushchev era. The fact that even after his death Vysotsky did not get recognition as a national singer, even though everyone from Siberian workers to Polit-buro members hummed his songs, evinced the immobile and ossified nature of the official ideology and cultural policy.

The myth about Brezhnev is that he was a mediocre politician pushed around by his aides and advisors. That image was basically the result of efforts by Khrushchev's team, who tried to spin a new historical narrative in the years of Gorbachev's glasnost: revenge for the defeat of their old boss. It is unlikely that Brezhnev was less of a master politician than

Khrushchev, otherwise he would not have lasted eighteen years in power (seven more than Khrushchev).

Brezhnev was not stupider than Khrushchev, but he was significantly more cautious and guarded. After Khrushchev's removal, the question of expanding cultural freedom was debated in an inner Party circle, and Brezhnev expressed his sympathy for the idea, adding that it was embarrassing to see Khrushchev yelling at artists and writers. The ladies' man Brezhnev was particularly upset at the ruthless treatment of the poet Margarita Aliger.

Brezhnev announced then that he wanted to establish "confidential relations" with the intelligentsia.[6] In 1964, a new film appeared in Soviet film theaters by the young director Elem Klimov. *Welcome, or No Admittance* was a sharp satire on Soviet society, depicted as a Pioneer summer camp, where the children are brainwashed, driving out all traces of independence, and turned into tiny mean-spirited robots.

The film was topical, because it was seen as a mockery of Khrushchev (the director of the camp, comically arrogant, kept trying to push corn on everyone, as did the former Soviet leader). The talented Klimov managed to catch the wave of change, because his father held a high position in the Party apparatus. At the time, the joke about him was: "It's handy to be a lefty when you have support from the right."

But his next comedy, *Adventures of a Dentist,* created serious problems for him with the authorities. It was an allegory about the place of talent in the Soviet Union, with a screenplay by Alexander Volodin, perhaps the most Chekhovian Russian playwright of the second half of the century.

Volodin, a strange, shy, and hard-drinking man who seemed to come out of a Chekhov story, went into film because his plays—*Factory Girl* and *Big Sister*—were attacked as "slander of Soviet life." His play *Five Evenings* (and I still remember Georgi Tovstonogov's 1959 deeply moving production at the Leningrad Bolshoi Dramatic Theater) was characterized as "spiteful barking from an alleyway," and the main charge against his popular *The Appointment,* produced by Efremov at the Sovremennik Theater, was that it "hammered a wedge between the people and the government."[7]

Misfortune followed Volodin in his move to film: the censors were reluctant to release *Adventures of a Dentist* because, allegedly, "everything in the film is upside down. In our society the *individual* is responsible to the society, but you have the *society* responsible before the individual."[8] With the help of his mentor, Mikhail Romm (and his father's connections), Klimov managed to get the film approved, but it was shown in very few theaters and hushed up. Klimov made no more comedies. In the West he would be known subsequently for his epic narrative about the fall of the Russian monarchy, *Agony*, and the violent antiwar film, *Come and See*.

Volodin once wrote perceptively about the Theater on Taganka: "Lyubimov hated the authorities and he did not hide it. . . . But he dressed his anger in such festive, fantastically inventive theatrical clothes that sometimes even the authorities wanted to think that his allusions were not to them."[9] In 1968, when Lyubimov was fired and expelled from the Party for yet another "slanderous" production, he wrote a letter to Brezhnev, who responded with the resolution, "Let him work," thereby reprieving the death sentence given to the theater by Minister of Culture Ekaterina Furtseva. As Lyubimov recalled, he was also immediately reinstated in the Party: "Sorry, we got overexcited."[10]

According to his aides, Brezhnev unlike Stalin had no great love for fiction or nonfiction, limiting his reading to newspapers and popular magazines, and his preferred films were nature documentaries. He was bored by serious feature films, although he liked, and shed a tear over, Andrei Smirnov's *Belorussian Station* (1971), a sentimental story of four former soldiers, which premiered Okudzhava's song "We Won't Stand for the Price," one of the best about World War II.

But Brezhnev could astound his entourage when he was General Secretary of the Central Committee of the Party by reciting a long poem by Symbolist classic Dmitri Merezhkovsky, or the poems of Esenin.[11] These works had been banned under Stalin, but as a young man Brezhnev had dreamed of becoming an actor and had performed with one of the many amateur theater groups popular in the early years of the revolution— whence his unorthodox poetic interests. Until his illness, Brezhnev liked to affect people emotionally. Once, in a moment of frankness, he told an aide that he considered his charm an important political tool.[12]

The culmination of Brezhnev's artistic ambitions was the publication in 1978 of his memoir trilogy: *Small Land, Resurrection*, and *Virgin Soil*. Naturally, the books were written by literary ghosts, paid by state funds—there is nothing unusual about that or the fact that despite their more than modest literary qualities, Brezhnev's books were published in printings of millions: after all, these were the memoirs of the leader of one of the two superpowers.

But his works, besides being made mandatory reading for the public and Party members especially, were praised as unsurpassed master-pieces in numerous reviews by leading writers, were given the Lenin Prize for literature, and their author was accepted into the Writers' Union with membership card No. 1. Films were hastily made based on the memoirs, plays written and oratorios composed; at the Tretyakov Gallery, the finest museum of Russian art, *Small Land,* a large painting by Dmitri Nalbandyan, a Soviet court painter since the Stalin days, depicted Brezhnev as one of the main heroes of World War II.

A popular joke of the time had Brezhnev telephoning members of the Politburo to get their opinions of his books; they, naturally, were unani-mous in their praise, and Brezhnev then wondered, "Everyone likes them. Maybe I should read them, too?" There is a transcript of a Politburo meeting on April 13, 1978, when Brezhnev, speaking of the publication of the first part of his memoirs, says that in meeting with leading officials, military men, and other comrades he was told that his books are extremely useful in bringing up the people.[13]

Brezhnev probably also enjoyed the fact his work had finally upstaged Khrushchev, whose "illegal" memoirs were published to great publicity in the West in 1970–1974 and declared "forgeries" in the Soviet Union. (Khrushchev's memoirs, like Brezhnev's, were taped and edited by others.)

Despite Brezhnev's personal benevolence, softheartedness, and even sentimentality, culture came under increasing pressure in his regime. The signals from above were mixed, like Khrushchev's. In the same month, September 1965, Leningrad poet Joseph Brodsky was released early from his exile in the North, where he had been sentenced in the last year of Khrushchev's rule to five years of forced labor for "parasitism" (fighting which was one of Khrushchev's favorite ideas), and the writers Andrei Sinyavsky and Yuli Daniel were arrested. Their crime was the publication in the West of anti-Soviet satirical prose. They apparently used Pasternak as a model, but unlike him, they hid behind the pseudonyms Abram Terts and Nikolai Arzhak, which the KGB eventually uncovered.

Pasternak had only been threatened with arrest and trial, but the authorities decided to go ahead with Sinyavsky and Daniel. Brezhnev with Petr Demichev, then ideology secretary of the Central Committee, made a special visit to Konstantin Fedin, head of the Writers' Union, for approval of these sanctions, reminiscent of Stalin's repression. Fedin, once a talented prose writer and favorite of Gorky's, had become totally ossified over the years, and it goes without saying that, flattered by the attention, he approved.

Under Brezhnev, cultural issues moved mostly into the supervision of apparatchiks; the general secretary rarely interfered in cultural affairs, usually only when he wanted to give an award to a favorite film actor.

The day-to-day work in the area was left to Furtseva (Minister of Culture between 1960 and 1974) and Demichev (Minister of Culture 1974 to 1986). The conservative Demichev was rather colorless; there were many colorful but unsubstantiated stories about Furtseva, a strong personality: that she had been Khrushchev's mistress, that she was an alcoholic, that she had slit her wrists after a Party demotion in 1961, and that she committed suicide by taking cyanide in 1974.

The work of both ministers was supervised and controlled in many ways by two much more influential figures—Politburo member Mikhail Suslov, who was in charge of ideology since the Khrushchev years and known as the Party's gray cardinal for his backstage machinations, and Andropov, who headed the KGB for fifteen years and became the country's leader after Brezhnev's death in 1982.

Tall, thin, and pale, Suslov was a Party ascetic, who dressed modestly and wore old-fashioned galoshes until his death in 1982. Andropov, who ostensibly loved jazz, whiskey, and Jacqueline Susann novels, was smart and personable. The two seemed polar opposites. But they were similar in believing in Communism and the primacy of Party ideology over culture and behaved accordingly. The decision to arrest and try Sinyavsky and Daniel had been prepared by these men, who felt that the intelligentsia was getting out of hand again and needed to be brought to heel. And once again, it led to unexpected results.

The arrest of Sinyavsky and Daniel itself was a warning, as the authorities had intended; at that moment people seriously feared that the two writers might be executed for their "subversive" works, already translated into many languages. It soon became clear that accused were no longer tortured behind bars, they were not beaten during questioning, and apparently they were in no danger of a death sentence. The trial was going to be open. This reflected the new tactics of the regime, intended to prove the guilt of Sinyavsky and Daniel strictly within the post-Stalinist "socialist legality" so that both Soviet intellectuals and the liberal West would be satisfied.

The defendants, Sinyavsky, of medium height, bearded, and cross-eyed, and Daniel, stoop-shouldered, black-haired, and charmingly talkative, did not repent. They quickly earned the sympathy of the skeptical Western journalists who flocked around the Moscow courthouse. Foreigners were not admitted into the courtroom, but when the defendants' wives came out during recess, they were ready to talk openly and give interviews to the Western press—for the first time in Soviet history.

Close contact was thus forged between Soviet cultural dissidents and the Western media. It was a historic breakthrough, which led directly to the daily dramatic reports on the Sinyavsky-Daniel trial on radio stations that broadcast to the Soviet Union.

The names of the disobedient writers became widely known; I remember a friend bringing an hour-long compilation he had taped of reports from Voice of America, the BBC, and Deutsche Welle to my dormitory at Leningrad Conservatory. We had the chance to hear the witty writings of the banned authors, because the radio broadcast excerpts from them.

Following the trial on a transistor radio in his village "hide-out" near Obninsk, Solzhenitsyn was working on *Gulag Archipelago*, which he defined as "an experiment in literary investigation" of the Soviet camp system. In his diary he noted that the "progressive West" had previously forgiven the Soviet Union for its cruel treatment of writers, but this time was upset over Sinyavsky and Daniel—"a sign of the times." The West was outraged by the sentence: seven years in hard-regime camps for Sinyavsky and five for Daniel.

But in the Soviet Union there were notables who were not ashamed to hail it; Sholokhov famously declared: "If those guys with black consciences had been caught in the memorable twenties, when trials did not depend on the strictly defined articles of the Criminal Code but were 'based on revolutionary righteousness,' oh, those werewolves wouldn't have gotten off so easily! But here, you see, there are complaints about the 'severity' of the sentence."[14]

Western radio stations carried news of a letter in defense of Sinyavsky and Daniel signed by sixty-two Soviet writers. Solzhenitsyn did not join them: "It is not fitting for a Russian writer to seek fame abroad." (That was how Maria Rozanova, Sinyavsky's wife, conveyed his explanation to me.) But by that time, Solzhenitsyn had, albeit with "bated heartbeat," smuggled out the manuscript of his novel *The First Circle*, and in 1968–1969 this novel and the other, *Cancer Ward*, which Solzhenitsyn could not get published in the USSR, either, came out in the West.

The appearance of these "polyphonic" (his term) works about the Stalin era suddenly made Solzhenitsyn, who had just turned fifty, a real candidate for the Nobel Prize. The action of *The First Circle* took place in a secret research institute for prisoner scientists, a *sharashka*, and *Cancer Ward* was set in a hospital—both autobiographical and at the same time symbolic.

Solzhenitsyn had proved to the Western cognoscenti that he was not a one-work wonder whose fame rested only on the political sensation caused by *One Day in the Life of Ivan Denisovich*. Now there was a mature master working in the best traditions of the great Russian novel and holding an independent position vis-à-vis the hostile Communist establishment.

The belligerent Soviet empire armed with nuclear weapons seemed a mysterious and ominous monolith to the West, so the smallest manifestations of contrary thought within Soviet society were regarded with lively interest. Even the timid desire for liberalization among Soviet intellectuals was hailed by their Western colleagues, because it gave them hope of moving the Soviet Union toward greater transparency and "normalcy." The post-Stalinist Communist leadership had offered the slogan of "peaceful coexistence" for socialism and capitalism, but still forcefully rejected coexistence in ideology, which increased the jitters in Europe and America about the reliability and stability of détente between East and West.

Hence, the arrival of a figure like Solzhenitsyn on the Soviet cultural scene was a gift for the West. Solzhenitsyn combined several attractive qualities: an enormous talent who presented the bitter truth about Soviet life, he wrote not from secondhand accounts but as a fearless eye-

witness using his own tragic experience as an inmate in a Stalin concentration camp. His future adversary, the satirist Vladimir Voinovich,
summed up the perception of Solzhenitsyn at that time: "He writes
beautifully, his behavior is valorous, his judgments independent, he does
not bow down to authority or fold before danger, he is always prepared
to sacrifice himself."[15]

The tall, broad-shouldered, blue-eyed Solzhenitsyn, with his memorable Nordic face, made a powerful impression. Akhmatova, not given to
raptures, was astounded after he visited her: "Fresh, smart, young, merry.
We had forgotten that such people exist. His eyes were like precious
stones." She concluded solemnly: "A bearer of light."[16]

According to Voinovich, that was when photos of Solzhenitsyn began
appearing on bookshelves of liberal Muscovites, moving aside pictures
of previous idols Pasternak and Hemingway. "Solzhenitsyn was persecuted and in great danger, so every holder of his portrait was not only
expressing his admiration for him but also demonstrating his own
courage."[17]

Solzhenitsyn, along with Andrei Sakharov, was the undisputed leader
of Soviet dissidents, undermining the authority of the state. This gave
rise to the Solzhenitsyn legend, which was created simultaneously by
various sides: the writer himself; the authorities, who only strengthened
his reputation by persecuting him; the growing circle of his supporters
and admirers inside the country; and the Western media. Voinovich said,
"In those days, whatever Western station you could tune to, Solzhenitsyn was the main story."

The legend acquired its final form when Solzhenitsyn was awarded
the Nobel Prize for Literature in October 1970: the culmination of at least
a quarter century of stubborn, one might even say fanatical, pursuit of
that goal. He had first thought about getting the Nobel when he was a
prisoner in the camps and heard of its existence, before he had published
a single line. That must be a unique example in the prize's history.

We know about the passions that consumed Solzhenitsyn, because he
described them in his remarkable autobiographical book *The Oak and the
Calf*. Probably no other Nobel laureate has revealed his emotions and his
strategy that frankly. Solzhenitsyn had decided to go for it from the start:
"Something in the spirit of our country, totally political: that is what I

need for my future Breakthrough." The Nobel was to become a weapon in Solzhenitsyn's hands.

Even as a provincial math teacher in 1958, Solzhenitsyn was passionate about Pasternak. Sitting in Ryazan, Solzhenitsyn imagined Pasternak traveling from Moscow to Stockholm and making a fiery anti-Soviet speech that "would change the entire world."

Given his temperament and prison savvy, Solzhenitsyn could not imagine that Pasternak would take a pass and refuse both the prize and the opportunity to burst onto the political stage. "I measured him by my goals, by my standards—and I cringed in shame for him. . . . No, we were hopeless!"[18] Solzhenitsyn decided on a strategy of active lobbying, which succeeded beyond anyone's wildest dreams: the Swedish Academy crowned the writer a mere eight years after his very first publication—an unprecedented event in the annals of the Nobel Prize.

Solzhenitsyn received it "for the ethical force with which he has pursued the indispensable traditions of Russian literature." This accolade underscored the view that Solzhenitsyn was working in the Tolstoyan tradition—the one that the Swedish Academy had found unacceptable at the dawn of the century. Subsequently, the Swedes evaluated Bunin, Gorky, Pasternak, Sholokhov, and Nabokov in terms of their adherence to the Tolstoyan line: the writers who were deemed to be close to it were rewarded, the others rejected. While the recognition of Sholokhov was seen by many as a concession to Soviet pressure, the Swedes particularly appreciated Pasternak and Solzhenitsyn for their Christian values.

Soviet reaction to Solzhenitsyn's award was totally predictable: in its top secret memorandum sent to the Central Committee, the KGB reported that "with this act the West has paid for Solzhenitsyn's 'political contributions.' "[19]

Through diplomatic channels, the Kremlin began pressuring the Swedish government to distance itself from the decision of the Swedish Academy; this time, the politicians held firm. As mentioned before, Solzhenitsyn observed: "Even though the Swedish Academy was always being accused of *politics,* it was *our* barking voices that made any other assessment impossible."

Andropov, by then chairman of the KGB, was the first to bring up the idea of "pushing out" Solzhenitsyn from the Soviet Union, which was then bandied about for the next three and a half years at Politburo meetings run by Brezhnev. The transcripts of these meetings, declassified in 1994 by Boris Yeltsin, make for entertaining reading, and it makes clear that the Politburo and Solzhenitsyn belonged on different planets.

In his "Letter to the Soviet Leaders," which Solzhenitsyn sent to Brezhnev on September 5, 1973, he proposed an ambitious program to save the country from what he saw as the looming catastrophes: war with Communist China and a global economic crisis due to a depletion of natural resources or overproduction. As a means of avoiding these mortal dangers, Solzhenitsyn recommended discarding Marxist ideology and the policy of excessive industrialization and returning to traditional values.

"Letter to the Soviet Leaders" is an amazing document: the first and probably the most impressive realization of Solzhenitsyn's maxim that the writer is a second government. Concise but saturated with information and clearly formulated global ideas, this memorandum could be the result of many years of study by some think tank, with the difference that Solzhenitsyn's text, presented in a compact form with urgency and passion, is also dynamic prose comparable to the antigovernmental declarations of Leo Tolstoy. (Solzhenitsyn's 1974 appeal "Live Not By Lies!" belongs to the Tolstoyan line, as well, being a call to ideological disobedience, directly oriented on Tolstoy's comparable ideas at the turn of the century.)

The eschatological prophecy of "Letter to the Leaders" has not yet come to pass, although at the time and subsequently, similar ideas were the subject of lively debate among the world intellectual elite. But Brezhnev and his colleagues would not consider discussing Solzhenitsyn's proposals, seeing nothing but "delirium" in his appeal.

In a separate letter to Brezhnev, Solzhenitsyn expressed the hope that the ruler, "as a simple Russian man with a lot of common sense," could accept his conclusions. And here Solzhenitsyn was wrong: for Brezhnev and his cohort, the writer was not a legitimate opponent but simply the "scum of society," by chance elevated by Khrushchev, whom they hated.

Andropov took a particularly intransigent position toward Solzhenitsyn. Rumors (probably originating in the KGB) made Andropov out to be a tolerant and quite progressive person. His dealings with the dissidents showed he was nothing of the sort. In his speeches at the Politburo and in his memoranda, Andropov insisted that by remaining in the

Soviet Union as an "internal émigré," a useful position for him, Solzhenitsyn was turning into an opposition leader. In a special personal letter
to Brezhnev dated February 7, 1974, Andropov expressed his concern that
Solzhenitsyn's ideas in his "Letter to the Soviet Leaders" were spreading
among workers and students, while earlier at a Politburo meeting he
warned that the writer could find support among tens of thousands of
"hostile elements" inside the Soviet Union.[20] After the KGB found and
confiscated the manuscript of his magnum opus, *The Gulag Archipelago,*
which the writer had been carefully hiding, Andropov's anti-
Solzhenitsyn rhetoric turned hysterical.

The work, written in 1964–1968, was unprecedented in scope, com-
pleteness, and vividness of description of the system of Soviet camps.
Dostoevsky's *The House of the Dead* (1860–1862) and Chekhov's *Sakhalin
Island* (1893–1895) were remarkable books, and they dramatically brought
to the attention of the Russian public the failures of the penitentiary system. But they did not have the great political impact of Solzhenitsyn's
work.

Only a future history, detailed and objective, documenting the creation of *The Gulag Archipelago* will be able to explain how Solzhenitsyn's
many years of labor on this monumental opus, which used not only his
own camp experiences but the reminiscences, stories, and letters of at
least another two hundred people, had gone unnoticed by the "all-
seeing and all-hearing" KGB, which only caught on, according to declassified documents, in August 1973.

When the KGB did learn of the work, Andropov's reaction was: "*The
Gulag Archipelago* is not a work of art, but a political document. This is
dangerous." His opinion was supported by Brezhnev. "This is a crude
anti-Soviet lampoon. . . . the hooligan Solzhenitsyn has gotten out of
hand . . . He has attacked the holy of holies, Lenin, our Soviet system,
everything that we hold dear."[21]

After vacillating for a rather long time, Brezhnev at last sanctioned
Solzhenitsyn's arrest. On February 12, 1974, the writer was charged with
treason and taken to Lefortovo Prison in Moscow, where he had already
spent 1945 and 1946. Solzhenitsyn, as he later recalled, was prepared for
the worst—even execution. But unexpectedly for him and the Western
media, which had speedily covered the sensational news of his arrest, he
was released the next day, stripped of his Soviet citizenship by special
decree, and placed on a charter flight to Frankfurt-am-Main. (As it was

later revealed, this came as the result of secret negotiations between cunning Andropov and German chancellor Willy Brandt.)

From West Germany, Solzhenitsyn went to Zurich and then to the United States, where he settled with his family in the small town of Cavendish, Vermont. This was the start of the twenty-year exile of the most famous and influential Russian writer of the late twentieth century.

Part Five

A TIME OF CHANGES

Chapter Thirteen

The authorities were sure that they were making a clever move in the cultural cold war by expelling Solzhenitsyn from the USSR. Brezhnev and Andropov obviously borrowed the idea of forcing political opponents out of the country from Lenin, who in 1922 had a large group of prominent intellectuals forcibly sent to the West, announcing, "We will purge Russia for a long time."[1]

Lenin's ideas were always considered the highest form of wisdom in the post-Stalin Soviet Union, besides which, in this given situation, from a purely political point of view, Lenin's solution was not at all stupid. The Russian antirevolutionary émigrés never managed to organize themselves into an effective political force.

General Dmitri Volkogonov studied the Soviet secret archives that were opened for him (and remain closed to this day for others), containing the innumerable reports by Bolshevik agents from Paris, Berlin, and other Western capitals and he concluded that the Soviet secret police succeeded in neutralizing the émigré community by "doing everything possible to 'corrupt' it through discrediting, bribing people to spy, and pitting factions against one another."[2]

According to Volkogonov, there was close surveillance on almost every famous Russian émigré: "Numerous special dossiers were kept to record every notable public step of the person, his statements and moods."[3] In the archives of the Foreign Directorate of OGPU, Volkogonov found reports on the writers, poets, and philosophers who had settled in the West—Zinaida Hippius and Merezhkovsky, Balmont, Mark Aldanov, Nabokov, Berdyaev, Georgy Fedotov, and many others. They even kept watch over the composer Igor Stravinsky and the ballerina Mathilde Kschessinska, the former mistress of the last Russian tsar, Nicholas II.

Andropov, who valued the early Bolshevik experience and had carefully studied the secret dossiers and the history of the KGB, which he headed, had apparently been eager to apply the Leninist methods of fighting ideological foes. When the West increased pressure on the USSR in the early 1970s about free emigration, the Soviet leadership decided to make some concessions, but placed the process under tight control.

Indeed, they permitted only Jewish and German emigration, which might not seem much. But for the first time in many years, thousands of people started leaving the Soviet Union on their own volition and legally. The majority of them belonged to the educated classes.

Among those who ended up in the West one way or another in the following years were a number of major cultural figures who "disturbed the peace" and whom the authorities decided to get rid of: the poets Joseph Brodsky and Alexander Galich; the writers Vladimir Maximov, Andrei Sinyavsky, Viktor Nekrasov, Vassily Aksyonov, Vladimir Voinovich, and Georgy Vladimov; the musicians Mstislav Rostropovich and his wife, Galina Vishnevskaya, and Rudolf Barshai; the sculptor Ernst Neizvestny; and the artists Oskar Rabin, Mikhail Chemiakin, and Oleg Tselkov.

Some cultural stars defected: the dancers Rudolf Nureyev, Natalya Makarova, Mikhail Baryshnikov, and Alexander Godunov; the pianist Vladimir Ashkenazy; the conductors Kirill Kondrashin and Maxim Shostakovich; the film director Andrei Tarkovsky; and head of the Moscow Theater on the Taganka Yuri Lyubimov.

Apparently the Soviets believed that once these irritants found themselves abroad and the first wave of heightened media interest in them subsided, they would lose their authority, which was based on being insiders, and their influence would come to naught, both in the Soviet Union and in the West.

The Soviets based their prognosis on the experience of the earlier waves of immigration: the "White," after the revolution, and the "displaced persons," after World War II. Even though they were much more numerous, they eventually dissolved into the countries where they settled and by the 1970s no longer posed a threat to the Soviet regime and Party ideology.

Moreover, the Communist apparatchiks developed quite cordial relations with some of the émigrés of the first two waves; they were permitted to come as tourists and even on business to the homeland, a privilege that the new immigrants could not even dream about. The departure of the latter was seen by everyone—the regime, the immigrants, and their relatives and friends who stayed behind—as "permanent" exile. When one of the friends seeing off Brodsky said, "Till we meet again," the customs guards corrected him: "It's 'good-bye.' "[4]

Solzhenitsyn may have been the only one to repeat stubbornly that he was certain of his return to Russia. The first volume of his *Gulag Archipelago*, published in the West in 1973, became an international best seller and was a powerful political statement that opened the eyes of the world to the repressive nature of the Soviet regime.

Some say that *The Gulag Archipelago* was not the first description of the Communist camp system to appear in the West, but that Solzhenitsyn was helped by felicitous timing: by the early 1970s the Western intellectual community was becoming disillusioned with the Communist experiment. In this case it would be difficult to distinguish the cause from the effect: did the change in the political climate make possible the rapturous reception for Solzhenitsyn and his writing, or did his work and activities accomplish an ideological breakthrough unseen since Tolstoy's time?

Some of his critics, like Voinovich, deny the literary value of *The Gulag Archipelago*. One can argue about the artistic merits of any politically motivated work, even Dostoevsky's *The Devils* or Tolstoy's *Resurrection*. *The Gulag Archipelago* belongs to a select company of landmark books, whose overwhelming effect on contemporaries depends as much on their strong artistic qualities (Solzhenitsyn used new, dense, expressive language and a new type of quasi-realistic narrative that was noted even by Brodsky, who was not a great admirer of Solzhenitsyn) as on the author's powerful personality and the special political circumstances in which the book appears.

In memoranda to the Central Committee after Solzhenitsyn's expulsion, the KGB concluded with obviously premature glee that the noise around the writer's expulsion and publication of volume one of *The Gulag Archipelago* was quieting down and "the opinion is more frequently expressed that Solzhenitsyn as an émigré will have a very difficult time preserving 'the glory of a great writer.' "[5]

Andropov's agency had overestimated the perspicacity and effectiveness of its methods of combatting dissent. True, the exile of Solzhenitsyn and other prominent dissidents and emigration in general had let off some steam from Soviet society. But this was a short-term effect; in the long run, moving all those people abroad had created the worst threat possible for a totalitarian system—a cultural alternative.

.   .   .

For a long time the authorities could label any manifestation of cultural independence "anti-Soviet." This tactic intimidated people from sympathizing with nonconformist ideas, and it worked domestically and in the West.

The émigrés hastened the process of transforming the binary opposition "Soviet/anti-Soviet" into a ternary system with a new element, "non-Soviet." This development, which began inconspicuously back in the mid-1950s, gave rise to several important figures, among them the film director Andrei Tarkovsky, the poet Joseph Brodsky, and the composer Alfred Schnittke.

The three are rarely grouped together, yet they had much in common, beyond the obvious differences. As far as I know, they had never collaborated, although Schnittke (who wrote scores for dozens of films and worked with the best directors of Tarkovsky's generation—Andrei Mikhalkov-Konchalovsky, Elem Klimov, Larissa Shepitko, and Alexander Mitta) once used Brodsky poems as a sort of phonetic layer in his short piano cycle "Aphorisms" (1990).

It is interesting that all three were "infected" by the West from childhood, by its culture and lifestyle, even though their family backgrounds differed. The oldest was Tarkovsky, born in 1932; Schnittke was two years younger, and Brodsky, eight. But Tarkovsky and Brodsky both were *stilyagi*: they loved to wear elegant Western clothes (even though they didn't have the money for it) and sit in fashionable cafés, sipping cocktails and listening to Western music, primarily jazz (later they both developed a love of Bach and Haydn).

Their longing for the West was influenced by literature and movies. (Brodsky always spoke of his admiration for American films, especially the Tarzan series.) Only Schnittke got to spend some time as a youth in the real Europe: in 1946 his father, a military interpreter and Party member, was sent to Vienna, where he worked for two years on a propaganda newspaper published in the Soviet occupation zone. Vienna had a magical effect on the provincial twelve-year-old boy from the Volga, and he described this as the "best time" of his life.[6]

Of the three, only Alfred was a diligent student; he was in the top of his class in grade school, music school, and the Moscow Conservatory, where he, like his classmate Sofia Gubaidulina, won the Stalin scholarship (a high honor indeed). Tarkovsky, rather short and with a chip on his shoulder, was a bad student and a troublemaker; red-haired and importunate Brodsky dropped out in eighth grade, where his formal education ended. Tarkovsky and Brodsky both found work in geological expeditions, wandering around the Siberian taiga. The expeditions attracted déclassé elements, hoboes, and adventurers, but also future poets. For Tarkovsky this period was "the best memory" of his life, as he later insisted; Brodsky recalled his geological work (they were searching for uranium) rather skeptically.

Cultural education in the USSR from the purely professional point of view was always highly effective, despite the required courses on Marxism-Leninism, which, in fact, talented students were permitted to ignore. The conservatories, still based on solid, prerevolutionary traditions, were particularly good. They graduated highly skilled performers, the best of which easily won the most prestigious international competitions. They also gave thorough grounding for composers. If a student demonstrated talent, the road to the Composers' Union, which conferred substantial privileges, was open.

The same held for the Moscow All-Union State Institute of Cinematography (VGIK). The Moscow Literary Institute, which prepared (as it does to this day) diploma-bearing writers, poets, and translators, was more hard-line. But even there, a "good fairy" could help out a student: in 1952, at the height of Stalinism, the Literary Institute accepted Yevtushenko, even though he had been expelled from school (on charges of vandalism and hooliganism) and did not have the required diploma.

Brodsky did not have influential mentors like Yevtushenko did; the way to the Literary Institute was closed to him. He became an autodidact. But Tarkovsky and Schnittke received the best professional education, and for free.

There is a legend that in 1954 when the venerable Mikhail Romm went "upstairs" for approval for the freshmen he had selected for his course on directing, he was told that two of the candidates would not be accepted at VGIK: Tarkovsky and Vassily Shukshin, who became a film actor, director, and writer, and the best-known representative of the "village" school in Russian culture of the 1960s and 1970s.

A secretive Siberian peasant, Shukshin showed up for the oral admissions examinations in a striped navy shirt (he had just been demobilized), and he did not please the high cinema board with his alleged lack of education ("He's a total ignoramus, he doesn't even know who Leo Tolstoy is!"). The dandified Tarkovsky, on the contrary, struck them as being "too smart."[7] But Romm knew how to get what he wanted, and both the *stilyaga* Tarkovsky and Shukshin, who proudly showed off his calluses, were accepted (and disliked each other instantly), going to the top of their class at VGIK.

Tarkovsky, like Schnittke, graduated from his school with honors. Tarkovsky was immediately hired as a director at Mosfilm, and Schnittke, after graduate school, went on to teach at the Moscow Conservatory. Schnittke was also accepted at the Composers' Union, and started moving up the ladder there: he became a member of the board and was even groomed to become one of the secretaries, an important bureaucratic position.

Yet the first performed works by Schnittke—Violin Concerto No. 1 and the *Nagasaki* Oratorio (about the Japanese city hit by U.S. atom bomb)—while basically well received (Shostakovich and Georgy Sviridov were among his admirers), did not cause the sensation created by Tarkovsky's first full-length film, *Ivan's Childhood,* made on a shoestring budget in five months in 1961.

Introducing *Ivan's Childhood* to its first audience at Dom Kino, the Cinematographer Union's club in Moscow, Tarkovsky's visibly nervous teacher Romm said, "Friends, today you will see something extraordinary, nothing like this has appeared on our screens before." The influential critic Maya Turovskaya recalled, "Two hours later we came out of the theater—agitated, bewildered, still not knowing whether to berate the filmmaker for that confusion or to set aside our usual perceptions and accept the strange world that had appeared and vanished on the screen."[8]

In Tarkovsky's hands, the banal plot (a teenage army scout heroically sacrifices himself during World War II) was transformed into an existential parable, receiving high praise from Jean-Paul Sartre and in 1962 winning the Gold Lion of St. Mark at the Venice Film Festival. Venice made Tarkovsky famous at thirty.

The black-and-white *Ivan's Childhood,* which subtly blurs the lines between reality, dream, and memory, is arguably Tarkovsky's most perfect work. But his most famous film is *Andrei Rublev,* an epic narrative of more than three hours about the great monk icon painter of the fifteenth century. No one had attempted a project as ambitious as this since

Eisenstein's day, but Tarkovsky was then the darling of the cinemato-graphic establishment, so they gave him what he needed, 1,250,000 rubles.

Rublev, like Ivan's Childhood, was made in record time—filming began in mid-1965 and ended in November, and despite the later legend, the bureaucrats accepted it with a cheer. The film was headed for Cannes when, as Tarkovsky told it, a denunciation from the influential film director Sergei Gerasimov led the Party culture curator Demichev to bring back Rublev from customs at Sheremetyevo Airport. Thus began Tarkovsky's misfortunes.

Tarkovsky was not an admirer of Eisenstein. His idols were Robert Bresson, Luis Buñuel, Ingmar Bergman, and Akira Kurosawa. Their influ-ence on Rublev is evident, but the unconscious resemblance to Eisen-stein's Ivan the Terrible is remarkable: both directors focus on the tragedy of an outstanding personality, with the historical events as mere back-ground.

Eisenstein was intrigued by the philosophy of power, Tarkovsky by the mysteries of creativity. His painter monk, naturally, is autobiographical, and Tarkovsky can be seen in some of the film's other characters, as well. This is particularly true in the episode of the bell casting, the best in the film, when the young apprentice desperately takes on the leadership of a whole army of adult subordinates—an allegory for filmmaking—and using only his intuition, against all expectation, creates his master-piece—a bell with a marvelous peal that unites the Russian nation, increasing the prestige of the prince and stunning the imagination of foreigners (an obvious parallel with the unexpected success of Ivan's Childhood).

The bell episode shows that Tarkovsky had no intention of fighting his Soviet masters. He wanted to serve Russia and glorify her. That is why the director was so stung by the demands to cut and re-edit Andrei Rublev, which was suddenly declared to be anti-Russian and unpatriotic. He was also accused of animal cruelty: during the filming of the Tatar attack on a Russian city, a horse was thrown from a belfry and a cow was burned alive (Tarkovsky always denied the latter, while arguing that the horse was going to be slaughtered, anyway).

Tarkovsky resisted in every way he could. In the end, the authorities put Rublev on the shelf for five and a half years, stating: "The film works against us, against the people, history, and the Party's cultural policy."[9]

The Soviet audience only heard rumors about *Rublev,* but the film was sold to France, where Tarkovsky's Western fans organized its showing out of competition in Cannes. It was a sensation (a banned film!) and won the Fipressi Prize.

The Soviet authorities pushed Tarkovsky away with their own hands, turning him into an international cultural hero in the Western press. Once again, they found themselves in a ridiculous situation, as they were accustomed to using the ideological cudgel that worked more or less inside the country but was useless against foreign public opinion.

The Iron Curtain was becoming more permeable, the Western media were more aggressive in reporting the harassment of Soviet cultural figures, and all that information seeped back into the USSR, leading to unexpected results.

The ossified Leningrad authorities embarrassed themselves when they put Brodsky on trial in 1964, charging the twenty-three-year-old with "malicious parasitism." They meant that at the moment Brodsky was not holding down any official job. This was prosecuted under a law passed on Khrushchev's initiative, as the Leningrad authorities were clumsily trying to show fealty to their Moscow boss.

It was intended to be a show trial, and indeed it was, but not as planned: it turned Brodsky, little known even in his own city, the author of complex, often sorrowful, but never political poems, into a symbol at home and abroad of the coercion of independent poetry by an ignorant and repressive apparatus.

Frida Vigdorova, a journalist, managed to make secret notes of the trial and smuggle them abroad. She artfully shaped the real questions and answers of the judge and the defendant into a parable play on the resistance of a lone genius against the cruel system (a dramatic version was later performed on the BBC).

The harsh sentence—"exile Brodsky to a remote region for five years with mandatory labor"—was the final touch. Akhmatova, Brodsky's mentor and great master of self-creation, clucked ironically: "What a biography they're creating for our red-haired one! It's as if he hired someone to do it."[10] The "martyr" biographical context magnified the resonance of Brodsky's sometimes elliptical poetry.

The Brodsky affair elicited a storm of outrage, which yet again came as a total surprise to the slow-witted Soviet authorities. Shostakovich, Akhmatova, the critic Chukovsky, and the poet Samuil Marshak all appealed on his behalf, but they were "homegrown" celebrities, and the Party functionaries ignored them.

It was a different story when they got a letter in 1965 from Jean-Paul Sartre, at the time an influential friend of the Soviet Union. Sartre hinted that the new leadership (Khrushchev had been sent off into retirement) could show generosity toward the young poet to avoid being suspected of "hostility toward the intelligentsia and of anti-Semitism"[11] (which in fact was the main charge in the Western media).

The authorities yielded, releasing Brodsky early, but that did not reduce tensions, and in 1972, Brodsky left the country, pushed out by the KGB. He wrote a letter to Brezhnev that was obviously meant to be historic: "Ceasing to be a citizen of the USSR, I do not cease being a Russian poet. I believe that I will return; poets always return: in the flesh or on paper."[12]

The friends (and even enemies) of Brodsky and Tarkovsky always characterized them, with delight or condemnation, as maximalists who behaved freely in an unfree society. In the beginning their differences with the Soviet state were, to use Andrei Sinyavsky's formula, stylistic rather than ideological: different language, a rare preference for brutal and pessimistic imagery, and an unwarranted tendency to philosophize. But in that unusual style, the authorities sensed an ideological threat and reacted accordingly.

Both Brodsky and Tarkovsky wrote letters "upstairs," trying to speak to the leaders as equals, like two high-ranking negotiating sides, but the rulers merely filed the letters, considering them pretentious babble from immature young men. Yet both Brodsky and Tarkovsky were consciously creating the appearance of a dialogue between artist and state, fitting themselves into an old Russian tradition.

In Brodsky's case, it is clear that he had studied Pasternak's letter to Khrushchev. The difference is also obvious. Pasternak appealed to Khrushchev, hoping to defuse the tense situation that arose over the Nobel Prize. Brodsky's letter to Brezhnev is a different matter. This is a purely rhetorical gesture, a page of writing that was intended from the start to be included in a future academic collection of the author's works. In that sense, Brodsky, who did not borrow Akhmatova's stylistics or aesthetics (he was more influenced by Tsvetaeva, Mayakovsky, and Boris

Slutsky), turned out to be her best student in the field of self-mythologizing.

Tarkovsky was no less adept than Brodsky at creating his own legend. When he began keeping a diary in 1970, he called it his Martyrology, that is, a list of suffering and persecutions. Of course, Tarkovsky like Brodsky had sufficient material: the officials of the State Committee on Cinematography sucked a bucket of blood out of the director, continually finding fault with his screenplays and his finished films (as happened with *Andrei Rublev,* which was not released in the Soviet Union until 1971, almost six years after it was made). But on the other hand, Fedor Ermash, chairman of the Cinema Committee, allowed Tarkovsky in 1977 to start over on his almost completed *Stalker* (in form, science fiction, in content, a Christian parable), writing off the expenses (300,000 rubles) for the material that Tarkovsky did not like and wanted to reshoot.

In his Martyrology, Tarkovsky demonized Ermash, creating a grotesque image of a Soviet culture boss whose only goal was to humiliate and trample the filmmaker. But there is evidence that Ermash sympathized with Tarkovsky and often supported him, while Tarkovsky had snit fits and behaved rather aggressively. A friend of Tarkovsky's, the Polish film director Krzysztof Zanussi, thought that no American producer would let Tarkovsky get away with such behavior, and used to tell him: "You would never have been allowed to make your *Rublev* in the West."[13]

But Tarkovsky felt stifled and hindered in the Soviet Union. According to his calculations, in more than twenty years of work in Soviet film, he was "unemployed" almost seventeen years. That is shaky arithmetic—in those years he made five major films (besides *Ivan's Childhood* and *Rublev,* there were *Solaris, The Mirror,* and *Stalker*)—but it helped Tarkovsky cement his image as a suffering and persecuted artist.

Tarkovsky's imagining that he could have made many more films is probably self-delusion. He spent several years preparing for each movie (except the spontaneous *Ivan's Childhood*), thoroughly planning each scene and detail, and then during filming trying to re-create exactly not only the outward appearance but the spiritual essence of pictures he had imagined: this was the source of the meditative, contemplative nature of his works, oversaturated with intuitive visual gestures. Every

Tarkovsky film is "one-of-a-kind," they could never have come off a conveyor belt.

Tarkovsky's other misapprehension was thinking that his hermetic, autobiographical works could have had box office success if not for the sabotage by the State Cinematography Committee, which allegedly did not release enough copies of the films or give them the proper publicity. In fact, the circulation of *Ivan's Childhood*, Tarkovsky's first full-length feature, was quite impressive—fifteen hundred copies. True, *The Mirror* played in only seventy-two houses. But *Ivan's Childhood,* for all its refinement, is his most accessible work while the subtle, almost plotless *Mirror,* an extended cinematographic Freudian self-analysis, was unlikely to become popular with a mass audience under the best of circumstances.

On the contrary, the dissident reputation of Tarkovsky's films increased their appeal in the Soviet Union. When they were shown, the theaters were full: forbidden fruit is sweet. The same effect worked for the intellectual and baroque poetry of Brodsky; after the Russian-language Western radio broadcasts about his trial, numerous typewritten copies of his poems began circulating in *samizdat.*

The greatest success of Schnittke's avant-garde music came in 1983, when his long-banned *Faust Cantata* at last was performed at the Tchaikovsky Concert Hall in Moscow. The premiere was in doubt until the last second, the concert hall was surrounded by police on horseback, and a large crowd waited outside, with people begging for tickets blocks away. Here, the excitement was fueled by the rumor that the contralto part of Mephistopheles in Schnittke's philosophical work was to be performed by the biggest pop star of the Soviet Union, the wild redhead Alla Pugacheva. Pugacheva, scared off by the music or the authorities, did not sing in the *Faust Cantata,* but the scandalous atmosphere helped to put Schnittke on the national cultural map.

Brodsky started trying on the exile's toga early. At the age of twenty, he wrote poetry with references to the fate of Ovid, and in 1962, he wrote: "Thank God that I am left without a homeland on this earth." The pose of exile, fugitive, or émigré ideally suited Brodsky's poetics; one of its central themes from the start was alienation, separation, emotional and philosophical distance. Later, Schnittke would speak of the same feeling: "There is no home for me on this earth, I understand that."[14]

On the other hand, Tarkovsky's works were always firmly rooted in Russia. Is there a more national film than *Andrei Rublev*? (Schnittke approached the Orthodox intensity of *Rublev* in his four instrumental Hymns, composed in 1974–1979, one of which is based on the traditional church Trisagion chant.)

But *Rublev* was criticized for being an "anti-Russian" film both by the Soviet cultural bureaucrats and Solzhenitsyn (joined in this by the ultra-nationalist artist Ilya Glazunov). They all must have felt something profoundly antipathetic in the film. What was it?

The film director Andrei Mikhalkov-Konchalovsky, who had worked with Tarkovsky on the screenplays for *Ivan's Childhood* and *Rublev,* recalled how their trip to Venice in 1962 turned their lives around: "I will never forget that sense of lightness, joy, light, music, holiday. All my subsequent ideological waverings and unpatriotic behavior came from there."[15] Aksyonov confirmed that even though at first no one from the artistic generation of the sixties thought about emigrating, internally many of them were prepared for it because of their "openness to the world."[16]

The idea that he could go abroad and make movies there was first formulated by Tarkovsky in his diaries in 1974, when Brodsky had been living in the United States for two years. The Martyrology makes clear that Tarkovsky always fell into a deep depression after a bout with the cinema bosses. Meanwhile, his new admirers in Italy were offering him work in the West, promising creative freedom, fame, and money—the last was not unimportant to the director, who was always complaining about being without funds.

(Brodsky, who had been rather stoic about his poverty in Leningrad, focused on financial problems in conversations with friends in America, where his salary as a college professor should have guaranteed him a comfortable existence. His worries over income must have stemmed from his late marriage and birth of a daughter—now he had to care not only for himself, but a family: "I have two girls on my hands," he would say.)[17]

When Tarkovsky finally ended up in the West, it did not happen as traumatically as it had for Brodsky: the Soviet authorities officially sent the director to work on his film *Nostalghia* in Italy. When he completed it, Tarkovsky did not return to Moscow, even though he commented ominously in his Martyrology: "I am lost. I can't live in Russia, but I can't live here, either . . ."[18]

Tarkovsky had always insisted that he was not a dissident, he had never attacked the regime in his films, because political issues did not interest him as an artist. But when he called a press conference in Milan in 1984 and publicly renounced his Soviet citizenship, it was an openly political move that the KGB qualified as "treason to the Homeland in the form of refusal to return from abroad and abetting a foreign state in implementing hostile activity against the USSR."[19] His films were banned in the Soviet Union and his name disappeared from the press and even from books on cinema.

After *Nostalghia* (which came out in 1983), Tarkovsky made only the Bergmanesque *Sacrifice,* in Sweden, where he was well liked and where Bergman praised him highly. (So came to pass the prophecy Tarkovsky heard at a séance in his youth from the spirit of the late Pasternak that he would make only seven films, "but good ones.") Some consider *Sacrifice* the peak of Tarkovsky's spiritual journey, while others deplore it as self-indulgent and too slow, verging on self-parody.

The film director Alexander Sokurov, a protégé of Tarkovsky, thought that the master had been on the brink of unheard-of artistic discoveries. But in 1985, while editing *Sacrifice,* Tarkovsky learned that he had lung cancer. He died in a Paris hospital on December 29, 1986. Until the end, when he was heavily sedated by morphine, he had hoped to survive.

Tarkovsky's death was especially painful for the Russian émigré community. Another exile, Yuri Lyubimov (he renounced his Soviet citizenship at the same press conference in Milan with Tarkovsky), was in Washington, D.C., staging *Crime and Punishment,* based on the Dostoevsky novel. With his friend, the writer Aksyonov, he had a service said for Tarkovsky in a local Russian Orthodox church. In Paris, where Tarkovsky's funeral was held at the Alexander Nevsky Cathedral, Mstislav Rostropovich played Bach, so beloved by Tarkovsky, on his cello right on the church steps: a fitting ritual gesture, of which Rostropovich was a master.

Tarkovsky was buried in the Russian cemetery at Sainte-Geneviève-des-Bois in a Parisian suburb. At that time, political changes began in the Soviet Union under Mikhail Gorbachev, who came to power in 1985. Dying, Tarkovsky learned from friends that his previously banned films were at last being shown in Moscow. The news did not please him; the director bitterly saw this as the start of a political struggle for his legacy.

The attempt by the Soviets to appropriate Tarkovsky culminated in 1990, when the director was posthumously given the country's highest award, the Lenin Prize. Not accidentally, the 1990 Lenin Prize was also offered to Schnittke, who was living in Germany by then: it was an olive branch extended by the state, which had only eighteen months to live.

Schnittke was surprised to learn that the Soviet authorities were intending to award the Lenin Prize for his Concerto for Mixed Chorus, one of his most religious works; he had converted to Catholicism in 1983, at the age of forty-eight. This gave him an excuse for refusing the now unwanted sign of attention; in his letter to the Committee on the Lenin Prizes, he noted, not without irony, that Lenin was an atheist and there-fore accepting the award "would be a manifestation of an unprincipled attitude toward both Lenin and Christianity."[20]

They say that Schnittke had still vacillated: after all, why not accept the Lenin Prize, as had done in their time (to name only musicians) Shostakovich, Mravinsky, Gilels, Oistrakh, Richter, and Rostropovich, for whom the highest Soviet cultural award (like the Stalin Prize before it) was a form of protection?[21]

Was Schnittke morally superior to these great artists? It's doubtful he presumed so. The new historical paradigm helped the composer. So did his financial situation; no longer dependent on the Soviet state (all his commissions came from the West by then), he could afford to take the high road.

Material support from the West also helped Tarkovsky and Brodsky. According to the American *Dictionary of Literary Biography*, the publica-tion of Brodsky's first book in Russian (which came out in the United States in 1965) was sponsored by the CIA.[22] His next book, *A Halt in the Desert*, was published in 1970 by the New York Chekhov Publishing House, created especially to support nonconformist authors from the Soviet Union.

In America Brodsky got a tenured professorship and also received several prestigious American awards, the most important financially being the MacArthur Foundation "genius award" in 1981 (around $150,000). Brodsky used to joke that being a Russian poet, English-language essayist, and American citizen he held the best of all possible positions in life.

The high point of Brodsky's Westernization was the announcement that he had won the Nobel Prize for Literature in October 1987. Solzhenitsyn had warned after his own Nobel that if the Soviet Union "did not wake up," the next Swedish prize to a Russian writer would be turned into a huge international political scandal, too. Solzhenitsyn could have been using a crystal ball, but the Gorbachev perestroika changed a few things.

At first, the old Soviet scenario was followed. A secret memorandum from the Culture Section of the Central Committee of the Communist Party to the leadership, using language that was indistinguishable from the reaction to Solzhenitsyn's award, described Brodsky's Nobel Prize as "a political action inspired by certain circles in the West. Its goal is to cast a shadow on Soviet policy, on the solution of humanitarian issues in the Soviet Union, to undermine the growing sympathy of the public and primarily of the artistic intelligentsia in the West toward our country." (Gorbachev saw this document, as evinced by his notation: "Agree.")[23]

But simultaneously another note was heard, reflecting the new policy of appropriating the émigrés whose views, not anti-Soviet, but merely non-Soviet, made them potential allies. That is why the KGB, also concerned with Brodsky's Nobel, in its secret analysis, characterized it as an attempt "to discredit our policy of open dialogue with noted loyal representatives of the creative intelligentsia who left the USSR for various reasons, and also to use every method possible to hinder the process of returning by certain intellectuals who have realized their misapprehensions and mistakes."[24]

Another secret memorandum emphasized that Brodsky in his public statements "shows restraint," stresses his being part of Russian culture, and refrains from anti-Soviet sloganeering. As a result, it was decided—on the highest level—in order "to deprive anti-Soviet propaganda of its main arguments and to neutralize the participation in it of Brodsky himself,"[25] to allow *Novy Mir* (which still retained a reputation as a liberal journal left over from Tvardovsky's day) to print several of Brodsky's poems. That was perhaps the first publication in a Soviet journal in almost sixty years of poems by an émigré who still lived abroad.

In the course of the next few years, numerous volumes of Brodsky's poems were published in the Soviet Union with huge print runs. My collection of "Brodskiana" includes his book *Nazidanie* [Exhortation], printed in 1990 in Leningrad and Minsk in an edition of 200,000 copies, which sold out instantly and went into a second printing. For Brodsky's esoteric poetry, that was a fantastic amount. His popularity brought his fellow poets in Leningrad—Dmitri Bobyshev, Yevgeny Rein, and Anatoly Naiman, who with him made up the "magical chorus" of Akhmatova's students in the 1960s—into the limelight.

Brodsky's poetry, especially the late works, showed a certain emotional aloofness, as did the oeuvres of Schnittke and Tarkovsky. There was an icy demeanor in Brodsky's last poems, making them even more difficult than Schnittke's postmodern works, in which at least the images of evil are more often than not represented by vulgar, albeit vivid and memorable, music. (As Leonard Bernstein once quipped, "If I hear a tango, foxtrot, or waltz in a Schnittke work, I like it very much, but if I don't, then I'm not so enchanted."[25])

When the ban was lifted in the Soviet Union on performing Schnittke's polystylistic compositions (that is, combining musical idioms of various eras—from baroque to atonal and dodecaphonic—in the same work), at first audiences literally pushed their way into concert halls and hung from the rafters. The Russian intelligentsia canonized Schnittke, as it had Tarkovsky and Brodsky.

Still, relatively few truly understood and appreciated the work of these new idols. People were buying not the cultural product itself, but the story behind it. They were attracted by the tragic nimbus around the heads of these "non-Soviet" heroes. Their lives were the stuff of legends: they had been attacked by the mighty state, forcing them to flee to distant shores, where they did not get lost but were celebrated for their exploits and then died prematurely far from home.

Of the three, the best candidate for secular saint would be Schnittke, who in person was like Sakharov, just as gentle, calm, attentive, and decent. No excesses here.

Brodsky and Tarkovsky, on the other hand, could drink a lot; the latter once polished off nineteen bottles of cognac in three days with a friend. The perceptive Tvardovsky noted after meeting the young Brodsky in his office at *Novy Mir:* "A rather repulsive fellow, basically, but definitely talented, perhaps more than Yevtushenko and Voznesensky taken together."[26] Many contemporaries were put off by the arrogance, alleged cruelty, and dictatorial demeanor of Brodsky and Tarkovsky, as well as their priapic appetites. Schnittke could never be reproached for anything of the kind.

The martyr image was helped by the relatively early deaths of Tarkovsky (at fifty-four) and Brodsky (at fifty-five, of a heart attack), and Schnittke's series of strokes, the last and fourth on July 4, 1998 (the composer died on August 3, at the age of sixty-three). The strokes gradually turned Schnittke into an invalid. He was half-paralyzed after mid-1994, unable to speak, his right leg and arm immobilized. But he continued writing music, with his left hand. The media reported this, and it made Schnittke seem even more heroic.

For comparison: neither Mandelstam nor Tsvetaeva were legendary personalities in their lifetime for any sizable audience; nor did they become cultural icons right after their tragic deaths, which were not publicized. Esenin's mythological status was assured by the unprecedented and persistent popularity of his love lyrics and secured by his suicide, which was widely discussed in the Soviet press. Mayakovsky was celebrated by the state on Stalin's orders.

The newness of the instantaneous deification of Tarkovsky, Brodsky, and Schnittke in contemporary Russia right after their deaths was that they were promoted (at least in part for political reasons) in the West. All three had been supported by a wide-ranging network of prestigious commissions, prizes, grants, and international festivals that were thoroughly covered by the Western media.

The irony lies in the fact that the influence of this trio on the current cultural process in the West is rather limited. Tarkovsky, Brodsky, and Schnittke have what is usually referred to as cult status, and they have their great fans, particularly Schnittke, whose music is played and recorded all over the world (the conductors Gennady Rozhdestvensky and Kurt Masur, the violinist Gidon Kremer, and the Kronos Quartet). But their works are perceived as concluding chapters rather than the start of something new. For today's fast-changing, global, and multicultural situation, the artistic legacy of Tarkovsky, Brodsky, and Schnittke seems too static, hierarchic, and eurocentric.

Chapter Fourteen

The rise to power of Mikhail Gorbachev in April 1985 is often described as the start of a totally new era in the country's life. It is true that after the final years of Brezhnev, who had fallen into senility and died in 1982, and the brief sojourns in the Kremlin of Andropov and Konstantin Chernenko (both died after long illnesses), the appearance on the political scene of the dynamic Gorbachev seemed to herald significant changes.

But that sense of historic shift increased in hindsight, when the true meaning of Gorbachev's leadership became apparent. Back in 1985, no one could have predicted what the seemingly routine change of general secretaries of the Communist Party, even for a younger and more energetic one, could portend.

"The country cannot go on this way." The famous words Gorbachev allegedly uttered to his wife, Raisa, on the eve of his election, sound apocryphal.[1] Gorbachev had not shown himself to be a bold reformer at that point. Even after he took over, he was a traditional Party big shot, as can be seen from some of his cultural interventions.

In 1983, while one of the secretaries of the Central Committee, he brought to the attention of the Secretariat the "ideologically harmful" play by a young author, Ludmila Razumovskaya's *Dear Elena Sergeyevna*, depicting "problem" schoolchildren. The play had already been shown in several theaters to thousands of viewers and had received mostly good reviews. But someone had denounced it to the Party leadership, and Gorbachev performed a ritual whipping of the suddenly popular young playwright.

Indignantly reading the lines of one of the characters from the play ("Come on, pop, what ideals are you talking about, there aren't any now, come on, can you name just one?"), Gorbachev fumed: "Just this speech should have alerted any Soviet person, much less a cultural worker or a censor. We must state that there has been a lack of supervision and an absence of political vigilance. . . . How long are we Communists going to be ashamed of defending our Party positions and our Communist morality?"[2] One could argue that at that time it was mimicry, with Gorbachev just pretending. But in late June 1989, four years after he became the country's leader (perestroika was at its height), Gorbachev summoned the Politburo to discuss the urgent problem of the publication in the USSR of the exile Solzhenitsyn's *Gulag Archipelago.* The transcript shows: Gorbachev agreed to the publication only under pressure of his more liberal colleagues Alexander Yakovlev and Edvard Shevardnadze.

At that meeting, Gorbachev sided with the arch-conservative Yegor Ligachev in denouncing Solzhenitsyn: "I don't think he will ever be our unconditional friend and perestroika supporter." When he saw that the majority was on Solzhenitsyn's side, he gave up, saying to Ligachev: "Well, are we the only ones left? I guess I'll have to read the book."[3]

Gorbachev is often called the father of perestroika. However, it did not spring from his forehead like Athena from the head of Zeus. The roots of the changes, including cultural ones, can be found in the Brezhnev era, which had been dubbed the time of stagnation.

Specifically, it was in the last ten years of Brezhnev's administration that emigration to the West was permitted, thus creating for the first time in many years an alternative paradigm of Russian culture. This occurred in great part because the new third wave of emigration was largely embraced by the Western media.

Contact and interaction between Western journalists and the previous émigrés had not developed. Solzhenitsyn mentioned it in his 1981 interview on NBC television: "In the 1930s, at the most terrible time of the Stalin terror, when Stalin destroyed many millions of people, at that time your main newspapers were proclaiming the Soviet Union as the country of world justice."[4]

Solzhenitsyn then insisted that if in those years the West had focused its propaganda on the Soviet Union, the global situation might have changed. The Soviet citizen, the writer said, exists in an information vacuum and is continually brainwashed by his own government: "That is why radio broadcasts from abroad are so important—he can get information about himself and what is happening to us."[5]

By the time of this interview, the West had been broadcasting to the Soviet Union for more than thirty years. Solzhenitsyn recalled that when he was released from prison camp in 1953, he used his first wages to buy a radio receiver and then "listened continually" (his words) to all Western broadcasts in Russian, trying to catch snatches of information that broke through the Soviets' powerful jamming: "I learned so well, that even if I missed half a sentence, I could construe it from the few words I got."[6] Dissidents inside the country were the first Soviet citizens to break the barrier of silence and mutual distrust with the West. They were followed by a significant number of cultural figures who left the country, giving a new impulse to Western broadcasting in Russia. Viktor Nekrasov, Aksyonov, Voinovich, and other popular writers and artists appeared regularly on Voice of America, Radio Liberty, the BBC, and Deutsche Welle. They spoke to their huge audience of fans, starting a confidential dialogue that helped dismantle cultural obstacles. This genre of frank and intimate conversation was new to Soviet listeners.

The broadcasts created new stars, like the writer Sergei Dovlatov, who moved to New York from Leningrad in 1979. In the Soviet Union, almost none of his prose got into print, while in the United States his works were published one after another, first in Russian and then in the most prestigious American publishing houses. Even *The New Yorker,* which of the Russian émigrés had previously printed only Nabokov and Brodsky, published ten of Dovlatov's ironic short stories, which described the tragicomic adventures of Soviet "little people." At *The New Yorker,* Dovlatov was justly considered a writer in the Chekhovian tradition, but they must have also sensed his connection with American prose: while in the Soviet Union, he had been influenced by Hemingway.

Dovlatov had an adventurous life: very tall, dark, and handsome, resembling the actor Omar Sharif, he was drafted into the army and served as a guard at a labor camp in the north, then worked as a guide, journalist, and black marketeer. He drank a lot and brawled often, but in the meantime absorbing the ideas of liberalism and individualism, which were debated in the narrow circle of intellectuals that he entered. Brodsky was part of that crowd, and he later remarked that he and his friends back in the Soviet Union were in a certain sense "more American" than many actual ones.

Dovlatov, who had an innate journalistic talent and temperament, put his ideas into action in New York in 1980, founding the Russian-language weekly *Novy Amerikanets* [New American]. It did not last for long (the usual lack of funds), but it became a milestone in the history of free

Russian journalism, primarily for its rejection of the obsolete methods of party polemics that Soviet émigrés continued to use out of habit in the West.

A born editor, Dovlatov, together with the young literary critics Peter Vail and Alexander Genis, purged his weekly from dogmatic and crude anti-Sovietism, which he found just as revolting as the pro-Soviet sermons in the media back in Russia. Dovlatov said with a shrug: "Fanatics have amazingly similar arguments, whether they're pro or contra." When a writer offered to cover the opening of a flower show "from an anti-communist position," Dovlatov replied, "Write it without any positions." His unorthodox stance upset many conservative émigrés and he was even accused of being a KGB agent.

After *Novy Amerikanets*, Dovlatov found himself at the New York bureau of Radio Liberty, where the essayist Boris Paramonov was already working. Vail and Genis soon followed. A small group of like-minded people formed at the bureau, which I later joined.

Those were happy days. The Liberty offices at 1775 Broadway were dominated by the gigantic, exotic figure of Dovlatov, who dropped sarcastic jokes and memorable bon mots; it was impossible to resist his charm, even if you did not agree with him. His radio scripts made him famous in the Soviet Union. His prose came harder to him; he wrote slowly, meticulously shaping every sentence. Even though he insisted that he was only a storyteller, he strove for an unreachable perfection, collapsing into frequent alcoholic binges. He died of a heart attack after one in August 1990, ten days before his forty-ninth birthday. After his death, the Dovlatov circle at Radio Liberty inevitably fell apart.

Aksyonov gave an ironic account of the effect of Western broadcasts on the life of the Soviet elite. At the writers' colonies, resorts for the privileged "creative workers," if you walked down the hallway in the evening "you couldn't help hearing from almost every room the twitter of transatlantic swallows. After listening, the writers came out into the fresh air to exchange news."[7] According to Aksyonov, "The persistent and active existence of some alternative lifted the spirits in the society of a permanent bad mood."[8] Yet, the broadcasts with their persistent prodemocratic and proliberal message annoyed a lot of people.

The negative reaction of the Communist leadership was predictable: the very existence of Western radio voices addressed to the Soviet Union was seen as a real threat. The boss of the Soviet secret services, Andropov, speaking at a Central Committee Plenum on April 27, 1973, indignantly quoted an American supervisor at Radio Liberty who told a KGB source: "We can't take over the Kremlin, but we can bring up people who can, and we can prepare the conditions that will make it possible."[9]

Andropov maintained that the alternative cultural figures promoted by Western radio, like Solzhenitsyn and Brodsky, "no matter how loudly they shout about them, are nothing but the dregs of society who do not make weather. But since the Western ideologues have nothing better, they have to fuss over these rejects."[10] At the same time, Solzhenitsyn, who had moved to the United States by then, complained that American radio "for several years banned quoting Solzhenitsyn," stopped broadcasting *The Gulag Archipelago* to Russia, and instead wasted precious time on "an incredible amount of piffle" like jazz and pop music. "Even worse, they find time to broadcast a 'hobby' show. . . . That's completely horrible!"[11]

Solzhenitsyn's opinion amazingly matched the official Soviet line when he warned that the Western broadcasts will "cause revulsion, nothing but indignation, in the Soviet listener, who will turn off the radio and never listen again."[12]

There was another point on which Solzhenitsyn's complaints coincided with that of the Soviet authorities. The writer was unhappy that "news about the Jewish émigrés from the Soviet Union is given incommensurable space."[13] In 1981, the same year that Solzhenitsyn made these remarks in an NBC interview, Ivan Artamonov's book *Weapon of the Doomed (A Systemic Analysis of Ideological Diversion)* was published in the Soviet Union. It explained that in the United States "Zionists controlled half the radio stations (including Voice of America, Radio Liberty, and Radio Free Europe) and magazines, and three-fourths of all foreign bureaus of American newspapers, magazines, and press agencies."[14]

This attitude toward Radio Liberty and other Western radio stations as organizations under Jewish control and oriented "on the breakup and total destruction of Russia as a state and Russians as a nation"[15] survived the fall of the Soviet regime with its propaganda myths and continues to dominate the discourse in Russian nationalist cultural circles today.

In the speech cited earlier, Andropov assured the Party leadership: "The KGB is implementing an entire complex of measures to suppress various forms of ideological diversion, to break up foreign ideological centers and to compromise them."[16] Until the secret archives are open, it would be difficult to gauge the involvement of the Soviet secret agencies in fanning divisions among new émigrés. The fact is, there were plenty of conflicts based on political, aesthetic, and simply personal disagreements.

The two Russian Nobel laureates in literature did not get along in exile. Solzhenitsyn rebuked Brodsky in *The New York Times Book Review* for his poetic vocabulary being limited to urban intelligentsia usage and lacking deep folk roots.[17] Brodsky, when I brought up Solzhenitsyn in a conversation, merely shrugged: "Well, I don't feel like talking about that gentleman."[18] Solzhenitsyn also questioned in print Sinyavsky's Christianity, calling him "the main Aesthete."[19] Sinyavsky responded with a swipe at Solzhenitsyn: "This all smells too much of Tartuffe, blasphemy, and the anti-Christ."[20]

Voinovich published his satirical novel *Moscow 2042*, which included a funny caricature of Solzhenitsyn, called Sim Simych Karnavalov in the book. Solzhenitsyn, who was already called the "Russian Ayatollah Khomeini" by some liberal observers, took umbrage: Voinovich, he claimed, had depicted him unfairly as a "terribly scary leader of looming Russian nationalism." Aksyonov, in his novel *Say Cheese!*, took a jab at Brodsky and complained to everyone that Brodsky tried to prevent the American publication of Aksyonov's masterpiece, the novel *The Burn*, which Brodsky, in turn, described as "written with a mop."[21] Sinyavsky called the influential émigré journal *Kontinent*, which was edited by Vladimir Maximov in France (and published with American money), "the Paris regional Party committee." Maximov told everyone that Sinyavsky collaborated with the KGB. And so on, and so forth.

If the KGB took pleasure in these intra-émigré arguments, it was in vain. Such open disagreements did not have a seriously detrimental effect on the émigrés' authority, either inside the Soviet Union, or in the West, where every faction had influential allies and patrons, who considered political debate a normal and healthy democratic process. Solzhenitsyn, who was not a big fan of "our pluralists," had to admit: "Their influence in the West is incomparable to the influence of all previous emigrations from Russia."[22]

So somewhere in Soviet Party think tanks, people began to realize that it would be good to have their own, controlled cultural "loyal opposition." Interestingly, the first person to propose this idea was none other than Stalin, back in 1947 in a conversation with a select group of writers, when he said that the weekly *Literaturnaya Gazeta* should be bolder and sharper than the official line on some issues: "It is quite possible that we will sometimes criticize *Literaturnaya Gazeta* for this, but it should not fear this."[23] (Simonov, who wrote down Stalin's words, remembered the chuckle with which he said them.) As a result *Literaturnaya Gazeta* for many decades functioned as Stalin had suggested: as a controlled place for the intelligentsia to blow off steam.

Apparently the similar role of "throwing stones in the permitted direction" was to be allotted to *Novy Mir,* but its editor, Tvardovsky, grew too independent, slipping out of the Party's control, and was eventually ousted from his position. In the meantime two notable groups appeared in literature, partially sharing the line of *Novy Mir* and in some ways diverging from it—the "villagers" and the "urbanists."

Among the most outstanding "villagers" who focused attention on the fates of villages destroyed by collectivization and war were Fedor Abramov, Vassily Shukshin, Boris Mozhaev, Viktor Astafyev, Vassily Belov, and Valentin Rasputin. Some of them were close to Tvardovsky, also a peasant poet, but the "villagers" were more conservative and anti-Western.

In the 1960s and 1970s this group, which stressed patriarchal values and idealized the contemporary Russian peasantry, was quite popular, being a powerful alternative to "industrial" literature with its cardboard characters and primitive plots. The villagers' prose was sincere, alive, and its heroes, usually simple but noble peasants, expressed themselves in juicy language. Their characters were presented as true representatives of the Russian people, unlike the innumerable "positive" Party functionaries that populated the dreary works of state-commissioned literature.

Alas, this talented prose, which played such a vital role in reviving the landscape of Soviet culture, barely reached the Western reader. Yevtushenko once tried to interest an American publisher in Rasputin's works. The publisher was excited at first, but faded when he realized it wasn't "that Rasputin."[24]

Solzhenitsyn explained the lack of success in the West of the village writers who were dear to him in spirit and style by the fact that their themes and language were incomprehensible to Westerners; that may be so. But his own story "Matryona's House," paradigmatic for village prose, nevertheless was integrated into the world cultural discourse, which does not in fact reject stylistic exotica outright.

Some works of writers in the rival "urban" group, particularly the prose of Yuri Trifonov and Vladimir Makanin, did find an opening in the Western book market, especially in Europe. Dying before the advent of perestroika at the age of fifty-five in 1981, the formidable Trifonov described the drab lives of the urban intelligentsia that would be most enthusiastic about the changes that came in the Gorbachev years—the moderately liberal middle class that balanced precariously between conformity and hidden opposition.

A writer in the Chekhov mode, Trifonov amazingly managed to get a Stalin Prize in 1951, even though his father had been executed in 1937 as an enemy of the people. Some of the other urban writers—Okudzhava, Aksyonov—were also children of Soviet luminaries who were repressed in the 1930s. Anatoli Rybakov, who won the Stalin Prize the year before Trifonov, had even spent time in Siberian exile before the war.

These black marks in their résumés did not keep the urbanists from taking a visible spot in censored Soviet literature, even if they got their feathers clipped every time they tried to go beyond the proscribed limits of plot and stylistic canon. Nevertheless, every important work by an urban writer elicited great interest among readers and lively discussion in the Soviet press. In that sense they competed successfully with the village writers.

Both camps carefully distanced themselves from émigré literature. The villagers acted out of conviction, because they had always considered the writers who eventually moved to the West to be alien and false. Trifonov, on the other hand, had been friends with many of the future émigrés, and he was forced in statements that appeared in print to cluck, "These writers are of course in a very bad way, because a Russian writer must live in Russia."[25] At the same time, in private conversations, he spoke harshly of the Soviet regime: "I think that the corpse will rot for a long time, although perhaps we will live to see the end of it."[26]

Music had its own "urbanists" and "villagers." The leader of the latter was the composer Georgy Sviridov, an important, complex figure: his

Oratorio Pathétique using Mayakovsky's revolutionary poems received the Lenin Prize in 1960; but a discerning listener could find in the music nostalgic feelings for prerevolutionary Russia. Sviridov also had a Stalin Prize, but at the same time, he almost single-handedly revived the Russian choral tradition, introducing palpably archaic and religious subtexts (mostly using poetry by Esenin, who was Mayakovsky's antagonist). In this Sviridov was helped by the prominent choir conductors Alexander Yurlov and Vladimir Minin.

Since Shostakovich, broken by clashes with the authorities and gravely ill, was writing mostly contemplative, darkly elegiac music of a requiem nature, like his Fifteenth Quartet or his final work, the Sonata for Viola and Piano with its enigmatic quotation from Beethoven's "Moonlight" Sonata, the most visible representative for urban music was Rodion Shchedrin, nicknamed "Cosmonaut" by his colleagues for his nimbleness. His ballets *The Little Humpbacked Horse, Carmen Suite, Anna Karenina* (based on Tolstoy), and *The Seagull* (based on Chekhov), essentially vehicles for his wife, the brilliant prima ballerina Maya Plisetskaya, were staged at the Bolshoi with great success.

Shchedrin was suspicious of Sviridov's nationalistic position. Sviridov, on the other hand, referred to Shchedrin as the "Rasputin of Soviet music,"[27] insisting that the urbanists' music "was sick with soullessness: it doesn't matter if it is simple or complex, primitive or sophisticated, our [Edison] Denisov, Shchedrin, and [Alexandra] Pakhmutova are equally lacking spirituality."[28] (The insult was in equating the avant-garde works of Denisov and Shchedrin with Pakhmutova's popular, quasi-official songs.)

Sviridov considered Soviet musical life a dead-end alley where "clever careerism and grandiose money-grubbing"[29] reigned. According to Sviridov, a clique from the Composers' Union board had "divided up" the country's main musical stages among them as their private fiefdoms: the Bolshoi Theater was Shchedrin's "personal property," Tikhon Khrennikov had the Stanislavsky and Nemirovich-Danchenko Musical Theater all to himself, and Leningrader Andrei Petrov basically ran the Maryinsky Theater.[30]

But Sviridov praised the conductors Kirill Kondrashin and Yevgeny Svetlanov, champions of Russian classics both in the Bolshoi Theater and on the philharmonic stage. (Svetlanov recorded a major anthology of Russian symphonic music, which included all twenty-seven symphonies by his favorite, Nikolai Myaskovsky.) Sviridov was less enthusiastic about the work of the great St. Petersburg conductor Mravinsky, reproaching him for "excessive" interest in Western music: Wagner, Bruckner, Mahler, and Hindemith. Mravinsky was also probably the best interpreter at the time of émigré Stravinsky's late works.

The Soviets since Stalin's day had considered their performing arts as the most successful areas of the "cultural front." Of course, there were problems there, too, especially with émigrés. Chaliapin, the most popular Russian classical artist of the twentieth century, died in 1938 in Parisian exile, an implacable foe of the Communist regime. His memoirs, *Soul and Masks*, could not be published in full in the Soviet Union until perestroika because of its anti-Bolshevik statements.

The greatest Russian pianist, Rachmaninoff, also emigrated. Another titan of Russian piano, Vladimir Horowitz, lived in New York, a fact that Soviets found annoying, as well. But new Soviet piano lions, the best of whom had been students of Genrikh Neihaus—Richter and Gilels— took the West by storm when regular cultural contacts were established after Stalin's death. The Soviet violinists Oistrakh and Kogan and the cellist Rostropovich were just as much a sensation in New York (where they were applauded by such Russian émigrés as Yascha Heifetz, Nathan Milstein, and Gregor Piatigorsky).

Outwardly the musicians appeared to be loyal Soviet citizens, and Gilels, Oistrakh, and Kogan even joined the Party. Privately, however, they expressed their dissatisfaction with the government's too strict cultural policy, but Rostropovich was the only one to air his complaints publicly. After he defended Solzhenitsyn (and even let him live in his dacha), Rostropovich was forced out of the country with his wife, the soprano Galina Vishnevskaya, in 1974, and stripped of his Soviet citizenship by a special decree in 1978.

Ten years before that, the winner of the 1962 Tchaikovsky Piano Competition, Vladimir Ashkenazy, moved to the West. So did the creator of the first Soviet chamber orchestra, Rudolf Barshai. In 1979 a new popular chamber group, Moscow Virtuosi, was founded by the young violinist Vladimir Spivakov, and a few years later the Moscow Soloists (headed by violist Yuri Bashmet) appeared. A new generation of talented musicians, the conductors Yuri Temirkanov, Mariss Jansons, Valery Gergiev, and the pianist Mikhail Pletnev, had more creative freedom.

Ballet, which along with music was traditionally considered the most successful export of Soviet culture, still caused the Party functionaries to keep looking over their shoulders at the émigrés. Even before the revolution a number of the greatest stars of the Russian ballet settled abroad: Anna Pavlova, Nijinsky, Karsavina, and the pioneer of plotless ballet, the choreographer Fokine. Diaghilev's ballet had Russian roots, but it was a solidly based Western business by the time it achieved world fame. It started the meteoric Western careers of two new choreographic geniuses—Léonide Massine and Georgy Balanchivadze, whose name the impresario simplified to George Balanchine.

Soviet ballet, which like the opera was under the personal patronage of Stalin (continuing the Russian imperial tradition in this sphere), managed to come up with a new generation of great performers, too: the dazzling ballerinas trained in Leningrad by Agrippina Vaganova—Marina Semenova, Galina Ulanova, and Natalya Dudinskaya—and the extraordinary Moscow dancers Plisetskaya, Vladimir Vasilyev, and his wife, Ekaterina Maximova. The innovations of such masters of choreography as the avant-garde Kasyan Goleizovsky and Fedor Lopukhov and the more traditionally inclined Vassily Vainonen, Rostislav Zakharov, and Mikhail Lavrovsky (*Romeo and Juliet*) were transformed by Yuri Grigorovich into a new monumental style, of which *Spartacus* was the most successful example. Leningrader Boris Eifman continued the experimental tradition of choreographer Leonid Yakobson.

Just when the international reputation of Soviet ballet was at its peak, it was badly shaken by a series of sensational defections: Rudolf Nureyev, Natalya Makarova, and Mikhail Baryshnikov stayed in the West. The dramatic fates of these celebrated dancers, who became the darlings of the Western media, served as yet more proof that in the cultural cold war, even an abstract art like classical ballet would inevitably be used as a political weapon.

In that sense, it was a symbolic gesture in 1979 when the American authorities stopped the departure from JFK Airport of a Soviet plane returning to Moscow carrying the wife of Alexander Godunov, premier dancer of the Bolshoi Ballet, who had just asked for political asylum in the United States. President Jimmy Carter and General Secretary Brezhnev were personally involved in this incident, which naturally got world coverage. Joseph Brodsky, in those tense days acting as interpreter for the fugitive dancer, described the drama of Godunov and his wife, separated by political circumstances, as the "Romeo and Juliet of the twenti-eth century."[31]

A major headache for the Soviet authorities was caused by unofficial art that functioned outside the state cultural paradigm. It appeared at the juncture of visual art and poetry toward the end of the 1940s. In that bleak time, when socialist realism seemed omnipresent, strange "stand-offish people with a tough individual streak,"[32] as they were later charac-terized by one of them, the abstract artist Vladimir Nemukhin, moved into action on the margins of orthodox culture.

After the war against Hitler, some members of the Moscow artistic elite got the impression, as one observer put it, that the Iron Curtain was "badly rusted." "We managed to get a gulp of air after the victory, espe-cially we school kids . . . even in Moscow beer halls you could hear the poetry of Esenin, Gumilev, Mandelstam from people who had known the poets personally, or at least, seen them."[33] All those poets were banned at the time.

Timidly, cultural traditions and connections destroyed by the Great Terror were re-established by the emerging cultural underground. In art this was primarily the domain of the small groups of young students of surviving old masters, like Vladimir Favorsky, Robert Falk, and Pavel Filonov. In Moscow the center of attraction was Malevich's former pupil Yevgeny Kropivnitsky, although he did not insist on his teacher's stark Suprematism as the mandatory dogma for his own students.

Kropivnitsky and his wife and daughter, also artists, moved to the bar-racks settlement of Lianozovo outside Moscow, where in the 1940s Oskar Rabin, who had become Kropivnitsky's son-in-law, joined his group; this was the first unofficial art movement in the postwar Soviet Union, and it became known as the Lianozovo Circle.

The survival of the Lianozovo Circle is one of the mysteries of Soviet cultural life in that period. Its members were marginal artists who some-how managed not to dissolve in the mainstream flow of official art. Moreover, in a strict system that denied outsiders the right to cultural activity, they fenced off a small private area for themselves where the authorities did not venture. Visitors from Moscow began frequenting the Lianozovians: there were celebrities like Ehrenburg and Konstantin

Paustovsky, the liberal prose writer and idol of the Soviet intelligentsia, but also young artists and poets and curious guests. Later, foreign diplomats and tourists came, too, although officially they were not allowed to travel outside Moscow city limits: another mystery.

The Lianozovo circle included abstract, expressionist, and neoprimitivist artists. Not everyone was pleased by their work—the conceptual artist Viktor Pivovarov later admitted: "I thought the paintings of the Kropivnitskys pathetically dilettante homegrown provincialism."[34] But people were attracted and surprised by the independent lifestyle of that bizarre artistic colony right under the allegedly all-seeing eyes of the secret police.

The artists were joined by underground poets—Igor Kholin, Genrikh Sapgir, Vsevolod Nekrasov—also colorful characters who wrote brutal, experimental verse that could never be submitted to Soviet publications. Kholin, wiry and with an equine face, was a captain in the Ministry of Internal Affairs, but was demoted for an ugly fight and sentenced to exile near Lianozovo, where he met the Kropivnitsky family. He started writing short, grim poems that were reminiscent of the banned work of the Soviet Dadaists of the 1920s and 1930s—Daniil Kharms, Alexander Vvedensky, and Nikolai Oleinikov, who were destroyed by Stalin.

Kholin's nascent underground fame grew and soon the former street kid with nothing but a brief time in military school for an education, a drunkard and a womanizer, became one of the leaders of a new movement in Russian poetry, known as "barracks writing." Like many people, Kholin lived in shanty-like barracks, where each tiny room (without plumbing and with a public outhouse) sheltered a large family.

The underground poets read their works in those barracks rooms and also in Moscow apartments. They were fed by the "patrons of the arts" of the period like the pianist Richter and the poet Pasternak; the latter usually stuffed an "honorarium" into a performing poet's coat pocket (amusingly, it was in strict accordance with the number of poems read). These were the first tentative hints at a developing system of private funding, as opposed to state financing.

But when the enterprising dissident Alexander Ginzburg began distributing the poems in typed anthologies (the *samizdat* journal *Syntaxis*, four issues in 1959–1960) he was imprisoned; in the logocentric Soviet Union, words were considered by far the most dangerous ideological instrument. The authorities traditionally regarded *samizdat* as an evil to be ruthlessly uprooted. One of the last highly publicized cultural-political cases of the Brezhnev era was *Metropol*, a *samizdat* literary almanac compiled in 1979 by a group of writers headed by Aksyonov; for this attack on the state monopoly, one boss of the Writers' Union called Aksyonov a CIA agent and another recommended applying wartime laws to the overly independent writer—that is, put him up against the wall. In 1980, Aksyonov wisely chose to leave for the West, which at the time suited both sides.

The underground artists, who were watched as closely as their literary brothers, managed to find themselves a more comfortable niche, nevertheless. One of them thought it was because Khrushchev considered avant-garde artists "run-of-the-mill swindlers, something akin to fleas under a shirt,"[35] so they were not squeezed until they jumped out too boldly onto the surface.

The first big news on Soviet nonconformist art came in 1960 from *Life* magazine, with the sensational headline "The Art of Russia . . . That Nobody Sees," a long report in which along with the paintings of the classics of the avant-garde, like Kandinsky, were reproductions of works by the new unofficial artists. (After that, they were also called "the second Russian avant-garde.")

Soviet private collectors began buying the watercolors by Anatoli Zverev, featured in *Life*. Self-taught, Zverev discovered Tachisme art (splattering paint on canvas) at the 1957 International Youth Festival in Moscow, where it was demonstrated by a visiting American artist, and he applied the technique in his still lifes and portraits, quickly developing a "mad creator" persona: he drank heavily, brawled, and showed off, while still managing to produce up to ten gouaches and watercolors a day.

When Zverev worked, it was a real show: he would come to someone's luxurious home, toss sheets of paper on the floor and then spatter paint on them, holding several brushes at a time. Cigarette dangling from his mouth, dancing a jig, Zverev growled and cursed, imitating a shaman, as he covered the papers with new color splashes and strokes, the final ones being his famous initials, AZ. His portraits, amazingly, bore quite a resemblance to the sitter, and it is not surprising that collectors (dentists, lawyers, engineers) picked them up by the bunch, since in the beginning they went for a trifle: three rubles apiece.

The big-time Soviet collectors, even those who, like the legendary Georgy Costakis, were already collecting Tatlin, Rodchenko, and Lubov Popova, did not pay attention to the second avant-garde until the West did. The sudden attention of the foreign press turned the underground artists into tourist destinations, along with the Kremlin and the Moscow metro, and their exotically grimy cellars were visited by foreign business-men, journalists, and Western diplomats.

Dip-Art (art for diplomats and other foreigners) burgeoned in the early 1960s, changing the position of unofficial culture. Private enterprise until then had existed quietly on the sidelines, where a few legal private dentists and tailors toiled. Culture, on the other hand, as an important part of ideology, was a total state monopoly.

Since the relevant documents are still classified, we can only guess why the ubiquitous secret police looked the other way as the Moscow Dip-Art scene (followed by Leningrad) expanded and flourished. It is a fact that this unofficial guild, which at its peak had at least several dozen participants (probably around two hundred people), gradually turned into a tempting alternative to the state system of rewarding artists.

The underground Dip-Art market grew more orderly and prices rose, evolving from primitive barter, when the artist traded a painting for a bottle of whiskey or a pair of jeans, to significant (by Moscow standards) sums in hard currency.

Outstanding among the first serious Western buyers was the American economics professor Norton Dodge, who wanted to create an exhaustive collection of Soviet nonconformist art. Traveling regularly to the Soviet Union, the stocky, mustachioed, walrus-like Dodge brought out around fifteen hundred works by underground artists, which became the basis of his permanent collection at the Zimmerli Museum at Rutgers University in New Jersey. The collection, now numbering approximately twenty thousand works by hundreds of artists, may be regarded as definitive.

Dodge began his purchases with Lianozovo artists, then added the works of the hyperbolic figurativists Vladimir Veisberg and Oleg Tselkov; the neoprimitivist Vladimir Yakovlev; the metaphysical surrealist Vladimir Yankilevsky; the abstract artists Eduard Shteinberg and Lydia Mast-erkova; the conceptualist Ilya Kabakov; and artists from the conceptual camp who differed in approach, like Erik Bulatov, Oleg Vassiliev, and Grisha Bruskin; the inventors of Sots-Art, Vitaly Komar and Alexander Melamid; and artists working in the same vein, Alexander Kosolapov,

Leonid Sokov, and Vagrich Bakhchanyan. Perhaps the best works of these artists are in the Zimmerli Museum.

Some Dip-Artists became well off, converting their hard currency and ruble earnings into cars, dachas, and co-op apartments. The boldest and most determined of them, like Oscar Rabin, started having one-man shows in the West with the help of foreign diplomats and Russophile gallery owners. This led Rabin, a born activist and leader, to the idea of a show of nonconformist art in Moscow, outdoors, like Paris exhibitions on the banks of the Seine.

Rabin's idea, when he first proposed it in 1969, was dismissed by his fellow artists. But by 1974, the underground artists felt confident enough to try it. They gathered on September 15, a Sunday, in a vacant lot for a happening, which they called "The First Autumn Painting Exhibition in the Open Air."

This was intended as a rather modest action, with perhaps a dozen participants, including Rabin and his wife and son, Komar and Melamid, and the Leningrad artist Yevgeny Rukhin. The overzealous authorities, intending to teach the disorderly artists a lesson, turned it into a symbolic event with international resonance.

When the artists began setting up their works on folding aluminum tripods, they were attacked by young toughs who had been waiting for them; they grabbed the paintings, broke them and tossed them into parked dump trucks. Some canvases were burned on the spot. The attackers beat up anyone who resisted, and finally unleashed several bulldozers and street-washing trucks, whose icy streams of water completed the destruction.

Rabin jumped in the path of a bulldozer to rescue a painting. Several Western correspondents, who had been invited to the happening by the artists, were also beaten up. The result was a series of Western reports with headlines like "Soviet Officials Use Force to Break Up Art Show. Painters, Newsmen Roughed Up in Turbulent Public Confrontation" and "Art Under the Bulldozers."

This altercation created friction between the secret police and the Party. As General Filipp Bobkov, chief of the Fifth Directorate of the KGB, created by Andropov in 1967 for "countering ideological diversions by the enemy," that is, supervision of culture, described it in his memoirs (which were published in post-Soviet times), the "absurd decision" to use bulldozers against paintings was not made by the KGB and those were not its brawny thugs punching artists in a Moscow empty lot. According to Bobkov, the initiative came from the local Party; KGB agents hurried out to save the paintings. The general, "stunned," as he described himself, told them: "Take care of the artists!"[36]

Alas, the paternal concern of the secret police for the avant-garde was too late, and the world media picked up the scandal. "To tell the truth, there was nothing we could say in justification," the KGB general lamented. "Our enemies were given a very wide field this way, and they used the platform for a new, thoroughly prepared attack. Disregarding cost, they helped 'banned' artists in every way possible to get abroad, thereby killing two birds with one stone; first, it started a new wave in the press: talented artists cannot work in the USSR and they flee abroad; and second, they had made a certain calculation: the artists who bene- fited would try to repay their patrons by participating in the Cold War. Their calculation turned out to be correct."[37]

The KGB general's dismay is understandable, considering the time, money, and effort the secret services spent on keeping unofficial culture under control. Even Bobkov admitted it: "The KGB should not have tried to act as arbiter in the rivalry among schools of art. However, there were circumstances that forced us to appear sometimes on that arena."[38]

The general is being too modest. One of the prominent noncon- formist artists maintained: "The old-fashioned, populous spy network entangled the underground, and colleagues in the arts readily denounced one another in order to hang on at the Dip-Art trough and earn as much as possible."[39]

The sphere of intensive interest for the KGB included not only the avant-garde, but such realist artists of a nationalistic bent as Ilya Glazunov, whose house in Moscow was a gathering place for Soviet and foreign dignitaries, diplomats, and correspondents. The writer Leonid Borodin, a close friend of the artist, wrote: "Undoubtedly, the appropri- ate agencies could not leave this oasis of socializing unattended, and everyone there understood that."[40]

According to Borodin, the parties at Glazunov's house were "a perma- nent object of rumor, gossip, suspicion, and accusations. And not with- out reason."[41] In that sense, the Glazunov circle could be seen as a microcosm of the elite of Soviet culture, existing with the morbid sense that it was in a bell jar of constant surveillance and interference from the KGB. (This sense has been confirmed by declassified documents, which are now being published less frequently and more selectively than in the early post-Soviet years.)

It was not easy living and working in that paranoid atmosphere. Everyone suspected everyone else of collaboration with the KGB, and that heavy fog of mutual distrust (probably quite beneficial for the secret police) was used to settle personal scores, when "the most reliable way to smear a rival was by calling him a KGB agent. . . . For some people such defamation ended in tragedy. But of course, real agents did exist."[42]

In the post-Soviet years intellectuals began making public admissions of having been forced to work with the KGB. We must assume that the number of these (self) exposés will grow, and we will find that the KGB used the most unexpected people. One surprise came in the memoirs of Stalin-era KGB boss Pavel Sudoplatov, published in the second half of the 1990s: the poet Boris Sadovskoy, who died in Moscow in 1952 and was known to family and close friends as a monarchist and implacable foe of the Soviet regime, had been recruited by Soviet counterintelligence back in the war years.[43]

It was also astonishing to read in Sudoplatov's book that the composer Lev Knipper, nephew of Chekhov's wife, had been enlisted by the secret services to assassinate Hitler should the Führer appear in Nazi-occupied Moscow.[44] Knipper, author of twenty symphonies (and the popular song "Polyushko-Pole"), was an impeccable gentleman of the old school. Knipper killing anyone? It seemed impossible. A similar surprise (and even shock) for old émigrés in New York was the mention in one of historian Dmitri Volkogonov's books that the Russian musicologist Alexis Kall, a friend of Stravinsky's and his secretary for a while, sent reports to Moscow from Los Angeles on the political situation in the émigré milieu.[45]

Andropov was proud that the KGB was implementing a "very cautious and flexible policy" toward the intellectuals. After the "bulldozer show," an agent came to the leader of the rebel artists, Rabin, with a message that "a bad peace is better than a good quarrel." A compromise was reached and the KGB "with great difficulty" (as General Bobkov recalled) got the Moscow Party officials to give permission for a large show of nonconformist art in Izmailovo Park for September 29, 1974.[46]

Perhaps the KGB did see this move as "cautious and flexible," but in Moscow in 1974 the exhibition in Izmailovo Park was perceived as a capitulation by the authorities. On a warm sunny day, on a huge green meadow, more than fifty artists showed hundreds of their works to thousands of Muscovites, dazzled by the spectacle. The attendees will never forget the rare atmosphere of an unsanctioned public festival, a people's celebration with an opposition undertone. The Izmailovo show was simultaneously an important cultural gesture, a picnic, and a demonstration—a breath of freedom and a harbinger of the changes that took place more than a decade later.

In the meantime, the KGB continued using the carrot and stick approach with unofficial art. On one hand, several "permitted" exhibitions by avant-garde artists took place, on the other, so did a series of searches, arrests, and "accidental" beatings. As the artist Kabakov recalled, "We were always under the threat of arrest or exile. . . . I cravenly refused when Oskar Rabin invited me to participate in the famous bulldozer exhibition."[47] Kabakov explained further: "Fear as a state of mind persisted in every second of our life, in every action, and like coffee and milk, that is, in any possible combination, there was not a word or deed that was not diluted by a certain dose of fear."[48]

Kabakov and his friends in conceptualist nonconformist art—the poets Prigov and Lev Rubinshtein, the prose writer Vladimir Sorokin—held the idea, unusual for Russian culture, that the artist need not participate in public life, "defend anything, speak out against anything."[49] According to Prigov, this was also "a great art—not falling into public scandals or provoking them. . . . Increasing tension did not lead to anything good. Therefore it was a very complex policy dealing with the authorities. . . . Our goal was to expand our zone of freedom little by little. It was not a sociopolitical or even an existential strategy, it was rather an aesthetic one."[50]

Paradoxically, a position of nonengagement on the part of the Soviet postmodern artists created additional problems for the KGB because it blurred the borders between permitted and not permitted. The nonconformist artists and poets were not openly anti-Soviet, yet the KGB felt it necessary to give them "prophylactic" talks every now and then: "They began calling us in a lot in the late 1970s, when they had put away all the dissidents, and the water level dropped sharply. That is, now the heads were visible of people who were not involved in politics or in any social protests at all."[51]

In Leningrad, the KGB gathered the avant-garde writers into a special association, the literary Club-81, "so they wouldn't have to drag themselves out to the outskirts to our readings,"[52] as one of the participants deduced. They herded them into the organization by various means: "some were intimidated, others persuaded, given promises. One woman poet . . . managed to get the ceiling of her room whitewashed in exchange."[53] Also in Leningrad, the first officially published almanac of underground literature, *Krug* [The Circle], appeared in 1985 under the "paternal supervision" of the KGB. (The Leningrad KGB had clearly learned from the negative fallout of the *Metropol* affair in Moscow in 1979.)

The secret police started to herd artists under the aegis of various quasi-official "covers." One of their plans was to supervise Dip-Art and the underground art market. The Soviets were always looking for new ways of adding revenues in hard currency. In 1971, KGB chairman Andropov suggested "studying the question of the possibility and conditions for selling modernist works created in our country to foreign consumers."[54] An active role in the organization of some exhibitions of unofficial Soviet artists in the West was played by Victor Louis-Levin, the Moscow correspondent of the London *Evening News* known for his close KGB ties, who also tried to sell manuscripts by Solzhenitsyn and Svetlana Alliluyeva, Stalin's daughter, and videotape of Sakharov and his wife, Elena Bonner, in exile in Gorky, being examined by physicians.

As prices in the West grew, nonconformist art became ever more acceptable for the Soviet authorities, comparable in hard-currency revenue with tours by the Bolshoi Ballet or the Igor Moiseyev Ensemble of Folk Dance. Mutually beneficial deals had been worked out in music and ballet with Western impresarios like Sol Hurok. Now the Ministry of Culture agreed to the auction run by Sotheby's in Moscow in 1988, where the heated bidding brought in sensational prices—for example, Grisha Bruskin's *Fundamental Lexicon* went for $412,000. The auction marked the emergence of the unofficial underground of Soviet art onto the open global art market—a step that some veterans of the underground ruefully considered "commercial and political."

Chapter Fifteen

Sergei Paradjanov stunned the audience at the New York Film Festival in 1988 when he announced that he wanted to film Gorbachev in the role of Hamlet. Some in the audience ascribed the statement to the director's well-known eccentricity.

But in November 1991, when Alexander Yakovlev was in New York, I asked him what he considered the main character trait of Gorbachev, who by then had lost his title of President of the USSR, and the country to boot. His reply was brief: "Hamletism." Yakovlev knew what he was talking about: that cunning fellow with prickly eyes was Gorbachev's leading liberal advisor. He was the polar opposite of the former chief ideologist of the USSR, Mikhail Suslov, the *éminence grise* of the Brezhnev era who had become a member of the Politburo under Stalin and died in 1982 still a Stalinist hard-liner.

Yakovlev changed rapidly, starting out with a solid career in the Party as a former military hero with a peasant background, a nondrinking, hardworking, and commonsensical man. When he was thirty-five, Yakovlev came to New York and spent two years in graduate school at Columbia University. Then he was the Soviet ambassador to Canada for ten years. Those experiences influenced him strongly. (The KGB even accused Yakovlev of being recruited by the American intelligence services, but Gorbachev ignored that report.)

It was in Canada, which Gorbachev visited in 1983 as a member of a Soviet delegation, where he became friends with Yakovlev, sensing that they shared the same ideas. In 1985, as the new leader of the Soviet Union embarking on a reform program of perestroika and glasnost, Gorbachev assigned Yakovlev to bring in the intelligentsia, for he saw that without its active support the country would be slow to change. Thus, Yakovlev became the Party patron of the liberals, even though he was not quite comfortable in that role at first, sometimes displaying the very Hamletism (that is, indecision and fear of change) for which he later rebuked Gorbachev.

Gorbachev's aim was socialism with a human face. He first thought he could achieve it relying only on Party cadres. But encountering fierce resistance to his reforms within the Party, Gorbachev decided to use cultural forces as a battering ram. As his aides attest, his plans regarding the intelligentsia were thoroughly pragmatic, even cynical: it was to service, theoretically and in practice, the new course of comparatively greater freedom of speech and limited relaxation of economic and political restrictions, reminiscent of Lenin's New Economic Policy of the 1920s.

The liberal Soviet intelligentsia responded to the call enthusiastically, describing themselves as the contractors of perestroika (which literally means "reconstruction"). For the first time in many years they felt needed by the state and they began attacking Gorbachev's opponents at meetings, in the press, on television—especially since the conservatives had long been their personal oppressors.

The liberals had good reason to see Gorbachev as their patron. He had begun to realize that the stubborn and influential conservatives, recovered from their original shock, would use the first opportunity to get rid of him, as Brezhnev and his friends had done to Khrushchev. He met with writers in 1986, and Anatoly Ivanov, a Hero of Socialist Labor and author of the patriotic potboilers *Shadows Vanish at Noon* and *Eternal Call*, demanded that the Politburo restore ideological order, condemning the out-of-control liberals the way Stalin and Zhdanov had handled Akhmatova and Zoshchenko in 1946. Gorbachev was staggered. "Where do people like that come from? They're like wood lice."[1]

Learning that the head of the Writers' Union, Georgy Markov, also a Hero of Socialist Labor, had managed to get his works printed in twenty-seven publishing houses in 1985 alone (and, as it turned out, had 14 million rubles in his savings account), Gorbachev was outraged. "Talentless, senile old men. They praise themselves. They offer their own candidacies for awards. They give themselves prizes and titles."[2]

Responding to my question in 2003 on which contemporary poets influenced his worldview, Gorbachev named Okudzhava, Yevtushenko, and Voznesensky. A response like that from Brezhnev or even Andropov would have been impossible. At the urging of Gorbachev and Yakovlev, administrators were replaced in the "creative" unions of writers, artists, and filmmakers, and new people appeared as heads of the leading newspapers and magazines. The weeklies *Ogonek* and *Moskovskie Novosti* [Moscow News] took a particularly aggressive pro-Gorbachev stand, printing increasingly bold muckraking and anti-Stalinist materials. They were sold out instantly; people lined up at the newsstands at six in the morning to pick up an issue of these suddenly liberal publications.

Journals and then book publishers unleashed an avalanche of previously unavailable literature. It began with the publication of poems by Gumilev, executed by the Bolsheviks in 1921, and then came other banned masterpieces—Akhmatova's *Requiem,* Platonov's *The Foundation Pit* and *Chevengur,* Bulgakov's *A Dog's Heart,* Vassily Grossman's *Life and Fate,* and, finally, Pasternak's *Doctor Zhivago.* (These were reprints of Western Russian-language editions. Possession of these books just a short time before could have led to a prison-camp term.)

As the list of officially rehabilitated figures once considered "enemies" (Bukharin, Trotsky, even Nicholas II) expanded in the political sphere, the cultural gates opened more widely, too: the Russian avant-garde was rehabilitated—Kandinsky, Chagall, Malevich, Tatlin, Filonov, and the Russian Dadaist writers Kharms, Oleinikov, and Alexander Vvedensky.

After that, conveniently deceased émigré writers, from Zinaida Hippius and Khodasevich to Yevgeny Zamyatin and Nabokov, and religious philosophers Berdyaev, Lev Shestov, Semyon Frank, and Ivan Ilyin were published in the USSR. The genius of Stravinsky and Balanchine was recognized in full. And then came the turn of living émigrés: Nureyev, Baryshnikov, Rostropovich and the writers Aksyonov, Voinovich, Sinyavsky, Maximov, Brodsky, and to top the list, Solzhenitsyn. A popular witticism of the time was, "Today reading is more interesting than living."

In hindsight, it might appear that this was a spontaneous, unstoppable flow. In fact, the "process went" (to use Gorbachev's favorite expression) in fits and starts, with the fear that liberalization could cease at any moment. Some people joked, "What will we do when perestroika and glasnost stop? We'll read old magazines and newspapers, if they're not confiscated."

The long-awaited leaps toward greater freedom were interrupted by sudden halts, and almost every publication of an important, previously banned work involved a tense behind-the-scenes struggle. The law on freedom of the press and the repeal of censorship was not passed until 1990.

. . .

An example of this struggle was the dramatic fate of *Children of the Arbat,* a novel by the popular writer Anatoli Rybakov: it is well documented, for the author and his widow both wrote memoirs[3] and Rybakov told me a lot himself.

Rybakov, a Stalin Prize laureate (despite having been exiled to Siberia in the 1930s for being a former Trotskyite), completed *Children of the Arbat,* an epic narrative about the Great Terror in which Stalin is a central character and is depicted as a devious tyrant, in 1966. He immediately offered it to Tvardovsky for his liberal journal, *Novy Mir;* the editor had a high regard for the novel, quite bold for those days, and planned to publish it the following year, in 1967. But the censors blocked *Children of the Arbat* and the manuscript remained in the author's desk for twenty years.

Throughout the Brezhnev era, Rybakov, a persistent and energetic former soldier, tried to get the book into print, without avail. The situation should have changed with Gorbachev's rise to power in 1985, but that was not the case at all: the Stalin theme continued to be a minefield. Under Brezhnev and Andropov, the Party bureaucrats told Rybakov that a novel like his about Stalin would be published only "when our entire generation is gone from this life." Under Gorbachev they demanded huge changes and cuts: "Stalin is shown in a one-sided way."

Stubborn Rybakov resisted in every way he could, gathering reviews of support of the novel from sixty famous writers, film actors, and directors. It was an old defense technique, but it was more effective in the glasnost era. Gorbachev recalled it grumpily in his memoirs: "The manuscript had been read by dozens of people who began showering the Central Committee with letters and reviews, calling it the 'novel of the century.' It became a public event before it was published."[4]

In the new political situation, Gorbachev had to take that into account, even though he stressed that Rybakov's book "did not impress us much" artistically. (Khrushchev read *Children of the Arbat* in manuscript in 1969 when he was retired, and he also criticized the Stalin episodes.)

The manuscript of *Children of the Arbat* became a litmus test for determining a person's political position. Tatiana Rybakov recorded a characteristic exchange. The poet Bella Akhmadulina: "If I wake up tomorrow and see that the journal with Rybakov's novel is out, I will say: that means the Soviet regime is over!" Her former husband, Yevtushenko, countered: "And I, on the contrary, will say: The Soviet regime is stronger and triumphant!" Yet he wrote the first letter of support for the book's publication.

In the end, the fate of *Children of the Arbat* was decided at the highest political level. At a Politburo meeting on October 27, 1986, the leading conservative Yegor Ligachev attacked the novel: "The meaning of this enormous manuscript of 1,500 pages boils down to denouncing Stalin and all our prewar policies. . . . Clearly, such a novel cannot be published, even though Rybakov is threatening to send it abroad." Gorbachev, as befits Hamlet, continued vacillating. "If we start exposing ourselves, acknowledging our mistakes, that would be the most expensive and most desired present for our enemy."[5]

Gorbachev's advisor, Yakovlev, even though less blinkered than his boss, still could not decide, either: having read it over several nights (the novel made a powerful impression on him), Yakovlev felt that the writer was wrong to treat Stalin "with prejudice." He recalled the three-hour conversation he had with Rybakov at his Central Committee office: "He responded to all my cautious comments on the book with ferocious objections, he reacted sharply, with blatant challenge . . . he rejected my right as a member of the Politburo to make any criticisms at all to a writer."[6]

Rybakov had the foresight to bring along a compilation of the letters in support for his novel to this audience with Yakovlev: "These are not simply raves, this is the mindset of the intelligentsia. The intelligentsia cannot abide Stalin." The roles had changed: no longer was the Party functionary pressuring the writer, but the writer, in the name of the cultural elite, was pressuring the functionary. Yakovlev knew that Gorbachev needed the support of those people and he surrendered: "It must be published, since we've taken the course for the freedom of creativity."[7]

When the journal *Druzhba Narodov* [Friendship of the Peoples] announced it would be printing *Children of the Arbat,* its subscription went from 100,000 to over 1,000,000. The total print run for the book, which came out in the Soviet Union in 1987 as a hardcover, was 10.5 million copies; *Children of the Arbat* was published in fifty-two countries, became an international best seller and a political signal of the Soviet leadership's intentions. In the United States, Rybakov's picture appeared (along with Stalin) on the cover of *Time* magazine, and President Reagan, speaking in Moscow in 1988, announced, "We applaud Gorbachev for bringing Sakharov back to Moscow from exile and for publishing Pasternak's *Doctor Zhivago* and Rybakov's *Children of the Arbat.*"[8] Thus the story of *Children of the Arbat* became one of the last examples of the huge importance of literature in political life during the Soviet era.

It seemed that the Soviet state had ideologized society to the limit. The irony was that after Stalin's death, politics was evaporating from the surface of cultural life. It was replaced by moribund official rituals, while the real political debate moved to the kitchens of the intelligentsia. The main requirement of the Brezhnev era was not to rock the boat. Even the orthodox Andropov complained that there were a lot of Communists but no Bolsheviks (meaning that people joined the Party pro forma, as a way to get ahead, but without conviction).

Under Gorbachev, the real discussions suddenly became public. The spectrum of political views among the cultural elite turned out to be unexpectedly broad—from monarchism to anarchism. Neopaganism and neofascism, appearing from out of nowhere, flourished like wildflowers, and Black Hundred and anti-Semitic views became fashionable. Conspiracy theories about the suicides of Esenin and Mayakovsky spread: some thought they were murdered, either by the Soviet secret police or by Jews or by both.

The cultural and political situation grew more complex: in the past, the central dichotomy had been "Soviet v. anti-Soviet." Now, there were also the "conservative-liberal" and "Slavophile-Westernizer" divides as well. For the first time there was a dizzying array of variants of these positions: one could position oneself as an anti-Soviet conservative or a Slavophile avant-gardist.

As Gorbachev relaxed Party control, a vacuum was created in cultural power, and elite groups tried to grab as much territory as they could. The division into spheres of power went on everywhere: literature, art, music, film, and even that icon of Russian culture, the Moscow Art Theater.

Founded in 1898 by Stanislavsky and Nemirovich-Danchenko as the "theater of Chekhov," the legendary company was driven before the revolution by Stanislavsky's motto: "Be neither revolutionary nor Black Hundred." This allowed MAT to remain above the fray and win a respect and an almost sacral authority among the intelligentsia.

After the Bolshevik revolution, Stalin became MAT's patron, regularly attending its performances. This assured the theater a privileged position and funding, but it destroyed its former independence. Yet some of MAT's Soviet productions were as refined as the legendary works of Stanislavsky and Nemirovich-Danchenko. One milestone was the premiere of Mikhail Bulgakov's play about the Civil War, *The Days of the Turbins* (based on his novel *The White Guards*), in 1926.

A direct connection to the Chekhov line of the old Art Theater was seen in this production. It was perceived, as *The Seagull* had been in its day, as the company's political and social manifesto, and audiences saw Chekhovian traits in the characters of Bulgakov's play, noble idealistic officers who defended the doomed "White idea" from the victorious Bolsheviks.

The Days of the Turbins at MAT had a difficult history. The public adored the play, it was sold out, but the orthodox critics were vicious. Stalin, by then the highest cultural arbiter of the land, was drawn to the play and saw it at least fifteen times; scenes from the production appeared in his dreams, he confessed.

In 1929, Stalin wrote about *The Days of the Turbins:* "The main impression that the audience is left with is an impression that is beneficial for Bolsheviks: 'if even people like the Turbins are forced to put away arms and bow to the will of the people, admitting their cause is completely lost, that means the Bolsheviks are unbeatable, and you can't do anything with them, the Bolsheviks.' *The Days of the Turbins* is a demonstration of the crushing power of Bolshevism," he concluded.[9]

Despite that, Stalin's attitude toward Bulgakov was unpredictable: sometimes he encouraged the writer, sometimes he punished him. Stalin would not reply to Bulgakov's letters, but once he telephoned him. The writer, anti-Soviet at heart and a sober, ironic person, nevertheless got drawn into this cat-and-mouse game to the extent that it became one of the central themes of his work, reflected in his exquisite novel about Molière and his patron Louis XIV (a very transparent parallel), a fine play on the same theme, *Cabal of Hypocrites,* and his phantasmagoric novel *The Master and Margarita,* his final statement and one of the peaks of twentieth-century Russian prose. One of the main characters of the novel, Woland, a Lucifer-like figure, enters into a complex relationship (not unlike the one between Stalin and Bulgakov) with the Master, a writer.

The Master and Margarita was not published in Bulgakov's lifetime, nor did he succeed in staging his last play, *Batum* (about Stalin's youth), which was written at the request of the Art Theater. The theater awaited *Batum* like manna from heaven and they were elated by the manuscript, which the author delivered in 1939. But Stalin told Nemirovich-Danchenko that while he considered Bulgakov's work "very good," it should not be staged: "All children and youths are the same. Do not put on a play about the young Stalin."[10]

This was a mortal blow for the vulnerable Bulgakov, and he died soon afterward at the age of forty-eight. As for the Moscow Art Theater . . . well, it had survived the death of Chekhov, the battle with Gorky, even the arguments, alienation, and then enmity (hidden from outsiders) of its two great founders, Stanislavsky and Nemirovich-Danchenko. MAT continued presenting *The Days of the Turbins* right up until the war in 1941 (almost a thousand performances), when the sets were lost in a fire during an air raid.

The Art Theater was awarded the title "Academic" by the state in 1920, which conferred substantial privileges. In 1923, Stalin added the name "Gorky" to the company. Russian émigrés were outraged, recalling how in 1904, Nemirovich-Danchenko publicly told Chekhov, "This company, Anton, is yours!" The émigrés could not resign themselves to the idea that those days when you could say fairly openly what you thought were gone forever; in the new reality, Stanislavsky, who had always disliked Gorky for his pro-Bolshevik sentiments, now had to address the writer in the name of the Gorky MAT this way: "From now on we will work together on Soviet theater, which alone can support theater perishing all over the world."[11]

Stanislavsky was more or less sincere at least about "theater perishing all over the world." Traveling to Europe for treatment (Stalin generously allotting hard currency for that), Stanislavsky became convinced that culture there was in free fall: "Hitler broke them all up. There is no theater." While in the Soviet Union, thanks to Stalin, not only was MAT declared the best and exemplary collective that all others should emulate, but his cherished Method of training actors was officially proclaimed The Only True Method, with all the concomitant consequences.

Stanislavsky was clearly pleased: "In places that in tsarist Russia were barren fields, impenetrable tundras and backwaters, now life is thriving, art is blossoming, and they are studying my Method."[12] For all that, Stanislavsky, who died in 1938 with every possible prize and honor under his belt, being made one of the first People's Artists and receiving the Lenin Order, had not crossed the threshold of the MAT in the last years of his life, citing declining health.

Locking himself in his Moscow mansion like a medieval monk, Stanislavsky doggedly worked on his Method, which spread all over the world in approximate retellings and versions and was received as if it were the Holy Grail by many actors; in particular, in the United States, students of the Method, which had been adapted by Michael Chekhov (nephew of the great writer and a former student of Stanislavsky) and Lee Strasberg, included Henry Fonda, James Stewart, Anthony Quinn, and then Marlon Brando, Paul Newman, and even Marilyn Monroe.

Stalin made MAT and the Bolshoi his official court institutions that could not be criticized (except on his own orders). No wonder that MAT ossified and after the deaths of Stanislavsky and Nemirovich-Danchenko gradually turned into an empty shell. During the 1950s and 1960s, when audiences fought to get into Oleg Efremov's Sovremennik Theater and Lyubimov's Theater on the Taganka, obtaining tickets for MAT was not at all difficult. Tourists made up most of the audience.

Even high officials realized it, and in 1970 a special decision of the Secretariat of the Central Committee appointed Efremov to shore up MAT, which seriously weakened the Sovremennik but did not return MAT to its former glory. Efremov, a talented actor and fine director, who often went off on Karamazovian drinking binges, remained artistic director of MAT until his death in 2000, trying to renew it as best he could. Still, he was obliged to produce officially approved works like *Steel Workers* or *The Party Committee Meeting* with lines like: "As they justly pointed out to us at the Twenty-Fifth Party Congress . . ."

The low point of the new MAT came with the infamous production of a play about Lenin called *Thus We Will Win!* in March 1982, which was attended by Brezhnev and an entourage of Politburo members. In the government box, furbished specially for Stalin, the general secretary sat surrounded by three future Soviet leaders: Andropov, Konstantin Chernenko, and Gorbachev.

Brezhnev was very ill (he died in November of that year) and had trouble both hearing and comprehending; in a loud voice, he kept asking his comrades, "Is that Lenin? Shouldn't we greet him?" It was a great embarrassment. The audience laughed openly at what was going on in the box and on the stage, and the sorry episode became a symbol of the situation not only at the Moscow Art Theater but in the USSR as well.

On April 30, 1983, just a bit over three years later, Gorbachev, now the new ruler of the country, returned for a performance at MAT. He had been general secretary less than two months, and he clearly wanted to send a signal to the capital's intelligentsia: he chose to attend Chekhov's *Uncle Vanya* (in Efremov's staging) rather than one of the "Party" plays. A week later he telephoned the director.

Efremov naturally remembered Stalin's phone calls to Pasternak and Bulgakov, which were part of the MAT lore, for it was after the ruler's condescending conversation with Bulgakov that the writer was hastily given a job as assistant director at MAT. Neither Khrushchev nor Brezhnev repeated Stalin's gambit. As a Party member, Efremov considered a call from his new boss, Gorbachev, a signal event; embarrassed by the sweat that appeared on his brow during the call, Efremov paraphrased Chekhov to explain apologetically to his assistant: "It is hard to squeeze the slave out of oneself."[13]

Gorbachev told Efremov that his production of *Uncle Vanya* was a "feast for the spirit." However, in Russian his words *"pir dukha"* could easily sound like a rude criticism, *perdukha,* which basically means "a big fart." The director tensed up, but when he realized that Gorbachev had meant no insult, he asked for an audience with the general secretary. In response, Efremov heard "historic words" from the leader, which were probably the reason he had called in the first place: "Let me get the flywheel going first."[14]

They got the flywheel going so fast that the whole state flew apart. In the process, MAT broke up, among many other things small and big. Under Stalin, or even later, the division of MAT was unimaginable, although Stanislavsky and Nemirovich-Danchenko had seriously considered it when they were feuding. (That hostility was depicted with a satirical edge by Bulgakov in his unfinished masterpiece, *Theatrical Novel.*)

In 1986, when Efremov realized that he would not be able to handle the overgrown and contentious company (more than 150 actors alone, of which Efremov used only three dozen or so in his productions), he presented his half-baked idea of dividing the MAT troupe into two parts.

The authorities unexpectedly gave him the go-ahead: it was in accord with the new spirit of total perestroika.

The more conservative group of actors, headed by the theater's prima donna Tatyana Doronina, rebelled. MAT did not survive the attempted reform from within and collapsed; on its ruins two totally separate troupes formed in 1987: MAT in Kamergersky Alley, under the direction of Efremov, and MAT on Tverskoi Boulevard, where Doronina ruled. In 1989, Efremov's theater added Chekhov to its name, while Doronina's company kept the Gorky name, given by Stalin. The lines were drawn.

In 1998, the centenary of the Moscow Art Theater was celebrated with pomp. The festivities, accompanied by heavy nostalgia for the olden days when MAT had been the pride and cultural symbol of the country, were one more excuse for the endless squabbling between the proponents and the opponents of political and economic reforms in Russia.

In an interview, Doronina readily agreed with the remark of a conservative journalist that the destruction of MAT was a conspiracy and the model for the subsequent collapse of the Soviet Union: "The entire collective of MAT stood for unity. And this unity should not have been destroyed. Just as our country should not have been destroyed. But there were people at the theater and in the state who took advantage of our nonresistance, our Christian meekness—and got their dividends. The schism of the theater was planned, just as the collapse of the country was planned and rehearsed."[15]

Conspiracy theories explaining perestroika and the subsequent collapse of the Soviet Union as an evil plan executed by the West's "fifth column" abounded among radical conservatives. The writer Alexander Zinoviev, a former dissident, spent many years living abroad where, he said, he was in contact with Western intelligence agencies, and he claimed that "Gorbachev's rise to power was not simply the result of the country's internal development. It was the result of intervention from outside. It was a grand subversive operation on the part of the West. Back in 1984, people who were actively working on destroying our country told me: 'Wait a year and our man will be on the Russian throne.' And so they've put their man on the Russian throne. Without the West, Gorbachev would have never reached that position."[16]

Zinoviev and his supporters called Gorbachev, Yakovlev, and other reformers "Soviet Judases" in the pay of the CIA, a view that was not shared by everyone in the ultraconservative camp. But Zinoviev went even further: since the Gorbachev reforms were implemented "before the eyes of the people, with its connivance and even approval," the writer branded the whole country as the "traitor nation."[17]

Valentin Rasputin, one of the respected leaders of "village" prose, was horrified by what he considered the evil mutation of the cultural landscape in Gorbachev's Soviet Union: the uncontrolled breeding of rock groups, playing music that caused "dangerous changes in the blood"; the proliferation of beauty contests; the formerly banned sex scenes now common in Soviet films and even the appearance of homosexuals in television programs, who, Rasputin reminded his audience, were still, thank God, illegal in the Soviet Union. All this, he insisted, was part of a planned program "to corrupt minds and souls."[18]

The transformations in the country, which for many decades had been isolated from the influence of Western mass culture, really could be seen as quite radical. Particularly annoying for the archconservatives was the ubiquitous presence of innumerable rock groups, finally let off the leash.

In Brezhnev's Soviet Union, rock music existed underground, and under the watchful eye of the KGB: it was considered ideologically harmful, replacing jazz, which had become respectable even in the eyes of the Party bureaucrats (it was said that Andropov was a jazz aficionado). Young people by now preferred disco music and then rock to jazz, and in big cities almost every building had its own amateur group that imitated Western models, especially the Beatles.

Some reasonable minds in the KGB understood they were unlikely to eradicate this mass underground movement and therefore tried to control it. In Moscow, Leningrad, and a few other large cities, the KGB—as an experiment in the 1970s—permitted several rock festivals to take place and rock clubs to be organized, the one in Leningrad becoming the most famous.[19]

The first popular domestic rock groups with original Russian-language repertoire appeared: in Moscow Mashina Vremeni, led by Andrei Makarevich, and in Leningrad, Akvarium, whose leader, Boris Grebenshchikov, was called the Soviet Bob Dylan, even though he preferred to be compared to David Bowie.

These and other early rock groups (DDT, created by Yuri Shevchuk in Ufa, Nautilus Pompilius from Sverdlovsk, Auktsion from Leningrad, and

Zvuki Mu from Moscow) existed in a parallel reality, on the edge of per-mitted and forbidden, legal and illegal. Makarevich, Grebenshchikov, and Shevchuk wrote songs that could be called proto-perestroika, like "The Turn," a hit from Mashina Vremeni that back in 1979 told people in allegorical terms not to fear extreme shifts in the country's life.

During perestroika, the frightened conservatives imagined that this music they so hated enveloped them; Rasputin declared that rock had a "destructive influence on the psyche" and fumed, "The news on televi-sion has rock music, music class in kindergarten has rock, the classics are given in a rock version, plays are given rock scores."[20]

For "villagers" like Rasputin, even more unacceptable was the sudden ubiquity of the new androgynous pop stars like Valery Leontyev or the openly homosexual theater productions by Roman Viktyuk, as well as the tolerance of works that used to be considered experimental. Many authors of such works, who had moved from the shadows to the center of attention, were women (the writers Ludmila Petrushevskaya, Tatyana Tolstaya, and Ludmila Ulitskaya, the poets Elena Shvarts and Olga Sedakova, the film director Kira Muratova, the artists Natalya Nesterova and Tatyana Nazarenko, the composers Galina Ustvolskaya and Sofia Gubaidulina), and this only added to the traditionalists' discomfort. This was new and powerful women's art, a vivid continuation of the "Ama-zons" of the Russian avant-garde at the turn of the century, and there were people who could not stomach it.

The conservative camp of Russian culture, sensing a threat to its exis-tence (or at least its well-being), panicked and moved even closer to the opponents of the Gorbachev reforms. On July 23, 1991, they published "A Word to the People" in the newspaper *Sovetskaya Rossiya,* and it became the anti-reform manifesto.

Composed by writer Alexander Prokhanov and signed by him and other foes of liberalization like the writers Rasputin and Yuri Bondarev, "A Word to the People" called for ousting the traitors from power and replacing them with patriotic leaders: "Let's wake up and come to our senses, arise old and young for the country. Let's say 'No!' to the destroyers and occupiers. Let's put an end to our retreat. . . . We are starting a popular movement, calling into our ranks those who have rec-ognized the terrible adversity that has befallen our country."

The critic Vladimir Bondarenko, who shared their views, called these people "flaming reactionaries." Their alarmist slogans were supposed to provide ideological cover for the coup planned by the counterreformers. On the night of August 18, 1991, the conspirators declared martial law and pushed Gorbachev aside. They brought tanks into the capital, assuming that this display of military might would scare off the populace, but it quickly became obvious that the putsch had failed. Thousands of Muscovites gathered at the House of Soviets of the Russian Federation (known as the White House) to demonstrate their support for charismatic Boris Yeltsin, who headed the resistance to the coup.

The conspirators' tanks did not dare storm the White House, and the troops loyal to Yeltsin arrested the putsch leaders three days later. The Soviet Union fell apart, and its president, Gorbachev, turned over his authority to Yeltsin. Soviet Communism collapsed after seventy-four years. "The empire ended, history ended, life ended—it didn't matter what came next. It didn't matter in what order firebrands and shards would come flying or at what speed," wrote Andrei Bitov.[21]

A cultural artifact of that historic moment is the poem Yevgeny Yevtushenko declaimed on the morning of August 20 from the balcony of the White House to the crowd of two hundred thousand defenders of democracy, in which he compared the White House to a "wounded marble swan of freedom." It was, according to Yevtushenko, his "very best bad poem."[22]

Gorbachev was better educated than Khrushchev or Brezhnev, but less well read than Stalin or Andropov. Yeltsin's cultural worldview was apparently much narrower than Gorbachev's. It's unlikely that Yeltsin could have recited a Lermontov poem extemporaneously or do chitchat about the latest play or novel, like Gorbachev. But Yeltsin could act as a battering ram at dramatic moments, which sometimes helped and often hindered the cause.

The liberal wing of the Soviet cultural elite, which had bet on Gorbachev, recoiled from its idol as soon as it became clear that the reforms were stuck, and followed Yeltsin as the more decisive leader. Yeltsin, even though he had been formed like Gorbachev in the depths of the Party nomenklatura, was initially more democratic and more accessible and appeared to be more pliable: Russian intellectuals assumed that he could be eventually shaped into a "good" ruler for Russia. And why not: after all, Yeltsin spoke respectfully to them, using the formal pronoun "*Vy*" and their name and patronymic, unlike Gorbachev, who used the familiar "*ty*" with everyone (a bad Party habit).

Yeltsin seemed to appreciate the imagination of his new liberal advisors, but unlike Gorbachev, he did not see high culture as his useful ally. In breaking the Soviet system, Yeltsin rejected its cultural policies as well. The new president must have considered (not without reason) all those thousands of writers, poets, artists, and musicians who, as members of the "creative" unions, had been supported by the Communist state, as wastrels and spongers, living off the people.

The Soviet cultural apparatus had been in place since the Stalin era, around sixty years. It was well oiled by state subsidies and controlled from top to bottom. Stalin knew why he needed high culture and he managed it with carrot and stick. The Soviet leaders after him did not have his clarity on the issue, but they followed in his wake—however, using the stick less and counting more on the edifying nature of carrots. Under Gorbachev the stick had turned into a twig that no one feared, and the intellectuals wanted to take over the allocation of carrots: this was their golden opportunity.

When the Soviet regime fell, the totalitarian stick vanished completely, but so did the carrots. The state-sponsored film industry withered; the circulation numbers of the traditional "thick" literary journals, which had climbed astronomically under Gorbachev, declined sharply; the publication of poetry and prose also fell; the only source of income for symphony orchestras and ballet troupes were foreign tours; thousands of Russian musicians and dancers moved to the West, since the borders were open for the first time in decades. New Russian stars like the singer Dmitri Khvorostovsky, pianist Yevgeny Kissin, and violinist Maxim Vengerov settled in Europe. Many people in Russia and the West had expected an immediate flowering of culture after the fall of the Communist regime. Almost the complete opposite occurred.

The catastrophic drying up of the cultural flow took place amid general impoverishment caused by the radical turn toward a market economy by the Yeltsin team. Prices rose thirty times over, salaries and pensions were paid irregularly, and savings became worthless. The silent dissatisfaction of the masses was used by the parliament leadership, which had turned into a center of opposition to Yeltsin; in the fall of 1993, parliament tried to overthrow him. As it had been during the failed coup of 1991, the sympathies of the intelligentsia were divided: the president was supported by those who wanted the reforms to continue, while the "flaming reactionaries" inspired the conservative parliament. Both sides thought their opponents were dragging Russia into an abyss.

Subsequent events brought the final splash of participation by the cultural elite in Russia's political life in the twentieth century. There was a whiff of civil war in the air, which both sides feared even as they realized that things were heading toward armed confrontation. The embattled sides needed ideological cover, which could be supplied only by the intellectuals. The reactionaries heated up rhetoric about Yeltsin's "criminally cosmopolitan regime" that was destroying Russian culture and the state. The reformers called on the president to deal forcefully with the "fascist" opponents.

Manifestos from both sides exacerbated the situation, but Yeltsin's tanks had the last word on October 4, 1993, firing on the opposition White House, which was then taken by storm. This confrontation between president and parliament ended in Yeltsin's victory, but the fact that there were many casualties, including civilians, shocked the country.

Yeltsin found determined supporters here, too, including influential ones like Academician Dmitri Likhachev and the poets Akhmadulina and Okudzhava. Yeltsin's firing on the White House united Communists with former dissidents like Zinoviev and Maximov against him. Sinyavsky complained bitterly, "Today the most horrible thing is happening: my old enemies are starting to tell the truth sometimes, and my own tribe of Russian intelligentsia, instead of creating some sort of opposition to Yeltsin and somehow correcting the mistakes of Yeltsin's rule, is once again hailing every move of the regime and supporting its harsh measures. All that has happened before. That is how the Soviet regime began."[23]

Among the defenders of the White House were the writers Alexander Prokhanov and Eduard Limonov. Only the bizarre zigzags of post-Soviet politics could have brought such disparate personalities together. Prokhanov, back in the Brezhnev era, burst onto the scene with his novel *A Tree in the Center of Kabul* (about the Soviet invasion of Afghanistan), which earned him a prize from the Defense Ministry and the nickname "Nightingale of the General Staff." Continuing to describe in a flowery, quasi-expressionist style events in hot spots around the globe (novels set in Cambodia, Mozambique, Nicaragua), Prokhanov quickly moved up the ladder, becoming secretary of the board of the Writers' Union.

Limonov, on the contrary, was always marginal. He started out as a sophisticated avant-garde poet, known in Moscow's bohemian circles also as someone who could sew a pair of durable jeans inexpensively. With many other nonconformists, Limonov ended up in the United States in the mid-1970s, and in 1979 published his first novel, *It's Me, Eddie,* which created a brouhaha in émigré circles with its sexual episodes, unusually frank for Russian literature (including the homosexual encounter between the novel's autobiographical hero and a black New Yorker in Central Park) and its free use of previously unprintable language.

In his New York years, he stood out in the rough-and-tumble Russian bohemian crowd with his neatness, punctuality, and reliability. Those qualities helped him get a job as butler in a millionaire's house. But, behind the polished servant's mask there lurked the adventurer and the neurotic mind of a Russian Louis Céline without the anti-Semitism. The artist Vagrich Bakhchanyan, a friend of Limonov's, recalled the writer's three suicide attempts (the first when he was still in school), all caused by failed love affairs.[24] Today, Limonov claims to have "iron mental health," but back then, it was a different story.

Like the experienced tailor he was, Limonov recut his personal myth many times. People who knew him in his youth say he was a mama's boy, while Limonov's nostalgic autobiographical prose *(Teenager Savenko, Young Scoundrel,* and *We Had a Great Epoch)* depicts him as an adroit and fearless gang leader. Limonov's father was an officer in the NKVD (KGB), but the young writer positioned himself among Moscow dissidents as staunchly anti-Soviet. When he immigrated, he tried to become a cosmopolitan author in the United States and later in France. Then, to the astonishment of his New York and Paris acquaintances, he declared himself a Russian patriot par excellence.

The biggest somersault came in the post-Soviet era, when Limonov moved back to Moscow, where in 1994 he founded the radical National-Bolshevik Party with the proclaimed goal of uniting extreme right and extreme left (in Limonov's terminology, "fascists" and "anarchists") to fight against democracy and the "new world order," which he described as the "total despotism of the U.S.A. and the European Community over the world."[25]

In 2001, Limonov was arrested and in 2003 he was sentenced to four years in prison on charges of illegally procuring firearms, but he was released on probation a month later. Limonov learned of the terrorist attack on the United States on September 11 while in prison, and the news "made him exult," because America "is a country of violence, dictating its will to everyone. It deserved to be punished."[26]

Over the two years in prison, Limonov wrote eight books, including his utopian manifesto, *Another Russia: Outline of the Future*, in which he proclaimed the collapse of the old Russian culture and presented his ideas of new, nomadic Russia. Now, Limonov said, "a writer's glory no longer excites me. My literary talent has received world recognition. Now I want my political gift to be recognized."[27]

The low-circulation opposition newspapers where Prokhanov and Limonov published their passionate anti-Yeltsin appeals were shut down by presidential decree after the White House capitulated on October 4, 1993, under the pressure of pro-Yeltsin troops. The reactionaries spoke of violation of freedom of the press. However, many of these publications reopened, but they continued to be unpopular: none of the opposition ideologists had national authority.

There was probably only one man at that time who did: Solzhenitsyn. People were waiting to hear his opinion of the traumatic events that shook the nation. But Solzhenitsyn, who had lived twelve and a half years in the West by then and had announced that he was planning to return to Russia, spoke unusually briefly and impassively, characterizing the clash of October 3–4 as a "completely unavoidable and expected stage in our tortuous and long path for freedom from Communism."[28]

Perhaps Solzhenitsyn was being cautious so as to retain room for political maneuver. He had just completed the major work of his life, the ten-volume historical epic *The Red Wheel*, planned when he was an eighteen-year-old student. His idea was to describe the February 1917 revolution, which brought down the tsar and opened the way for the eventual Bolshevik victory, which he always considered the most significant and fateful event in Russia's history, changing the destiny of the country and the world.

Solzhenitsyn explained the symbolism of the title this way: "Revolution is an enormous cosmic Wheel, like a galaxy . . . that begins unfolding—and all the people, including the ones that started it turning, become grains of sand. And they die there in multitudes."[29] In order to describe the causes of revolution, Solzhenitsyn also tackled World War I and its roots, concentrating on four "knots": August 1914, October 1916, March 1917, and April 1917.

This historic canvas of colossal scope (Solzhenitsyn worked on it for a solid eighteen years) presented complex narrative problems, which the author attempted to solve by compressing enormous documentary material through various devices: there are psychological profiles of political leaders of the period (the portraits of Lenin and Nicholas II are outstanding), chronicles of events, documents (letters, telegrams, leaflets), and ample quotations from newspapers.

It is all painstakingly organized, particularly with the help of rhythmically active prose. Solzhenitsyn manipulates the narrative rhythm, constantly changing it, juxtaposing contrasting sections and small episodes. This is musical prose, comparable not to *War and Peace,* as it sometimes is, but to the operas of Mussorgsky or Rimsky-Korsakov.

When I wrote to Solzhenitsyn in 1985 about this (in connection with *October 1916*), he replied: "You felt it very correctly: frankly, my favorite 'literature' teacher is Beethoven, I somehow always hear him when I write."[30] *The Red Wheel,* contrary to the popular perception of Solzhenitsyn as a heavily didactic writer, has no central hero to express the author's point of view—it is dialogical (to use Mikhail Bakhtin's terminology), or even symphonic.

Solzhenitsyn clearly wanted to give the reader a maximum amount of "objective" information to consider: hence the stress on describing real events instead of love triangles, so beloved in the novel genre. Trying to comprehend what led Russia to revolution, which he considered a national tragedy, Solzhenitsyn came to the conclusion that "everyone was at fault, including the ordinary people, who easily fell for the cheap infection, the cheap trick, and rushed to loot, to kill, rushed to join the bloody dance. But the guiltiest of all, of course, were those in charge."[31]

This point of view precluded the acceptance of *The Red Wheel,* Solzhenitsyn's life work, both among liberals, who still considered the February revolution an important milestone in the failed history of democracy in Russia, and among conservatives, who thought that all the country's woes were caused by outsiders, Jews being the main culprits.

Solzhenitsyn's relations with the Western political elite were not very good. He was always a fierce opponent of détente with the Soviet Union. Feeling that Western compromises would inevitably lead to catastrophe, Solzhenitsyn came up with an astonishing thesis that "World War III has already taken place and it ended with the defeat of the West."[32]

With this polemical slogan, the writer thrust himself into the very center of American political debate. His moral capital in the West was substantial at the time, and Solzhenitsyn decided to use it to make a difference in US foreign policy. His 1973 "Letter to the Soviet Leaders," an ambitious program of reforms for Communist Russia, was never answered. Apparently, he expected US politicians to heed his advice more readily. He was mistaken.

The West did exploit Solzhenitsyn to the hilt in the Cold War. But the writer wanted to be more than an ideological weapon in someone else's hands. He aspired to a position of real political power, without getting American citizenship first. (Congress had discussed making him an honorary citizen but then quietly dropped the idea.)

There were many European and American politicians, especially conservatives, who listened to Solzhenitsyn attentively. In 1976 the election platform of the Republican Party included a reference to Solzhenitsyn as a great beacon of human valor and morality. But when it came to real actions, the Americans were very cautious.

No American president—not Gerald Ford, Jimmy Carter, Ronald Reagan, or Bill Clinton—met with Solzhenitsyn; they were not ready for even this symbolic gesture. Reagan did invite Solzhenitsyn to visit the White House in 1982 as part of a large group of other Soviet dissidents, some of them the writer's implacable foes, which made it unacceptable for Solzhenitsyn; the press reported that the reason the president was not eager to meet separately with Solzhenitsyn was that the writer allegedly was a "symbol of extreme Russian nationalism."

The real reason for American wariness of Solzhenitsyn was that they did not see any real alternative to negotiating with the Soviet Union, while the writer denounced such dealings as useless and even harmful. In the eyes of Western pragmatists, Solzhenitsyn was acting beyond his area of competence.

When he attacked the Soviet Union and its gulag, it was perceived as a truthful account by a fearless eyewitness and a great writer. But in his interviews and speeches, the most famous being the Harvard graduation address in 1978, Solzhenitsyn started criticizing the West, offering his profoundly conservative advice, and the attitude toward him changed markedly.

The Western press began referring to Solzhenitsyn as an outsider, an old-fashioned moralist, anti-Semite, monarchist, and religious fanatic, and even compared him to the Ayatollah Khomeini. (Many of these arguments came from recent immigrants from Russia; Solzhenitsyn tried to counter them, but in vain.) He repaid the Western press (and more broadly, Western culture as a whole) in kind, accusing it of arrogance, cynicism, irresponsibility, and immorality.

In the end, the gap between the writer and many of the Western intellectuals who had put in a lot of effort to publicize Solzhenitsyn as an international prophet, the new Leo Tolstoy, widened dramatically. By the time perestroika had begun in the Soviet Union, the peak of Solzhenitsyn's influence in the West was behind him.

Back home, however, Solzhenitsyn's reputation was higher than ever. Gorbachev was wary of him but was forced by public opinion to appear better disposed toward the writer, and in the fall of 1989 the Politburo gave permission to publish *The Gulag Archipelago* in the journal *Novy Mir,* where Tvardovsky had printed *One Day in the Life of Ivan Denisovich* in 1962.

The subscription to *Novy Mir* instantly rose to 2,710,000. Sergei Zalygin, the editor, hurried to declare 1990 "the year of Solzhenitsyn," proudly stating: "This concentration on a single author has perhaps not been known in any literature before and will not be known again."[33]

Fourteen years before that moment, in the West, Solzhenitsyn had predicted that if his *Gulag Archipelago* were widely distributed in the Soviet Union, "things would get very tough for the Communist ideology in a very short time." As it happened, Solzhenitsyn's most famous work became widely available to Soviet readers at a time when that ideology was already crumbling. That is why it is difficult to assess accurately the degree to which *Archipelago*'s publication (it sold a hundred thousand copies in book form in 1990, too) helped Yeltsin's victory and the collapse of the Soviet Union.

Solzhenitsyn imagined Soviet readers to still be the way he had known them many years earlier, when every important book was pored over by the public, read thoroughly and thoughtfully and then discussed heatedly. In the new reality, readers were bombarded by formerly banned and "subversive" books and were restless and inattentive. In addition, the pitched battle in politics, covered round the clock by television, also distracted even the most fervent book lovers.

Solzhenitsyn's long stay in exile was an obstacle as well. The loss of contact was bilateral. The writer had spent his eighteen years in Vermont in great isolation, working up to fourteen hours a day. In all those years, he came to the phone only a few times, he claimed; the connection with the outside world was maintained by his indefatigable wife, Natalya.

Neither Leo Tolstoy in Yasnaya Polyana nor even Gorky, when he was on Capri, lived in such isolation. Therefore, they had a better idea of the evolution of their Russian audience. Also, both understood how the capitalist press worked (Gorky had been a reporter in his youth) and how to use it.

Eighty-year-old Tolstoy in Yasnaya Polyana readily received correspondents even from tabloids, if he felt he needed to express his position on a current issue, and he did not take offense at their pushiness. But Solzhenitsyn stopped giving interviews in 1983, explaining huffily, "I realized that no one was asking for my criticism and that I was wasting my time, which is precious to me, on nothing. I decided: enough, from now on I will concentrate only on my literary work."[34]

Solzhenitsyn's political manifestos in the Soviet period had one serious flaw: there was no clear addressee. Solzhenitsyn as polemicist worked in one genre, appeals *urbi et orbi*. His statements could have a powerful public resonance when they appeared (also leaving potentially fascinating material for future historians), but their immediate practical effect usually remained nil. That was the fate of Solzhenitsyn's famous texts "Letter to the Soviet Leaders" (1973) and "Live Not By Lies!" (1974).

A similar fate befell his next important manifesto, *Rebuilding Russia* [in Russian, *How Shall We Organize Russia?*], when he finally decided to break his silence for the first time in the years of perestroika. He finished the long article in the summer of 1990 and immediately responded to the invitation of Prime Minister of Russia Ivan Silayev to come to Moscow (he declined then, feeling it was premature) by asking him to publish his latest manifesto in a large edition.

His not-so-subtle hint was picked up instantly and *Rebuilding Russia* was printed simultaneously in *Komsomolskaya Pravda* and *Literaturnaya Gazeta*, with a total circulation of twenty-seven million. Solzhenitsyn's manifesto could be purchased at any newspaper kiosk in the land for a few kopecks. The writer later admitted that he "had never dreamed" of something like that. For the government, which still had direct control of the leading publications, it was a generous gesture, which, as it became clear, obliged it to nothing.

The ideas Solzhenitsyn expressed in *Rebuilding Russia* were radical for the times: he proposed liquidating the Communist Party, getting rid of the KGB, moving to a market economy, and privatizing land. His main point was immediately disbanding the Soviet Union, giving independence to the Baltics, the Caucasus, and Central Asia. Instead of the Soviet empire, the author proposed creating a new Russian Union that would include Russia, Ukraine, and Belorussia, as well as the northern regions of Kazakhstan, settled by Russians.

The implementation of these ideas would be in the hands of the Supreme Soviet of the USSR, but none of its leading factions supported Solzhenitsyn's proposals in the fall of 1990—they did not suit Gorbachev, who was trying to preserve the Soviet Union, nor the political elites of Ukraine, Belorussia, or Kazakhstan. Solzhenitsyn's article was rejected almost without discussion by both Communists and democrats.

Gorbachev announced then that the ideas of "the great writer were unacceptable," since Solzhenitsyn "was all in the past." The suggestion of obsolescence was prompted by the deliberately archaic style of Solzhenitsyn's text, which, as one reader put it, "makes you think Solzhenitsyn is addressing our great-grandfathers in 1913."[35]

His opponents called *Rebuilding Russia* a retrospective utopia. Anti-Solzhenitsyn demonstrations were organized in Ukraine and Kazakhstan, and newspapers with his article and his pictures were burned.

Solzhenitsyn had made a tactical error once again: instead of trying to influence concrete political leaders or deputies of the Supreme Soviet, he addressed himself to the people in general, the abstract masses, which, he felt, would read his work and in some mysterious way implement all his suggestions (there were more than two hundred in *Rebuilding Russia*).

But his manifesto did not interest the mass reader at all: it seemed too long, boring, and affected. He chose not to formulate his ideas in a simple, clear, and effective slogan-like style, preferring to use a highfalutin vocabulary. This was the conflict between Solzhenitsyn the writer and Solzhenitsyn the politician, in which the former won to the detriment of the message. Solzhenitsyn never did acknowledge this, explaining away the failure of his proposals by the fact that "first Gorbachev suppressed them, forbidding discussion . . . and then many people, busy with daily life and sitting by the television, as was fashionable then—they kept watching and watching the deputies give speeches, waiting for something to happen there—they missed these ideas . . . this means that the country at that time had not matured enough for those thoughts."[36]

When in his opinion Russia had matured enough for his thoughts, Solzhenitsyn returned to his homeland. It took place in May 1994, and his popularity and prestige in Russia was still incredibly high. He was even asked to run for president (he refused) and some people seriously thought that if he wanted, Solzhenitsyn could become a new Russian tsar.

But Solzhenitsyn did not want the burden of power or the responsibility, although he did not refuse the right to influence policy at first: "I, for as long as I have the strength, will try to help the people with my words, written and spoken. For we are in a crisis."

From all appearances, Solzhenitsyn had only a vague idea of his part in the solution of that crisis. He did not want to join any existing movement in Russia or start his own party: "I am against parties in general. There are heavenly creations—nation, family—but a party . . . I not only have never belonged to any party—I reject on principle creating parties and a party system."[37] Still, he maintained that "morality must not only influence the hearts of politicians, but it must have a certain advisory function. Not legislative, not executive power, but simply an advisory influence."[38]

That position on the eve of his return to Russia was yet another modification of his old idea that "a great writer is like a second government." The model here for Solzhenitsyn was Leo Tolstoy, with his attempt to influence politics by the force of his colossal moral authority.

But when Solzhenitsyn gave a long speech televised live on October 28, 1994, to the parliament, the event was not reminiscent of Tolstoy, who avoided solemn meetings with the powers-that-be, but of Gorky's pomp-filled return in 1928 to Stalinist Moscow from Italy.

For all the outward similarity, the substantive difference was great. Stalin, who was by then the dictator of the Soviet Union, saw in Gorky a potential powerful ally. The cultural programs of Stalin and Gorky did not always correspond, but the ruler and the writer demonstrated their solidarity to the world, each secretly hoping to use the other for his own goals. In exchange for Gorky's public approval of his policies, Stalin conferred on him the unprecedented power of influencing the country's cultural transformation.

Precisely because Boris Yeltsin was no Stalin, Solzhenitsyn could not have played the role of Gorky with him, even if he had wanted to. Yeltsin did not even have the dictatorial powers of Khrushchev. Without Khrushchev's sanction, *One Day in the Life of Ivan Denisovich* could not have appeared in the Soviet Union of that time. It is unlikely that Brezhnev actually read anything by Solzhenitsyn; Andropov definitely did, and hated it. Gorbachev's aide recorded Gorbachev's passionate reaction in January 1989 to Solzhenitsyn's "Lenin in Zurich" (a chapter from *August 1914*); the ruler recounted what he had read at length and with emotion: "Strong stuff! Angry, but talented!"[39]

While in power, Yeltsin could not be suspected of a passion for reading, but he was the first leader of Russia to publicly demonstrate his respect for Solzhenitsyn. According to his press secretary, Yeltsin considered few of his contemporaries his equal, but he valued the power of moral authority, and so he was quite anxious before his first meeting with Solzhenitsyn face-to-face on November 16, 1994.[40]

By that time, Yeltsin permitted himself to meet even high-ranking guests while tipsy. But the president sensed that this would not do for Solzhenitsyn, who while not a teetotaler, did not approve of alcohol. Hard-drinking Viktor Nekrasov, author of the war classic *In the Trenches of Stalingrad*, recalled the time that Solzhenitsyn invited him over for a talk "about the future of Russian literature," which turned into a half-hour monologue on the evils of drink: "When will you stop drinking? You're not a writer anymore, you're a writer plus a bottle of vodka."[41]

The president's aides tried to encourage him: "Who is Solzhenitsyn, anyway? He's not a classic, no Tolstoy. And everyone is sick of him. So, he suffered from totalitarianism, yes, he knows history. But there are thousands like him! And there is only one of you."[42] Yeltsin's foes tried to pit Solzhenitsyn against him when the meeting was announced. "Will Solzhenitsyn settle for the pathetic role of private confidant to an obstinate drunken fool who is consciously and ruthlessly destroying our common home, Russia?"[43]

Yeltsin decided not to tease the bull and appeared for the meeting as sober as a judge and surprisingly well prepared. The conversation (without any witnesses) lasted more than four hours, and apparently went well—despite the obvious political disagreements—since both participants ended up having a drink, to the president's great relief. When a journalist asked Solzhenitsyn to comment on his visit, the writer remarked: "He's very Russian." And added, "Too Russian."[44]

Despite the temporary cease-fire, Solzhenitsyn's influence on real politics remained a phantom in Russia, as well. His "historic" speech at the parliament in 1994 was received sourly: the members of the government and a good half of the deputies did not show up, the audience reacted wanly and applauded sparingly (mostly the Communists). Some of the younger deputies laughed openly during his speech: the familiar moaning about "our woes and our wounds" did not touch them.

Relations between Solzhenitsyn and Yeltsin quickly deteriorated. At first the authorities gave the writer a platform for his views: in April 1995 on ORT, national Channel One, Solzhenitsyn began his talk show, in which he criticized the parliament, the Russian electoral system, grumbled about the horrible situation in the villages and attacked the government for its war in Chechnya.

His television appearances were not particularly popular, but they did irritate the authorities, who waited six months (there had been twelve fifteen-minute broadcasts in that period) and then blocked the writer's access to television with a lame excuse about "low ratings" (while everyone knew that ratings were manipulated in Moscow). A commentator noted sarcastically: "Imagine Leo Tolstoy bringing an article to a magazine, and hearing, 'Sorry, Count, your rating is too low! We're going to put a page of police jokes in your slot.' "[45]

The unceremonious canning of Solzhenitsyn's program, which pleased some, was seen as a sad symbol of the era by others. It signaled major changes in the country's cultural situation. It was becoming ever clearer that the old Russian logocentrism, with its idolization of the word and its magical properties, was waning.

That great Russian tradition had had its high points. One was Solzhenitsyn's heroic resistance to the Soviet political system in the 1960s–1970s. In 1978, Maximov, then editor of the leading émigré journal *Kontinent* and no apologist for Solzhenitsyn, summarized the general perception of the writer's importance: "You can accept Solzhenitsyn or

not, listen to him or not, love him or hate him, but the tragic era in which
we live is passing under his sign and without any consideration of our
wants will be named for him."[46]

Maximov's statement seemed more indisputable then than it did some
twenty years later. In 1991, a revolution took place in Russia, whether you
consider it for better or worse. The émigré philosopher Georgy Fedotov,
watching the tectonic shifts in Stalinist Russia from Paris in 1938, said
with a sigh: "No nation comes out of a revolutionary catastrophe in the
same shape that it went into it. An entire historic epoch, with its experience, tradition, and culture, is crossed out. A new page of life is turned
over."[47] Among the causes for radical cultural changes in the 1930s,
Fedotov listed the people's loss of religious faith and the quick absorp-
tion by the masses "of civilization at its most superficial: Marxism, Dar-
winism, technology."[48]

By the end of the twentieth century, a somewhat similar situation had
developed in Russia: the hollow pyramid of Communist ideology had
collapsed, and the country embarked on a new, dizzying spiral of Westernization, which in many ways turned out to be a mixed blessing. The
Soviet censors had diligently sifted the cultural product coming from the
West. Now, a huge flow of bad American movies, bland pop music, and
pulp fiction rushed into the country. At the same time, the state made
severe cuts in financing national theaters, serious films, opera, ballet, and
symphony orchestras.

Literature in particular lost ground, after playing such a visible role in
perestroika. The Soviet Union used to call itself "the most reading country in the world." In contemporary Russia, as in the entire world, people
read less and less, therefore print runs for books, the traditional "thick"
journals, and highbrow periodicals were falling. The public idols were no
longer writers and poets but pop musicians, film actors, and television
celebrities, as it is everywhere else.

One of the last serious authors who made his way into the pantheon
of cultural heroes was the eccentric Venedikt Erofeyev, who in his popular novella "Moscow-Petushki" (which had circulated in manuscript for
years in the USSR and was at last published in 1988, only two years
before his death at fifty-one) created an autobiographical image of an
alcoholic and tramp traveling the commuter train from Moscow to the

end of the line, Petushki, that resonated with pages from Dostoevsky and Rozanov. Erofeyev, an erudite and subtle stylist in the surrealistic vein, managed, as had Sergei Dovlatov who died the same year, to intrigue the reader, creating a memorable image of an ordinary guy, who with the help of a bottle of vodka turns into an existentialist philosopher commenting acidly on Soviet absurdity.

As Russian literature in the 1990s ceded its former central role, poetry in particular lost its former public significance, becoming, in the wry observation of critic Viktor Toporov, a marginal occupation within a marginal profession: "One poet has written several thousand poems but still is famous only for screaming like a banshee. Another reads from catalogue cards, cursing under his breath, which due to his profoundly intellectual appearance creates a comic impression. A third composes one mediocre poem a year—and is proud. A fourth tells boring stories in a booming voice, hoping they pass for poetry."[49]

These lampoon portraits of prominent contemporary poets (respectively, Dmitri Prigov, Lev Rubinshtein, Sergei Gandlevsky, and Yevgeny Rein) were manifestly unfair, but they reflected the marginal status of the poets, which the writers themselves recognized, using it to justify their position as observers rather than participants and certainly not arbiters of public life.

Gandlevsky (a serious poet who in fact does write very little) admitted, "With the years, I came to terms with the notion that I do not belong to the same civilization as nine-tenths of my countrymen. This narrows my ambitions. You understand as a writer: you are not the spokesperson of those people."[50] Paradoxically, Gandlevsky connects his refusal to take a public stand to the same Soviet experience that produced the larger-than-life figures of Solzhenitsyn and Brodsky, stressing "the danger of overestimating the importance of one's message, a supergoal, becoming a missionary—pride always finds a loophole: we may have ended up in a puddle, but at least it's the deepest one in the world."[51]

The postmodernist Prigov also rejected the traditional great claims made by Russian writers: "The intelligentsia fought for the minds of the masses. I don't do that. I only fight for my personal spot in the cultural marketplace."[52]

With Russian culture atomized along the Western model, writers focused on finding comfortable genre or stylistic niches. Vladimir Sorokin brilliantly parodied the classic unhurried Russian novel and the placid socialist realist industrial fables ("boy meets girl and tractor"), exploding the traditional schemes with scenes of wild sex and sadism. (The pioneer in this field was Yuri Mamleyev, the grandfather of the contemporary Russian literary mysticism.)

The disturbing sex descriptions were particularly shocking when Sorokin read them aloud, being a quiet, pleasant-looking man with a stutter. Another prose writer, Viktor Pelevin, first cultivated an image as a homegrown eccentric (walking around Moscow in a gorilla mask), then became a recluse in the manner of Thomas Pynchon (refusing to give interviews or have his photograph taken, communicating only by email), while writing stylish science fiction in the manner of Philip K. Dick. He claimed, like Prigov, that he wrote not to lead his readers anywhere but rather to entertain himself.

Broader audiences were addressed by Edvard Radzinsky, the author of popular historical novels and plays, by Grigory Chkhartishvili, a Japan scholar, who under the pseudonym B. Akunin was the first to offer a cycle of "retro" detective novels, based on popular British models, but with a whiff of Dostoevsky, and by the much less pretentious (and therefore even more popular) authors of contemporary police procedurals and chick lit like Darya Dontsova, Alexandra Marinina, and Maria Arbatova.

The Soviet and even the post-Soviet value systems became irrelevant. When a group of influential critics was asked to name the most important works of the 1990s at the end of the decade, Sorokin got as many votes as Solzhenitsyn (two), and Gandlevsky was even with Brodsky (both got four votes). The leaders among poets were the slick parodist Timur Kibirov and the philosophical ironist Lev Losev, and among prose writers, Pelevin came right behind Makanin and Georgy Vladimov, whose historical novel about Nazi collaborator Andrei Vlasov, hanged in 1945 on Stalin's orders, was the literary sensation of 1994.

On December 31, 1999, on the eve of the twenty-first century and the third millennium (a date to which many at the time attributed mystical significance), Yeltsin appeared with a televised address to announce to the stunned nation that he was retiring early and handing the presidency to Vladimir Putin, forty-seven, a previously little-known former KGB officer who became head of the Federal Security Service in 1998 and in August 1999 was named prime minister.

Yeltsin's departure, which had been secretly prepared for a long time but came as a total surprise to the country, drew a line under an entire era. During his turbulent administration, Russia came dangerously close to an economic crash and political collapse. Yeltsin confessed: "I am tired and the country is tired of me."[53] Solzhenitsyn summarized it all in 2000 even more forcefully: "There is nothing left that had not been ruined or embezzled."[54]

Yeltsin, unlike Gorbachev, truly did want to end the Communist regime in Russia. But like Gorbachev, he often improvised, with disastrous results. Masses of people were impoverished and disillusioned in the concepts of democracy and the market economy. The crash of liberal ideals led to words like "democrap" and "piratization." In the new ideological vacuum, as it had been at the turn of the century, bearded (and shaven) intellectuals diligently set about finding national identity, the elusive "Russian idea."

Early in perestroika the philosophical works of the great fumbler Berdyaev, who died in exile in France in 1948, became fashionable. His book *The Russian Idea*, written during World War II, defined the main trait of the Slavic soul as religious Messianism: "The Russian nation was not a nation of culture primarily, as were the nations of Western Europe, it was more a nation of revelations and inspiration, it knew no measure and easily fell into extremism."[55] But Berdyaev with his essays on Russian ambivalence always looked suspiciously cosmopolitan to nationalists.

Some of them now made historian Lev Gumilev (1912–1992) their new idol. The son of two famous poets—Nikolai Gumilev, who was shot by the Bolsheviks in 1921, and Akhmatova—he was a complex, truly tragic figure. I met him in 1966, after Akhmatova's death. As a young violin student at Leningrad Conservatory, I was asked to select music for the memorial service at the Writers' Union. I suggested Bach, knowing how much she loved his music. Gumilev, who resembled Picasso and rolled his Rs, countered aggressively: "No, only Russian Orthodox composers!" As a compromise I played Prokofiev's First Violin Sonata; naturally, neither Gumilev nor I could have known then that the Eurasianist composer was a follower of Christian Science.

Lev Gumilev was arrested four times—as he and most people presumed, because of the anti-Soviet stance of his parents—and he spent a total of fourteen years in prisons and camps, during which time he developed an original theory of ethnogenesis, according to which the biological dominant in the development of a nation was its *passionarnost'* ("passionarity"), which he explained as a heightened drive to exploits and self-sacrifice, created by the influence of the biosphere.

Gumilev liked to boast that the idea of passionarity ("like all ideas of genius," he would add with a chuckle) came to him in the camp. According to him, "every ethnos appears as the result of a certain explosion of passionarity, then, gradually losing it, enters a period of inertia, which ends eventually with the ethnos breaking down."[56] He defined the life-span of an ethnos as approximately fifteen hundred years, and contemporary Russia, he suggested, was close to the inertia phase, which would give her in the near future "three hundred years of a golden autumn, an era of harvest, when the ethnos leaves behind a unique culture for coming generations."[57]

This comforting idea, popular in the post-Communist chaos, had Eurasianist roots. Gumilev positioned Russia between Europe and Asia, in a role of uniting force, and insisted that Russia had always been on good terms with the Turks and Mongols: he believed that the Mongol invasions in the eighth century and later were not the historical disasters textbooks made them out to be. This made some traditionalists call Gumilev a Russophobe, but on the other hand, it was useful for the influential opponents of closer ties with the West. They repeated Gumilev's casual phrase that the "Turks and Mongols can be sincere friends, while the English, French, and Germans, I am certain, can only be cunning exploiters."[58]

Contemporary Eurasianists call for the creation of a new empire on the ruins of the Soviet Union, with Russia at its center. The United States is the great Satan for the neo-Eurasianists, and they see the mission of the Russian people as stopping the American-sponsored expansion of the Western liberal model of economic and cultural development.[59] They propose creating new geopolitical axes: Moscow–Beijing, Moscow–Dehli, and Moscow–Tehran, and also uniting with the Arab world. Consequently, they argue, Russia's cultural priorities must be Eastern, not Western.

For Solzhenitsyn, the idea of building a new global empire headed by Russia was always alien, despite the widespread perceptions to the con-

trary. "The grandeur of a nation is in the high level of its inner develop-
ment, not the external," he wrote. Solzhenitsyn dismissed the neo-
Eurasianists as "good-for-nothing theoreticians."[60] But he, too, perceived
American cultural expansion into Russia as a clear and present danger.

In his 1998 book, *Russia Collapsing,* which can be seen as the final
manifesto and spiritual testament of the octogenarian writer, Solzhenitsyn passionately warned that the twenty-first century could become
"the last century for Russians" because of the looming demographic catastrophe (he pointed out that Russia's population was decreasing by a
million a year) and the degradation of the national character: "We are
facing irreversible loss of the spiritual traditions, roots, and organic
nature of our life," which he defined as the "whole of our faith, soul, and
character, our continent in the world cultural structure."[61]

At the time, few people paid attention to Solzhenitsyn's desperate
warning about the national cultural crisis, which he considered more terrible than any political or economic failures. Solzhenitsyn was still seen
as an important figure, but one that belonged to the past, to the eras of
Khrushchev and Brezhnev. At the end of the century in Russia, he was
seen by some as a tragic patriarch, a Russian King Lear.

Other observers also found theatrical comparisons but of a more
skeptical nature—for them, Solzhenitsyn was a great director and actor
who had a successful run in the show called *Struggle Against Communism*
playing prophet and ascetic moralist. The essayist Boris Paramonov, who
had visited Solzhenitsyn in Vermont, even suggested that "if Solzhenitsyn is going to play a role now, let it be a role that coincides as much as
possible with his real image as diligent homeowner, who lives in a house
of plenty. Those are the images he must project in Russia now, those are
the ideals to present, instead of talking about morality, repentance, and
salvation through suffering."[62]

As he had in Vermont, Solzhenitsyn isolated himself in his estate in
Troitse-Lykovo outside Moscow, coming into the capital rarely, and as he
had lived in exile in the United States, not coming to the telephone. Age
took its toll on the writer, whose enviable stamina for many years had
allowed him to work tirelessly and without days off. A stroke disabled
Solzhenitsyn's left arm. It became difficult for him to get up, to walk, to
receive visitors. This curtailed his contacts with the outside world even
more and increased the perception that he was an isolated, lonely, and
tragic figure.

The sense that "time is out of joint" was increased by the general decline of "high" culture, painful for the intelligentsia. Public opinion polls suggested the rapid deterioration of the influence of intellectuals on the masses. Solzhenitsyn was the only writer still named regularly as a moral compass and cultural leader, even though the number of his loyal fans had decreased drastically. The other moral models mentioned were Andrei Sakharov (who died in 1989) and Dmitri Likhachev (who died in 1999), an expert on ancient Russian culture.

Tellingly, in the last years of the century, this short list of cultural icons included the actor and director Nikita Mikhalkov, a member of a contro-versial clan. His father, Sergei, a popular children's poet and a three-time Stalin Prize winner, was the author of the lyrics approved by Stalin for the Soviet anthem in 1943 and who then reworked them in 2000 at the request of President Putin; his brother, Andrei Mikhalkov-Konchalovsky, a film director, worked successfully both in the Soviet Union and in the United States (*The First Teacher,* his debut in 1965, was Eurasianist in spirit; *The Story of Asya Klyachina, Who Loved but Did Not Get Married,* with Iya Savvina's unforgettable performance as the lame country girl, was banned in 1967 and released only eleven years later; and in Holly-wood, *Runaway Train,* with screenplay by Akira Kurosawa).

The writer Leonid Borodin suggested, with tongue only partially in cheek, that "the unparalleled endurance of the Mikhalkov clan is noth-ing less than a signal of Russia's 'unsinkability,' even if the country were to be in the worst possible state both in spirit and in flesh,"[63] announcing that "were our people on the level of a monarchist worldview, I person-ally would have nothing against a Mikhalkov dynasty: Russia's age-long goal has been to stupefy the world."[64]

Nikita Mikhalkov, who considers himself an enlightened conserva-tive, also prefers a constitutional monarchy for Russia, maintaining that a monarchy "is the only way for our country, no matter how loud the liber-als laugh,"[65] but demurs when asked if he means a return of the Romanov dynasty.[66]

In such films as *Oblomov* (with Oleg Tabakov in the eponymous role) and *The Barber of Siberia* (where the director pointedly appeared as Tsar Alexander III), Mikhalkov consistently presents a nostalgic view of the sweet life of old Russia.

Tall, charmingly mustachioed, and terrifically charismatic, Mikhalkov cuts a prominent political figure, chairing for many years the post-Soviet

Filmmakers' Union of Russia and the Russian (formerly Soviet) Cultural Foundation, created by the late first lady Raisa Gorbachev. Back then the foundation, with enormous funding and actually an alternative to the staid Ministry of Culture, was headed by the more authoritative academician Dmitri Likhachev. Mikhalkov's proclaimed goals are modest: to support cultural life in the provinces, where he believes the true Russian spirit still lives, uncorrupted by Western influences.

His popularity is not due so much to his public profile (he is criticized fiercely by many for his moves in that area) but to his movie work: three of his films were nominated for the Oscar: the Chekhovian pastiche *Black Eyes* in 1988; the Eurasianist manifesto *East of Eden* in 1993; and the anti-Stalin melodrama *Burnt by the Sun,* which won the award for best foreign film in 1995. This impressive thriller, once again strangely imbued with Chekhovian nostalgia, nevertheless pales as a cinematic depiction of the horrors of the Stalin era in comparison to Alexei Guerman's masterpiece, *Khrustalev! Bring the Car!* (1998), a brutal black and white phantasmagoria about the twilight days of the Stalin regime.

Guerman's film, which passed unnoticed in the West, was perhaps equal to the best works of Eisenstein or Tarkovsky, summarizing the entire post-perestroika period of Russian film. Guerman rejected nostalgia for the Soviet past, but that past—horrible for some but still attractive for many others—permeates his *Khrustalev* like a nightmare from which you can't wake up.

In *Khrustalev,* Guerman poses the eternal Russian question: is Russia capable of freeing itself from the vestiges of totalitarianism while overcoming the allure of anarchy? And what will happen with its national identity? In cinematic form, Guerman paraphrased Solzhenitsyn's anxious statement that "our highest and most important goal is to preserve our nation, which is totally exhausted, to maintain its physical existence, its moral existence, its culture, and its traditions."[67]

Another important artistic commentary on Solzhenitsyn's message was *The Russian Ark,* a cinematographic tour-de-force by Tarkovsky's protégé Alexander Sokurov, in preproduction for four years but shot in one day, December 23, 2001. It is a melancholy, poetic meditation on the zigzags of Russian culture and state in the last three hundred years, compressed into ninety minutes and shot in the halls of the Hermitage in St. Petersburg in a single, continuous take.

Reserved and almost tongue-tied, Sokurov—the polar opposite of the high-strung and voluble Guerman—has always argued that culture meant more for Russia than for any other nation. One of the film's characters maintains that the authorities only want to have acorns from the oak: they don't care if the cultural oak is dead or alive. But if the oak were to fall, any and all authority will perish with it. Sokurov also describes *The Russian Ark* as a film about the meeting of Russia and the West after the end of the Cold War. "The West should regret that it treats Russia with such cold indifference and arrogance."

Sokurov's philosophy (in the West he is best known for his trilogy about twentieth-century political leaders—Lenin, Hitler, and Emperor Hirohito of Japan) is expressed in the final words of *The Russian Ark:* "We will sail forever and we will live forever." That idea at the end of the twentieth century, an era of national catastrophes and unheard-of upheavals, sums up the subconscious fears and hopes of the majority of Russians, both the common people and the cultural elite. The country faces grave cultural and demographic challenges that threaten its very existence. There are no easy answers. Once again, as it was at the start of the twentieth century, Russia—anxious, brooding, enigmatic—is at a crossroads, choosing its way.

NOTES

Introduction

1. To see reviews of a typical work in that sense, *Natasha's Dance: A Cultural History of Russia* by Orlando Figes: *The Times Literary Supplement*, October 5, 2002; Lynn Garafola, *Legacies of Twentieth-Century Dance* (Middletown, CT, 2005), p. ix.
2. Aleksandr Solzhenitsyn, *V kruge pervom* [First Circle] (New York, 1968), p. 320.
3. Solomon Volkov, *Dialogi s Iosifom Brodskim* [Dialogues with Joseph Brodsky] (Moscow, 1998), p. 198.
4. See David Caute, *The Dancer Defects: The Struggle for Cultural Supremacy During the Cold War* (Oxford, 2003).
5. Aleksandr Solzhenitsyn, *Bodalsia telenok s dubom: ocherki literaturnoi zhizni* [The Calf Butted the Oak: Sketches of a Literary Life] (Paris, 1975), p. 314.
6. Abram Efros, *Profili* [Profiles] (Moscow, 1930), p. 75

Part One: THE GATHERING STORM

Chapter One

1. Maxim Gorky, *Literaturnye portrety* [Literary Portraits] (Moscow, 1983), p. 175.
2. Quoted in: *Russkaia literatura kontsa XIX–nachala XX v., 1908–1917* [Russian literature of the late nineteenth and early twentieth century: 1908–1917] (Moscow, 1972), p. 467.
3. Quoted in: *L. N. Tolstoi v vospominaniiakh sovremennikov* [L. N. Tolstoy in reminiscences of his contemporaries], in two volumes, vol. 2 (Moscow, 1978), p. 458.
4. *V. I. Lenin o literature* [V. I. Lenin on literature] (Moscow, 1971), p. 108.
5. Gorky, *Literaturnye portrety*, p. 204.
6. Viktor Shklovsky, *Khod konya. Sbornik statei* [Knight's move: collected articles] (Moscow and Berlin, 1921), pp. 117–118.
7. Viktor Shklovsky in conversation with the author.
8. Quoted in: Semen Pozoiskii, *Istoriia otlucheniia L'va Tolstogo ot tserkvi* [History of Leo Tolstoy's excommunication] (Moscow, 1979), p. 82.
9. *Lev Tolstoi i russkie tsari* [Leo Tolstoy and the Russian tsars] (Moscow, 1995), pp. 106–107.
10. A. Suvorin, *Dnevnik* [Diary] (Moscow, 1992), p. 316.
11. Boris Eikhenbaum, *Moi vremennik. Marshrut v bessmertie* [My diary. Route to immortality] (Moscow, 2001), p. 108.
12. *Lenin o literature*, p. 104.
13. *Novoe vremia*, November 16, 1910.
14. I. A. Bunin, *Sobranie sochinenii* [Collected works], in nine volumes, vol. 9 (Moscow, 1967), p. 207.
15. Ibid., p. 63.
16. *Literaturnoe nasledstvo* [Literary heritage], vol. 72: *Gor'kii i Leonid Andreev. Neizdannaia perepiska* [Gorky and Leonid Andreyev, unpublished correspondence] (Moscow, 1965), p. 217.
17. A. P. Chekhov, *Sobranie sochinenii* [Collected works], in twelve volumes, vol. 12 (Moscow, 1957), pp. 49–50.

18. Quoted in: *Chekhov i Lev Tolstoi* (Moscow, 1980), pp. 144–145.

19. Quoted in: Bunin, *Sobranie sochinenii,* vol. 9, p. 207.

20. Quoted in: A. Anikst, *Teoriia dramy v Rossii ot Pushkina do Chekhova* [The theory of drama in Russia from Pushkin to Chekhov] (Moscow, 1972), p. 571.

21. Alexander Blok, *Sobranie sochinenii* [Collected works], in eight volumes, vol. 8 (Moscow and Leningrad, 1963), p. 281.

22. Osip Mandelstam, *Sochineniia* [Works], in two volumes, vol. 2 (Moscow, 1990), p. 302.

23. *Teatral'naia gazeta,* May 28, 1905.

24. Quoted in: I.Vinogradskaia, *Zhizn' i tvorchestvo K. S. Stanislavskogo. Letopis'* [Life and works of K. S. Stanislavsky: chronicle], in four volumes, vol. 1 (Moscow, 1971), p. 341.

25. Quoted in: Gorky, *Literaturnye portrety,* pp. 137–138.

26. V. V. Vorovskii, *Estetika. Literatura. Iskusstvo* [Aesthetics, literature, art] (Moscow, 1975), pp. 406–407.

27. Ibid., p. 277.

28. Chekhov, *Sobranie sochinenii,* vol. 12, pp. 318, 308.

29. Quoted in: *Russkaia literatura kontsa XIX–nachala XX v., 1901–1907* [Russian literature of the late nineteenth and early twentieth century: 1901–1907] (Moscow, 1971), p. 360.

30. Quoted in: *Perepiska A. P. Chekhova* [Correspondence of A. P. Chekhov] in two volumes, vol. 2 (Moscow, 1984), p. 356.

31. *Sankt-Peterburgskie vedomosti,* April 9, 1903.

32. *Birzhevye vedomosti,* April 6, 1903.

33. *Perepiska Chekhova,* vol. 2, p. 274.

34. V. I. Nemirovich-Danchenko, *Izbrannye pis'ma* [Selected letters], in two volumes, vol. 1 (Moscow, 1979), pp. 318–319.

35. Quoted in: Il'ia Erenburg, *Liudi, gody, zhizn'. Vospominaniia* [People, years, life: reminiscences], in three volumes, vol. 3 (Moscow, 1990), p. 81.

36. Quoted in: A. Turkov, *A. P. Chekhov i ego vremia* [A. P. Chekhov and his time] (Moscow, 1980), p. 379.

37. Chekhov, *Sobranie sochinenii,* vol. 12, p. 557.

38. Quoted in: Turkov, *Chekhov,* p. 389.

39. *Rus',* April 3, 1904.

40. K. S. Stanislavsky, *Sobranie sochinenii* [Collected works], in eight volumes, vol. 7 (Moscow, 1960), p. 227.

41. Ibid., p. 307.

42. Quoted in:Vinogradskaia, *Zhizn' i tvorchestvo Stanislavskogo,* vol. 1, p. 537.

43. *Novyi put',* 1 (1904), p. 254.

44. *Novosti,* March 27, 1905.

45. Quoted in: A.V. Ossovskii, *Muzykal'no-kriticheskie stat'i* [Musical criticism articles] (Leningrad, 1971), p. 82.

46. I. F. Stravinsky, *Perepiska s russkimi korrespondentami. Materialy k biografii* [Correspondence with Russian correspondents: materials for a biography], vol. 1 (Moscow, 1998), p. 152.

Chapter Two

1. Quoted in: Vadim Kozhinov, *Rossiia. Vek XX-i (1901–1939)* [Russia: 20th century (1901–1939)] (Moscow, 1999), p. 22.

2. V.V. Shul'gin, *"Chto nam v nikh ne nravitsia. . . ." Ob antisemitizme v Rossii* ["What we don't like about them is. . . ." On anti-Semitism in Russia] (Moscow, 1992), p. 47.
3. Ibid., p. 45.
4. V.V. Rozanov, *Sredi khudozhnikov* [Among artists] (Moscow, 1994), p. 398.
5. V. V. Rozanov, *Mysli o literature* [Thoughts on literature] (Moscow, 1989), pp. 394–395.
6. Quoted in: Alexander Etkind, *Khlyst* [*Sekty, literatura i revolutsiia*] [*khlyst* (sects, literature, and revolution)] (Moscow, 1998), p. 10.
7. Alexandre Benois, *Moi vospominaniia* [My reminiscences], in five volumes, vols. 4–5 (Moscow, 1980), p. 291.
8. Mikhail Vrubel, *Perepiska. Vospominaniia o khudozhnike* [Correspondence, reminiscences about the artist] (Leningrad, 1976), p. 293.
9. Ibid., p. 295.
10. Alexander Blok, *Sobranie sochinenii* [Collected works], in eight volumes, vol. 5 (Moscow and Leningrad, 1962), p. 435.
11. B. Eikhenbaum, *O literature. Raboty raznykh let* [On literature: works of various years] (Moscow, 1987), p. 355.
12. Yu. N. Tynianov, *Poetika. Istoriia literatury. Kino* [Poetics, history of literature, film] (Moscow, 1977), pp. 118–119.
13. Quoted in: Dmitri Merezhkovsky, *Bol'naia Rossiia* [Ailing Russia] (Leningrad, 1991), p. 221.
14. Mandelstam, *Sochineniia*, vol. 2, p. 157.
15. *Apollon*, 11 (1910), p. 3.
16. Quoted in: I. V. Nest'ev, *Vek nyneshnii i vek minuvshii. Stat'i o muzyke* [The present century and the past century: articles on music] (Moscow, 1986), p. 102.
17. Quoted in: Yu. D. Engel', *Glazami sovremmennika* [Through the eyes of a contemporary] (Moscow, 1971), pp. 216–217.
18. Anna Akhmatova in conversation with the author.
19. S. Lifar, *Diagilev* (St. Petersburg, 1993), p. 51.
20. *Sergei Diagilev i russkoe iskusstvo* (Sergei Diaghilev and Russian art), in two volumes, vol. 2 (Moscow, 1982), p. 309.
21. Ibid., p. 26.
22. *Peterburgskii listok*, May 12, 1907.
23. Boris Mikhailovich Kustodiev, *Pis'ma. Stat'i, zametki, interv'iu. Vstrechi i besedy s Kustodievym. Vospominaniia o khudozhnike* [Letters, articles, notes, interviews. Meetings and conversations with Kustodiev. Reminiscences about the artist] (Leningrad, 1967), p. 115.
24. *Diagilev i russkoe iskusstvo*, vol. 2, p. 80.
25. Ibid., p. 85.
26. *Novyi put'*, 4 (1904), p. 243.
27. *Le Matin*, May 19, 1908.
28. F. I. Chaliapin, *Maska i dusha. Moi sorok let na teatrakh* [Mask and soul: my forty years in the theater] (Paris, 1932), p. 289.
29. A. V. Lunacharsky, *V mire muzyki. Stat'i i rechi* [In the world of music: articles and speeches] (Moscow, 1958), p. 343.
30. Ibid., pp. 343–344.
31. Ibid., p. 345.
32. Kirill Kondrashin in conversation with the author.

33. *Neva,* 6 (1989), pp. 145–146, 158–159.

34. Ibid., p. 146.

35. Fedor Lopukhov in conversation with the author.

36. Benois, *Moi vospominaniia,* vols. 4–5, p. 530.

37. Quoted in: Vaslav Nijinsky, *Chuvstva. Tetradi* [Feelings: notebooks] (Moscow, 2000), p. 151.

38. Quoted in: E. Poliakova, *Nikolai Rerikh* (Moscow, 1985), p. 172.

39. *Utro Rossii,* August 17, 1914.

40. *Zavety,* 6 (1912), p. 67.

41. Quoted in: *I. Stravinskii-publitsist i sobesednik* [I. Stravinsky, columnist and inter-locutor] (Moscow, 1988), p. 22.

42. Ibid.

43. Blok, *Sobranie sochinenii,* vol. 6, p. 11.

44. Ibid., p. 10.

45. A. N. Benois, *Moi dnevnik* [My Diary] (Moscow, 2003), p. 75.

46. Ibid., p. 107.

47. A. Blok, *Dnevnik* [Diary] (Moscow, 1989), p. 210.

48. Benois, *Moi dnevnik,* p. 228.

Part Two: A TIME OF CATASTROPHES

Chapter Three

1. A. V. Lunacharsky, *Ob izobrazitel'nom iskusstve* [On fine arts], in two volumes, vol. 1 (Moscow, 1967), p. 129.

2. Ibid.

3. *Na literaturnom postu,* 22–23 (1927), p. 18.

4. *Novaia zhizn',* November 10, 1917.

5. Benois, *Moi dnevnik,* p. 273.

6. A. Rylov, *Vospominaniia* [Reminiscences] (Leningrad, 1977), p. 193.

7. Ibid.

8. *Iskusstvo kommuny,* December 7, 1918.

9. Natan Altman in conversation with the author.

10. Alexander Blok, *Zapisnye knihzki. 1901–1920* [Notebooks: 1901–1920] (Moscow, 1965), p. 429.

11. Kazimir Malevich, *Chernyi kvadrat* [Black square] (St. Petersburg, 2001), p. 49.

12. Quoted in: A. Fevral'skii, *Pervaia sovetskaia p'esa. "Misteriia-buff" V. V. Maiakovskogo* [The first Soviet play: V. V. Mayakovsky's Mystery Bouffe] (Moscow, 1971), p. 70.

13. Ibid.

14. Ibid.

15. *Zhizn' iskusstva,* November 11, 1918.

16. *Petrogradskaia Pravda,* November 21, 1918.

17. Quoted in: Alexander Gladkov, *Teatr: Vospominaniia i razmyshleniia* [The theater: reminiscences and considerations] (Moscow, 1980), p. 308.

18. V. E. Meierkhol'd, *Perepiska. 1896–1939* [Correspondence: 1896–1939] (Moscow, 1976), p. 29.

19. Ibid.

20. Gladkov, *Teatr,* p. 306.

21. Georgy Chulkov, *Gody stranstvii* [Years of Wandering] (Moscow, 1930), p. 221.

22. Blok, *Dnevniki,* p. 248.

23. *Literaturnoe nasledstvo,* vol. 89: *Aleksandr Blok. Pis'ma k zhene* [Alexander Blok: letters to his wife] (Moscow, 1978), p. 256.

24. Blok, *Dnevnik,* p. 199.

25. Ibid, p. 173.

26. Gladkov, *Teatr,* p. 307.

27. Quoted in: K. Rudnitskii, *Rezhisser Meierkhol'd* [Meyerhold the director] (Moscow, 1969), p. 237.

28. Ibid., p. 244.

29. Sergei Mikhailovich Eisenstein, *Memuary* [Memoirs], in two volumes, vol. 1 (Moscow, 1997), p. 220.

30. Quoted in: K. Rudnitskii, *Meierkhol'd* [Meyerhold] (Moscow, 1971), p. 285.

31. Gorky, *Literaturnye portrety,* p. 45.

32. *Literaturnoe nasledstvo,* vol. 65.

33. *Literaturnoe nasledstvo,* vol. 80: *V. I. Lenin i A. V. Lunacharskii. Perepiska, doklady, dokumenty* [V. I. Lenin and A. V. Lunacharsky: correspondence, reports, documents] (Moscow, 1971), p. 717.

34. Ibid., p. 718.

35. Benedikt Livshits, *Polutoraglazyi strelets. Stikhotvoreniia. Perevody. Vospominaniia* [The one-and-a-half-eyed archer. Poems, translations, reminiscences] (Leningrad, 1989), p. 413.

36. Alisa Koonen, *Stranitsy zhizni* [Pages of a life] (Moscow, 1985), p. 222.

37. Efros, *Profili,* p. 228.

38. Igor Stravinsky and Robert Craft, *Conversations with Igor Stravinsky* (Berkeley and Los Angeles, 1980), p. 99.

39. Alexander Rodchenko, *Opyty dlia budushchego. Dnevniki. Stat'i. Pis'ma. Zapiski* [Experiments for the future: diaries, articles, letters, notes] (Moscow, 1996), p. 60.

40. Ibid.

Chapter Four

1. *Vlast' i khudozhestvennaia intelligentsia* [The regime and the artistic intelligentsia] (Moscow, 1999), p. 21.

2. Ibid., p. 28.

3. See: Vasilii Stavitskii, *Za kulisami tainykh sobytii* [Behind the scenes of secret events] (Moscow, 2004), pp. 5–7.

4. *Lenin o literature,* p. 242.

5. A. V. Lunacharsky, *Vospominaniia i vpechatleniia* [Reminiscences and impressions] (Moscow, 1968), p. 192.

6. *Literaturnoe nasledstvo,* vol. 80, p. 313.

7. Lunacharsky, *Vospominaniia i vpechatleniia,* p. 195.

8. *Pravda,* September 19, 1922.

9. Ibid.

10. *Krasnaia nov',* 1 (1924), p. 179.

11. *Pechat' i revolutsiia,* 3 (1925), p. 10.

12. Quoted in: N. N. Primochkina, *Pisatel' i vlast'* [The writer and the regime] (Moscow, 1998), pp. 42–43.

13. Gorky, *Literaturnye portrety,* p. 27.

14. D. S. Mirsky, *Uncollected Writings on Russian Literature* (Berkeley, 1989), p. 213.

15. Sergei Esenin, *Sobranie sochinenii* [Collected works], in five volumes, vol. 5 (Moscow, 1962), p. 13.

16. Gorky, *Literaturnye portrety,* p. 296.
17. Esenin, *Sobranie sochinenii,* vol. 4, p. 266.
18. Ibid., p. 265.
19. *Pravda,* January 12, 1927.
20. Ivanov-Razumnik, *Pisatel'skie sud'by. Tiurmy i ssylki* [Writers' destinies. Prisons and exile] (Moscow, 2004), p. 47.
21. I.V. Stalin, *Sochineniia,* vol. 12 (Moscow, 1952), p. 146.
22. Quoted in: Vitalii Shentalinskii, *Raby svobody. V literaturnykh arkhivakh KGB* [Slaves of freedom: in the literary archives of the KGB] (Moscow, 1995), p. 268.
23. Ibid.
24. Quoted in: Nikolai Kluyev, *Stikhotvoreniia i poemy* [Verse and narrative poems] (Leningrad, 1977), p. 61.
25. K. Chukovsky, *Dnevnik* 1930–1969 [Diary 1930–1969] (Moscow, 1994), p. 9.
26. Ibid.
27. Shentalinskii, *Raby svobody,* p. 38.
28. Mirsky, *Uncollected Writings,* p. 204.
29. Valentin Kataev, *Almaznyi moi venets* [My diamond crown] (Moscow, 1981), p. 242.
30. Mirsky, *Uncollected Writings,* p. 110.
31. Quoted in: Lazar Fleishman, *Boris Pasternak v tridtsatye gody* [Boris Pasternak in the 1930s] (Jerusalem, 1984), p. 145.
32. Emma Gershtein, *Memuary* (Memoirs) (St. Petersburg, 1998), p. 51.
33. Nadezhda Mandelstam, *Vospominaniia* [Reminiscences] (New York, 1970), p. 35.
34. Quoted in: Nikita Zabolotskii, *Zhizn' N. A. Zabolotskogo* [Life of N. A. Zabolotsky] (Moscow, 1998), p. 215.
35. Ibid., p. 216.
36. Ibid., p. 567.
37. Ibid., p. 281.
38. V. Kaverin, *Epilog. Memuary* [Epilogue: memoirs] (Moscow, 1989), p. 281.

Chapter Five
1. *Vlast' i khudozhestvennaia intelligentsia,* p. 739.
2. Ibid., pp. 110, 112.
3. Quoted in: Evgenii Gromov, *Stalin: vlast' i iskusstvo* [Stalin: power and art] (Moscow, 1998), p. 113.
4. Quoted in: *Poetika. Istoriia literatury. Lingvistika. Sb. k 70-letiu Viacheslava Vsevolodovicha Ivanova* [Poetics, history of literature, linguistics: a collection for the 70th birthday of Vyacheslav Vsevolodovich Ivanov] (Moscow, 1994), p. 184.
5. Maxim Gorky, *Nesvoevremennye mysli. Zametki o revoliutsii i kul'ture* [Untimely thoughts: notes on revolution and culture] (Moscow, 1990), p. 151.
6. Ibid.
7. Quoted in: Dmitrii Volkogonov, *Lenin,* in two volumes, volume 2 (Moscow, 1994), p. 184.
8. Stalin, *Sochineniia,* vol. 3, p. 386.
9. Ibid.
10. Konstantin Fedin, *Sobraniie sochinenii* [Collected works], in ten volumes, vol. 10 (Moscow, 1973), p. 41.
11. *Vesy,* 4 (1905), p. 50.
12. Blok, *Sobranie sochinenii,* vol. 6, p. 92.
13. Gorky, *Nesvoevremennye mysli,* p. 136.

14. Vladislav Khodasevich, *Belyi koridor: Vospominaniia. Izbrannaia proza* [White corridor: reminiscences and selected prose], in two volumes, vol. 1 (New York, 1982), p. 265.
15. Gorky, *Nesvoevremennye mysli*, p. 257.
16. *Vlast' i khudozhestvennaia intelligentsia*, p. 138.
17. Ibid., p. 125.
18. Ibid., p. 107.
19. Ibid., p. 104.
20. Stalin, *Sochineniia*, vol. 6, p. 188.
21. Ibid., pp. 187–188.
22. N. Punin, *O Tatline* [On Tatlin] (Moscow, 1994), p. 21.
23. Valentina Khodasevich, *Portrety slovami* [Portraits in words] (Moscow, 1987), p. 155.
24. Rodchenko, *Opyty dlia budushchego*, p. 235.
25. Ibid., p. 282.
26. Grigory Alexandrov in conversation with the author.
27. Sergei Eisenstein, *Izbrannye proizvedeniia* [Selected works], in six volumes, vol. 2 (Moscow, 1964), p. 55.
28. Vladimir Mayakovsky, *Polnoe sobranie sochinenii* [Complete collected works], in thirteen volumes, vol. 12 (Moscow, 1959), pp. 358–359.
29. Ibid., p. 95.
30. Boris Pasternak, *Vozdushnye puti. Proza raznykh let* [Aerial ways: prose of various years] (Moscow, 1982), p. 452.
31. *Pravda*, December 5, 1935.
32. Quoted in: Lenin, *O literature*, p. 226.
33. Ibid.
34. Alexander Gladkov, *Pozdnie vechera. Vospominaniia, stat'i, zametki* [Late evenings: reminiscences, articles, notes] (Moscow, 1986), p. 261.

Chapter Six

1. *Kratkaiia literaturnaiia entsiklopediia* [Short encyclopedia of literature], vol. 8 (Moscow, 1975), p. 57.
2. More on this in: Solomon Volkov, *Shostakovich i Stalin: khudozhnik i tsar'* [Shostakovich and Stalin: artist and tsar] (Moscow, 2004), pp. 252–261; *Shostakovich and Stalin: The Extraordinary Relationship Between the Great Composer and the Brutal Dictator* (New York, 2004), pp. 102–106.
3. *Pravda*, January 28, 1936.
4. *Pravda*, February 13, 1936.
5. More on this in Volkov, *Shostakovich i Stalin*, pp. 358–360; Volkov, *Shostakovich and Stalin*, pp. 153–154.
6. Lev Trotsky, *Stalin*, in two volumes, vol. 2 (Vermont, 1985), p. 211.
7. Quoted in: Ilya Ehrenburg, *Ludi, gody, zhizn'. Vospominaniia* [People, years, life: reminiscences], in three volumes, vol. 3 (Moscow, 1990), p. 211.
8. *Voprosy literatury*, 3 (1989), p. 221.
9. Ibid.
10. D. Merezhkovsky, *Ne mir, no mech* [Not peace, but the sword] (Kharkov and Moscow, 2000), p. 330.
11. Ibid., p. 576.
12. *Literaturnoe nasledstvo*, vol. 70: *Gor'kii i sovetskie pisateli. Neizdannaia perepiska* [Gorky and Soviet writers: unpublished correspondence] (Moscow, 1963), p. 568.

13. *Novyi mir,* 9 (1997), p. 188.
14. *Literaturnoe nasledstvo,* vol. 84: *Ivan Bunin,* book 2 (Moscow, 1973), p. 7.
15. Ibid., p. 34.
16. Ivan Bunin, *Velikii durman. Neizvestnye stranitsy* [Great delirium: unknown pages] (Moscow, 1997), p. 152.
17. Marina Tsvetayeva, *Sobranie sochinenii* [Collected works] in seven volumes, vol. 6 (Moscow, 1995), p. 407.
18. Boris Eikhenbaum, *O literature* [On literature] (Moscow, 1987), p. 440.
19. Vladislav Khodasevich, *Koleblemyi trenozhnik. Izbrannoe* [Unstable tripod: selected works] (Moscow, 1991), p. 362.
20. *Literaturnoe nasledstvo,* vol. 84, book 2, p. 375.
21. Quoted in: Oleg Mikhailov, *Zhizn' Bunina* [Life of Bunin] (Moscow, 2001), p. 387.
22. *Sankt-Peterburgskie vedomosti,* December 8, 1901.
23. Galina Kuznetsova, *Grasskii dnevnik* [Grasse diary] (Moscow, 1995), p. 201.
24. Ibid., p. 210.
25. *Ustami Buninykh* [In the words of the Bunins], in three volumes, vol. 2 (Frankfurt-am-Main, 1981), p. 256.
26. Kuznetsova, *Grasskii dnevnik,* p. 293.
27. Bunin, *Velikii durman,* p. 168.
28. *Ustami Buninykh,* p. 290.
29. *Novoe literaturnoe obozrenie,* 40 (1999), p. 276.
30. Quoted in: Viktor Fradkin, *Delo Kol'tsova* [Koltsov case] (Moscow, 2002), p. 227.
31. Ibid., p. 211.
32. Ehrenburg, *Ludi, gody, zhizn',* vol. 2, p. 53.
33. Oleg Platonov, *Gosudartstvennaia izmena. Zagovor protiv Rossii* [State treason: the conspiracy against Russia] (Moscow, 2004), p. 9.
34. *Istoriia Rossii. XX vek* [History of Russia: twentieth century] (Moscow, 2000), p. 386.
35. *Teatral'naia zhizn',* 5 (1989), p. 3.

Part Three: RENDEZVOUS WITH STALIN
Chapter Seven

1. *Kratkaia literaturnaia entsiklopediia,* vol. 7, p. 93.
2. *Voprosy literatury,* 2 (1989), p. 148.
3. *Pravda,* March 16, 1941.
4. Nadezhda Mandelstam, *Vospominaniia,* p. 156.
5. *Pervii Vsesoiuznyi s'ezd sovetskikh pisatelei. Stenograficheskii otchet* [First all-Union congress of Soviet writers: stenographic transcript] (Moscow, 1934), p. 10.
6. A. Lunacharsky, *Iskusstvo kak vid chelovecheskogo povedeniia* [Art as an aspect of human behavior] (Moscow, 1931), p. 15.
7. Antonina Pirozhkova, *Sem' let s Babelem* [Seven years with Babel] (New York, 2001), p. 46.
8. Aleksandr Solzhenitsyn, *Publitsistika* [Articles], in three volumes, vol. 2 (Yaroslavl, 1996), p. 186.
9. Quoted in: Valentin Osipov, *Tainaia zhizn' Mikhaila Sholokhova . . . Dokumental'naia khronika bez legend* [The secret life of Mikhail Sholokhov . . . documentary chronicle without legends] (Moscow, 1995), p. 40.
10. For more on Sholokhov's recollection of meeting Stalin, see: Osipov, *Tainaia zhizn',* pp. 38–40; Ivan Zhukov, *Ruka sud'by. Pravda i lozh' o Mikhaile Sholokhove i Aleksandre*

Fadeeve [Hand of fate: the truth and the lies about Mikhail Sholokhov and Alexander Fadeyev] (Moscow, 1994), p. 224.

11. Quoted in: Osipov, *Tainaia zhizn'*, p. 224.

12. *Pisatel' i vozhd'. Perepiska M. A. Sholokhova s I. V. Stalinym. 1931–1950 gody. Sbornik dokumentov iz lichnogo arkhiva I. V. Stalina* [Writer and leader: correspondence between M. A. Sholokhov and I.V. Stalin, 1931–1950. Collection of documents from Stalin's personal archives] (Moscow, 1997), p. 17.

13. This and subsequent quotations from Sholokhov's letters from *Pisatel' i vozhd'*, pp. 24, 29, 49, 58, 68, 102–103.

14. Lili Brik in conversation with the author; Nadezhda Mandelstam, *Vospominaniia*, p. 342.

15. See B. V. Sokolov, *Narkomy strakha* [People's commissars of fear] (Moscow, 2001), p. 107.

16. Quoted in: Vitalii Shentalinskii, *Donos na Sokrata* [Denunciation of Socrates] (Moscow, 2001), p. 422.

17. Mikhail Romm, *Kak v kino. Ustnye rasskazy* [Like in the movies: oral tales] (Nizhny Novgorod, 2003), p. 136.

18. See *Istochnik,* 5 (1995), pp. 156–158.

19. See *Znamia,* 12 (1996), p. 164.

Chapter Eight

1. Pasternak, *Vozdushnye puti,* p. 452.

2. Ibid.

3. Georgii Efron, *Dnevniki* [Diaries], in two volumes, vol. 1 (Moscow, 2004), pp. 179–180.

4. Quoted in: Irma Kudrova, *Gibel' Mariny Tsvetaevoi* [Death of Marina Tsvetayeva] (Moscow, 1995), p. 269.

5. Shentalinskii, *Donos na Sokrata,* p. 276.

6. Quoted in: Kudrova, *Gibel' Tsvetaevoi,* p. 276.

7. Georgii Adamovich, *Somneniia i nadezhdy* [Doubts and hopes] (Moscow, 2002), p. 311.

8. Quoted in: Kudrova, *Gibel' Tsvetaevoi,* p. 258.

9. Efron, *Dnevniki,* vol. 2, pp. 51–52.

10. Ibid., p. 109.

11. Pavel Filonov, *Dnevnik* [Diary] (St. Petersburg, 2000), p. 343.

12. Ibid., pp. 316–317.

13. Ibid., p. 310.

14. Quoted in: Ales Adamovich and Daniil Granin, *Blokadnaia kniga* [Blockade book] (Leningrad, 1989), pp. 32–33.

15. *Panorama iskusstv,* issue 11 (Moscow, 1988), p. 125.

16. Ehrenburg, *Ludi, gody, zhizn',* vol. 2, p. 242.

17. Joseph Brodsky in conversation with the author.

18. *Literaturnoe nasledstvo,* vol. 70, p. 313.

19. *Vlast' i khudozhestvennaia intelligentsia,* p. 150.

20. For Sutyrin's recollections, see *Andrei Platonov: Vospominaniia sovremennikov. Materialy k biografii* [Andrei Platonov: reminiscences of contemporaries. Materials for a biography] (Moscow, 1994), pp. 270–271.

21. Shentalinskii, *Raby svobody,* pp. 283–284.

22. Ibid., p. 293.

23. *Platonov: Vospominaniia sovremennikov,* p. 69.

24. *Znamia,* 6 (2002), p. 159.

25. *Platonov: Vospominaniia sovremennikov,* p. 85.

26. *Pravda,* July 8, 1943.

27. *Literaturnaia gazeta,* January 4, 1947.

28. *Platonov: Vospominaniia sovremennikov,* p. 84.

Chapter Nine

1. See http://idf.ru/15/doc.shtml

2. *Literaturnoe nasledstvo,* vol. 84, book 1, pp. 53–54.

3. M. Iof'ev, *Profili iskusstva* [Profiles of art] (Moscow, 1965), p. 205.

4. *Znamia,* 7 (2004), p. 153.

5. *Moskovskie Novosti,* September 24, 2004.

6. *Vlast' i khudozhestvennaia intelligentsia,* p. 583.

7. Milovan Djilas, *Besedy so Stalinym* [Conversations with Stalin] (Moscow, 2002), p. 119.

8. *Vlast' i khudozhestvennaia intelligentsia,* p. 491.

9. Ibid., p. 488.

10. *Den' poezii* [Poetry day] (Leningrad, 1967), p. 169.

11. *Istochnik,* I (1999), p. 77.

12. *Anna Akhmatova v zapisiakh Duvakina* [Anna Akhmatova in the notes of Duvakin] (Moscow, 1999), pp. 312, 330.

13. Anna Akhmatova, *Requiem* (Moscow, 1989), p. 294.

14. D. L. Babichenko, *Pisateli i tsenzory* [Writers and censors] (Moscow, 1994), p. 47.

15. Ibid., p. 48.

16. Anna Akhmatova in conversation with the author.

17. Anna Akhmatova in conversation with the author.

18. *"Literaturnyi front." Istoriia politicheskoi tsenzury 1932–1946 g.* ["The literary front": the history of political censorship 1932–1946] (Moscow, 1994), p. 53.

19. Solomon Volkov, *Dialogi s Iosifom Brodskim* [Dialogues with Joseph Brodsky] (Moscow, 1946), p. 13.

20. Ibid., p. 7.

21. Cited in Akhmatova, *Requiem,* p. 174.

22. *Doklad t. Zhdanova o zhurnalakh "Zvezda" i "Leningrad"* [Comrade Zhdanov's report on the journals *Zvezda* and *Leningrad*] (Moscow, 1946), p. 13.

23. Ibid., p. 7.

24. *Druzhba Narodov,* 3 (1988), p. 174.

25. Anna Akhmatova in conversation with the author.

26. *Prokof'ev o Prokof'eve. Stat'i i interv'u* [Prokofiev on Prokofiev: articles and inter- views] (Moscow, 1991), p. 220.

27. Sergei Prokofiev, *Dnevnik. 1907–1933* [Diary: 1907–1933], part 2 (Paris, 2002), p. 292.

Part Four: **THAWS AND FREEZES**

Chapter Ten

1. Yevgeny Yevtushenko, *Volchii pasport* [Wolf's passport] (Moscow, 1998), p. 81.

2. Armen Medvedev, *Territoriia kino* [Cinema territory] (Moscow, 2001), p. 41.

3. Yevtushenko, *Volchii pasport,* p. 435.

4. Vassily Aksyonov, *V poiskakh grustnogo bebi* [In Search of Melancholy Baby] (New York, 1987), p. 20.

5. G.V. Aleksandrov, *Epokha i kino* [The era and film] (Moscow, 1976), p. 107.

6. *Sochineniia Iosifa Brodskogo* [Works of Joseph Brodsky], vol. 6 (Moscow, 2000), p. 16.

7. Aksyonov, *V poiskakh grustnogo bebi,* p. 20.

8. Joseph Brodsky in conversation with the author.

9. Dmitrii Shepilov, *Neprimknuvshii* [The nonjoiner] (Moscow, 2001), pp. 232–234.

10. Ibid., p. 234.

11. Arch Puddington, *Broadcasting Freedom: The Cold War Triumph of Radio Free Europe and Radio Liberty* (Lexington, KY, 2000), p. 9.

12. Ibid., p. 11.

13. *Muzyka i zhizn'. Muzyka i muzykanty Leningrada* [Music and life: music and the musicians of Leningrad] (Leningrad and Moscow, 1972), p. 127.

14. Kirill Kondrashin in conversation with the author.

15. Frances Stonor Saunders, *The Cultural Cold War: The CIA and the World of Arts and Letters* (New York, 1999), p. 142.

16. *The New York Times,* December 25, 1977.

17. Yevgeny Yevtushenko, *Ne umirai prezhde smerti* [Don't die before your death] (New York, 1993), pp. 496–497.

18. *Lubyanka: organy VChK-OGPU-NKVD-MGB-MVD-KGB. 1917–1991. Spravochnik* [Lubyanka: the agencies VChK-OGPU-NKVD-MGB-MVD-KGB, 1917–1991: a directory] (Moscow, 2003), p. 718.

19. Shepilov, *Neprimknuvshii,* p. 69.

20. Andrei Voznesensky, *Na virtual'nom vetru* [In a virtual wind] (Moscow, 1998), p. 79.

21. *Doklad N. S. Khrushcheva o kul'te lichnosti Stalina na XX s'ezde KPSS. Dokumenty* [Khrushchev's speech on the cult of personality of Stalin at the Twentieth Party Congress: documents] (Moscow, 2002), p. 97.

22. Voznesensky, *Na virtual'nom vetru,* p. 242.

23. *Russkie sovetskie pisateli. Poety. Biobibliograficheskii ukazatel'* [Russian Soviet writers: poets—biobibliographical directory], vol. 7 (Moscow, 1984), p. 347; see also: *Kratkaia literaturnaia entsyklopediia* [Short literary encyclopedia], vol. 2 (Moscow, 1964), p. 866.

24. Yuri Nagibin, *Dnevnik* [Diary] (Moscow, 1996), pp. 272–273.

25. Yevtushenko, *Volchii pasport,* p. 90.

26. Ibid., p. 83.

27. Anna Akhmatova in conversation with the author.

28. *Literaturnaia gazeta,* March 19, 1953.

29. *Kogda fil'm okonchen. Govoriat rezhisery "Mosfil'ma"* [When the film is finished: talking with Mosfilm directors] (Moscow, 1964), p. 116.

30. Lidia Chukovskaya, *Zapiski ob Anne Akhmatovoi* [Notes about Anna Akhmatova], vol. 3 (Moscow, 1997), p. 419.

31. Vladimir Lakshin, *"Novy mir" vo vremena Khrushcheva* [*Novy mir* in the Khrushchev era] (Moscow, 1991), p. 153.

32. Konstantin Simonov, *Glazami cheloveka moego pokoleniia. Razmyshleniia o I. V. Staline* [Through the eyes of a man of my generation: thoughts on I. V. Stalin] (Moscow, 1990), p. 159.

Chapter Eleven

1. Nikolai Bukharin, *Revolutsiia i kul'tura. Stat'i i vystupleniia 1923–1936 godov* [Revolution and culture: articles and speeches of 1923–1936] (Moscow, 1993), pp. 218–268.

2. N. Vil'mont, *O Borise Pasternake. Vospominaniia i mysli* [About Boris Pasternak: remi-

niscences and thoughts] (Moscow, 1999), p. 218; Zoya Maslenikova, *Portret Boris a Pasternaka* [Portrait of Boris Pasternak] (Moscow, 1995), pp. 86–87; Nadezhda Mandelstam, *Vospominaniia* [Reminiscences] (New York, 1970), pp. 152–156; Emma Gershtein, *Memuary* [Memoirs] (St. Petersburg, 1998), pp. 330–332; Isaiah Berlin, *Personal Impressions* (New York, 1981), pp. 181–182.

3. *V krugu Zhivago. Pasternakovskii sbornik* [In Zhivago's circle: a Pasternak anthology] (Stanford, 2000), p. 63.
4. *Vlast' i khudozhestvennaia intelligentsiia*, p. 275.
5. Ibid.
6. Lidia Ginzburg, *Literatura v poiskakh real'nosti* [Literature in search of reality] (Leningrad, 1987), p. 318.
7. Alexander Fadeyev, *Pis'ma i dokumenty* [Letters and documents] (Moscow, 2001), p. 286.
8. Boris Pasternak, *Perepiska s Ol'goi Freidenberg* [Correspondence with Olga Freidenberg] (New York and London, 1981), p. 267.
9. Czeslaw Milosz, *Emperor of the Earth: Modes of Eccentric Vision* (Berkeley and Los Angeles, 1981), p. 80.
10. Olga Ivinskaya, *V plenu vremeni. Gody s Borisom Pasternakom* [In the thrall of time: years with Boris Pasternak] (Paris, 1978), p. 113.
11. Quoted in: V. Kaverin, *Epilog: memuary* [Epilogue: memoirs] (Moscow, 1989), p. 514.
12. Simonov, *Glazami cheloveka moego pokoleniia*, p. 146.
13. *Komsomol'skaia Pravda*, October 30, 1958.
14. Vladimir Semichastny, *Bespokoinoe serdtse* [Turbulent heart] (Moscow, 2002), pp. 72–73. Khrushchev's son, Sergei, casts doubt on Semichastny's account: see William Taubman, *Khrushchev: The Man and His Era* (New York and London, 2003), p. 744.
15. *Pravda*, November 2 and November 6, 1958.
16. Quoted in: E. Pasternak, *Boris Pasternak. Biografia* [Boris Pasternak: a biography] (Moscow, 1997), p. 712.
17. Kaverin, *Epilog*, p. 374.
18. Semichastny, *Bespokoinoe serdtse*, p. 74.
19. "*A za mnoiu shum pogoni . . .*" *Boris Pasternak i vlast'. Dokumenty. 1956–1972* ["Behind me the chase . . ." Boris Pasternak and the regime: documents, 1956–1972] (Moscow, 2001), p. 221.
20. Medvedev, *Territoriia kino*, p. 112.
21. "*A za mnoiu shum pogoni . . .*" p. 255.
22. Osipov, *Tainaia zhizn'*, p. 339.
23. A. V. Blum, *Sovetskaia tsenzura v epokhu total'nogo kontrolia. 1929–1953* [Soviet censorship in the era of total control, 1929–1953] (St. Petersburg, 2000), p. 192.
24. Quoted in: Brian Boyd, *Vladimir Nabokov: The American Years* (Princeton, 1991), p. 371.
25. Quoted in: *Boris Pasternak and His Times* (Berkeley, 1989), p. 169.
26. Max Hayward, *Writers in Russia: 1917–1918* (San Diego, New York, and London, 1983), p. l.
27. *Solzhenitsyn. Publitsistika* [Solzhenitsyn: articles], vol. 2, p. 44.
28. Ibid., p. 184.
29. Boyd, *Nabokov*, p. 656.
30. Valentina Chemberdzhi, *V dome muzyka zhila* [Music lived in the house] (Moscow, 2002), p. 230.
31. Lakshin, "*Novy mir,*" p. 75.
32. Ibid., p. 84.

33. Ernst Neizvestny, *Govorit Neizvestnyi* [Neizvestny speaks] (Frankfurt-am-Main, 1984), pp. 13–14.
34. Romm, *Kak v kino,* p. 185.
35. Sergei Khrushchev, *Pensioner soyuznogo znacheniia* [Federal pensioner] (Moscow, 1991), p. 362.
36. Voznesensky, *Na virtual'nom vetru,* p. 78.
37. Ibid., pp. 79–81.
38. Ibid., p. 85.
39. Romm, *Kak v kino,* p. 203.
40. Ibid., p. 214.

Chapter Twelve

1. Marianna Volkova and Solomon Volkov, *Iurii Liubimov v Amerike* [Yuri Lyubimov in America] (New York, 1993), p. 122.
2. Ibid.
3. Quoted in: Yuri Lyubimov, *Rasskazy starogo trepacha* [Tales of an old blowhard] (Moscow, 2001), pp. 261–262.
4. Voznesensky, *Na virtual'nom vetru,* p. 133.
5. Quoted in: Pavel Leonidov, *Vladimir Vysotskii i drugie* [Vladimir Vysotsky and others] (New York, 1983), p. 158.
6. Quoted in: Georgii Arbatov, *Chelovek sistemy* [Man of the system] (Moscow, 2002), p. 208.
7. Alexander Volodin, *Tak nespokoino na dushe* [I Feel Such Unease] (St. Petersburg, 1993), p. 55.
8. Ibid., p. 28.
9. Ibid., p. 57.
10. Yuri Lyubimov in conversation with the author.
11. Arbatov, *Chelovek sistemy,* p. 356.
12. A. M. Aleksandrov-Agentov, *Ot Kollontai do Gorbacheva* [From Kollontai to Gorbachev] (Moscow, 1994), p. 118.
13. Dmitrii Volkogonov, *Sem' vozhdei* [Seven leaders], vol. 2 (Moscow, 1996), p. 73.
14. Quoted in: Mark Altshuller and Elena Dryzhakova, *Put' otrecheniia. Russkaia literatura 1953–1968* [Path of renunciation: Russian literature 1953–1968] (New Jersey, 1985), p. 333.
15. Vladimir Voinovich, *Portret na fone mifa* [Portrait on a background of myth] (Moscow, 2002), p. 52.
16. Lidia Chukovskaya, *Zapiski ob Anne Akhmatovoi,* vol. 2 (Paris, 1980), p. 449.
17. Voinovich, *Portret na fone mifa,* p. 44.
18. Solzhenitsyn, *Bodalsia telenok s dubom,* p. 316.
19. *Kremlevskii samosud. Sekretnye dokumenty Politburo o pisatele A. Solzhenitsyne* [Kremlin lynching; secret Politburo documents about the writer A. Solzhenitsyn] (Moscow, 1994), p. 133.
20. Ibid., pp. 353, 439.
21. Ibid., pp. 352–353.

Part Five: A TIME OF CHANGES

Chapter Thirteen

1. Dmitrii Volkogonov, *Lenin. Politicheskii portret v dvukh knigakh* [Lenin: a political portrait in two books], vol. 2 (Moscow, 1994), p. 186.

2. Ibid., p. 191.
3. Ibid., pp. 191–192.
4. Yakov Gordin in conversation with the author.
5. *Kremlevskii samosud,* p. 491.
6. Alfred Schnittke in conversation with the author.
7. Nikolai Boldyrev, *Stalker, ili trudy i dni Andreia Tarkovskogo* [Stalker, or the works and days of Andrei Tarkovsky] (Chelyabinsk, 2002), pp. 95–96.
8. Maya Turovskya, *Pamiati tekushchego mgnoveniia* [In memoriam of the current moment] (Moscow, 1987), pp. 230–231.
9. Ibid., p. 137.
10. Solomon Volkov, *Istoriia kul'tury Sankt-Peterburga s osnovaniia do nashikh dnei* [Cultural history of St. Petersburg from its founding to our times] (Moscow, 2001), p. 457.
11. Quoted in: *Literaturnaia gazeta,* May 5, 1993.
12. Quoted in: Yakov Gordin, *Pereklichka vo mrake. Iosif Brodskii i ego sobesedniki* [Calling out in the dark: Joseph Brodsky and his interlocutors] (St. Petersburg, 2000), p. 219.
13. Quoted in: Boldyrev, *Stalker,* p. 162.
14. Quoted in: *Literaturnaia gazeta,* March 8, 1995.
15. Andrei Konchalovsky, *Nizkie istiny* [Base truths] (Moscow, 1998), p. 115.
16. Vassily Aksyonov in conversation with the author.
17. Joseph Brodsky in conversation with the author.
18. Quoted in: Boldyrev, *Stalker,* p. 309.
19. Ibid., p. 336.
20. *Besedy s Al'fredom Shnitke* [Conversations with Alfred Schnittke] (Moscow, 1994), p. 233.
21. See *Moskovskie novosti,* October 1, 2004.
22. *Dictionary of Literary Biography,* vol. 285: *Russian Writers Since* 1980 (Farmington Hills, MI), p. 28.
23. *Literaturnaia gazeta,* May 5, 1993.
24. Ibid.
25. Leonard Bernstein in conversation with the author.
26. *Znamia,* 11 (2000), p. 154.

Chapter Fourteen

1. Mikhail Gorbachev, *Zhizn' i reformy* [Life and reforms], vol. 1 (Moscow, 1995), p. 265.
2. Volkogonov, *Lenin,* vol. 2, pp. 198–200.
3. Volkogonov, *Sem' vozhdei,* vol. 2, p. 413.
4. Solzhenitsyn, *Publitsistika,* vol. 2, p. 556.
5. Ibid., p. 563.
6. Ibid., p. 554.
7. Vassily Aksyonov, *Desiatiletie klevety (radiodnevnik pisatelia)* [Decade of lies (a writer's radio diary)] (Moscow, 2004), p. 235.
8. Ibid., p. 236.
9. *Lubyanka,* p. 727.
10. Ibid.
11. Solzhenitsyn, *Publitsistika,* vol. 2, pp. 564, 567–568.
12. Ibid., p. 567.
13. Ibid., p. 568.
14. I. I. Artamonov, *Oruzhie obrechennykh (sistemnyi analiz ideologicheskoi diversii)*

[Weapons of the doomed (systematic analysis of ideological sabotage)] (Minsk, 1981), p. 166.

15. Valery Konovalov, *Vek "Svobody" ne slykhat'*. *Zapiski veterana kholodnoi voiny* [Haven't heard "Liberty" in ages: notes of a Cold War veteran] (Moscow, 2003), p. 5.

16. *Lubyanka*, p. 728.

17. *The New York Times Book Review,* May 11, 1980.

18. Volkov, *Dialogi s Brodskim,* p. 564.

19. A. I. Solzhenitsyn, *Na vozvrate dykhaniia. Izbrannaia publitsistika* [Breathing again: selected articles] (Moscow, 2004), pp. 305, 315.

20. Abram Tertz (Andrei Sinyavsky), *Puteshestvie na Chernuyu rechku i drugie proizvedeniia* [Journey to Black River and other works] (Moscow, 1999), p. 346.

21. Joseph Brodsky in conversation with the author.

22. Solzhenitsyn, *Na vozvrate dykhaniia,* p. 311.

23. Simonov, *Glazami cheloveka moego pokoleniia,* p. 116.

24. Yevgeny Yevtushenko in conversation with the author.

25. Quoted in: *Novoye Russkoye Slovo,* August 27, 2005.

26. *Yuri i Ol'ga Trifonovy vspominaiut* [Yuri and Olga Trifonov recall] (Moscow, 2003), p. 26.

27. Georgii Sviridov in conversation with the author.

28. Georgii Sviridov, *Muzyka kak sud'ba* [Music as destiny] (Moscow, 2002), p. 231.

29. Ibid., p. 438.

30. Ibid., p. 437–438.

31. More on this episode in: Volkov, *Dialogi s Brodskim,* pp. 182–188.

32. *Argumenti i fakty,* 2005, No. 4 (international edition).

33. Quoted in: Vladislav Kulakov, *Poeziia kak fakt* [Poetry as a fact] (Moscow, 1999), pp. 352–353.

34. Viktor Pivovarov, *Vlublennyi agent* [Agent in love] (Moscow, 2001), p. 50.

35. Valentin Vorobyov, *Vrag naroda. Vospominaniia khudozhnika* [Enemy of the people: reminiscences of an artist] (Moscow, 2005), p. 175.

36. Filipp Bobkov, *KGB i vlast'* [The KGB and the regime] (Moscow, 2003), p. 297.

37. Ibid., p. 299.

38. Ibid., p. 298.

39. Vorobyov, *Vrag naroda,* p. 274.

40. Leonid Borodin, *Bez vybora. Avtobiograficheskoe povestvovanie* [Without a choice: an autobiographical account] (Moscow, 2003), p. 192.

41. Ibid., p. 190.

42. *Novoye Russkoye Slovo,* May 15–16, 2004.

43. Pavel Sudoplatov, *Spetsoperatsii* [Special Operations] (Moscow, 2002), p. 243.

44. Ibid., pp. 210–211.

45. Volkogonov, *Lenin,* vol. 2, p. 192.

46. Bobkov, *KGB i vlast',* p. 300.

47. Ilya Kabakov and Boris Grois, *Dialogi (1990–1994)* [Dialogues (1990–1994)] (Moscow, 1999), p. 62.

48. Ilya Kabakov, *60-e–70-e . . . Zapiski o neofitsial'noi zhizni v Moskve* [60s–70s . . . Notes about unofficial life in Moscow] (Vienna, 1999), p. 206.

49. Kabakov and Grois, *Dialogi,* p. 62.

50. Irina Balabanova, *Govorit Dmitrii Aleksandrovich Prigov* [Dmitri Alexandrovich Prigov speaks] (Moscow, 2001), pp. 11–13.

51. Ibid., p. 16.
52. *Novoye Russkoye Slovo,* May 15–16, 2004.
53. Ibid.
54. Quoted in: Vorobyov, *Vrag naroda,* p. 488.

Chapter Fifteen

1. A. S. Chernyaev, *Shest' let s Gorbachevym* [Six years with Gorbachev] (Moscow, 1993), p. 98.
2. Ibid., pp. 95–96.
3. Anatoli Rybakov, *Roman-vospominanie* [Memoir novel] (Moscow, 1997); Tatiana Rybakova, *"Schastlivaia ty, Tania!"* ["You're lucky, Tania!"] (Moscow, 2005).
4. Gorbachev, *Zhizn' i reformy,* vol. 1, p. 322.
5. Quoted in: Rybakov, *Roman-vospominanie,* pp. 335–336.
6. Alexander Yakovlev, *Omut pamiati* [Vortex of memory] (Moscow, 2001), p. 260.
7. Anatoli Rybakov in conversation with the author.
8. Quoted in: Tatiana Rybakova, *"Schastlivaia ty, Tania!"* p. 352.
9. Stalin, *Sochineniia,* vol. 11, p. 328.
10. Quoted in: Vladimir Lakshin, *Literaturno-kriticheskie stat'i* (Moscow, 2004), p. 480.
11. Quoted in: I. Vinogradskaya, *Zhizn' i tvorchestvo K. S. Stanislavskogo, Letopis' v chetyrekh tomakh* [Life and work of K. S. Stanislavsky: chronicle in 4 volumes] (Moscow, 1976), p. 291.
12. Quoted in: Anatoli Smeliansky, *Ukhodiashchaia natura* [Departing nature] (Moscow, 2002), p. 12.
13. Ibid., p. 480.
14. Oleg Efremov in conversation with the author.
15. Quoted in: Vladimir Bondarenko, *Plamennye reaktsionery. Tri lika russkogo patriotizma* [Flaming reactionaries: three faces of Russian patriotism] (Moscow, 2003), p. 667.
16. Ibid., p. 51.
17. Alexander Zinoviev, *Gibel' russkogo kommunizma* [Death of Russian Communism] (Moscow, 2001), p. 91.
18. *Sovetskaia kul'tura,* May 27, 1989.
19. Boris Grebenshchikov in conversation with the author.
20. *Sovetskaia kul'tura,* May 27, 1989.
21. Andrei Bitov, *Oglashennye* [Possessed] (St. Petersburg, 1995), p. 364.
22. Yevtushenko, *Ne umirai prezhde smerti,* p. 412.
23. *Nezavisimaia gazeta,* October 13, 1993.
24. Vagrich Bakhchanyan in conversation with the author.
25. Eduard Limonov, *Anatomia geroia* [Anatomy of a hero] (Smolensk, 1998), p. 55.
26. *Moskovskie novosti,* September 16, 2003.
27. Ibid.
28. *Russkaia mysl',* October 28, 1993.
29. Solzhenitsyn, *Publitsistika,* vol. 3, p. 324.
30. Letter from Aleksandr Solzhenitsyn to the author, October 10, 1985, Volkov archives.
31. Solzhenitsyn, *Publitsistika,* vol. 3, pp. 264–265.
32. Solzhenitsyn, *Publitsistika,* vol. 1, p. 226.
33. *Novyi mir,* 1 (1990), p. 223.
34. Solzhenitsyn, *Publitsistika,* vol. 3, p. 341.
35. Eduard Limonov, *Limonov protiv Zhirinovskogo* [Limonov versus Zhirinovsky] (Moscow, 1994), p. 127.

36. *Ogonek,* 27–28 (1994), p. 22.
37. Ibid.
38. *Novoye Russkoye Slovo,* September 24, 1993.
39. Cherniayev, *Shest' let s Gorbachevym,* pp. 277–278.
40. Vyacheslav Kostikov, *Roman s prezidentom* [Novel with a president] (Moscow, 1997), p. 339.
41. Mikhail Kozakov, *Risunki na peske* [Drawings in the sand] (Tel-Aviv, 1993), p. 254.
42. Kostikov, *Roman s prezidentom,* p. 339.
43. *Nash Sovremennik,* 11–12 (1998), p. 185.
44. Quoted in: Zhores Medvedev, Roy Medvedev, *Solzhenitsyn i Sakharov. Dva proroka* [Solzhenitsyn and Sakharov: two prophets] (Moscow, 2004), p. 213.
45. *Sintaksis,* 36 (1998), p. 149.
46. *Kontinent,* 18 (1978), p. 345.
47. G. P. Fedotov, *Sud'ba i grekhi Rossii. Izbrannye stat'i po filosofii russkoi istorii i kul'tury* [Fate and sins of Russia: selected articles on the philosophy of Russian history and culture], vol. 2 (St. Petersburg, 1992), p. 167.
48. Ibid.
49. Viktor Toporov, *Pokhorony Gullivera v strane liliputov* [Gulliver's funeral in the land of Lilliputians] (St. Petersburg and Moscow, 2002), pp. 180–181.
50. Sergei Gandlevsky, *Poeticheskaija kukhnia* [Poetic kitchen] (St. Petersburg, 1998), pp. 68–69.
51. Ibid., p. 57.
52. Dmitri Prigov and Sergei Shapoval, *Portretnaya galereia D. A. P.* [D. A. P. portrait gallery] (Moscow, 2003), p. 92.
53. Boris Yeltsin, *Prezidentskii marafon* [Presidential marathon] (Moscow, 2000), p. 127.
54. *Sovetskaia Rossiia,* May 16, 2000.
55. *O Rossii i russkoi filosofskoi kul'ture* [About Russia and Russian philosophical culture] (Moscow, 1990), p. 44.
56. L. N. Gumilev, *Ritmy Evrazii* [Rhythms of Eurasia] (Moscow, 1993), p. 24.
57. L. N. Gumilev, *Ot Rusi do Rossii* [From Rus to Russia] (St. Petersburg, 1992), p. 250.
58. Gumilev, *Ritmy Evrazii,* p. 31.
59. Alexander Dugin, *Proekt "Evraziia"* [Project Eurasia] (Moscow, 2004), p. 349.
60. Aleksandr Solzhenitsyn, *Rossiia v obvale* [Russia collapsing] (Moscow, 1998), p. 149.
61. Ibid., pp. 159, 175–176.
62. *Segodnya,* September 7, 1993.
63. Borodin, *Bez vybora,* p. 403.
64. Ibid., p. 404.
65. *Chaika,* 21 (2005), p. 27.
66. Ibid.
67. Solzhenitsyn, *Na vozvrate dykhaniia,* p. 519.

INDEX

A Note About the Author

Solomon Volkov is the award-winning author of several notable books about Russian culture, including *St. Petersburg: A Cultural History* and *Shostakovich and Stalin,* published worldwide. After moving to the United States from the Soviet Union, he became a cultural commentator at the Voice of America and then Radio Free Europe/Radio Liberty, broadcasting to the USSR (and later, Russia), discussing contemporary artistic developments in his former homeland. He lives in New York City with his wife, Marianna, a pianist and photographer.

A Note About the Translator

The prizewinning translator Antonina W. Bouis is known for her work with contemporary Russian literature. She and her husband, Jean-Claude, live in New York City and travel to Russia regularly.

A Note on the Type

The text of this book was composed in Palatino, a typeface designed by the noted German typographer Hermann Zapf. Named after Giovanni Battista Palatino, a writing master of Renaissance Italy, Palatino was the first of Zapf's typefaces to be introduced in America. The first designs for the face were made in 1948, and the fonts for the complete face were issued between 1950 and 1952. Like all Zapf-designed typefaces, Palatino is beautifully balanced and exceedingly readable.

Composed by North Market Street Graphics,
Lancaster, Pennsylvania
Printed and bound by Berryville Graphics,
Berryville, Virginia
Designed by Anthea Lingeman